# PRIMATE POLITICS

*Edited by*
*Glendon Schubert*
*and*
*Roger D. Masters*

Foreword by Albert Somit

Southern Illinois University Press / Carbondale and Edwardsville

94  93  92  91    4  3  2  1

Library of Congress Cataloging-in-Publication Data
Primate politics / edited by Glendon Schubert and Roger
D. Masters.
    p.  cm.
    Includes bibliographical references: p.
    Includes indexes.
    1. Primates—Evolution. 2. Primates—Behavior.
    3. Human behavior. 4. Political anthropology.
    I. Schubert, Glendon II. Masters, Roger D.
    GN281.4.P69 1991
    306.2—dc20                   90-9611
    ISBN 0-8093-1611-0           CIP

For Adrienne, Biruté, Dian, Jane, Shirley, and Thelma
as exemplars of all primate women of valor
who have contributed to this work

And to all whose observations of primate behavior
have illuminated human nature

# Contents

# Foreword

## Albert Somit

About a quarter-century ago, a small handful of political scientists, understandably viewed as eccentric by even the most charitable of their colleagues, began to use biological concepts and techniques in an effort to better explain and study political behavior. That movement, quickly dubbed "biopolitics," has since flourished. Today, biopolitics is recognized as an official sub-area of the discipline by both the International Political Science Association and the American Political Science Association, the profession's two largest and most prestigious organizations.

As the bibliography to this book abundantly testifies, Professors Schubert and Masters have played leading roles in the development of this new field. *Primate Politics*, their first joint effort, reflects the same qualities that have characterized their previous work, that is, a concern with theory, whether evolutionary or political, on the one hand, and an insistence on relating theory to empirical research, on the other. These dual interests are reflected in the organization of the volume. The first section provides an excellent overview of contemporary primatological theory. The second poses what is essentially an empirical question—are there meaningful similarities between human politics and primate social behavior? The third, taking the next logical step, deals with the extent to which an "ethological perspective" can help us better understand political phenomena in our own world.

Inevitably, since it ventures into terra incognita, *Primate Politics* raises more issues than it settles—the hallmark, I should add, of a successful book. Many readers will be struck, as I was, by the description (in the first section) of the way in which a discipline can be literally transformed by the entry of a new breed of practitioner. The appearance of women in primatology, starting in the 1960s, was followed by a major change in the type of questions posed and, eventually, in a far-reaching revision of long-established beliefs and concepts.[1] Primatologists no longer focus exclusively on adult males, especially dominant males; and, as one consequence, our notions of the structure of primate societies (and possibly those of our early ancestors) have been profoundly altered. Will the arrival of increasing numbers of women in political science, I wonder, eventually have a similar impact upon that discipline in terms of the issues addressed and the kinds of answers accepted?

Whether chimpanzees, baboons, and macaques engage in *political* behavior or, as Professor Schubert argues, only in *pre*political behavior, turns, as we might expect, on one's definition of "political." But if the issue is left unresolved, two valuable points nonetheless emerge: first, and especially for political scientists, the realization that other primate species to which we are very closely related (and with whom we share a common evolutionary ancestry) display many, if not all, of the behaviors that we associate with "political"; second, and especially for those in primatology, the importance of defining "political" with greater care and, ideally, with an awareness of how that term is used by social scientists.

Can an ethologically oriented approach help cast new light upon human political behavior? Here, I think, we should distinguish between ethological *concepts* and the research *method* traditionally associated with ethology—careful, systematic field study of actual behavior. Both have already demonstrated their value, as evidenced in the studies described in the book's third section. Still, given the resistance to change repeatedly documented by historians of science, I suspect that the ethologists' research techniques will find much more rapid acceptance among political scientists than their conceptual apparatus. In either case, *Primate Politics* will have served a further useful purpose in propelling the profession appreciably closer to a true, rather than a surrogate, behaviorism.

Professors Schubert and Masters have sought, on balance quite successfully, to build a bridge between two previously separate fields, politics and primatology. They have erected a solid structure. I would hope, with them, that there will now be increasing movement across that bridge—with traffic flowing in both directions.

1. "Observing is subjective: the animal described is only an illusion created out of a personal perspective, based on which questions are raised, which facts written down, which information ignored. Another biologist asking different questions will create a different animal" (George B. Schaller, in Strum, 1987:xi).

# Editors' Preface

The preface contains three sections. The first two are concerned with the development and the organization of this book. The third records the obligations—intellectual and otherwise—of the co-editors.

## DEVELOPMENTS

Atlthough the contributors to this book are equally divided between primatologists and social scientists, both editors are political scientists. For us, this book is the fruit of two decades of research, teaching, and dialogue with scholars in many disciplines. The history of those developments is useful as a preface to what follows.

A dozen years ago, one of us (Glendon Schubert) became a charter member of the American Society of Primatologists and also a member of the International Primatological Society. During the next six years, he was a regular participant in ASP annual meetings, becoming socialized through panels and informal discussions into an orientation toward primate behavior that was quite exceptional for a political scientist (G. Schubert 1978, 1980, 1982b, 1982d, 1983a, 1983b, 1984a; G. Schubert and Somit 1982).

In 1967–68, the other of us (Roger Masters) received a Guggenheim Fellowship to study the relationship between political philosophy and modern biology. In subsequent years, he became editor of the "Biology and Social Life" section of *Social Science Information*, served for several years as a Fellow of the Hastings Center, participated actively in meetings and publications sponsored by the Gruter Institute for Law and Behavioral Research, and pursued interdisciplinary research applying an ethological approach to the study of politics (Masters 1973a, 1974, 1975, 1976a, 1981; chap. 8, below).

By the early eighties several other political scientists (e.g., Barner-Barry 1977, 1978, 1981, 1982; J. Schubert 1983, 1984b; Somit 1984; Watts 1981; Willhoite 1976), quite independently of each other as well as of primatologists, had begun research on human behavior, using methods (G. Schubert 1981c) that ethologists and experimental animal behavioralists had developed for the study of nonhuman animals. When a professional subfield linking evolutionary biology and political science emerged, it was natural that both co-editors play a central role in forming the Association for Politics and the Life Sciences; each of us continues to serve on its Executive Council. Thus political science is being enriched by studies in what can be called human primatology, because primatology consists of ethology and animal behavior research done with primates as the subject animals—and humans are primates, though of course unique ones in many respects (see chap. 10, below).

Given this background, in the early 1980s it seemed particularly desirable to promote face-to-face contact between primatologists and interested political scientists who had little direct contact with them. The first co-editor (Glendon Schubert) realized that a scheduled convention of the International Primatological Society in East Africa offered an ideal forum for the organization of an interdisciplinary discussion of primate politics. Thus this book began as a two-session, day-long symposium on "Political Behavior as a Primate Social Strategy" that convened on July 24, 1984, in the Louis Leakey Auditorium of the National Museum of Kenya, as part of the Xth Congress of the International Primatological Society in Nairobi, hosted by Richard E. Leakey.

The symposium was jointly organized and chaired by a political scientist (Glendon Schubert) and a primatologist (Shirley Strum). It had been explicitly planned to bring together a mixed group with half of the participants scholars trained in political science and the other half in primatology (either as zoologists, as physical anthropologists, or as physiological psychologists), to discuss before an international audience of primatologists the communality of interests between biopolitical scientists (concerned with developing a better understanding of the genesis of human political behavior among pre-historical humans, possibly among their hominid forebears, and conceivably among other-than-human primates); and primatologists (many of whom had explicitly used the metaphor of human "politics" to describe aspects of the social behavior of several nonhuman primates, especially chimpanzees, baboons, and macaques).

The primatological papers at the symposium were presented by Shirley Strum, Frans de Waal, Jonah David Western, and William Mason (who at that time was the president of the International Primatological Society); the political science papers were presented by Glendon Schubert and James Schubert; Albert Somit was moderator of both symposium sessions. A third paper in political science, co-authored by Denis Sullivan, Roger Masters, and their colleagues, was written and scheduled for the symposium, but not presented because neither senior author was able to make the trip to Nairobi and their paper, although mailed in time, became lost in the Kenyan customs mazes. Of the symposium papers, three (by Strum, G. Schubert, and J. Schubert) were subsequently published in the "Biology and Social Life" section of *Social Science Information* (edited by Masters), as were two additional papers by Thelma Rowell and Nicholas Blurton Jones, both of whom participated in the Nairobi Congress as contributors to other symposia; these papers, plus the one by Sullivan and Masters et al., are now brought together and integrated in *Primate Politics*. Two additional chapters are included in this volume: one, by Jane Goodall, is selected from her book *The Chimpanzees of Gombe* (published in 1986, two years after the Nairobi Congress); the other is by de Waal, who participated in the original symposium but presented a different paper than the one included here.

This volume thus attempts to continue the dialogue, begun in Nairobi among a handful of political scientists and a larger aggregation of primatologists, extending it to a more diverse, public audience. In our experience, the topic of primate politics is of interest to social scientists as well as biologists, to students as well as professors, and to the general public as well as to academic professionals. It is timely to expand the circle of those who understand human life from an evolutionary perspective.

This is, of course, not the only work relating primatology and political science. Among efforts to promote the dialogue between scholars who do research on human politics and those studying nonhuman primate behavior are two books recently published individually by the co-editors of this volume, and a symposium they organized at the 1989 annual meeting of the American Political Science Association in Atlanta. One of the books (G. Schubert 1989a) focuses on the implications of evolutionary theory for political theory and behavior; the other (Masters 1989a) defines human nature by relating evolutionary biology, social psychology, linguistics, and game theory to political philosophy. The general theoretical orientation of the co-authors, developed in these two books, are applied in the present volume to the analysis of the relationship between human politics and similar behaviors among other primates.

The 1989 symposium at the American Political Science Association—obviously a counterpart for political scientists of its 1984 IPS predecessor in Nairobi—took the format of a round-table discussion organized and chaired by the co-editors of this volume, with participants including anthropologists Melvin Konner and primatologists Sarah Gouzoules and Caroline Ehrhardt. A large audience of political scientists engaged in lively discussion with the panelists, expanding the dialogue to include most of the fifty-odd persons present. Many of their questions and comments influenced the co-editors in their final revisions of this volume.

As the foregoing indicates, *Primate Politics* has a history. The book arises out of the progressive development of scholarship extending evolutionary perspectives to the study of human social life. This emerging field, now often called "biopolitics," has not been imposed by biologists seeking to conquer enemy territory. Nor does it result from an attempt to borrow isolated bits of information from biology and import them to political science (as a device to entertain the reader and enhance the author's own status). Rather, this approach has entailed a long and careful process of interdisciplinary collaboration, in which the co-editors have sought to demonstrate that scholars in one field can indeed gain enough insight and knowledge of another discipline to make intellectual exchange both scientifically well-grounded and fruitful.

## ORGANIZATION

The structure of this book reflects that of both of the symposia just described, although its content is of course derived from the earlier one. Among the contributors, the five social scientists (four political scientists and one sociologist) are balanced by five primatologists (two physical anthropologists, two zoologists, and one physiological psychologist). More than two-thirds of the ten participants do their research under field rather than laboratory conditions: three of the social scientists (Latour and both Schuberts) and four primatologists (Blurton Jones, Goodall, Rowell, and Strum). In contrast, two social scientists (Masters and Sullivan) and one primatologist (de Waal) have done experimental research.

This diversity of scholarly approaches is paralleled by cultural differences among the contributors. Half of the participants are European (Blurton Jones, Goodall, and Rowell are English; de Waal is Dutch; and Latour is French), while the others were raised in the United States. Of the six chapters not presenting the research of the co-editors themselves, three are authored or co-authored by women. It is often claimed that scholarly approaches represent narrow cultural or academic bias. We hope that the breadth of approaches and origins of the contributors will preserve our work from this critique.

The book itself is divided in three major parts. The first is concerned with theories of primate behavior and its study; the second is an empirical examination of chimpanzee behavior from the perspective of both field and captive conditions; and the third focuses on primatological studies of human behavior. The Introduction (by Glendon Schubert) seeks to situate the study of *Primate Politics* in the context of contemporary academic life; the conclusion (by Roger Masters) asks how this perspective relates to the tradition of political philosophy and the central concepts of political science.

## ACKNOWLEDGMENTS

Each of the co-editors has many obligations that deserve to be recognized.

*Glendon Schubert.* I thank particularly the two women who have been most influential in shaping my own thinking regarding what I discuss in this book.

Shirley Strum knows me over a period of several years, but only slightly. Yet her ideas and writing (esp. 1975a, 1975b, 1987, and chap. 4, below) have contributed greatly to my understanding of the literature of primatology in general. Adrienne Zihlman probably knows me not at all, although we were for a few days part of the same small group in a Land Rover tour of the Masai Serengeti—but I did not know who she was then, either. However, her creative scholarship in regard to both human evolution theory (e.g., Zihlman 1982, 1983, 1987; Zihlman and Lowenstein 1983) and likewise feminist primatology (Tanner and Zihlman 1976; Zihlman and Tanner 1978; Zihlman 1981) has inspired my teaching as well as my thinking about the sexual and primate politics of humans.

In recent years I have had three political science doctoral students whose intellectual interest engaged mine transactionally, and to my benefit. Dr. Ra Chong Phil (Ra 1989), now of Seoul, Korea, enrolled in the first course in primatology taught at the University of Hawaii at Manoa; and subsequent discussions with him have helped me in my work in this book. Of the other two, Micheal V. Loh has worked with my co-editor at Dartmouth on the extension of the project described in chapter 8, organizing an experimental study at Southern Illinois University at Carbondale just before the 1988 presidential election; his sudden return to Malaysia for personal reasons, shortly after that election, appears to have preempted the dissertation he had expected to write on biosocial theory of charismatic political leadership. The other SIUC student, Steven Parmenter, brought to my attention the great importance of the nineteenth-century Russian school of cooperative evolutionary theorists (Kropotkin 1925; Capouya and Tompkins 1975) as a counterpoise to the overweening emphasis in twentieth-century American and British evolutionary theory on conflict, competition, dominance, and aggression as the main evolutionary ingredients of contemporary male human political nature. That dissertation remains a challenging idea of uncertain outcome; but I am indebted to Parmenter for having made the contribution that he did to my own continuing socialization.

I must also thank two colleagues in administrative roles for their material support of my work on this book. Dean John Jackson of the College of Liberal Arts at Southern Illinois University at Carbondale assisted me with research funds for, among many other things, helping to pay for the typing and retyping of my contributions to this book, and likewise for my trip to Atlanta for the symposium in 1989. At the University of Hawaii at Manoa, former Social Science Faculty Dean Deane Neubauer, and incumbent Dean Richard Dubanowski, provided funds for, inter alia, my trip to Kenya in 1984 and my sabbatical leave during 1988–89 to complete, again inter alia, the revision of my contributions to this book.

*Roger D. Masters.* My chief intellectual debt is to the late Leo Strauss who, in addition to teaching his students how to read (and think), impressed on me the primordial importance of the question of human nature and of the need to relate political philosophy to modern natural science. Among many others who have been invaluable to my scholarly career, two are particularly deserving of mention in relation to the current volume. Without Denis Sullivan, my colleague at Dartmouth, the experimental research on the facial displays of leaders described in chapter 8 would never have been possible; our sharing of ideas, dialogue, and teaching over the years has been incalculably to my benefit. Without Dr. Margaret Gruter, President of the Gruter Institute for Law and Behavioral Research, personal contacts with a fascinating variety of evolutionary biologists, primatologists (including Jane Goodall and Frans de Waal), legal theorists, and social scientists would not have occurred; her remarkable ability to bring together exceptional scholars in diverse disciplines, her support, and her own conceptualization of the implications of ethology for the study of human law and behavior, have both inspired and helped me without measure.

Many other scholars have shared their insights—and borne with my attempts to integrate their different perspectives and disciplines. While none has responsibility for the result, I have especially appreciated the opportunity to meet, know, and exchange ideas with (in alphabetical order); Dick Alexander, David Barash, Alan Bloom, Hiram Caton, Ivan Chase, Frans de Waal, Henry Ehrmann, Don Elliott, Robin Fox, Jane Goodall, John Lanzetta, Mike McGuire, Paul MacLean, Heinrich Meier, Tom Pangle, Lionel Tiger, and Edward O. Wilson. Finally, thanks to my co-editor, who originally conceived of the symposium and this volume, and was kind enough to invite me to work with him.

A number of institutions have generously funded the research without which my work would have been impossible. As noted above, a John Simon Guggenheim Fellowship in 1967–68 provided a year for uninterrupted study of evolutionary theory and its implications for politics. Other foundations have funded the experimental research on nonverbal behavior, emotion, and cognition in responses to leaders: the Harry Frank Guggenheim Foundation, the National Science Foundation, the Maison des Sciences de l'Homme (Paris), the Rockefeller Center for the Social Sciences at Dartmouth College, and the Gruter Institute for Law and Behavioral Research. All those individuals responsible for this support, without which my academic endeavors could not have borne fruit, deserve my sincere appreciation and thanks.

For both co-editors, finally, we thank our colleagues who have contributed to this volume as well as those at Southern Illinois University Press who have seen it through production. As the collective nature of this enterprise indicates, many of the most important things in human life depend on cooperation.

*Primate Politics*

# 1

## *Introduction*
## *Primatology, Feminism, and Political Behavior*

Glendon Schubert

The first two sections of the preface discuss the developmental and theoretical aspects of the organization of this book. The emphasis here will be brief, empirical, and practical. The intent of this first chapter is to introduce social scientist, general, and student readers to primatology as an academic field of knowledge and of praxis. Emphasis is given to changes during the past quarter of a century due to the infusion of human females as field observers of nonhuman primates; and of feminist theorists upon primatological theory. This introductory chapter also offers a précis of the content of the remaining nine chapters.

Each of the three parts of the book begins with an introductory essay, which provides an overview of, and raises critical questions concerning, the subset of chapters included. The subject of each part is different from that of the other two; and none of the part introductions duplicates what is discussed in the present chapter, which introduces the book in relation to the theory of primatology.

This introduction includes five sections, of which the first suggests the kinds of theoretical questions that currently interest primatologists and considers how and why many contemporary primatologists—field and laboratory alike—deem various aspects of the social behavior of the nonhuman primates whom they study to be *political*. The next section deals with taxonomy and is therefore also theoretical, but its focus shifts from living primates to their ancestors millions of years ago, from whose behaviors came the adaptations leading to the punctuational speciation (Stanley 1986) that resulted in earlier hominids and modern humans. The third section returns to contemporary primatology, asking: what difference did it make to both the theory and praxis of field primatology when substantial numbers of women began to enter the fields of physical anthropology and zoological ethology as observers of apes and monkeys in (what then

3

remained of) their natural habitats? The fourth section follows up by asking what effects female primatology has had upon *both* evolutionary *and* political theory. The concluding section provides an overview of the book's three parts in terms of the differing approaches of the life and the social sciences and discusses the major commonalities and differences among the eight substantive chapters, two through nine.

## 1. PRIMATE THEORY AND POLITICAL BEHAVIOR

Primatologists turn to evolutionary theory to help explain the behavior of primates, ranging from mouse-sized prosimians through a diverse array of both New World and Old World monkeys, to the apes: simiangs, gibbons, and the much larger pongids and humans (see Leutenegger 1982). As biologists familiar with the paleoanthropological and genetic evidence on human evolution, primatologists have no doubt that humans are primates, mammals, and animals; therefore, they assume that there are homologies between the social behaviors of humans and other apes. Primatologists tend to specialize, and particularly for purposes of making field studies, in one or a few closely related species of primates; however, anthropology in general covers the spectrum of primates, living and dead: cultural and some medical anthropologists study live humans; paleoanthropologists study extinct primates, human and nonhuman alike; and physical anthropologists carry out much of the field study on living nonhuman primates although some physical anthropologists do experimental research in primate centers or laboratories. Zoologically educated ethologists also have contributed much to field primatology, whereas physiological psychologists have tended to undertake laboratory studies of captive monkeys and apes. Alison Richard (1985, 35–36) has commented as follows on this entire field of study.

> For the psychologist, nonhuman primates provided access to the human mind and served as good subjects for studying links between physiology and behavior in complex social animals. For the physical anthropologist, nonhuman primates presented reflections of ourselves or our past selves; in particular, nonhuman primate societies provided an opportunity to study possible antecedents of our own social structures. For the zoologist, primates were a group of mammals about whose natural history little was known, and their relatively large size and social complexity, though disadvantages in the eyes of many, made them particularly interesting and challenging subjects.

The kinds of research questions that field primatologists investigate are probably best exemplified by surveying a few of the best recent textbooks in primatology on the subject of primate social organization and behavior. I have picked four such textbooks, plus one monograph that is not technically a text, for that purpose; of these, four are authored or edited by women, while the man who edited the fifth has done much to encourage and facilitate the graduate education and research of female field primatologists. (This may constitute a biased selection on my part, but if so, it represents the right kind of bias to make the points that are important in the presentation that follows.)

Dorothy Cheney and her coauthors (1987, 3) introduce an almost encyclopedic symposium on research in primate social behavior with a series of fundamental generalizations in response to their opening query, "What Makes Primates Different from Other Animals?"

> 1. *Primates have unusually varied and diverse ways of expressing themselves socially.* Although it is always dangerous to pretend to know the limits of animal communicative repertoires . . . we can say that the touching, hugging, mouthing, mounting, lip smacking, vocalizing, greeting, and grooming of primates allow them many subtly different ways of expressing affinity and perhaps more means of developing complex social relationships than are found in most other species. Moreover, primates seem to move easily from one behavioral "currency" to another, often apparently "trading," for example, a mount for tolerance at a food source, or a bout of grooming for later support in an alliance. . . .
>
> 2. *The social organization of many primate species is unusually complex.* A typical primate group contains individuals of different ages, sexes, dominance ranks, and kinship. Although this in itself is not unusual, primates also form temporary alliances, subgroups, and even long-term associations that cut across such categories. The result is (1) a complex network of interactions, with many alternative strategies for survival and reproduction, and (2) social groups in which individuals are likely to pursue a number of different strategies during their lifetimes. . . .
>
> 3. *Primates form various kinds of long-term social relationships.* As is the case with other animal species, the function of some types of competitive and cooperative behavior in nonhuman primates can often be described in terms of their direct consequences for reproductive success. For example, aggressive behavior may allow a male to maintain a high dominance rank, thereby increasing his access to estrous females. Because primates are long-lived, intelligent creatures, however, there are also many more subtle, indirect ways in which a given pattern of behavior can affect fitness.
>
> Ample evidence, for example, shows that primates groom or form alliances not only for their immediate benefits but also to establish and maintain particular social relationships. For instance, close kin groom one another after fighting, males sometimes groom and maintain close proximity to pregnant and lactating females, and female vervets and baboons often form alliances against animals that already rank lower than they do. . . .

Linda Fedigan (1982, 44) points out that primate social organizations may vary, and thus be categorized, with respect to at least the following factors:

1. the group size;
2. the group composition;
3. the mating system;
4. the social roles, especially for adult females and adult males, in relation to socialization, resource and predator defense, group movement leadership, etc.;
5. the major internal structuring principles, be they various types of dominance hierarchies, kinship networks, age/sex class associations, or alliance systems, etc.;
6. the permanence versus instability of group membership;

7. the tendency or ability of one level of social group to aggregate into larger social groupings;

8. the presence of only heterosexual reproductive units; or the additional presence of all-male groups; all-female groups; single individuals;

9. the pattern of interactions—who does what to whom, how often and under what circumstances?

What will no doubt strike most readers of the above list of criteria of social organization is that any *cultural* anthropologist would immediately recognize the relevance of Fedigan's categories—whether in the fast-disappearing traditional "field" and studying some remnant quasi-aboriginal tribal group, or in the modern field in some urban ghetto studying disintegration in public education in relation to public housing. Indeed, if I had not slanted the discussion by mentioning that the subject is *primate* social organization (and were the general context here something less precise than "primatological theory"), very few social scientist readers would have been likely to think first of monkeys and apes as the obvious subject of Fedigan's discussion.

Drawing upon his earlier very influential and widely cited article (1981; cf. also 1979), Richard Wrangham (1983, 261) proposes a model of primate behavior that emphasizes ecological theory and the basic importance of female social structure (cf. van Hooff 1982):

> Individuals who are familiar from birth have repeated opportunities to test each other's reliability as partners, allowing the development of a reciprocally beneficial relationship. . . . Within groups, nested subgroups occur and compete together for access to group resources. Again, these subgroups tend to consist of close kin, who thus cooperate against more distant kin. . . . A critical feature in each case is that females are bonded by the need for support against outside alliances. Relationships thus contain both competitive and cooperative elements, a condition conducive to complex social manoeuvers. . . .
>
> With groups viewed as founded on female alliances, males enter the scene as secondary players, adapting to and not substantially changing the pattern of female relationships. Nevertheless, male strategies of course bring much complexity to social structure, principally through competition for mating rights. Males compete with and occasionally support other males . . . develop long-term and short-term affiliative bonds with females . . . and threaten infanticide, which thereby favours male protection of infants they may have fathered. . . . How far male relationships can be explained in terms of sexual competition remains an open issue but it is surely the predominant factor. An important component of male strategies is that males leave their natal groups to breed, both because of the costs of inbreeding in their natal groups and because of the increased mating opportunities elsewhere. . . . An understanding of the forces influencing female relationships is thus the key to explaining the ultimate sources of monkey social structure.

Sarah Blaffer Hrdy agrees (1981, 17):

> Among langurs, it is females, not males, who comprise the stable core of social organization; as with most monkeys, langur society is given its shape by the relationships between overlapping generations of related females. In all but a few species, females are

permanent residents in social groups, males mere transients. In fact, the first evolutionary step toward social life for any mammal is thought to have taken place when related females began to develop mutual tolerance and to cooperate with each other. In those primates where rank is inherited from the mother, female dominance relations have far more long-term influence than does the ephemeral power politics of males, and the rank an individual's mother happens to hold may be the single most important fact of its biological existence.

Alison Richard, like Wrangham, emphasizes the importance of ecology to a better understanding of primate social behavior (1985, 36–38):

> For the ecologist bent on experimentation in the laboratory, prohibitive costs are compounded by the difficulty of re-creating within the confines of the laboratory an environment resembling the wild. For the field ecologist, the problems arising from the expense of reaching a study site in the topics when one could be studying squirrels on one's own temperate-zone doorstep are compounded by conditions at the end of the trip. Primates, tree-living forms in particular, are often elusive, and the tropical and subtropical forests where most are found tend to be inhospitable as well as inaccessible. . . . The difficulties of locating and following arboreal animals living at low densities, let alone of doing field experiments in a capture-release program, mean that built-in methodological constraints generally limit the kinds of questions one can hope to answer. . . .
>
> This book is primarily about the findings of the growing number of researchers more interested in the nonhuman primates as mammals than as relatives. If a range of factors discouraged this approach in the past, then what precipitated the change in the last 15 years or so? I would suggest two contributing factors, one affecting primarily those trained as physical anthropologists, whose numbers have increased dramatically in the last 20 years . . . and the other affecting those trained as ecologists in departments of biology, who make up most of the balance of primate field-workers. The first factor results from the change in how we think about our ancestors. Where once even our remotest ancestors were envisioned as humanlike in many features, today the fossil evidence suggests that during much of their evolution, our ancestors were more like other mammals than like us. . . . This changed perception makes the study of nonhuman primates as mammals in their own right much more compelling for physical anthropologists, who have turned to the discipline of ecology and increasingly contributed to research on the ecology of medium- and large-bodied mammals.

However, Robert Hinde (1983, 7) introduces the volume that he edited on primate social relationships by mentioning that although the "comparative methods pioneered by [classical ethologists] have been used to formulate hypotheses about the evolution of certain aspects of the social behaviour of individuals, most especially the behaviour used in social communication in interactions . . . yet practically nothing is known about *the course of evolution* of the behavioural propensities that lead to the formation of long-term relation-ships or to social structures of particular kinds" (emphasis added). There are actually two quite different points involved in what Hinde says about present lack of knowledge concerning the evolutionary *development* of behaviors found — in one form or another — in many different social species, including some whose genetic relationship to any primates is so remote that their concurrence with behaviors that can also be observed in modern humans (or modern gibbons) must be due primarily to similar environmental influences rather than to shared genetic opportunities and constraints. In the first place, *all* behaviors *per se* are remarkably ephemeral, in the sense that they leave no direct physical trace (unlike seeds or shells or even coprolites); and since behavior (in all species) is the first thing to change due to environmental stress (Geist 1978; Waddington 1957: G. Schubert 1985), it varies tremendously from individual to individual— certainly among primates—and among individuals during their ontogeny (Ra 1989)—and again, markedly among primates. So behavior is intrinsically extremely difficult to study in terms of evolutionary continuity and/or change (but see Potts 1987, 1988; Foley and Lee 1989), except for the simplest animals that tend to display the least flexibility in their behaviors. Secondly, and quite possibly because it is so hard to pin down, even attempts to study "the course of evolution of the behavioural propensities" of primates other than humans—not to mention those of mammals other than primates or of animals other than mammals—have been relatively few and far between. Even in the case of humans, most of what is known is about the (mostly) literally hard data of human evolution (stone tools, teeth, bones, chromosomes, and genes) as distinguished from considerably "softer" inferences and educated guesses that must be made (if very much is to be said) about behavioral evolution in pretransition gathering-hunting groups of modern humans, Neanderthals, Archaic *Homo sapiens*, *Homo erectus*, or australopithecines. So we have to begin any discussion of primate politics with the recognition that we know substantially less about how and why modern chimpanzees (or gorillas, orangs, gibbons, baboons, etc.) evolved into their present genomic possibilities than we do about humans (but see, e.g., Corruccini and Ciochon 1983; Ciochon and Fleagle 1985; Fleagle 1988). Hominoid cladistics (see Sarich and Wilson 1967; Sarich 1983; Ciochon 1983) helps tremendously, of course; however, gene mapping is only a way of describing those possibilities: it is not a description of any specific behaviors, let alone of how any specific *behavior* evolved through time *and* space.

That leaves us with the alternative of trying to learn what we can by examining comparatively both similarities and differences in the behaviors of modern primates, using paleoanthropology and behavioral genetics as guides to the probabilities that, in the context of equally painstaking studies in the comparative ecology of the subject species, scientific investigators will be better able to distinguish homologies from analogies in the observed behaviors. Humans are presumed to be most similar genetically to the extinct species of hominids from which *Homo sapiens sapiens* evolved during the past 4 million years, but especially the direct ancestors and first cousins who became extinct only within the past half million years: Neanderthals, Archaic *Homo sapiens*, and *Homo erectus* (Eldredge and Tattersall 1982). Modern humans are now deemed (cf. Sarich 1983) to share 99 percent of their specific genome with chimpanzees ("The DNA and proteins show chimpanzees and humans to be 99 percent similar—as closely related . . . as . . . grizzly bears to polar bears" [Zihlman 1982, 88]), but that discovery raises complex questions of epigenetic develop ment discussed later in the Introduction. Almost as closely related to humans genetically are gorillas and possibly orangutans (although that involves dispute between molecular and skeletal cladists).

Contemporary research provides quite explicit inventories of, for example, the interspecific variation in sexual signaling and behavior among seventy-eight species of primates, including humans (Hrdy and Whitten 1987, 372–78); studies that are at least cognate in spirit have been made of humans by social scientists (Henley 1977; Henley and Freeman 1984; Henley and Harman 1985). Neverthe less, it is premature to attempt to present an analogous catalogue of primate political behaviors. In lieu of that, I have endeavored to identify a few criteria, all of which recur frequently in the papers in this book. Indeed, each of them is discussed in one of the initial four sections of this introductory chapter.

The remainder of this chapter considers questions—for they will be posed as such—related to the methodology of undertaking to compare nonhuman pri mates with humans in regard to their respective and at least putatively political behaviors. Several other questions could also be considered to be methodologi cal but will be grouped separately: these concern the sexual politics of either the subject nonhuman primates or their human observers in constructing or criticizing nonhuman primate social structure.

1. Should the origins of human political behavior be sought via comparative primatology, paleoprimatology, paleoanthropology, or archaeology? Which are the most suitable role models: modern apes, modern aboriginals, pretransition *Homo sapiens*, or extinct hominids?

2. If nonhuman primates are to be employed as models of human political behavior, where should the former be studied—in the field or in the labora tory—and why? (William C. McGrew, a highly respected field primatologist who works primarily with chimpanzees but who is also a child psychologist, states quite bluntly [1981, 36] that "however fascinating and provocative the implications of laboratory studies, they tell us nothing *directly* about adaptive responses by chimpanzees or early humans to natural selection.")

3. Unless we are to wait until (as some primatological linguists and primate cognitive ethologists think possible) the language competence of selected and highly learned chimpanzees and gorillas improves to the point where they can go beyond ordering Cokes (see G. Schubert 1989a, chap. 16) and design and carry out primatological studies of their conspecifics, we are probably stuck with human observers and analysts of nonhuman primate social and "political" behavior. If so, how can human primatologists take and keep the pledge to extirpate, instead of cultivating, rampant anthropomorphism, whether conscious or un conscious, in the perception, conceptualization, understanding, description, and analysis of the behavior of nonhuman primate subjects, whether in the field or the laboratory? And lest those readers who are humans (and social scientists

to boot) forget, it was none other than the godfather of behavioralism in political science, Harold D. Lasswell, who *defined* political behavior psychologically as a matter of socialized, but neo-Freudian *projection*, asserting that it consists of the displacement of private interests upon public objects and then rationalizing the result as being in the public interest. There is no doubt that in their general behavior—not just in their political behavior—humans anthropomorphize each other; and equally doubtless, it is necessary and appropriate that they should do so. The question is whether it is helpful for their own understanding, to say nothing of the understanding of the consumers of their research, for *primatologists* to anthropomorphize in their thinking about nonhuman primates. (For a spirited defense of the virtues, not just the necessity, of such anthropomorphism, see de Waal 1987, 421.) If *not*, how can primatologists make their own behavior less political in regard to their subject nonhuman primates?

4. Pretransition humans rarely congregated, other than temporarily and for specific limited purposes, in groups larger than a hundred individuals; nonhuman primates almost never do so, except for baboons while asleep and chimpanzees on a basis similar to that of gathering-hunting humans. Although it seems true that most human political behavior still takes place in groups much smaller than one hundred, even in industrialized societies, various modes of conventional as well as "nonconventional" (such as violent) behavior involve groups of much larger size, such as presidential nomination conventions in the United States and massed audiences for the harangues of dictators, popes, and revolutionary assemblages. But what is the relationship between the magnitude and complexity of social structure and that of political behavior?

5. What are the implications for primatological observations, findings, and theory, whether primatologists anthropomorphize for nonhuman primates (not the animals this time, but rather their social structure) by postulating for them a stereotyped version of sociological structure and function, with "primate society" determining (by means of processes that are assumed rather than explained) a set of roles to which the members of a primate group are expected to learn how to conform, primarily from the threats or violence of animals superior to themselves in the dominance structure? Alternatively, what difference does it make if primatologists take their cues from constructional biology (Wheeler and Danielli 1982) instead of from human sociology, and postulate that each member of a primate social group, beginning in infancy, creates his or her own role in relation to others in the group out of a combination of each individual's kin relationships, physical strengths and weaknesses, intelligence, personality, and unique experiences?

The remaining three questions focus explicitly on the sexual politics of nonhuman primates and/or their human observers:

6. How does the social behavior of male primates differ from that of females in many of the best-studied and most social primate species; and how are such differences related to the social structure of primate groups of conspecifics (Lancaster 1984, 1985; R. Hall 1982, 1985)?

7. How, why, and with what consequences for primatology have female observers modally reached different conclusions about the social behavior of nonhuman primates in the field than have male observers of the same primate groups? Why is it that ever since women began to undertake work in field primatology beginning in the early 1960s, they have by consensual acclaim had much greater success than have male primatologists in establishing and maintaining rapport for an extended period of time with a primate group in the field? When second-wave feminism began (in the early 1970s) to have an influence upon the socialization of undergraduate and graduate women in anthropology and psychology, and somewhat later and to a lesser extent in zoology (see Hubbard, Henefin, and Fried 1979; Birke 1986), what effect did this have upon female primatologists; and vice versa (see sections 3 and 4 below).

8. The renaissance in field primatology that began in the earliest 1960s was accompanied by widespread professional support, on the part of male physical anthropologists and paleoanthropologists alike, for the overarching theoretical paradigm of "Man the Hunter," including its spinoff scenarios of "Killer Apes" and an innate and instinctive human male love of killing as well as of hunting, with dominant, hypercompetitive males ruling hierarchies through violence but providing "protection" for grateful females whose sexual favors are monopolized by the dominants. Women entered physical and paleoanthropology in the 1960s but in the major conferences (on "early man") participated only as secretaries or clerks and coffee servers (see G. Schubert, in press, chap. 2.3.A, para. 1).

To what extent and how did Man-the-Hunter become transformed into Woman-the-Gatherer? The 1960s was also the decade of the Vietnam War, civil rights marches, and the radicalization of a generation of American college students, including female graduate students in physical anthropology at the University of California, Berkeley, such as Shirley Strum and Adrienne Zihlman. At the same time that female primatologists began to develop studies of and shift attention to modern female primate social hierarchies (Small 1982; Hrdy 1981; Fedigan 1982), the feminist reconstruction of premodern human evolutionary behavioral development also began, and the two parallel developments strongly stimulated and reinforced each other. By the end of the 1970s, female primatologists and evolutionary biologists (including by then more than a few feminist biologists) had succeeded in getting widespread acceptance of the alternative paradigm of "Woman the Gatherer" (see Zihlman and Tanner 1978; Dahlberg 1981; Tanner 1981) as a hypothesis at least as important as that of "Man the Hunter" (see Potts 1988, 203–4; but cf. Zihlman 1987). That, however, directly affected the implications for political (including feminist) theory of assumptions taken from evolutionary biology about "human nature," which would be based on the predominantly cooperative behaviors of female primates (human as well as nonhuman) instead of relying exclusively upon the predominantly competitive behaviors attributed to male primates in their relationships to each other as well as to females (see section 4 below). Furthermore, the studies by human females of nonhuman primate female social structure directly and positively influenced the reconceptualization of human evolutionary development theory at the same time that biochemical genetic cladistics was demonstrating how recently hominids diverged from pongids, and how extremely genetically close are modern humans and the other great apes. The conjoint implications were revolutionary both for evolutionary political theory and feminist political theory (see G. Schubert 1989a, 1989b, in press).

## 2. PRIMATE EVOLUTION: A BIBLIOGRAPHICAL PREFACE

All living primates have evolved from tiny ancestors about the size of the modern tree-shrew prosimians that coexisted with dinosaurs when the latter became extinct about 65 million years ago; but only the most recent 20 percent of that period—about the last 13 million years—is relevant here. Paleoprimatologists—a notoriously contentious group—generally agree that it was about then, in the mid-Miocene geological era, that the most probable common ancestor of all hominoids (and therefore of all living gibbons/simiangs, pongids, and hominids) was the widely dispersed fossil ape *Sivapithecus*. Dating the hominoids as originating 13Mya (million years ago; see Corruccini and Ciochon 1983, 9n.4), more than half of the time since then elapses until the mid-Pliocene (i.e., $5 \pm 1$ Mya) when the earliest hominid ancestor *(Australopithecus afarensis)* parted company from the pongid ancestors of modern chimpanzees, gorillas, and orangs; the Hylobatidae (gibbon ancestor) had already split off several million years earlier.

The subsections below will deal with the following topics: (1) nonhominid hominoid evolution for the eight million years from 13Mya to 5Mya; (2) hominid evolution during the past five million years; (3) homin*oid* models of the evolution of humans; (4) premodern band models of the evolution of humans; and (5) modern apes.

1. Corruccini and Ciochon (1983, 3–17) provide an excellent overview of the phyletic relationships of the Hominoidae from the mid-Miocene through the early Pliocene. There is agreement that the hylobatids diverged first, possibly very early in the Miocene, and that "during the period of the late Miocene-earliest Pliocene a common ancestor of *Homo*, *Pan*, and *Gorilla* existed" (Cronin 1983, 131). *Homo* and *Pan* (human and chimpanzee ancestors) were probably the latest to separate, with gorillas diverging somewhat earlier, although some molecular biologists claim that gorillas separated from hominids more recently than did chimpanzees. On this latter point, the difference in view reflects the kind of evidence and the training of the researcher (see Cronin 1983; Sarich 1983; Lewin 1987, chap. 6): paleoprimatologists rely on fossil teeth and bones which are dated in part by methods of estimating radioactive decay and in part

on the sedimentary context in which they are found; molecular biologists work with observable genome differences from which estimates of time as a function of species generation are calculated, and their cladistics are consistently substantially more accelerated than ones based on more traditional paleoanthropological skeletal discoveries (on the development of the method, see Sarich 1983). Consequently, there is also a dispute about orangs, with Schwartz (1984a, 1984b) positing a separate clade of hominids and orangs, making orangs the pongid closest genetically to humans today; this view is disputed by Andrews and Cronin (1982). A summary review of hominoid cladistics as of the early 1980s is presented by Ciochon (1983).

2. The origins of hominids about 5Mya are discussed in Reichs (1983); subsequent extinction in hominid evolution is discussed by A. Walker (1984). Stanley (1986) asserts that human evolution has been punctuational (i.e., stepwise) rather than gradual (i.e., smooth and continuous); for a discussion of punctuationism in relation to human evolution and politics, see G. Schubert (1989b). According to Eldredge and Tattersall (1982), there were four successive species of Australopithecines: *A. afarensis*, a gracile (relatively small and light) species, appeared about 4Mya and disappeared about a million years later, being replaced by *A. africanus* (also gracile), which also lasted for about a million years. *Africanus* was succeeded by two different but both much more robust species; the first to appear was *A. boisei*, and the second *A. robustus* about 200,000 years later. For discussion of the complexities of taphonomic inference (to evaluate the geologic/skeletal/cultural evidence on which cladistics is based), see T. White (1988) and Vrba (1988); Potts (1988) offers a detailed analysis of Olduvai hominid paleocommunities circa 1.85Mya. Both of the robust australopithecine species coexisted—although not necessarily in precisely the same locations—for almost 700,000 years, with *A. robustus* disappearing first and *A. boisei* perhaps 200,000 years later, slightly more than 1Mya. In the meantime, however, the first two species of the genus *Homo*—*habilis* and *erectus*—also evolved about 1.8–1.7Mya; so that for at least 600,000 years, four hominid species were extant simultaneously: *A. boisei*, *A. robustus*, *H. habilis*, and *H. erectus*. *H. erectus* proved to be the most durable, surviving the longest of any hominid species, until perhaps 300,000 years ago, to overlap for 200,000 with the Archaic *Homo sapiens* that survived it. Archaic *Homo sapiens* was succeeded by two subspecies which coexisted in different regions for fifty to a hundred thousand years, when *Homo sapiens sapiens* migrated into and through Europe to come into increasing contact with *Homo sapiens neanderthalensis*. Mostly during the first half of the last 100,000 years—and in a process that humans were to repeat many times and in diverse subcontinents among the subpopulations (races) of the modern species— *H. sapiens sapiens* incorporated some of the Neanderthals into their gene pool while exterminating the remainder by means of competitive exclusion.

Australopithecines are discussed by Wolpoff (1983), Zihlman and Lowenstein (1983), and especially by Grine (1988); *H. erectus* by R. Leakey and Walker

(1985); and Neanderthals by Kurtén (1986). Several aspects of hominid behavior have been the focus of considerable interest and attention from an evolutionary perspective, especially bipedalism (M. Leakey 1981; La Lumiere 1981). Parker and Gibson (1979) present a developmental model for the evolution of language and intelligence in early hominids, concluding that in terms of Piagetian stages, prosimians never progress beyond the first two stages; Old World monkeys go through the initial level of stage 5; the great apes through the initial level of stage 6 ("preoperational intelligence"), and the early hominids through all of the remaining categories of Piagetian stage 6. Falk (1987) discusses a different approach to hominoid intelligence: sex differences in brain lateralization in primates and its evolution in hominids.

The late Glynn Isaac (who in 1985 died suddenly and mysteriously at age forty-seven and at the very peak of his career, of a very high and undiagnosed fever that he might have contracted at Koobi Fora in Kenya en route to a professional conference in China [*Harvard Crimson* 1985]) was the leading proponent of the "home base" theory, including the hypothesis (Isaac 1978a,b) that food was shared among hominids 2Mya, at the very threshold when *A. boisei*, *A. robustus*, *H. habilis*, and *H. erectus* were about to replace *A. africanus*—or, stated somewhat differently, when *Homo* was beginning to displace *Australopithecus*. Potts, however, has concluded (1988, chap. 9) that home bases in the sense of the social structure and behavior of the San and other indigenous nineteenth- and twentieth-century gathering-hunting peoples (the apparent basis for Isaac's conceptual model) were not found at Olduvai Bed I (1.85–1.70 Mya) and probably did not appear until a million years later.

3. During the 1980s, considerable attention has been given to theorizing about the most probable phyletic pathway, back through the early Pliocene into the Miocene, to evaluate the available evidence in support of a common ancestor for contemporary humans and one of the contemporary pongids. As indicated above, the route back to and through *A. afarensis* seemed reasonably clear by the end of the 1970s; no doubt that was a major catalyst to the subsequent endeavors to push back to the next missing "link" (see Reader 1981)—actually, missing "node" would be better nowadays—to connect *A. afarensis* explicitly with *its* predecessor (see Ciochon 1983, 821, 828, 836). The most ambitious and best developed of these efforts was foreshadowed by Zihlman and Tanner (1978) and is found in a book by Nancy Makepeace Tanner (1981), appropriately entitled *On Becoming Human;* in a subsequent paper she presents a chart (1987, 11) suggesting a split about 7.5Mya between *Pan* and *Homo*, with a further division for *Pan* about 5My later between common and pygmy chimpanzees that puts *P. paniscus* (pygmy chimps; see Zihlman and Lowenstein 1983; de Waal 1989, chap. 5; and for a rare photograph of one, see Richard 1985, 36, fig. 1.19) adjacent to *Homo* (with *Gorilla gorilla* on the adjacent side). Her evidence—not consummate poetic license—required that Tanner put common chimpanzees, not *Homo sapiens sapiens*, at the pinnacle of her "Molecular Phylogeny of Old World Primates," a *tour de force* reminiscent

of the frontispiece to Stephen Jay Gould's *Ontogeny and Phylogeny* (1977), where a cartoon by Saul Steinberg is reproduced depicting an Olympics awards ceremony type of pedestal on which a beetle-browed eagle (see Kurtén 1988) perches rampant in glorious victory, with an Airedale in the three-piece business suit of a (contemporary to the cartoon) member of the Soviet Politburo (or an American union leader during the 1930s depression) tied for second place with a crocodile; and a human white-collar male worker tied with a fish for fourth-and-a-half place. (For discussion of Tanner's models and hypothesis, see her book [1981], McGrew [1981], Tanner [1987] and Wrangham [1987] Cf. Clarence Day's [1920] fantasy of life with—instead—superintelligent dogs, or cats, etc.)

4. The leading work on the model and hypothesis of Woman the Gatherer is Dahlberg (1981), and see especially therein Zihlman (1981); and see also Zihlman and Tanner (1978). For more general focus on the ecological and behavioral parameters of social life in contemporary (necessarily, remnant) gathering-hunting bands, the most extensive as well as intensive, highly interdisciplinary, research has related to the San (who before their rediscovery at the end of the 1960s were called "Bushmen") of southwest Africa, whose investigators (i.e., Blurton Jones and Konner 1973) include one of the contributors to the present volume. Among the many published studies of the San now available, the most relevant here is Lee (1979); more generally, see Leacock and Lee (1982) and A. Barnard (1983).

5. Chevalier-Skolnikoff and Poirier (1977) provide a unique introduction to comparative primate learning, socialization, and development. More recent and general surveys of the social structure and behavior of contemporary primates include Smuts et al. (1987), Richard (1985), Small (1982), Hinde (1983), and Fedigan (1982). The most voluminous research literature relates to chimpanzees: Goodall (1986; see also chap. 5 in this volume) is the most complete and outstanding report; but see also McGrew (1977), Nishida and Hiraiwa-Hasegawa (1987), Ghiglieri (1984, 1988), Zihlman and Lowenstein (1983), Tanner (1981), Susman (1987), and de Waal (1989, chaps. 2, 5). Gorillas are discussed by Stewart and Harcourt (1987); but see also Fossey (1983) and Schaller (1963). The leading field researcher of orangs (see section 3 below) has been Biruté Galdikàs (1975, 1984; and as a coauthor of Chevalier-Skolnikoff, Galdikàs, and Skolnikoff 1982); but see also Rodman and Mitani (1987) and Horr (1977). On gibbons, see Leighton (1987); on guenons and patas, Cords (1987); on baboons, see Strum (1987), a recent book by a contributor to this volume (chap. 4), Strum and Mitchell (1987), and Stammbach (1987).

## 3. FIELD PRIMATOLOGY BY FEMALE PRIMATOLOGISTS

*Women Primatologists Looking at Female Primates*

Most of the early best-known female primatologists were sent into the field during the 1960s and 1970s, primarily into Africa and almost entirely by three men: an

African paleoanthropologist, an English zoologist, and an American physical anthropologist. The latter two were and are career academics with lifelong prestigious academic chairs; the African, Louis Leakey, was, like most of his "ape girls" (see Cole 1975, 333–50) a person who endured only as much academia as was essential to support an always only marginally fiscally feasible career in the field, working most closely with his wife Mary and other native Africans in the wildest and most inaccessible habitats still available. Louis was born free, and he remained a lifelong romantic. He recruited and anted into the field a stable of young women, including Jane Goodall, Dian Fossey, and Biruté Galdikàs, of whom the first two started doing field primatology and only later on acquired Cambridge doctorates under the supervision of Robert Hinde and with Leakey's assistance. It was no coincidence that chimpanzees came first (with Goodall, of course), mountain gorillas next (in the lifelong fulfillment of what became Fossey's obsession), and orangs third (with Galdikàs), thereby touching all bases for the largest, most spectacular, and best-known great apes other than humans themselves. It was quite an accomplishment for a man (not to mention the young women who did it) for whom field primatology was only a sideline: Leakey himself did not study living apes, pursuing instead his lifelong quest for the earliest human ancestor—the missing hominid link.

Neither Leakey nor the American academic, Sherwood Washburn of the University of California, Berkeley, was feminist in orientation (see also Strum 1987, 9–13), although Robert Hinde became much more so. All three agreed, however, that women make good field observers of apes and monkeys, and all three strongly advocated the best possible field primatology. The present volume is fortunate to include a chapter by a leading protegé of each sponsor: Hinde's student Thelma Rowell (chap. 3); Washburn's, Shirley Strum (chap. 4); and Leakey's, Jane Goodall (chap. 5). And there were, of course, dozens of others (Haraway 1986, 106–7; 1989), plus female primatologists who took doctorates elsewhere than at Cambridge, Stanford, Berkeley, or Harvard; several are cited or quoted elsewhere in this volume (see also Small 1982; Smuts et al. 1987).

## The Kuhnian Paradigm Change in Primatology

The male primatologist "baboon primatology" of the 1960s and earlier is epitomized by DeVore and Hall (1965, 54: "The baboon group is organized around the dominance hierarchy of adult males") and subsequently memorialized in a typical (and certainly putatively authoritative) statement by E. O. Wilson (1980, 259, 264):

> The males are twice the size of the females, their appearance made still more striking by a large mane of wavy gray hair. This dimorphism is related to the feature of the hamadryas behavior that makes the species uniquely interesting: the extreme dominance of the adult male over females, who are kept forcibly in a permanent harem. This relationship influences virtually every other aspect of the social organization. . . . The harems contain from one to as many as ten adult females. At their physical peak most males control from two to five of these

adult consorts. The relationship is easily the most "sexist" known in all of the primates. The male herds the females, never letting them stray too far, associate with strangers, or quarrel too vigorously with one another. He employs forms of aggression that vary from a simple hostile stare or slap to a sharp bite on the neck. . . . The chastized female responds by running to the male. Since the males sequester their harems with such jealousy, they are also responsible for most of the interactions with other hamadryas units. Young male leaders tend to initiate band movement by moving out with their families closely in tow. Older male leaders then either follow or remain seated, and their actions decide the issue for the band as a whole. When preparing to change position, the males notify one another with special gestures. Fighting between the bands is also conducted by the males.

Washburn and DeVore (1961, 100) were among the first to report that "dominance in baboons is ultimately based on the ability to fight. Fighting within the troop seldom occurs, because the position of each animal is recognized by the others, and these positions remain stable for considerable periods of time. Adult male baboons are much larger than the females and have large canine teeth. When danger is near, *it is they that protect the troop*, and as a result they are actively sought out by the younger and weaker troop members" (emphasis added; for a recent defense of the dominance model, see de Waal, 1987a, 425–26).

In the section "The Role of Women Researchers" in a discussion on "the myth of the coy female," Sarah Blaffer Hrdy (1986, 135) queries this model:

Assuming bias, a preconstituted reality in which males played central roles, what factors motivated researchers to revise invalid assumptions? What changes in the last decade brought about the new focus on female reproductive strategies and, with it, the recognition that certain assumptions . . . were seriously limited and even, if applied universally, quite wrong. . . . To understand male-male competition for mates is to understand only a small part of what leads to the evolution of particular primate breeding systems. We need also consider the many sources of variance in female reproductive success, including a whole range of female behaviors not directly related to "mothering" that may have repercussions on the fates of their infants. Polyandrous mating with multiple males, mating with males when conception is not possible—what from the males' point of view might be termed "excessive" matings—can only be understood within this new framework, but it requires a whole new set of assumptions and research questions. As a result, sexual selection theory is currently in a state of flux; it is being rethought as actively as any area in evolutionary biology. What processes contributed to this destabilization of a long-held paradigm? And in particular, what led us to rethink the myth of the coy or monandrous female?

Signe Hammer (1988) discusses Strum's *Almost Human* (1987), remarking that when Shirley

first went to Kenya as a graduate student in 1972, the "killer ape" view of man held sway, based entirely on early studies of baboons. . . . What Strum found completely contradicted the model. But then, her method of study was different. Her predecessor at the 20-square-mile site had never left the security of a white VW van; parked a safe distance away from the troop, he had studied baboon communication through binoculars. Strum not only got out of the van; she spent several months edging her way, on foot, into the troop.

Hrdy (1981, 126–27) points out, on the basis substantially of her own research, that

> Females arrange themselves in space and time so as to maximize food intake while minimizing competition for food from either individual females or from other groups of females. Within the limits compatible with survival, males arrange themselves singly or in bands so as to control access to these dispersed females. Males may shift strategies with age, physical condition, and opportunities, but the basic constraint upon them remains the deployment of females. Where females clump together . . . fierce contests between males over access to these harems develop. Where females are solitary, a male will either settle in with a single mate and help defend their common territory . . . or move singly across ranges of several mother-offspring units.

Fedigan (1982, 119–20) concludes that

> there has been some discussion in primatology of a division of tasks such that females are infant-raisers and males are group protectors. . . . However, ideas about predator defense are largely theoretical as little actual predation on these primates had ever been observed. In a situation where I was able to observe a group of ground-dwelling macaques repeatedly defend themselves against predators, and on one occasion, chase a bobcat running off with an infant monkey in its mouth . . . animals of many ages and both sexes participated effectively in the defensive action. This species is one in which adult males only are traditionally thought to perform a specialized defense role.
>
> The common baboons are probably the most widely-publicized example of large males protecting their groups and yet Rowell reports: "Baboon males are often described as defending their troop, but this I never saw and find difficult to imagine, since Ishasha baboons always reacted to any potential danger by flight . . . the whole troop flees from any major threat, the males with their longer legs at the front, with the females carrying the heaviest infants coming last (1972, 44)."
>
> . . . Most important of all, longitudinal studies have shown that it is females who generally remain in their home groups and home areas for life, while males of many species have a tendency to wander . . . [and such studies also] have shown us that females are often the social foci of the group, and that female-offspring units form the "core" of many primate societies. . . . Primate young are very dependent for long periods of time, and the survival of offspring is considered *the* major criterion of success in evolutionary theory. In addition to performing what is the most important task for any animal, female primates also feed themselves and they may protect themselves, use their knowledge of their own range, control their own intragroup conflicts, and through their affinitive ties with friends, relatives, and mates, establish and maintain bonds which are the cement of primate social life.

In a little more than a decade—that of the 1970s—female primatologists gathered the observations, reported the evidence, and challenged the ideology of male dominance theory as the nature of primate social structure with such diligence and success that by the 1980s—as signaled by Richard Wrangham's leading article and model (1981)—the *primary* importance of primate females in assuring the organization and indeed the "fitness" (in the sense of evolutionary genetics) of their respective species-specific groupings had become widely accepted both as the dominant paradigm (cf. Kuhn 1970) of professional primatology and also among its diverse audiences (such as second-wave feminism: see Haraway 1978, 1983b; Small 1982; and Eckholm 1984).

## 4. FEMINIST EVOLUTIONARY AND POLITICAL THEORY

The change in how primatologists would observe and understand the social behavior of nonhuman primates is of course important per se; but what about its implications for bioanthropological and paleoanthropological understanding of sexual selection in relation to hominid (including human) evolution? Does the transformation of nurturant and socially active and effective female apes and monkeys from merely coy ones, and the consequent diminution (at least in relative importance vis à vis females) in the predominance of male dominance hierarchies, require that Man the Hunter make room for Woman the Gatherer?

Sherwood Washburn and Chet S. (not Jane) Lancaster (1968, 299) assert that male human killing of other animals for food, an essential part of the hunting adaptation of the species, has further evolved into the love of killing for its own sake, as best exemplified by the delights of warfare: "Men enjoy hunting and killing, and these activities are continued as sports even when they are no longer economically necessary. . . . War has been far too important in human history for it to be other than pleasurable for the males involved."

Haraway (1978, 51–53) comments that Sherwood Washburn and David Hamburg (1968)

saw aggression as a fundamental adaptation or functional complex, common to the entire primate order, including human beings. "Order within most primate groups is maintained by a hierarchy, which depends ultimately primarily on the power of males. . . . Aggressive individuals are essential actors in the social system and competition between groups is necessary for species dispersal and control of local populations." The biology of aggression has been extensively studied and seems, they argue, to rest on similar hormonal and neural mechanisms, modified in primates, and especially in humans, by new brain complexes and extensive learning. In nonhuman primates, aggression is constantly rewarded, and, the authors maintain, aggressive individuals (males) leave more offspring. So they argue for selection of a system of coadapted genes involving complex feedback among motor anatomy, gestural anatomy, hormones, brain elements, and behavior. Presumably, all parts of the aggressive complex evolve. The functions requiring aggression did not abate for humankind, Hamburg and Washburn believe. Protection, policing, and finally hunting all required a continued selection for male organisms who easily learned and enjoyed regulated fighting, torturing, and killing. "Throughout most of human history societies have depended on young adult males to hunt, to fight, and to maintain the social order with violence." Even when the individual was cooperating, his social role could be executed only by extremely aggressive action that was learned in play, was socially approved, and was presumably gratifying.

But then, as Bleier (1984, 121) recounts,

In a landmark paper first appearing in 1971, Sally Slocum (1975) discussed the problem of male bias in anthropology, pointing out that the choice of asking certain questions *and not others* grows out of the cultural context in which anthropologists exist. While by 1971 Western anthropologists had begun to recognize their ethnic, racial, class, and academic biases, Slocum first demonstrated the *male* bias in the Man-the-Hunter theory of evolution. She described her alternative version of evolution, which takes into account the participation of women as gatherers and mothers, and suggested the critical role such activities may have played in the evolution of food-sharing, cooperation, and the invention of containers and tools, all essential features for the evolution of the cooperative activity of large-scale social hunting. This line of investigation and writing has been carried forward by Nancy Tanner and Adrienne Zihlman (1976; and see also Zihlman and Tanner 1978) and others as will be described in succeeding pages. During the past decade, it has become clear that there is a paucity of data either to support any theory of the signal importance of large-scale hunting as a driving force in evolution millions of years ago or to suggest that it even existed earlier than about 100,000 years ago. Furthermore, studies from a number of disciplines suggest a variety of interpretations of data bearing on our evolutionary history.

Zihlman (1981, 93–94, 103, 110–11; cf. Dahlberg 1981) expands upon the implications of the gathering model:

> Gathering and not hunting was the initial food-getting behavior that distinguished ape from human. This was an innovation whereby human females used tools to obtain food for themselves, as well as to sustain their young through the long period of dependency, walked long distances, and carried food bipedally on the African savannas. . . . From the beginning of the human adaptation, a woman's role encompassed reproductive, economic, and social components. Furthermore, rather than a leading force, hunting must have emerged late in human evolutionary history from a technological and social base in gathering. . . .
>
> With the use of tools, sufficient food could be collected and transported to permit sharing with offspring and perhaps others. A nomadic way of life, in which female mobility was critical, was facilitated by bipedal locomotion, permitting long-distance walking even while carrying infants, food, and tools. Children raised in the gathering way of life remained dependent on adults until they could walk long distances, master the skills of collecting and processing food with the use of tools, and acquire sufficient knowledge of the social and physical environments. . . .
>
> There is no specific character in male or female physique in ancient or modern humans that can be interpreted to signify that only males must hunt and females gather. . . . Gathering and preparing food with tools made it possible for the early hominids, especially the mothers, to exploit the abundant savanna resources: it was a new feeding pattern in a new environment for obtaining, transporting, and preparing foods to share. . . . Women's critical contribution to shaping the human adaptation must be integrated into [the] evolutionary picture . . . [and advancing] our understanding of sex roles in prehistory . . . may further understanding of the sexes today.

Bleier (1984; 131) concludes that "the value of the controversy as posed by Slocum and Tanner and Zihlman is immense, since it opens the mind to the possibility of alternative arguments that are at least as plausible and logical as traditional androcentric versions."

The correlated paradigm shifts in primatology and paleoanthropology to more-feminist theories of nonhuman primate societies and of human evolution have additional implications for political theory. From Adam Smith to Ronald Reagan, repeated and insistent emphasis has been given to the virtues of successful competition and the vices of failure, or even of coming in second best. (In the deathless words of Vince Lombardi, a lion in the streets of Green Bay, Wisconsin, a generation ago, "Winning is not the main thing. Winning is *every*thing!") Much of this ideology of free enterprise stems from cultural sources: consider the great importance attached throughout Western societies to Marxist dialectical materialism (but cf. Kropotkin 1902), to Freud's inner struggle between ego and id, and (especially nowadays) to valuing nothing less than a gold medal from the Olympics. Social Darwinism certainly contributed to such thinking—as well it might, given not only the popularity of such imputed Darwinian notions as "the struggle of the fittest" for survival in a "Nature red in tooth and claw" but also the contemporary popularity of sociobiological and ecological theories that feature econometric games and zero-sum calculations of the utility of altruism, which is considered to be an "unnatural" alternative to universally natural selfish behavior that can be sacrificed only in trade-offs for even greater ultimate self-aggrandizement (cf. Caporael et al. 1989).

In spite of such continuing reinforcement of the traditional competitive models, one direct consequence of female primatology has been a refocusing of attention, in research on captive primates as well as in field primatology, on female primate social behavior as something different from that of males among other primates as well as among humans. This is exemplified by a recent chapter by de Waal (1987a, 427–29; cf. de Waal 1989), "Dynamics of Social Relationships," in which he concludes that "the evolutionary approach has put too much emphasis on competitive aspects; we also need to study dominance in the context of reconciliation, social tolerance, and group cohesiveness. These new approaches are illustrated with selected examples from the literature and from the author's observations on captive macaques and chimpanzees. Special attention is paid to the role of cooperation in agonistic situations and its attenuating effect on power differences between dominants and subordinates." The new feminist paradigms of primatology and paleoanthropology strongly support cooperative attitudes in several strands of contemporary feminist thinking, in which nurturance, environmentalism, well-fare-ism, and the valuing and protection of life define female nature, while technocracy, militarism, and the desecration of the biosphere generally are the opposite attributes of male nature. At this level of ideology, what I call "Third-wave feminism" (G. Schubert in press, chap. 7.2; cf. Merchant 1980) is replete with direct implications for politics and public policy, and for political theory, that provide more justification for cooperative social behavior and less for competitive individualistic behavior.

## 5. THE STRUCTURE OF *PRIMATE POLITICS*

The next eight chapters of this volume are organized into three major parts, each of which is introduced by one of the coeditors. The purpose of these introductory essays is to comment on the chapters included in the part, discussing questions of both theory and fact raised by the contributors and putting their conclusions into the broader context of other work in the fields of primatological or political inquiry. The purpose of this concluding section of the introduction is to discuss briefly the major differences in emphases among the three parts of this book.

The primary emphasis of the first part is upon research theory, from the perspectives of both primatology and political science. Political scientists are mostly classified as social scientists; and social scientists study human behavior, including human politics—although human politics is also studied by humanists, including artists and philosophers, of whom many (including probably most "political scientists") range from neutral to hostile in their attitudes toward political *science*. Anthropology is similarly bifurcated between a physical branch (including paleoanthropology) that embraces biology and other natural and physical science and a cultural ("social" in the United Kingdom and its cultural derivatives) branch that, like political science, embraces the humanities and some social science. But most doctorates in anthropology must take at least some graduate courses in the branch *other than* the one in which they major, with the result that most physical anthropologists have some familiarity with social science theory and methods. Most field primatologists of the past generation have trained as physical anthropologists; therefore, most contemporary primatologists have some training also in the study of human behavior. The same is true of the physiological psychologists who, although in smaller numbers, also study primates, but usually in laboratories rather than in the field.

The other disciplinary source of primatologists has been ethology, where the zoological curriculum emphasizes both biological and physical science, but correspondingly deemphasizes social sciences and humanities alike. Ethologically trained primatologists tend to have a strong background in evolutionary biology, but little educational background in political science or social science generally.

These socialization differentials begin to make a difference when scholars of such different backgrounds as zoologically trained primatologists and political scientists appraise each other's work in a subject of common interest—such as the political behavior of nonhuman primates. Such scholars see the subject through quite different eyes and with quite different conceptual tools because of the fundamental differences in the theories and methods (not to mention the substantive "knowledge") that each deems relevant.

Thus, political scientist Glendon Schubert directs attention to the difference of meaning in conceptualizing "political" on the basis of empirical research in human societies as the basis for trying to understand the roles of "political" leadership in small, basically kinship bands of nonhuman primates. The authors of most of the cases he examines (Chance, de Waal, and Hrdy, but conspicuously *not* Strum) purport to do that, although modern human societies are vastly different in size and scale from any nonhuman primate aggregations that have been observed in the field, "in nature." Ethologist/primatologist Thelma

Rowell goes outside of the nonhuman primates—to sea lions—in order to proffer an example of a mammalian habitat for which the constraints on but opportunities for mating behavior differ markedly from what is typical for monkeys. She thereby provides empirical evidence to confute the methodological fallacy committed by (mostly male) primatologists who are as insensitive to the implications of applying a sociopolitical concept such as "harem" to humans as they are when they misapply it to nonhuman primates. Possibly they do that unconsciously in attempts to glorify machoistic male patriarchal power over primate females (and thereby, by implication), with regard to the human females (whom they do *not* study), as well as the nonhuman primate females included in the groups containing the males whom they *do* study (see sections 3 and 4 above).

Anthropologist/primatologist Shirley Strum, in association with sociological theorist Bruno Latour, uses data from her field observations of baboons—which might conceivably have been used by Rowell as her foil for guenons, since baboons live in open plains where all of their behavior, and surely not least mating behavior, occur in full view of the entire troop at virtually all times. Strum and Latour are interested in the similarities and differences in the behavior of baboons and the hominids that, for millions of years, were their competitors in the plains of Africa, under circumstances such that baboons and hominids alike confronted similar problems of learning social skills in order to adapt to their respective conspecifics (see also Fedigan 1982, 117). Such adaptations take place under conditions of great social *complexity*, which these authors think contrasts sharply with the much less *complex* (as they define it) but vastly more *complicated* (like a modern automobile with computerized ignition, as compared to a Model T with a magneto) social choices that confront contemporary humans. For baboons in "field" habitats, life may now (due to human predation on themselves and their ranges; see the introduction to part II) be even more complex, but it remains no more complicated than in times past. But political scientist Schubert would argue that this is precisely his point: that it is a mistake to take concepts associated with the complications of contemporary, first-world human political life and to plaster them without change onto the social behaviors of nonhuman primates in small kinship groups.

Part II focuses on a single species, the common chimpanzees who, as Zihlman and Tanner and several molecular biologists assert, are *not* our sibling species (as Neanderthals surely once were [Kurtén 1986, chap. 13] and pygmy chimpanzees may be [de Waal 1989, chap. 5]) but *are* our first cousins, as it were. Chapter 5 provides a detailed condensation of Goodall's elaborate report on chimpanzee behavior, focusing on those segments that provide a direct metaphor or a clear simile to human behavior, particularly to pretransition behavior. De Waal is the author of both chapter 6 and a book (1982) that is replete with comparisons to the behavior of contemporary humans, based on his extensive observations of an enclosed, highly synthetic group of captive chimpanzees in a Dutch zoo.

Chapter 6 focuses particularly on the question of sexual differences in the social organization of the Arnhem chimpanzees that de Waal observed (cf. Van Hooff 1982), so that his data bear directly upon many of the theoretical questions posed by female and feminist primatologists (including some that were directed to de Waal, as his book discusses [1982, 58]; see also the preceding sections of the present chapter). The juxtaposition of Goodall's work with that of de Waal, which part II accentuates, invites examination in depth of the second question of primatological theory (adumbrated in section 1 above) concerning the relative strengths and weaknesses of field and laboratory observations of primate social behavior; but this juxtaposition also makes possible a further exploration of the even more fundamental substantive questions: how, why, and to what extent does human behavior resemble that of common chimpanzees?

The first two parts of the book are almost exclusively concerned with the question: how and why do nonhuman primates behave, at least in the judgment of primatologists, politically; and to what extent do such behaviors resemble those of either gathering-and-hunting bands or contemporary human societies? In part III, we turn to its converse; in what ways does the political behavior of modern humans resemble that of nonhuman primates; and in what ways can political scientists improve their own understanding of modern political behavior by learning how to apply primatological theory and methods and substantive knowledge about primates, especially in studies of verbal as well as nonverbal behavior in small groups of humans? The three chapters of part III illustrate several of the ways in which such an approach can be developed empirically. In chapter 7, Blurton Jones builds upon Isaac's (1978a, b) theory of food scrounging (as well as sharing) by applying it to pretransition (or what might be called "archaic" modern human) gatherer-hunting band societal behaviors. The evolutionary theory in terms of which Blurton Jones undertakes to evaluate his data stems from sociobiological theory, as developed by W. D. Hamilton in his dissertation (1964) and popularized by E. O. Wilson (1975) and various of his students (e.g., Trivers 1971, 1974) and then also by various of *their* students (e.g., Hrdy 1977a). This theory has also been applied (Axelrod 1984) and critiqued (E. White 1981) by political scientists; for a recent anthropological critique, see Harpending, Rogers, and Draper (1987). For present purposes, it suffices to say that sociobiological theory constitutes an isotope of econometrics, attempting to evaluate all behavior (of humans, chimpanzees, or whatever) in terms of quantifiable (at least, in principle) *genetic* units rather than economic units; and that oversimplification is both its virtue and its vice. For an amplification of that critical stance, see G. Schubert (1981b); for a somewhat more sympathetic restatement and appraisal of sociobiological theory, see the introduction to part III.

There is an extensive research literature by now in political science as well as in primatology (and ethology) on facial displays as an aspect of nonverbal communication. Chapter 8 by Sullivan, Masters, et al. is a research report taken from their participation throughout much of the 1980s in an extensive, highly interdisciplinary research project into political leadership and followership examining the reactions of surrogate followers to the nonverbal as well as the verbal stimulation communicated by photographic plus sound images projected by real political leaders. This is, of course, laboratory research; there is a somewhat smaller but growing body of field ethological research on small groups of human political leaders (e.g., G. Schubert 1982d; J. Schubert 1983; and J. Schubert, Wiegele, and Hines 1986). Naturally, any ethological research on human political behavior is by definition a form of primatological research. Chapter 9, by James Schubert, employs theory and methods developed by nonverbal communication experts Scherer and Ekman to focus on the relationship between verbal and nonverbal (voice-track) data, computer-coordinated and analyzed, in the disagreement and disapproval behavior of a five-member village-council group whose decision making was extensively observed over a period of a year. The paralinguistic dimensions of this human group's social communication were vitally related to their emotional involvement in the discussion; this is likewise the perception of anyone who has observed at first hand the Arnhem chimpanzees or any other small, uncaged group of nonhuman primates. Such connections exemplify the kinds of communalities between human and nonhuman behavior that political and other social scientists can and ought to examine (see Hinde 1987) in order to get political science in closer touch with its biopolitical roots.

Chapter 10 concludes the book by exploring the relationship between primatological research and the theories with which most political scientists are familiar, discussing the extent to which human political behavior as understood by political scientists is *not* based on biological or other life-science data, but rests instead overwhelmingly upon cultural sources such as the understandings and discussions of "human nature" by distinguished and still very influential political philosophers, throughout the past two and one-half millennia. In so doing, the book concludes with a survey of basic concepts in the study of politics, assessing what we can—and what we cannot—hope to learn about the foundations of human politics through the scientific study of nonhuman primates.

# PART I

*Primatology and Politics*

# Introduction
## *Primatological Theory*

### Glendon Schubert

The three chapters that comprise part I are primarily theoretical in their focus, but each represents a different disciplinary perspective: chapter 2 looks at primate politics from the point of view of political science, chapter 3 is ethological in perspective, while chapter 4 is distinctly sociological.

The emphasis in part I is thus broadly interdisciplinary. Political scientists borrow from history, law, and philosophy (among the humanities) as well as sociology, psychology, anthropology, and economics (among the social sciences); and as this book indicates, political science is now in the process of integrating ethology, evolutionary theory (see also G. Schubert 1989a; Masters 1989a), and psychobiology from the biological sciences. Strum and Latour (chap. 4) explicitly lament the partitioning of sociology from anthropology during the past century and a half and seek to reunite them. The study of primate politics obviously requires a broad focus on social science theory in relation to primatological theory.

### 1. DID POLITICS BEGIN AMONG APES?

Glendon Schubert raises questions about the genesis of political behavior in primates in terms of the respective phylogenetic evolution of modern humans and of other modern primates. He therefore emphasizes that evolutionary comparisons between or among any contemporary primate species—including humans—should be based on parallel studies of the compared species' phylogenies, unless statements on that subject are to be deemed as merely speculative. An empirical constraint that immediately arises, however, is that more attention has been paid, and therefore more presently is known, about the evolution of hominids (Fleagle 1988; Lewin 1987; Kurtén 1986; Reichs 1983; and Ciochon and Fleagle 1987; but cf. Ciochon and Corruccini 1983; Tanner 1981, 1987; and Zihlman 1982) than of other primates (but see Ciochon and Corruccini 1983; Schwartz 1984a, b; and Andrews and Cronin 1982).

Schubert proposes that homological continuities include many aspects of physiology and behavior genetics; these continuities probably extend to vocalizations and other nonverbal communication, and may extend to anticipatory socialization into leadership roles, sex role differences, and the cognitive primatology of both emotions and conscious—but not necessarily *self-conscious*—thought. He suggests that due to the greater extension of neoteny in humans (cf. Gould 1977, chap. 10; Chevalier-Skolnikoff and Poirer 1977), there may be many apt homologies between the behavior of juvenile chimpanzees or baboons and of human adults (see also Richard 1985, 38, fig. 1.20).

Although intentional anthropomorphism undoubtedly provides many economies in recognition and interpretation of cognate-primate behavior by human observers, this is achieved at the high cost of unintentional biasing of observations and data alike. The result has negative consequences for the validity and reliability of primatology to the extent that it purports to be biological *science*. Schubert's assertion in chapter 2 is echoed by Rowell in chapter 3, who gives considerable empirical evidence in support of that claim; for a forthright defense of anthropomorphism as a primatological virtue, see de Waal (1987a, 421). Indeed, linguistic anthropomorphism has gone so far in North American feminist circles (cf. G. Schubert in press, chap. 3) that female primatologist Linda Fedigan (1982, 22), obviously feeling somewhat on the defensive, explains why she refers

> to behavioral and physical differences between female and male primates as "sex" rather than as "gender" differences. The latter term is usually used to denote societal or culturally-derived differences; one's gender related behavior may be characterized as "feminine" for example, and cognition concerning the differences between females and males is implied in the term. "Sex" however, is a term which usually refers to "aspects of maleness and femaleness of an organic kind". . . . Since in many cases . . . the derivation of differences between females and males is itself in question, or is considered to be both organic and societal, the dichotomy represented by sex versus gender is false, I have chosen the term "sex differences." . . .

It is sex, not gender, that is subject to natural selection—and at that it is subject to only very weak selection pressure, at least in the human species during recent millennia. Fedigan certainly is correct in not wanting to be anthropomorphic about her monkeys; and of course it is all right for many purposes for humans to be anthropomorphic about their conspecifics; but there are other and excellent reasons for eschewing the sex/gender dichotomy, while still speaking for some purposes of either sex differences or gender differences between human males and females. Even in regard to human subjects, it is better to begin with the biological distinction; and for nonhuman primates and other animals, it is best to both begin and end with sex rather than gender.

Primate politics is a two-way street: political scientists must indeed study primatology, but primatologists also need to study political science if the two previously disparate academic specialties are to join in effective communication and mutually supporting research. Moreover, primatologists and political scientists are most likely to find communality in the genesis and epigenesis of political behavior if both constrain their ethological observations by testing them against evolutionary theory.

Schubert's most radical proposal is that primate politics can be observed when analysts of either simian or human behavior deal with attempts to aggregate a plurality of diverse consanguinous subunits (in human terms, extended families) in cooperation or competition with each other for control over policies that may effect the joint collectivity. Strum and Latour, however, argue that Schubert's definition for intergroup politics is too restrictive because it leaves unresolved the question of political leadership and followership within individual groups and therefore might exclude behavior that mainstream primatologists study when observing apes and monkeys. Certainly that is true; but Schubert's point is precisely that the leadership of small kinship groups of humans is studied by cultural anthropologists, social psychologists, and sociologists rather than by political scientists, who study small group behavior *as politics* only when the members are governmental elites or the group is a subunit of a larger social organization. Obviously, politics is defined differently by political scientists than by other social scientists and primatologists. Schubert's proposed definition emphasizes human politics as understood by political scientists.

## 2. WHY DO MONKEYS COPULATE?

Thelma Rowell analyzes "harem" as an anthropomorphic concept. However dubious its validity as a theory of how polygyny relates to the facts of sexual behavior in human societies, anthropomorphism clearly constitutes a projection of human ideas upon animals; and this has the effect of obfuscating rather than clarifying our understanding of their behavior. She describes the theory of the harem as a means of (what men think of as) "resource" hoarding (i.e., permitting one dominant male exclusive sexual access to multiple females). But she points out that even among humans harems function primarily to subserve political and economic rather than sexual goals. Moreover, she points out that other animals are presumed to have no economic or political considerations although humans do; and it is that assumption that she challenges.

As Rowell remarks, human polygyny seems to reduce the direct (genetic) fitness of harem women because of the long period of recusal from copulatory obligation following each birth, with greater birth spacing reducing their effective fertility; indeed, the increase of monogamy is frequently invoked as the explanation for rapid population growth in Africa. It is usually assumed that large aggressive males with "better weapons" have the highest reproductive success because of competition for access to females, in the absence of (or as a prelude to) "harem" arrangements. Most of this conventional thinking is more ideological than ethological; and as Zihlman (1981, 81) has pointed out (and as Strum and Latour strongly agree [chap. 5]), "There may be little correlation between high rank and reproductive success of males, and dominance behavior may have little adaptive significance (Rowell, 1974). 'Dominance' is more correlated with length of tenure in a social group than with winning fights, and reproductive success correlates with living to maturity (Lancaster, 1978)." The facts of paternity among other animals are even more in doubt than among humans, for whom—as Rowell notes, quoting Cicero—it is typically a matter of opinion.

Rowell's discussion of seals and sea lions establishes the requirement of good visibility, for the subject animals and their human observers alike, in order for dominant males to be able to control the reproductive behavior of either females or subdominant competitor males. On this basis, Rowell undertakes an analysis of the mating behavior of nonhuman primates, with special attention to guenon monkeys, whom she has studied extensively in field conditions. She does not assume that male monkeys "are trying to cause conceptions when they mate," and anyhow very few copulations result in conceptions. One might certainly question whether such an assumption is either necessary or important: if humans did not until fairly modern times understand the relationship between copulation and conception, it seems improbable that monkeys would be more intelligent than, say, humans in gathering-hunting bands. Is it necessary for guenons to understand the function of copulation in order to be able, and to want, to do it?

More generally, Rowell assumes that the apparent control of the behavior of other conspecifics does not in itself confer reproductive success on male animals. But why then, she asks, do they go to such extraordinary lengths to behave as though their goal is to maintain a harem? Of course, one possiblity may be that what seems to even a trained and sophisticated observer to be a demonstration of dominance in sexual behavior may nevertheless have very different origins and functional consequences for the subject animals (cf. the discussion in chapter 1 of how a difference in the sex of equally well-trained and intelligent human observers results in extremely different observations and interpretations of the social behavior of female *nonhuman* primates).

### 3. WHY IS LIFE MORE COMPLEX FOR BABOONS THAN FOR HUMANS?

Strum and Latour take a perspective that is unusual for primatology: they distinguish between *ostensive* and *performative* concepts of society. The former is the conventional sociological stance, which reifies *society* as the model into which humans are poured via acculturation. The latter is a diametrically op-posed ethnomethodological view that sees humans (or other animals) as defining their own scripts, their roles, and a tentative image of immanent society through their behavior in social relationships. Turning from ethnological to ethological theory, they credit the renewed emphasis on social biology (e.g., Wilson 1975) with having provided a genetic evolutionary paradigm that at least in principle paved the way for the acceptance by human observers of *group* variations in ba-boon behavior, in sharp contrast to the stereotyped portrait of male-dominated baboon hierarchies that prevailed during the middle decades of this century; but compare the argument in chapter 1, that female primatology has had a fundamental and pervasive impact on social biology in primatological theory.

It certainly is true that the persistent emphasis throughout the present volume is that, with very few exceptions (of which male orangs are a conspicuous example) that are now believed to represent ecological pressures on food availability (see also the discussion of food sharing in section 4 below), most primates live most of the time *only* in groups; and primate social grouping constitutes a principal behavioral adaptation that evolved because it is critical to the survival and successful reproduction of primate taxa. Furthermore, and notwithstanding the faddish overemphasis upon individual competitiveness due to "selfish genes" (cf. chapter 1, section 4, and G. Schubert 1980, 1981b, 1982b, and in press; with Williams 1966; Trivers 1971; Dawkins 1976), group selection receives far better empirical support than does individual selection from the data of field primatology. Group selection also better explains primate evolution generally; but human evolution does it best (see Goodall's discussion of the annihilation of the Kamaha splinter group and her use of Bigelow [1969] in chapter 5; and see especially Caporael et al [1989]).

Chapter 4 then asks, what are the proximate causes (i.e., physiological, behavioral) that explain the observed variations among baboon groups? And the answer, Strum and Latour assert, is to be found in *learned social skills*, making due allowance for individual differences. Indeed, they assert that both baboons and scientists "ask the same questions" about how baboon society is created. To be sure, for the baboons the questions are implicit: observations of baboon behavior are conceptualizations in the minds of the human observers, not self-consciously verbalized plans in the minds of baboons. Even if it were otherwise, then a great deal of simian psychobiological experimental research would remain to be done to investigate the possibility of adducing empirical support for such attributions of human intelligence to baboons. It is true that the title of Marais's precocious field study (1967; completed before 1936) was *The Soul of the Ape*, but most of his readers thought that he was indulging in poetic license rather than denoting scientific fact.

Strum and Latour distinguish between *complexity* ("to simultaneously em-brace a multitude of objects") and *complication* (to make "a succession of simple operations"). Baboons are said to live in complex societies because of their limited resources, which consist primarily of their own "bodies," their acquisition of "social skills," and their imputed capacity to develop and carry out social "strategies." Modern humans in technological societies have shifted from the leading of complex, to less complex but more complicated, lives. Given the importance of these two major types of social life, and the difference in type between the subject baboons and their human observers, it follows that primatologists, in their conceptualizations of baboon behavior and their attempts to understand it, *project* human complication upon and try to substitute it for the complexity of what is natural in baboon society.

Strum and Latour also expound a theory of how the "performative social bond" has evolved through several classes of aggregation among animals, for whom the initial choice is either to become isolated from conspecifics (except spasmodically for reproductive purposes) or else to learn how to live with conspecifics in a social group. The next major evolutionary dichotomy is between those animals (such as eusocial insects) that develop genetic manipulation of categories of phenotypes and those (like mammals generally) that rely upon behavioral manipulation of phenotypes through the learning of social skills. The third level distinguishes among primates, with apes and monkeys constrained to rely upon their noncultural somatic resources, whereas humans exploit tools and other aspects of culture as resources for social control. Finally, human societies can be distinguished as "primitive" (with minimal resources, relatively speaking), or "modern" (technocratic, postindustrial, nuclear-powered, etc.; cf. Green 1986; Tiger 1987).

Strum and Latour assert that primate behavior is the result of individually varied adaptations to the *social* environment of conspecifics, the ecological setting, and the mode of adaptation to these external factors that has evolved as the species-typical behavioral repertoire. Such varied responses are the result of performed social roles, reflecting individual intentionality (as behaviors derived from learned skills of tactical adaptations to social life). Thus, Strum and Latour's theoretical framework for explaining primate social behavior focuses on what they deem to be the foundations of human politics.

## 4. WHY DO BABOONS SHARE FOOD?

In her book, Shirley Strum (1987, 131–32) discusses her observations of food sharing among baboons as an unexpected and surprising anomaly, associated only with meat eating (on baboon plant eating, see Strum 1987, 19–20). She describes meat eating as a function of a combination of ecological pressures on food availability that necessitated more time being spent on hunting as compared to scavenging. (On hunting versus scavenging by various predators in the Serengeti today, see Potts 1988, 205–08, 218–21; cf. his discussion of paleoscavenging: Potts 1988, 209–18.) Strum emphasizes the importance of both chance and skill in shaping the experience of individual males (and thereby entailing their friendship entourage) in successful hunting and the gaining of direct access to meat. She points out that

> when males made a capture and brought it closer, females and youngsters would rush to the carcass and eventually have their turn at it. . . . The baboons were changing fast. The predatory rate climbed: In 1973, a hundred kills were noted in twelve hundred hours of observation, not much by the standard of traditional human hunters like the [San], but *almost ten times the rate of the Gombe Stream chimpanzees* [emphasis added]. In terms of real meat consumed, the baboons were probably doing even better, since their prey [infant gazelles] was heftier than chimpanzee prey [monkeys or infant baboons]. The baboons were beginning to *share* their kill—a previously unheard-of development. Baboons never share food. A mother won't even share food with her infant. The two might eat from the same patch, but no giving took place. Chimpanzees *did* share food: a discovery that challenged one of the bastions of human uniqueness. Now the Pumphouse baboons had become sharers. No one ever simply handed the meat over, but a male would scoot aside to allow a female friend a turn at the carcass, or a mother would let her infant join in the meal. As usual, Peggy was in the forefront. She exploited her good relations with Sumner and Carl, two of the key predators, and was the first to see they would share. Sumner did so graciously, but Peggy always chose the exact moment that he looked away to grab her big pieces. Surprisingly, none of the males ever shared with one another, not even with males who might have wittingly or unwittingly helped in a chase and capture.

Although some of the paleoanthropological dating of hominids in his article of more than a decade ago has been revised (now being considered up to twice as old as was believed even then), the provocative theory presented by Glynn Isaac (1978a, 92–93, 99, 102, 109) has been very influential upon hominid ecologists. Isaac points out that

> in *Homo sapiens* societies the acquisition of food is a corporate responsibility, at least in part. Among members of human social groupings of various sizes the active sharing of food is a characteristic form of behavior, most commonly family groups are the crucial nodes in a network of food exchange. [As Adrienne Zihlman points out (1981, 82), "women and children constitute at least 75 percent of human society; women are the primary social-izers; the human diet is omnivorous, not carnivorous; and meat and other protein can be obtained in numerous ways besides hunting."] Food is exchanged between adults, and it is shared between adults and juveniles. The only similar behavior observed among the great apes is seen when chimpanzees occasionally feed on meat. The chimpanzees' behavior, however, falls far short of active sharing: *I suggest it might better be termed tolerated scrounging* [emphasis added]. Vegetable foods, which are the great apes' principal diet, are not shared and are almost invariably consumed by each individual on the spot. . . . [But human social groupings maintain a home base, and characteristically] a proportion of [the] foodstuffs [collected] is not consumed until the return to the home base. This behavior is in marked contrast to what is observed among foraging great apes, which almost invariably feed at the spot where the food is acquired.. . . [Furthermore,] human beings actively share some of the food they acquire.

Isaac states, in regard to the transport of food as a protohuman attribute, that "Sherwood Washburn . . . observed some years ago [that] such an action would strike a living ape as being novel and peculiar behavior indeed. . . . [So this was one of the] fundamental shifts [that] had begun to take place in hominid social and ecological arrangements." Isaac also quotes Richard B. Lee as having "suggested that a carrying device was the basic invention that made human evolution possible." And not least, Isaac quotes Jane Lancaster as having "pointed out [that] the hominid life systems of two million years ago have no living counterparts."

Almost a decade later, Richard Potts (1987, 38–39; cf. Potts 1988, chap. 9) remarked that "the dominant interpretation of the Olduvai sites is that they were home bases—i.e., spatial nodes of social activity and food sharing among early hominids. . . . The early archeological sites from Olduvai are often believed to be the best evidence for early hominid home bases, characterized by both safety and food sharing"; Potts cites Isaac as his primary authority, among several others, on these points. In regard to *safety*, however, Blurton Jones (1987, 40, 45; see also chap. 7 below) has made the interesting suggestion (also following Isaac) that "the argument about tolerated theft [scrounging] is simple and adds . . . the individual selection argument of avoidance of [conspecific fights and therefore of] injury, to the traditional anthropological view of sharing meat." He also argues that "full-time scrounging is more likely to occur in larger groups and it is very unlikely indeed to occur in smaller groups"—which makes scrounging probable among contemporary common baboons and common chimpanzees as well as among early hominids (not to mention the contemporary species!).

Potts (1987, 42) observes also that

> it is important to note that living primates still offer numerous plausible models of Olduvai hominid socioecology. For example, did early hominids at Olduvai move in social groups resembling those of hunter-gatherers—ie., changeable in composition but composed of several family units [for a reasonably spectacular example in living color, see the front cover of the paperback edition of G. Schubert 1989a] which consistently reunited at a social base to which artifacts and bones were not taken? Were they like common chimpanzees, living in communities of males and females which ranged independently throughout an area and formed short-lived parties [see Goodall, chap. 5 below]? Were they like pygmy chimps, which form more stable parties of males and females than do common chimps . . . ? Or do multiple male-female groups (as in common baboons) or "family units" (hamadryas baboon) which shift as a cohesive unit while foraging best portray the social groups of Olduvai hominids?

Part I of this volume questions the prevailing distinction between social science and ethology on several different grounds. On the one hand, ethological analyses of nonhuman primates often err by imputing specifically human concerns or experiences to nonhuman animals (chap. 2 and 3); and on the other, social scientists frequently ignore the homologies between nonhuman and human primates (chap. 4). By avoiding the twin fallacies of anthropomorphism when studying nonhuman primates, and of ignoring primate biology when analyzing humans, primatologists and political scientists can gain a more realistic understanding of primate nature and primate politics.

# 2

# *Primate Politics*

Glendon Schubert

During the past decade, there has been a convergence in the work of primatologists and political scientists as their common interest in the epigenetic roots of social behavior has gradually become recognized (G. Schubert and Somit 1982). While a few political scientists have explicitly sought an evolutionary alternative to the contemporary research designs that prevail in their discipline, primatologists have independently invented concepts of human political behavior in order to interpret the complex and dynamic structures of roles that they observe in small groups of contemporary pongids. Thus there has been an assymetry in this convergence that deserves more critical attention than it has received.

Until a decade and a half ago (Corning 1970), political scientists had ignored the modern evolutionary theory that resulted early in this century from the synthesis of the Darwinian and Mendelian theories (see Williams 1966). Their persisting fascination with classical political philosophy was limited to "the great books," even though Aristotle (G. Schubert 1973, 240n.1) and Rousseau (Masters 1967, 1968), to say nothing of Darwin himself (1965 [1872]), should have led political scientists to the evolutionary approach to political theory that has now clearly emerged (Masters 1977, 1982a; Corning 1977, 1983; G. Schubert 1983d).

For primatologists, the problem was not to discover evolutionary theory, but rather to consider the relevance of formal theories of human political behavior to questions of pongid social behavior. The major resurgence of modern primatol-

This article is a revised version of a paper presented by the author at a symposium of the International Primatological Society meeting in Nairobi, Kenya, on 24 July 1984. The symposium, "Political Behavior as a Primate Social Strategy," was jointly organized by political scientist Glendon Schubert and primatologist Shirley Strum. It was originally published in *Social Science Information* 25 (1986): 647–80; reprinted by permission.

ogy was catalyzed by the "nine-months 'Primate Project' . . . at the Center for Advanced Study in the [Human] Behavioral Sciences, Stanford, California, during 1962–1963" (DeVore 1965a, viii). At first, the emphasis was upon the putatively homological use of field studies of contemporary baboons (Lee and DeVore 1968; Loy 1975) and chimpanzees (Goodall 1977) as models—or metaphors (Landau 1961)—for understanding the social life of early hominids. The primatological quest for political theory began later, as a younger generation of scholars noted that the earlier approach was substantially analogical (Hrdy 1981).

## 1. FOUR CASES OF "PRIMATE POLITICS"

This paper will present and discuss four of the most important examples of theory about primate politics from the perspectives of both primatology and political science. These examples can be conceptualized as each constituting a benchmark on a continuum extending from monkeys that are born, raised, and experimented on in captivity, subject to the unceasing constraint of indoor cages and behavioral manipulation by their human controllers, to relatively freely ranging simians in a savanna-type ecology. These examples will be described here in terms of specific works by individual primatologists, although the discussion will include related work by other primatologists and by political scientists.

First we shall consider Michael Chance's theory of "attention structure," which was initially proposed primarily on the basis of his secondary analysis of other researchers' reports of their data. That idea became further refined over the course of the next decade (by Chance himself and various of his students and other associates) and was mostly based on observations of the Basle Zoo colony of long-tailed macaques and/or the much smaller satellite group of monkeys and their offspring imported from the Basle colony to the Uffculme (Psychiatric) Clinic laboratory in Birmingham, England.

The recent publication of Frans de Waal's (1982) book *Chimpanzee Politics* is an obvious choice for discussion, especially in view of the circumstance that both Albert Somit and I had together visited de Waal at the Arnhem Zoo in the Netherlands when his postdoctoral research was still in process. The Arnhem chimpanzees slept in indoor cages at night but were usually let loose in an enclosure of about an acre during daytime hours (from mid-April to late November); the social behavior that was observed for the purposes of de Waal's study took place under these conditions.

Next comes Sarah Blaffer Hrdy's model of regime change among hanuman langurs at Mount Abu in western central India; the "ground" monkeys with which she worked cohabited symbiotically with the humans, whose presence and artifacts they tended to exploit and (of course) be affected by.

Lastly we shall consider Shirley Strum's use of ecological and evolutionary theory in presenting her observations of the olive baboons that she described as "The Pumphouse Gang" (Strum 1975a), on Kekopey Ranch in Kenya's East African Rift country beyond the eastern shores of Lake Victoria.

### Hedonic Macaques

The three succeeding sections of this paper all deal with primatological theories of politics based on more or less extensive—more in the instances of Strum and de Waal, less in the case of Hrdy—observations of the behavior of groups of nonhuman primates. In each of those instances, primatologists developed hypotheses about what they had conceptualized to be political behaviors of the animals, in all instances relying heavily upon evolutionary and ecological theories that had been proposed by zoologists or comparative psychologists. None of these primatologists had undertaken to explore the professional political science literature to examine what formal political theory might propose regarding the human political behavior that the primatologists, in every instance explicitly, analogized in describing nonhuman primate data (G. Schubert and Somit 1982, ix).

Although Michael Chance's "theory" of attention structure also failed to reflect any study of political theory, the third component of his model—which he designated as "advertence/abvertence"— was derived not from observations of monkeys but rather was based on observations of the behavior of human patients in psychiatric wards of English hospitals. As a pharmacologically trained lecturer in ethology whose subdepartment was housed, both literally and figuratively, in the Department of Psychiatry of the Medical School of the University of Birmingham, it is understandable that Chance was in a position to make the observations on which his hypothesis was based. And one can agree that the practice of anthropomorphism in studying nonhuman primates ought to be undertaken as explicitly as possible (which is surely what Chance and de Waal do), rather than unconsciously and *sub rosa* as is often the case among both field and experimental primatologists. Moreover, if human patients who are emotionally and behaviorally disturbed are to be used as a model in studying nonhuman primates, then Chance was entirely right in applying his model to the particular collection of macaques upon which his laboratory observations are based (G. Schubert 1983a, 1984a, 1979; cf. Goffman 1961; Rubenstein and Lasswell 1966).

Problems arise, however, when the advertence/abvertence hypothesis is employed to model *either* the modal behavior of feral monkeys (as in the case of Strum's baboons) *or* what political scientists presume to be the "normal" political behavior of humans (e.g., Barner-Barry 1978, 1979; Masters 1978, 1981; Wingerson 1982). Perhaps one should use advertence/abvertence to guide observations of the behavior of putatively psychotic politicians such as those described more than half a century ago by the first political scientist cum lay psychoanalyst (Lasswell 1930; cf. Lasswell 1948, 61–68, and especially his contrast between "Judge X" and "Judges Y and Z"). Furthermore, if primates all live now in environments where human cultures result increasingly in such intolerable stresses that there are now more and more crazy monkeys and crazy humans alike (see Foucault 1965; Szasz 1965, 1970, 1973), then Chancian abvertence may well supply the most appropriate model of social behavior. But in a world of mad primates, who will remain sane to be a scientific observer?

The first two components of Chance's model are familiar to primatologists and social scientists alike. Since I have recently commented on them (G. Schubert 1983a, 1983b, 1984a), I shall be succinct here. The first dimension (centric/acentric) describes dichotomously the degree of dominance in hierarchical structure. The role of leaders in centric groups is defense against predators, which surely is reminiscent of the conventional "baboon primatology" of the 1950s and before; Chance's only distinctive contribution here was his suggestion that in acentric groups subordinates "escape into the environment" rather than "to the center of the group" where the centric leader can protect them.

The second dimension of Chance's model, which distinguishes agonism from hedonism, is more important. "Agonism" is a more hedonic word than "antagonism," the latter having become common currency among primatologists—to say nothing of psychologists, sociologists, and political scientists. Agonism, like antagonism, denotes leaders who dominate through physical force or threats, whereas hedonic leaders dominate through persuasion, and not least because their appearance and manner are appealing to subordinates who willingly follow (and are led by) such "attractive" leaders.

Hedonism, thus defined, may seem reminiscent of Max Weber's concept of charismatic political leadership; and it is not inconceivable that Chance's development of his ideas might have profited from some familiarity with the considerable literature, in political science and related social science disciplines, that discusses political charisma (e.g., Weber 1964; part 3, "The types of authority and imperative co-ordination"; Hummel 1973). Chance himself never mentions or cites Weber, although the late Ray Larsen, in the chapter that he contributed to the book he coedited with Chance, explicitly advocates that "the Weberian typology" including charisma "should be incorporated into . . . the attention structure model of primate social structure" (Larsen 1976, 270). Larsen, in explicating Weber's theory, points out that "the external proof of the presence of charisma [in a political leader] is the visible *emotional* state of followers . . . [and that] charismatic leaders . . . are thought to appear most readily in situations of distress and crisis when prevailing institutions are likely to be perceived as inadequate and *followers are inspired with emotions* born of distress" (Larsen 1976, 254: emphasis added). Larsen was an anthropologist; political scientist Ralph Hummel and Robert Isaak (1980, 178–84, esp. 180; see also Hummel 1974) agree that charisma defines the experience of a follower in distress, who projects love through his complete personal devotion to a leader perceived to be extraordinary or supernatural. The follower "resolves personal suffering and agony by subconsciously projecting love onto another individual (potential leader) from whom he or she then perceives his or her love returning in the form of an uncanny attraction." Larsen concludes (1976, 269) that "charismatic leader—follower behavior can . . . be interpreted to be an expression of a primal adaptive process which facilitates group cohesion, integration and stress reduction."

Chance himself treats the hedonic mode of behavior as a positive, affirmative, and desirable alternative to the negativism of agonism, with its impedimenta of dominance structure, the threats and use of force, and the involuntary insubordination of followers. This undoubtedly explains why a number of political scientists, not excluding myself, were initially attracted to Chance's model of attention structure as a potentially liberating democratic alternative to the intragroup authoritarianism of the older primate model of dominance by force; as applied to humans, it seemed to offer a breath of fresh air in a primatological room filled with the stale smoke of aggressive dominance and subservient subordinance. Three out of every four political scientists identify themselves as either "liberal" or "very liberal" in political ideology (Cattani 1981), so it is understandable that they should be more interested in a primatological theory of politics that proffers democratic as well as authoritarian alternatives, at least for the purposes of cross-species comparison in which the primate models are going to be applied to human societies, in which political scientists (like other citizens) have to live.

Attention structure "theory" fails to develop the necessary linkages for application to humans, either via the physiological route of the psychology of arousal and brain science (which Chance ignores) or through the political-sociological route of Weber, Parsons, structural functionalism, and ultimately role theories of political leadership (which Larsen recognized as a possible route but unfortunately did not explore before his premature death). That leaves us with a literature on charisma that describes followership as neurotic behavior, with leaders such as Adolf Schicklgruber who, in the consensual judgment of most appraisers of his political career, was not only highly neurotic but also centric, *both* agonic and hedonic, and abvertent to boot. Attention structure discussion of hedonic behavior says virtually nothing about followers, except that they "look at" and "pay attention to" their displaying leader. Thus the "theory" likewise pays attention only to leaders, which may constitute another example of art imitating life. It may also constitute a major defect of the theory, since it fails to say anything about the motivations of the hedonic followers; the hedonic leaders presumably get psychic income from being looked at. But if hedonic monkey leaders display to the fearful, emotionally disturbed, anomic animals that charisma theory denotes as the human followers of charismatic political leaders, then what we seem to have in Chance's second dimension is a preincarnation of his third dimension: advertent leaders in confrontation with abvertent followers. There seems to be very little that political science can either learn from, or teach to, such a theory of political leadership.

*Dominant Chimpanzees*

Both Frans de Waal (1982) and his mentor Jan van Hooff (1982) report an unabashedly anthropomorphic analysis of the leadership behavior of chimpanzees of the Arnhem Zoo colony. They employ the flamboyant rubric of "chimpanzee politics," an arresting metaphor suggested to them by Desmond Morris, himself an old hand at that sort of thing (e.g., *The Naked Ape, The Human Zoo,* etc.) and a godfather (of sorts) to the Arnhem chimp project. Since I shall return to the matter of anthropomorphism in section 2, here I deal with the concept of politics utilized by de Waal and van Hooff. The Arnhem colony consisted of approximately two dozen chimpanzees during most of the time when de Waal's data were collected. Of these, the number of adult males ranged from none to four; adult females, from about six to nine; and the rest were juveniles or infants. The colony was constructed by the aggregation of individuals or pairs or small maternal-family groups of animals, culled from various sources but apparently mostly from European zoos. The original leadership was necessarily female because the first males old enough to be potential leaders (two adults and one adolescent) were introduced together after the colony had become established as a new synthetic social structure. It was deemed necessary to remove temporarily the incumbent female leadership in order for the dominance of the oldest male to become accepted by the group.

DeWaal and van Hooff describe sexually discrete patterns of leadership motivations, styles, strategies, structures, and aggressive behavior, which they believe are the consequence of genetic/physiological differences between male and female chimpanzees. It is normal among feral chimpanzees for one or more adult males to be associated for more or less extended periods of time with several adult females plus the latters' offspring. Under such circumstances, the adult females are born into and tend to perpetuate a highly stable structure of subordinance relationships among themselves. At Arnhem there was one principal female leader but no simple linear pattern of subordinance in the interrelationships of the other adult females. The female substructure was based partly on genetic relatedness, but also partly on affection.

Females are described as being content to accept their respective statuses, as distinct from sexually mature males, who are said to "*strive* for higher status." Moreover, status is determined ultimately by successful aggression—manifest or potential—in dyadic encounters; but in social groups such dyadic conflict usually can, and often does, involve other members of the group. Therefore the social structure of dominance among mature males is highly dynamic and under continuing pressure for change. With three (or more) males in competition, leadership among them typically requires the dominant male to prevent the subdominants from cooperating in a coalition to oppose him. There is also a developmental dynamic in the process: usually (as was the case for de Waal's data), the pattern of succession is for younger males to displace older ones.

The female dominance structure presumes the coexistence of a male structure, and vice versa. The males do not compete in a social vacuum, and therefore their competition with each other is acted out against the background of the rest of the colony, so that it explicitly involves also the affective relationships between individual males and individual females and their offspring.

For insight into political science theory of coalitional behavior, de Waal might have consulted such appropriate sources as Riker (1962) or Riker and Ordeshook (1973); instead, he relied (de Waal 1982, 177) on Martin Wight, whom de Waal quotes as advising that "the alternatives to the balance of power are either universal anarchy or universal dominance." Although de Waal himself was evidently surprised that he failed to find Wight very useful, he was looking for a theory of power politics in all the wrong places. In some forty years as a political scientist I had never even heard of Wight, but I was provoked by de Waal's reference to look him up. Martin Wight's *Power Politics* (1946) is a tract of traditional political science by an English writer whose approach is institutional rather than behavioral and whose implicit theoretical paradigm is Newtonian mechanics—not Darwinian selective evolution (Landau 1961; G. Schubert 1983c). The "powers" with which he deals are nation-states, such as the United Kingdom, the United States, and the Netherlands.

By invoking this outdated and considerably outmoded pamphlet as a source of political theory, de Waal is compounding his anthropomorphic problems, which would be serious enough if he were saying only that the social leadership behavior of chimpanzees can best be understood by discussing chimps as though they are like *individual* humans. Instead, de Waal is implicitly asserting that the behavior of individual chimpanzees can be understood in terms of the competitive/cooperative relationships among nation-states that are aggregates of tens of millions of humans (cf. his listing [1982, 218] of Zinnes [1970] as a reference). The maximum size of chimpanzee groups—natural or unnatural—rarely exceeds 100 individuals. Humans in groups of 100 behave, are organized and are led very differently from humans in aggregations of 400 million—or even those in aggregations of 14 million, the approximate population of the Netherlands at the time of de Waal's research. To compare, whether explicitly or implicitly, the behavior of an aggregation of even 1 million persons with that of 100 chimpanzees is to commit an egregious error of scale (or of "level of analysis").

De Waal's use of Wight as a source of political theory is consistent with the hypothesis that when a person in one discipline attempts to make initial (and unprofessionally guided) excursions into some other discipline, she/he typically cuts into the unfamiliar discipline approximately a generation—three decades, not an *academic* generation—behind its contemporary cutting edge. Wight's pamphlet is typical of the pre-World War II literature of international politics. There are thousands of much better, behaviorally oriented works on international politics now available (including Zinnes [1970], which de Waal cites as a reference but otherwise neither mentions nor appears to use); for example, it would have been more useful for de Waal to have cited Quincy (the brother of Sewall) Wright's *The Study of International Relations* (1955). But even if de Waal had selected Wright instead of Wight, used Zinnes, or picked a more ethologically oriented political science work on the political theory of international politics (such as Ralph Pettman's *Human Behavior and World Politics*, 1975), his problem of the level of analysis would have remained.

*Infanticidal Langurs*

Probably the most dramatic, and certainly one of the best-known, empirical examples of sociobiological theory is that provided by Sarah Blaffer Hrdy's theory of regime change in hanuman langur troops. Actually, she has argued on behalf of a very much broader theory of mammalian infanticide (Hrdy 1977a, 1979) that focuses on the extent to which claims of infanticide among various animals have been made by a variety of observers, informants, and retrospective correspondents, many of which have no manifest nor even discernible latent implication for social structure or political behavior among the animals concerned. The discussion here will focus instead on her own field study of several adjacent troops of hanuman langurs whose ranges overlapped partially with each other, and in some cases considerably with the resort town of Mount Abu in northwest India, about 210 miles due south from Jodhpur. In her reports of these studies (Hrdy 1974, 1977b), male infanticide is a crucial and indispensible element of the theory of change in the "political" leadership of the langur troops that she observed.

The scenario that she sketches is truly elegant in relation to the sociobiological theory that she invokes. Hrdy assumes that langurs act (for genetic reasons) so as to maximize each individual monkey's inclusive fitness. Both male and female adult langurs improve their reproductive success by producing as many offspring as possible; their success in that endeavor is enhanced by several elements of the social structure of the group. Usually there is only one resident adult male in a hanuman langur troop, although Hrdy does discuss transitory situations in which a coalition of several adult males cooperates to oust an incumbent resident male. But in the latter circumstance, one among the cooperators soon becomes dominant over the other members of the recent coalition, and the dominant drives them out of the troop. The resident adult male is dominant over all adult females and over younger hanumans of either sex. At puberty, juvenile males are ejected from the troop by the resident adult male. Surplus males, including such juveniles and also adults who are not at the time acting in the role of the dominant resident of a heterosexual troop, combine to form all-male troops. Hanuman langurs occupy strictly defined territories, although the range boundaries of both all-male troops and other heterosexual troops not infrequently coincide or intersect slightly with the boundaries of heterosexual troops. As a resident male ages, or becomes injured, or sometimes as a consequence of other similar circumstances, he can expect to be challenged by another male. Sometimes the challenger comes from an all-male troop; sometimes he is a neighboring resident who undertakes to lead a new band in addition to, or instead of, his present one. The challenger sometimes succeeds (sooner or later) in driving out the incumbent resident.

Most of the time during most of his incumbency—and Hrdy's book mentions many exceptions and explains how and why they happened—the resident has exclusive sexual access to the estrous females in his troop. This means that he sires virtually all of the infants conceived during his incumbency; and conversely, troop infants and juveniles of corresponding ages will all (or almost all) be at least half-sibs, in same-mother clusters with full-sibs. Hrdy asserts that the dominance system evolved to guarantee the monopolistic breeding system— from the point of view of the dominant male. The more adult females that he can collect in the troop and the longer he can remain in the position of resident male of the troop, the more he will improve his direct fitness (in the sociobiological sense). If his incumbency persists for the few years that it requires for a female infant to mature sexually, then producing female offspring is one way to acquire females with which to breed.

Langur infants perish for many reasons: the predation of dogs and other carnivores, poisoning and other degradation of the environment, falls, and sometimes aggressive attacks by conspecific males, including (but by no means limited to) the resident male of the infant's troop. According to Hrdy such attacks by adult male langurs upon langur infants are associated with high states of psychophysiological arousal (cf. McGuire 1982) that is usually both sexual *and* explicitly aggressive (but see Vogel and Loch 1984). Hrdy's theory is that when a new resident takes over a troop he kills off all unweaned infants, which in hanuman langurs has the effect of causing the mothers of these infants to resume ovulation and become estrous within a month or two so that the newly dominant male can impregnate all of the adult females of the troop as rapidly as possible with his own genes (instead of having to wait a year or two for that to happen). Hrdy herself does not assert (1977a) what her sometime mentor and graduate research advisor, Robert Trivers, explicitly claimed (G. Schubert 1982b, 228n.3; 1981b, 225–27): that the new resident continues to kill off all infants born into the troop during the initial seven months of his presence there, but, after that, avoids killing his own offspring. The killer male thereby improves his fitness in two ways: (1) he procreates a larger number of offspring than would otherwise have been the case; and (2) he avoids wasting his energies providing "protection" for, and engaging in competition (however marginal) for food with, infants carrying genes of males other than himself. Hrdy's theory, if it were supported by the weight of evidence available, would constitute a striking example of the power of sociobiological theory to explain the behavior of primates.

Although Hrdy's methodology and use of empirical evidence have been criticized (Curtin and Dolhinow 1978; Boggess 1979; Vogel 1979; Eibl-Eibesfeldt 1980; G. Schubert 1982b; Wheatley 1982), I do not propose to restate that argument here. What I do want to do now is reexamine Hrdy's purported political theory, which she invokes as an additional prop to help "explain" the data produced by her field investigations of langur behavior.

The short of the matter is that Hrdy's theory of politics is highly anthropomorphic, metaphorical, and *ad hoc*. She refers to the period of the incumbency of a particular adult male resident, in a specific heterosexual langur troop, as a "regime." When some other adult male drives the resident out of the troop, she describes this as a "political change" involving the "usurpation of power." A succession of male leadership changes in a particular troop is the "political history" of the troop. But there is no politics in what she describes (cf. G. Schubert 1981b, 225), except possibly in her motivation for inappropriately invoking concepts of politics to theorize about the relatively small-scale and socially uncomplicated relationships among the primates with which she is concerned (at least, as compared to an equivalent number of humans). When behavior results from cultural evolution—rather than high-speed genetic evolution (Lumsden and Wilson 1981, 1983; G. Schubert 1982a, 1984b)—and the social group involves interactions among adult males and females alike, who are organized for breeding purposes into some substantial number of only partially related families that must agree upon common social policy in order for the multifamily group as a whole to survive in the available ecological niche, then it may be appropriate to speak of the beginnings of political behavior, at least in prototypical form. For Hrdy, this would require that she had observed a system of social control that was developed and operated *by langurs* to deal with the interrelationships among all of the langur troops in a given locality—not merely the social relations within each langur troop considered individually. A necessary, although by no means sufficient, condition for the construction of such a theory would be systematic observations of the behaviors that occur in the relationships *between* troops; "among" apparently does not occur.

The postulation of a cultural rather than a direct genetic basis for animals to behave politically is in diametric opposition to Hrdy's sociobiological premises (see Manicas 1983). Such a requirement by no means restricts, by definition, political behavior to humans alone; many other animals, including probably all other primates, act as they do in part—in small part, as compared to humans, it is true, but still in part—for cultural as well as for genetic reasons (Bonner 1980; Mainardi 1980). Much of species-specific behavior must be learned, by wolves as well as by chimpanzees, and Hrdy describes many aspects of langur behavior that must be learned to be acquired. (Maternal care of infants, adequate to permit the survival of the infants, clearly must be learned by most, if not all, monkeys and apes—not just by *human* mothers.) In section 2 of this paper, I shall present a more detailed discussion of what ought to constitute the minimal requirements of a political theory of primate behavior.

## Baboon Strategists

For more than a decade Shirley Strum has been working with a particular troop of olive baboons in north-central Kenya. There were about sixty individuals in the group when her field work began, including seven adult males and three times as many adult females; the other troop members, a majority of the total, included both male and female immature individuals. Female olive baboons are born into, and remain in, their natal troop; beginning at adolescence, males migrate from troop to troop, although usually with more or less extended periods of residence in the troops with which they become affiliated. Each adult male develops a consort relationship with as many of the adult females as he can manage, although sooner or later changes in consortship are the rule rather than the exception. After seven or eight years of field observations and coding of her data had produced a fairly substantial basis for making statistical analyses, Strum began to ask a number of questions all drawn from important and persisting issues in primate evolutionary and ecology theory, which could be tested with her accumulated data. These included: Is there a consistent hierarchy of dominance among adult males in PHG (as she came to refer to her troop "The Pumphouse Gang")? Is male dominance positively correlated with sociobiological fitness? Do dominant males preempt the meat that becomes available through predation or scavenging? Is the achievement and retention of high dominance status over other males best achieved through success in agonistic encounters?

Strum's answers (1982b) were as follows: Instead of finding a linear dominance hierarchy among males, she found numerous reversals in status and a poor basis (in dominance status) for predicting the outcome of any specific agonistic encounters and the acquisition of resources. The males who were most dominant were least—not most—successful in establishing consort relationships with females and in gaining access to estrous ones. Neither did dominance rank predict the extent of meat consumption by males. Recently immigrant males outranked in dominance status males with substantial residence; but resident males *did* attract more consorts than did the immigrants, evidently not because of greater dominance status but rather because of the residents' better knowledge and understanding of the social psychology of the group (cf. Reynolds 1984). Correspondingly, resident males obtained more resources—both females and meat—than did immigrants. However, immigrant males do initiate relationships with troop females, and all adult males develop similar relationships with troop infants. Such social relationships, which are nonaggressive and cannot be based (in this species) on agonism, are much more important to an adult male's access to resources than is dominance rank *per se*. On the other hand, the agonistic encounters of immigrant males probably accelerate their acceptance by the other males of the troop. Strum concludes (1982b, 199; cf. Strum 1982a) that her findings demonstrate "the limitations in the heuristic value of the concept of dominance hierarchy, at least for male baboons."

Strum therefore proposes that it is essential for males to learn to exercise social skills in circumstances where agonism and dominance do not assure preferential access to conspecific and environmental resources. She suggests that her data exemplify the behaviors of cooperation, strategy, division of labor, and certain cognitive abilities that would have been essential to a primate preying on other animals larger than the hunter. These skills are found in contemporary nonhuman primates and surely should be hypothesized to have had to evolve among hominids (Strum 1981; Baldwin and Baldwin 1979; Durham 1979). But she does not think that such a premise presumes any model of "Man the Hunter"; on the contrary, her data show that a sexual division of labor appears at the *earlier* collector/predator stage. That division could be a consequence of male and female differentials in the social structure and reproductive strategies characteristic of different primate species. Thus a sexual division of labor, with adult males specializing in predatory behavior, may have evolved even earlier than has been thought likely, *before* the shift from collector/predator to gatherer-hunter modes of hominid adaptation. With Jonah Western (Western and Strum 1983, 25) she speculated that natural selection may have acted directly on social skills, accelerating the encephalization of primates (and especially of hominids). "It is in humans," they remark, "that social manipulation has attained its greatest sophistication, *as evidenced by human political systems*" (emphasis added).

As noted above, Strum's work focused on nonhuman primates in the most natural—that is, relatively least disturbed by humans—setting of the four cases discussed in this paper. In her analyses and interpretation of her data, she also makes the most sophisticated use of formal primatological theory of the four cases considered here; indeed, there is a perfect, positive, and by no means necessarily spurious correlation between the two scales of naturalness of the primate group studied and of data analysis in terms of primatological theory that is both mainstream and formal. Strum is sufficiently interested in the possible political implications of her work to have presented a paper at the meeting of the Western Political Science Association in 1982, and also to have become further involved with political scientists at a symposium of the International Primatological Society in Nairobi in 1984. Like Chance, de Waal, and Hrdy, Strum makes no attempt to relate her primatological theory to contemporary formal political theory about relevant political behavior; but unlike them, she does not purport to be describing or analyzing political behavior per se in her reports on olive baboons. She is careful to restrict her claims to what is manifestly supportable in her data: that the behaviors she observed among baboons are of social strategies, many of which were nonaggressive and complementary to agonism and dominance (Strum 1983b); and that her data are consistent with the necessarily speculative hypotheses that she suggests about selection for encephalization among primates, about the dynamic relationship between scavenging and predation as primate responses to rapid ecological change, and about sexual selection for a division of labor prior to the emergence of a gatherer-hunter adaptation among some hominids.

## 2. REQUISITES FOR A BEHAVIORAL THEORY OF PRIMATE POLITICS

Interpretations of simian social behavior should not, for several reasons, be based on Shakespeare's plays, on Machiavelli's advice to Italian princes of the Renaissance, or on observations of the anomie and social isolation of human neurotics and psychotics. It is just as biasing of their observations, findings, and interpretations for primatologists deliberately to anthropomorphize their investigations of simian behavior—"political" or otherwise—as it is for political scientists to "simianize" their investigations of human behavior—political or otherwise—by purporting to understand war, aggression generally (Kortlandt 1972), the campaigning behavior of candidates for the presidency of the United States, or sex differences in participational and other political behavior on the basis of simplistic analogies with the behavior of simians. So we must first examine what "primatizing" involves.

If we want to compare the imputed political behavior of simians with that of humans, analysis should begin with inquiries into parallel evolution (R. Hall and Sharp 1978) between hominids and the simian species being compared; not with linguistic analogies with the behavior of whatever species is alternative to the one being studied. We can appropriately begin such a homological comparison by discussing a matter of *cultural* evolution: the changes in the political structure of human populations and groups that have taken place during the most recent 10,000 years since the transition from gathering-hunting to agriculture/pastoralism for mainstream human populations; such a transition was still in process for a few isolated—including some regressed—groups during the present century. Then we can turn to my main thesis: the requisites for the construction of behavioral political theory about simians. In considering the extent to which this can be modeled upon the political behavior of modern humans, surely we ought to understand something about how political behavior developed among humans. Such a phylogenetic model of human politics ought also to be related to the phylogenetic evolution of social behavior in each simian species to which comparison is to be made; but I leave that task to primatologists, whose specialization in one or another of the relevant simian species gives them a head start in pursuing such inquiries (and see Ciochon and Corruccini 1983).

### Primatizing

Although it can be conceded that simianism in the analysis—and even more so, in the prescription—of political behavior is much more dangerous to humans than is anthropomorphism in the study of primates, the issue of anthropomorphism is important.

There are three principal aspects of anthropomorphism in primatology to which I shall direct attention: (1) the cognitive consequences, not for the subject animals but rather for their human analyst(s), of the mode of their designation; (2) the consequences of naive (and truly uninformed) lay use of professional concepts (or, "Doesn't everybody understand politics intuitively?"); and (3) the methodological consequences of anthropomorphism, with particular regard to levels of analysis, the use (or nonuse) of evolutionary theory, and the dangers of insider analysts becoming blinded by the transitorily dominant paradigm in their field of personal academic socialization. (The latter—knowing too much about too little—is of course the converse of the question of interdisciplinary borrowing, where the problem typically is one of knowing too little about too much.)

First, to name an object is to know it; and to misname it is to fail to recognize it—for what it is in terms of alternative grammars, rhetorics, and systems of thought and discourse (see Peterson and Lawson 1982; Graber 1982; Peterson 1982, 1983a, b, c; and G. Schubert 1983e). The failure to recognize such risks and consequences, which is so evident in most of the cases considered above, indicates that many primatologists might profit, in both the conduct and interpretation of their field, from a more intimate acquaintance with contemporary scholarship in cognitive psychology and psychobiology (e.g., Secord 1982; and especially Manicas 1982). For starters, they would then certainly be more self-conscious about the consequences for themselves of bestowing the names of human children upon the animals they purport to study. Such names are not scientifically neutral; every one of them comes (for the user) equipped with the experience of the user's lifetime in previous associations with humans, whether they were known personally or vicariously through literature and television. Such associations influence what the user "sees" in the named animal's behavior, and also what the user subsequently "finds" to be significant about that observed behavior. It would be impossible for any primatologist to repress such entailments—and what good would that do anyhow?—but there is no apparent evidence that many of them even try to do so. The behavior observed may survive as an electronic impulse keyed into a particular locus in the memory of a portable data-events-recording instrument; but the name, identity, and character of the designated animal live on in a much more complex recording instrument: the memory of the primatologist observer. And this is especially true of the affective, as distinguished from the effective, traces in human memory.

Second, the facile use by some primatologists of political concepts, wrenched out of the context for which they were designed and in terms of which they make some (at least, limited) sense, is associated with no supporting evidence to suggest that they have troubled themselves to consult the relevant primary political science research literature through which political scientists themselves become socialized into an understanding of the range of meanings, theoretical contexts, and necessary limitations to the use of political concepts. To facilitate such primatological excursions, half a dozen of the best available contemporary introductory undergraduate political science textbooks on political behavior can be cited: Kavanagh (1983), Manheim (1982), Gianos (1982), Pettman (1975), Rosenbaum (1975), and Jaros and Grant (1974). These works discuss the relevant questions of theory, methodology, and substance, and they list an extensive research literature in the primary sources upon which they rely.

This process cannot be viewed as a one-way street, of course. Political scientists who study primatology and related fields of animal behavior need a good comprehension of how field ethologists do their research. My own case indicates the kind of interdisciplinary work needed to become *less* of an amateur in using the research theory of ethology and primatology to help convert political science into a more biologically based (e.g., a less exclusively culture-bound) academic discipline. As an active member of such professional organizations as the Animal Behavior Society (United States), the American Society of Primatologists, and the International Primatological Society, I spent a postdoctoral year (during 1977–78) at the ethology laboratory of the University of Groningen in the Netherlands, studying communication behavior in birds with Niko Tinbergen's first doctoral student, Gerard Baerends. A dilettantish social scientist does not bother to devote a year of his life to such research behaviors as getting up at 4 A.M. in order to beat the sun in arriving at a blind on a wet, freezing Dutch polder. What I have learned about the process ought to be worthy of consideration by primatologists approaching *political* theory from the opposite direction. There are, by now, at least a hundred political scientists with similar convictions and activities with regard to the relevance of the biological sciences to political science (Somit 1976; Wiegele 1979; Watts 1981; E. White 1981; Schubert and Somit 1982; Somit, Peterson, Richardson, and Godfischer 1980, as updated by Peterson, Somit, and Slagter 1982, and by Peterson, Somit, and Brown 1983).

Third, there are the methodological implications of anthropomorphism, of which I shall begin with the question of levels of analysis. Clearly what Reagan does in both his verbal and nonverbal communication in a virtually worldwide televised "news conference" functions at a different level, for their respective populations, from Luit's grimacing from an electrified treetop in the Arnhem Zoo. Whatever the analogical similarities in the appearance of the two subject primates (cf. Masters 1976b, 1978), it is naive to assume homology between events of such different scale (see also Somit and Peterson 1980; and Somit 1984).

Another question of methodology concerns the use of evolutionary theory, with a mind sufficiently open to be willing to entertain seriously the possibility of alternative explanations of the phenomena observed—even though such alternatives may not support, and might even detract from, the theoretical approach with which one is preoccupied at any given moment. This is a problem for many primatologists, just as it is certainly a problem for many political and other scientists (see G. Schubert 1982b, 233–35; A. Kaplan 1964, 351). An alternative way of stating this matter is to focus on the emotional implications for any scientific analyst—thereby including, of course, both primatologists and political scientists—of intellectual human bondage to what may be the most pernicious form of mood convection: the dominant paradigm that motivates the observer-analyst's field of inquiry at a particular time (Kuhn 1970; G. Schubert 1983c).

## Politicking

How does political behavior differ from any other aspect of social behavior? It is easy for nonspecialists to define the core subject of any discipline; but it is no more reasonable to expect political scientists to agree upon what politics is than to expect agreement among psychologists about the mind, sociologists about society, economists about the economy, biologists about the nature of life, or astronomers on whether the ultimate fate of the universe is to continue to expand or to contract. A preeminent political scientist defined politics as "who gets what, when, and how" (Lasswell 1936). A position that many biopolitical behavioralists would accept is that politics deals with the sociopsychological processes of human individuals and groups seeking to influence or control others who are not closely related to them in regard to any questions about which humans are, or might become, interested. The restriction of genetic heterogeneity means that politics does not occur other than metaphorically *within* families. Human intrafamilial relationships are studied by sociologists and cultural anthropologists, not by political scientists; social scientists are agreed that "families" consist of individuals who live and breed and raise offspring in intimate spatial and psychological proximity to one another (see Spiro 1975; Tiger and Shepher 1975; and Rossi 1977; but cf. Breines, Cerullo, and Stacey 1978). Discussions of "family politics" reflect simile and metaphor, like discussions of "langur politics" or of "chimpanzee politics," and substantially for the same reason. When the units of social structure become sufficiently large and diverse to encompass many different consanguinous (extended family) subunits in cooperation or competition with each other for control over the policies that are important for the group overall, *then* it is possible to recognize the beginnings of political behavior.

The first three cases discussed above involve primatologists who invoke selected political concepts about the behavior of modern humans—modern in the sense of cultures that evolved long, long after the transition to agriculture circa eleven to twelve thousand years ago in the Fertile Crescent and Meso-potamia. Whatever may be their cultural differences in politics and *Weltan-schauung* (Rosenbaum 1975), Plato and Machiavelli and Shakespeare are, like

us, modern humans; the relevant time scale is evolutionary rather than historical (Pettersson 1978), in the sense that "history" is understood and measured by
social scientists. Primatologists are surely right in presuming that the genesis of
political theory must be sought in the bones of Lucy and the footprints left in the
volcanic ash of East Africa by what may have been three of her conspecifics some
3.75 million years ago—not in such latter-day political writings (whatever their
merit otherwise may be) as Aristotle's *Politics* (G. Schubert 1983d; 1973, 240n.1).

Of course, the simians whose behavior is discussed in the four cases here are
also moderns—just as modern as we are. Discussing several lines of evidence
from different disciplines (primarily the electrophoresis of detectable substitu-
tions in the comparison of polypeptides, and bipedalism versus knuckle-walking
in the muscle system and skeletal structures of both living and fossil primates),
the behavioral geneticist Alan Templeton (1984) asserted that chimpanzees and
gorillas diverged from a common ancestry with hominids at least five million
years ago and *subsequently* evolved their unique knuckle adaptation. That
evolutionary change occurred while hominids were evolving their unique
extremities of feet, and brain size and cortical structure, especially after about
1.8 million years ago (Kurth 1976; Brace 1979). Whether or not a scientific
consensus comes to agree with the details of Templeton's scenario concerning
primate evolution (Cherfes and Gribbin 1981a, 1981b; Yunis, Sawyer, and
Dunham 1980; Yunis and Prakash 1982), it is no more justifiable for primatologists to homologize from the political behavior of living humans in order to
interpret the behavior of living simians than it would be for political scientists to
do the opposite (but see Willhoite 1976; Tiger and Fox 1971; Loy 1975). Strum
(1981; cf. Geist 1978; G. Schubert 1981a) has demonstrated how volatile such a
fundamental change in strategy as a shift from scavenging to much greater
predation can be, in response to extremely rapid and extraordinarily extensive
ecological change. Whatever may be assumed about progress in the social
behavior of modern simians in relation to their respective ancestral species, the
authors of the other three cases evidently presume that either (1) social behavior,
of the species each has studied, has remained essentially static—at least in
relation to human social behavior—or (2) phyletic evolution in the social
behavior of simian species is irrelevant in making comparisons to the political
behavior of modern humans.

To understand the evolution of political society, it is necessary to go back to a
time before the earliest classic books of traditional political philosophy, before
the earliest surviving political symbols such as the pyramids, and even before
the invention of written language in the early city states of Mesopotamia some
five thousand years ago. It is necessary to turn to the evolutionary anthropologists and botanists who have specialized in the study of the artifacts of human
prehistory (Fried 1967; Carneiro 1970; E. Fisher 1979). The most generally
accepted model is that of Kent Flannery (1972; cf. Alexander 1979, 250; and
Corning 1983, 346). Flannery, following Service (1962), distinguishes four levels

of human political organization: the band, the tribe, the chiefdom, and the state. Bands are characterized by local group autonomy, egalitarian status, ephemeral leadership, and ad hoc rituals. Bands typically include only about forty persons, who tend to be relatively highly interrelated genetically, belonging to one — or at most, very few — extended family lineages. Living examples of bands during the past two centuries include mostly gatherer-hunters, such as the Kalahari San. All humans were organized in bands prior to the transition to agriculture (Struever 1971; Cohen 1977; for a good review of recent work on political evolution, see Corning 1983, 345–75).

A tribe included about one hundred individuals, with more lineages than a band and a lower average level of genetic relatedness and much more stable and specialized social organization. Tribes evolved in synchrony with the domestication of plants and animals, which so stabilized food supplies that larger populations could be sustained. The economy of tribes initially was mixed, but some of them subsequently became based primarily on the domestication of plants, while others specialized in the domestication of animals for food consumption and developed pastoral economies if the animals they domesticated foraged on wild rather than domesticated plants.

As the density of population increased, so did competition between tribes for access to land, whether for use in horticulture or grazing, and this resulted in intertribal warfare (Durham 1976; Borgia 1980, 187). This began to result, possibly as early as six thousand years ago in some desirable Near Eastern locales, in the subjugation of some tribes by others; and the labor of the subjugated slaves or serfs shifted resources to their conquerors. The latter became supertribes or chiefdoms with an even more complex hierarchical political structure, corresponding divisions of social and economic status, and populations ranging in the hundreds. Tribes with an agricultural economic base had developed permanent residential sites as early as 9000 B.P., and many such sites came to be fortified for defense against attack by rivals. Some of the villages of 9000 B.P. became the towns of 7000 B.P.; and by 5000 B.P. the earliest states, which were hierarchically organized aggregations of a dominant city with many towns and villages extending over a relatively large area, began to be established. For present purposes I do not need to continue summarizing (but see Schubert 1986a) increasingly more familiar political history concerning the establishment of "states" (which happened almost invariably through military conquest and aggrandizement), as recounted in works of scholarship beginning two and one-half millennia ago with Herodotus' history of the rise of the Persian Empire and its attempted conquest of the Greek city-states and their confederations.

It is evident that the most complex level of social organization found in simians corresponds to the level that humans had achieved 100,000 years ago at the beginning of the Würm-Wisconsin Glacial — not at its end, which helped to catalyze the transition in the Fertile Crescent and elsewhere (Darlington 1969,

70). Occasionally in contemporary times chimpanzee bands have been observed to congregate in temporary aggregations of one hundred individuals, and troops of baboons may spend the night in contiguous territories that result in hundreds of animals sharing the same cliffs. But no student of chimpanzee behavior has reported any evidence of a system of social control—other than, perhaps, "mood convection"—by the leadership of such a temporary aggregation of chimps; it does not appear that sleeping baboons require or utilize any system of social control external to the troop groupings, each of which occupies its customary nocturnal territory just as it occupies its customary—though much more widely decentralized—daytime territory (Marais 1969). Thus the highest level of complexity in social organization and behavior for simians corresponds to the *pre*political band level among humans.

No doubt it would be better, if possible, to compare early *Homo sapiens* of the Paleolithic (Geist 1978, 354–55) with then-contemporary simians. Not having such an opportunity, at least we can restrict comparison with humans to what characterizes the band stage of human social unit organization. And there we find (under "natural" conditions) heterosexual but highly consanguinous groups of perhaps forty persons, living much like the Kalahari San did thirty years ago. For the San we now have continuous multidisciplinary observations, by primatologists as well as by cultural anthropologists, over a period of more than a human generation (e.g., Lee 1972; Lee and DeVore 1976). Such studies of the San and other gatherer-hunter bands suggest a model of small human groups that are egalitarian in their social leadership and structure—that is, *a*political in social organization and behavior. There are no dominant, aggressive, male bosses of status hierarchies. There are, therefore, no regimes to be usurped, no tyrants to be displaced, and no strategies necessary to the construction of minimal winning coalitions, so that the political victory can be divided among an optimally small number of "winning players" in a zero-sum game (Riker 1962; Riker and Ordeshook 1973; Axelrod 1981, 1984). There is, in sum, virtually no political behavior worthy of being imitated by—or, what amounts to the same thing, attributed to—the murderous langurs described by Hrdy, de Waal's power-hungry chimps, or the hedonistic macaque leaders who display to their attentive followers in Chance's scenario. At least prior to 15,000 years ago, humans at the band level were not yet filling a niche that would either require or permit them to develop the complex social and political structures and behaviors that stemmed from their successive domestication of plants, other animals, and finally themselves (for details of that process, see G. Schubert 1986a).

Even if primate politics as a subject of scholarly inquiry cannot be pursued by nimbly skipping back and forth between the social behaviors of contemporary apes and humans, this does not signify that the topic is an unworthy one, nor that primatologists and political scientists have little to share with each other. It clearly remains possible to consider the question of homologies in the prototypical behaviors of humans and of simians, even if it should be the case that these become manifest at different developmental stages in the ontogeny of contemporary simians and humans. Given the neoteny of contemporary humans, it should hardly be surprising that the behavior of our adults has the most in common with the behavior of juvenile chimpanzees or baboons (Barner-Barry 1977, 1981, 1982; Strayer 1981; Jones 1983; Omark, Strayer, and Freedman 1980). Furthermore, we ought to expect (or to have expected) that the route to our common goal, as students of the roots of political behavior, must be found in the study of the parallel evolution of primate species, and not merely in linguistic exegeses on the apparent social behaviors of living apes and humans. Such observations can just as well denote analogies or metaphors rather than homologies (G. Schubert 1983c; Hall and Sharp 1978; Thompson 1975; Campbell 1979; Harding and Tekeli 1981).

Nevertheless, there must be many important homological continuities between the substrata of social (including, when and where it occurs, political) behavior in humans and social behavior in simians. These must include many aspects of physiology and behavior genetics. Endorphins must operate similarly for all primates (Tiger 1979), and arousal may well be related to attention in the psychophysiology of perception for simians as well as for humans (Pribram and McGuinness 1975). Whether anticipatory socialization into leadership roles operates similarly for human as it does for rhesus males (McGuire 1982) appears not yet to have been studied (but see Madsen 1985). Notwithstanding important sex differences between humans and simians (and among different species of simians) in regard to sexual dimorphism, sexuality, and mating behavior (Hrdy 1981; H. Fisher 1982; Watts 1983; R. Hall 1985), there appear to be important questions about sex role differences (in both social structure and social behavior) for which continuities can be observed between humans and simians, as the de Waal and Strum case studies imply.

Of particular importance will be further inquiries into the wellsprings of human speech (e.g., Andrew 1963), more sophisticated and extensive studies of human nonverbal communication (e.g., van Hooff 1972), and the cognitive primatology of both emotions and conscious thought (Reynolds 1984). In time these will enhance considerably our understanding of the psychobiology of simians as well as of humans, notwithstanding the extent to which the respective brain sizes and cortical structures constitute what is probably the most important difference between us and other primates. After all, strong selection on the human brain is considered to have stopped 20,000 years before (Kurth 1976) politics began, as political science understands and studies it.

Primatologists and political scientists are most likely to discover common ground for their mutual interest in the genesis—and epigenesis (G. Schubert 1985)—of political behavior through the more deliberate use of evolutionary theory to keep their ethological observations in better perspective.

# 3

## On the Significance of the Concept of the Harem When Applied to Animals

Thelma E. Rowell

### INTRODUCTION

It is a human habit to project onto animals our own social organization, or at least our conception of the organization of neighboring cultures perceived as somewhat inferior. When early European naturalists saw groups of female mammals accompanied by a single adult male, and when they saw fights between males, they described these observations by analogy with human institutions. Both the observation and the knowledge of the institutions with which they were compared were sometimes reported secondhand, and it is also important to remember that the naturalists were men, who naturally interpreted from a male perspective of their time and culture. Thus we gained an impression of helpless females of many species being won by heavily armed males. The herd bull defended his harem for many years until challenged and beaten by a younger male, whereupon he went and moped away his declining years in solitude. Although the old image fits well with modern ideas of intrasexual competition, which should be extreme among male mammals which make little or no parental investment (Wittenberger 1961), it sometimes seems as if theorists are basing their ideas on the nineteenth-century stereotypes without questioning whether there are observations that are acceptable by modern standards which confirm them.

The harem is a human marriage arrangement, an extreme form of polygamy. A senior wealthy man marries several women: a woman is added to the harem by transaction with her male relatives. She is unlikely to have any choice in the matter or to have close kin among other members of the harem. The system emphasizes the owner's control of the women and his exclusive mating right, guaranteed by employing castrated men as guards. (I am deliberately using here the popular European conception of human harem polygamy that is likely to be in the back of the mind of the ordinary biologist.) Like other human matrimonial systems, harem polygamy is primarily a politico-economic arrangement. It is a system of resource retention and acquisition, of display, and of inheritance of wealth. It is symptomatic of inequality of possession and can arise only in economic systems in which wealth can be hoarded and exchanged.

The political and economic functions of a harem, which are the maintenance and advertisement of a man's power and influence among other men, can be achieved whether or not it also assures the paternity of the womens' children: it is only necessary that acceptable social conventions are deemed to have been followed. It would not be unduly cynical to question how far this or other marriage systems reflect the actual mating pattern of the population in which it occurs. Traditional stories of adultery suggest otherwise, as among the Masai described by Llewellyn-Davies (1978); the harsh penalties for adultery in societies where women are sequestered suggest both the need for a strong deterrent and an incentive for connivance by sympathizers.

Human polygamy is often much less spectacular than this special case. In much of Africa, a successful man, in the economic sense, may have two or three wives. Some of them join his household because he has a social obligation to them—for example, the wife of a dead older brother, who will have no more children herself. In a society in which each woman cultivates to provide food for herself and her dependent children, the household is not burdened by the addition and may even benefit where more hands can make light work. Again, this is polygamy with social rather than reproductive implications. It is common for a polygamist to have only one childbearing wife at a time, allowing comparison with the serial polygamy practiced in modern industrial society.

Polygamy is declining in the modern world (*Economist* 1984), and whereas the reasons given are often moral or religious, it seems probable that the underlying cause is a change in economics. Nonetheless, harem polygamy represents a way in which success in the human economic or political sense might be translated into success in the biological sense of leaving more than the average number of surviving descendants (cf. Dickemann 1979).

Human polygamy seems to reduce the number of children born to women, presumably because it permits the custom of a long interval between birth and resumption of sexual activity: the increase of monogamy has often been held to be responsible for the rapid population increase in parts of Africa. It can increase the children born to some men more than it decreases those born to most women. Thus, if the marriage system actually reflects the mating system, a polygamous society should increase more slowly than a monogamous one, with greater differences between men in their reproductive success.

When a human marriage system is projected onto animals, it is presumably intended to represent the animal's mating system. While the human marriage system is partly, perhaps primarily, economic and political, it is assumed that, for animals, only the mating system with its immediate and direct implications for selection and evolution is relevant; animals are presumed to have no economic or political considerations comparable to those of people. It is this assumption which I would like to reconsider here.

Of course, it will be argued that the use of a word like "harem" is only a convenient shorthand. I do not believe, however, that biologists are so sophisticated that they can use the word without carrying with it the whole portmanteau of *Arabian Nights* associations with which they grew up. The word "harem" is used, in reference to animals, to describe polygynous mating systems in which one male is able to control several females and be their exclusive mating partner, excluding competing males. The concepts of exclusive mating and control of females seem to derive from the political definition of human harem marriage. We have seen that there may be some legitimate doubt about the reality of these concepts in the human mating system, and we will now consider how far they can be used for other animals.

Consideration of mating systems begins from the assumption that males have a far higher reproductive potential than do females, not only in the limited physiological sense that more sperm than eggs are produced, but also in a real demographic sense. Total production of offspring by all males is limited by the output of the females, so it is possible for males to vary far more widely than females in their reproductive success. The physiological basis for the assumption is clear, even when limitations on sperm production and effectiveness are taken into account (Avery 1984); among domestic animals, enormous differences in male reproductive success can be realized with drastic human intervention. There are very few data about wild animals. Clutton-Brock and his coauthors (1982) showed that red deer stags did indeed have a wider variation in number of offspring produced than did the hinds, but the difference was much smaller than most people would have assumed.

Since male reproductive success can vary to zero from high levels, the assumption follows that males compete to an extreme degree, mainly by fighting, which leads to intense selection for greater size, better weapons, and aggressiveness. Many male mammals are larger, better armed, and more aggressive than the females (but see Ralls 1976), and it is assumed that competition for mates between males has given rise to these sex differences even where the sexual behavior of the species has not been investigated: from larger males polygyny is inferred, and extremely large males, harem polygyny.

These inferences may often be true, although it is interesting that among domestic animals the most extreme sexual dimorphism occurs in selected breeds in which males are not allowed to fight for access to females. As a man increases his harem by negotiation with a woman's male relatives, so females of other polygynous species are assumed to exert no direct choice of mate but to accept the outcome of "negotiations" between males. Females supposedly connive at this arrangement for the sake of successful sons who will inherit their father's ability to acquire a harem and so make them into successful grandmothers (in the biological sense).

These ideas, which are well reviewed by Wittenberger (1981), all rest on the assumption that paternity can be determined through male competition, and to test them it would be necessary to know the paternity of young born into a population over a period about as long as the reproductive life of males. This is very difficult information to obtain: there are few studies which record who copulates with whom, and copulation itself, in most species, is only an indicator because it is a necessary but not sufficient condition of paternity. Apart from a handful of paternity exclusion studies we are left, with Cicero, to observe that paternity is a matter of opinion; if so, ideas about mating success must similarly be open to question.

## THE MATING SYSTEM OF ELEPHANT SEALS

Seals and sea lions are perhaps most widely recognized among mammals as having harem mating systems. The long-term studies of LeBoeuf and his coworkers on the California coast have provided a description of the behavior of elephant seals during their breeding season, an appropriate starting point for a consideration of mammalian harems. No social system makes sense unless it is considered in the context in which it developed and in which it functions, so we must begin by considering the constraints on and advantages of this particular species in its environment.

Seals and sea lions are among the largest mammalian carnivores, but unlike land carnivores they are not at the top of the longer oceanic food chain: in the ocean they are preyed upon by still larger carnivores like sharks and killer whales (LeBoeuf, Riedman, and Keyes 1982). While anatomical and physiological adaptations for swimming in a cold ocean have made available a superabundant fish food supply, they make seals and sea lions less agile on land, and so vulnerable to predation there. Thus, there is a double predation pressure leading pinnipeds to breed on land, away from their marine predators, but in remote places inaccessible to land predators—often offshore islands. As LeBoeuf (1978) points out, good breeding sites are limited, so that many pinnipeds are forced into highly gregarious breeding and are thus set up for intense competition at breeding beaches. Seals and sea lions are probably limited by predation at sea (except for those species still hunted for fur as pups), and in this they are unlike the terrestrial carnivores which seem to be largely limited by food supply. Pacific elephant seal populations are expanding rapidly at present, since they are no longer hunted for blubber.

Elephant seals cannot be regarded as having a "typical" pinniped mating system, since seals and sea lions are being found to show great diversity of social organization, but they are at present the best understood. Mating and births occur in a short period between November and February; the adults do not feed during the breeding season, but live on fat stored during the rest of the year. Elephant seal bulls arrive before the females at the breeding beaches and fight with each other. A hierarchy is established in which lower-ranking males avoid higher-ranking males when challenged or even merely approached (LeBoeuf and Peterson 1969). Females form groups or "pods" as they arrive. High-ranking males stay with the female pods while they give birth and suckle and mate with them before they return to the sea after about five weeks. The size of the female pods seems to be limited only by the available space on a well-established breeding beach. A small pod, of fewer than forty females, may be accompanied by a single large male. Several males accompany a larger pod, and females mate with the highest-ranking males, with mating extending further down the male hierarchy as the pod gets larger (LeBoeuf 1974). Mating by highest-ranking males is probably limited by physiological constraints, while lower-ranking males are limited by interference from other males. The males make no attempt to control females directly, but because the females stay together in pods, they can prevent access to a small group of them by chasing away other males. As females leave the pod to return to the sea, they are at the height of estrus and do not resist copulation (Cox and LeBoeuf 1977), and at that time males lower in the hierarchy have some chance of mating, although the high-ranking males also follow such females down to the sea and copulate with them as they leave. The majority of males at a beach do not mate at all during the breeding season, and the great majority of copulations are by the males in the top half-dozen rank positions. Clearly, male reproductive success must vary a great deal. Male success in fighting has been assumed to determine copulation frequency and hence reproductive success. This would be analogous to a human harem system in which transactions between men determine, at least officially, by whom women have children, even though direct control of females turns out to be lacking in the elephant seal system.

Unfortunately, elephant seals are not convenient subjects for reproductive physiology; we do not know if copulation early in the five-day estrus is actually more likely to lead to conception, as Cox and LeBoeuf assumed, and this is an important point, since copulations by lower-ranking males are more likely late in estrus. There is also a problem in that females arrive for their first breeding season already pregnant, and it is not known when and where they conceive (theoretically, 10 to 12 percent of all conceptions in the population should be by virgin females since the females breed for about ten seasons if they survive). These factors introduce a tantalizing uncertainty, but do not necessarily invalidate the conclusions.

Male elephant seals continue to grow: the older a male the larger he is, and generally the largest males are the oldest males. Nonetheless there is variation in size within a cohort, which begins to develop while the male pups are still nursing: some of them develop the habit of stealing milk from several females and get fatter and grow more rapidly than do the others (Reiter, Simpson, and LeBoeuf 1978). Perhaps they can maintain this differential until they are old enough to breed, but a male's weight will also depend on his skill at catching fish. Fights are almost always won by the larger male, as is generally true among fighting mammals: elephant seals are difficult to weigh, but in dogfights the outcome of a fight is predictable by weight to within a few ounces.

Although very old, very large males may drop out of the hierarchy altogether (LeBoeuf pers. comm.), age, weight, rank, and frequency of copulation are highly correlated. Age is achieved by survival, and most mortality happens at sea, where the seals are preyed upon especially by white sharks. LeBoeuf and his colleagues have been able to mark elephant seal pups at birth and follow their entire life history. The following figures are from LeBoeuf (in preparation): even in a population which has been expanding very rapidly, less than a quarter of all male pups weaned survive to age 5, the first year they are capable of breeding. First mating occurs during years 6–8, and 93% of mating is by males between 9 and 12. Eight and one-half percent of males weaned survive to age 10, the prime mating age. Of adult males present on the breeding beach in one year, about half will not return the following year and may be presumed dead. Although a few males that survived to breeding age were never seen to mate, survival is probably the most important single element determining male reproductive success and would be even more important were the population static or decreasing.

The next most important determinants of success are probably those which can cause differences in weight within cohorts, including skill at getting food, which already varies before weaning. Only after all these factors is it possible for individual differences in ability to compete by fighting with other males to have any effect on reproductive success. It seems to me that this will be a relatively small part of the total selection pressure acting on the individual male: the outcome of fights, and whether the individual survives to fight at all, are both largely determined by events before the "competition" occurs. Thus, even in this species in which male competition is so dramatic, and differences in mating success during one season so extreme, the mating partners of females are not directly determined to a great extent by transactions (fights) between males.

Human marriage systems have politico-economic functions, and we may wonder whether male elephant seals have any interactions away from the breeding beaches which might affect or be affected by their breeding season interactions. Might they, for example, hunt cooperatively? In that case we should have to drastically alter our view of them as individuals whose interactions are solely antagonistic and competitive. We do not know, and it is frustrating that such elegant data on reproductive behavior cannot be related to the rest of the species' life.

## VISIBILITY

A striking feature of pinniped breeding beaches is visibility. Before an animal can try to influence the behavior of another, that behavior must be perceived:

monitoring is a prerequisite of control. Pinnipeds have the most public of breeding grounds, and the possibility of intervention is limited mainly by problems of locomotion on land. It seems possible for males of any species to sequester females into harems only if they have a clear view of the area in which the females are and if the females are gregarious among themselves. The extreme gregariousness of female seals on the breeding beaches is possible because they do not feed there. Most terrestrial carnivores are, in contrast, secretive, cryptic, nocturnal animals. A partial exception is the lion: in the Serengeti plains, where visibility is spectacular, Bertram (1975) describes lions defending prides of lionesses from other lions. Lions also live, however, in areas of dense vegetation where visibility is limited; is it reasonable to assume that in such places they have the same social organization?

This brings us to the confounding variable of observation conditions. To study social interaction, it is sensible to choose a site where you can see a lot of animals and follow individuals for long periods. But if the observer can see all the interacting animals, so can the animals themselves. That in itself makes some forms of interaction more likely and some forms of organization possible. The result must be that we have a distorted view of animal social organization, in which those systems made possible by clear and continuous monitoring of others' behavior are overemphasized.

The red deer provides a good example. It is a species built to live in woodlands or thickets (Gambaryan 1974), and over much of its range it inhabits forests. In Scotland it lives on deforested moorlands and survives there in spite of rather marginal nutrition, probably because natural predators have been eliminated. The excellent visibility in the moorland habitat allowed the first modern study of mammalian breeding behavior (Darling 1937) and, more recently, the long-term population studies of Clutton-Brock and coworkers. Clutton-Brock and coauthors (1982) describe a harem-type organization of mating, with a rapid turnover of males controlling small groups of females. They express doubt, however, as to whether such a system exists in the original forested habitat.

I suggest that harem-polygynous mating systems may arise in response to breeding sites with unusually good visibility. They are, in fact, possible only in conditions of good visibility since males must be able to monitor the behavior of others and to respond instantly. Use of other sensory modalities would propose problems for which I find it difficult to imagine solutions.

The second requisite of a harem mating system is that females must aggregate, and a high level of female gregariousness is possible only if the exigencies of foraging provide no constraints. Breeding sites with good visibility are therefore occupied for reasons other than the sake of the social system: for pinnipeds, because of the safety from predators which they provide; for red deer, because they have no choice in a uniformly bare habitat.

I shall now consider some social systems of nonhuman primates, and the determination of paternity within them, in the context of the requirement for monitoring the behavior of others in order to control it and the visibility provided by their environments.

## THE MATING SYSTEMS OF MONKEYS

In the majority of monkey species, females live in stable groups with their offspring. In most species studied so far, recruitment to the group is by maturation, so the groups are composed of matrilineal kin. In some other species the females leave at adolescence and join other groups, which are thus composed of females that are not particularly closely related. This pattern has been found in chimpanzees, gorillas, and red colobus *(Colobus badius)*, and it may be more common, since there has been a general presumption of matrifocality in less well known species which may not be justified (Moore 1984a). Movement of girls to an unrelated group at adolescence is also characteristic of human polygamous societies, including those where harems can be formed. Gregarious female groups provide a prerequisite for harem polygyny among primates.

Groups of female monkeys are almost always associated with one or more adult males. The degree of spatial and temporal association of these males, the number present at one time, and the way they interact among themselves vary strikingly between and sometimes within species. In species with matrifocal female groups, young males leave their natal groups, usually before they mate. They accompany other female groups for variable periods throughout their lives, and they may return later to their natal group (Sugiyama 1976). In species where young females leave, males usually stay in their natal group, forming associations with close male relatives (Wrangham 1981).

Our concern is to see whether, among this variety of male-female association patterns, there is opportunity of or evidence for harem-style polygyny. Most of the best-studied species, both in the wild and in captivity, are baboons or macaques, in which groups of females may be large and are accompanied by several males. The males will fight among themselves, allowing the observer to identify a more or less linear hierarchy based on the outcomes of fights and of approach-avoidance interactions. Males can be ranked also on the frequency of observed copulation. In a review of studies in which correlations were made between agonistic rank and copulation-frequency rank, Dewsbury (1982) found a positive correlation in about half the studies and concluded that there was evidence that high agonistic rank could allow greater access to the "resource" of fertile females. This implies some control, albeit incomplete, of the mating behavior of others by high-ranking males. In small groups of captive talapoins, *only* the highest ranking male was seen to mate even though other fertile males were present (Dixson and Herbert 1977), but this is not true in wild groups (Rowell and Dixson 1975).

Frequency of copulation observed has been taken as a measure of reproductive success, and it is often the only available measure in a field study. This measure is, however, unsatisfactory, even when refined by weighting copulations according to their closeness to time of ovulation, where this can be estimated by changes in the perineal skin or to the time of conception as estimated from birth date and average gestation length. The inadequacy of the approach has been demonstrated by paternity exclusion studies by Duvall, Bernstein, and Gordon (1976), Curie-Cohen et al. (1981), and Stern and Smith (1984). Stern and Smith, for example, found that in three large, long-established macaque groups, paternity was not correlated with frequency of copulation, with other commonly used measures of reproductive success, or with agonistic rank observed in observation periods lasting several hours each day. Some fathers were never observed to copulate with the mothers of their offspring. In these cases it would appear that an apparent ability to control the mating of other animals in the group and gain preferential access to fertile females did not provide reproductive success.

Is there a parallel with human marriage systems whose socioeconomic functions are not dependent on their apparent guarantee of paternity being realized? It is of course possible that, in these studies of captive animals, some essential ingredient was missing which would, under natural conditions, allow paternity to be determined by interactions between males. It is also possible, however, that interactions between males, including real or apparent competition between them for receptive females, may have a functional significance on survival value in the rest of their lives, and that these interactions have little or no influence in determining the number of conceptions the male achieves at the time.

The hamadryas baboon *(Papio hamadryas)* has a unique social organization which in some respects seems to parallel that of human polygamous societies (Kummer 1971). Hamadryas baboons live in large groups including many adult males, in a semidesert habitat with excellent visibility. Each adult male within a rather narrow age range in middle age controls and mates with a harem of from one to eight adult females (usually two or three). Control of females is achieved by catching and biting a straying female in the neck, upon which treatment the female learns to follow her male closely. Such direct control of the behavior of another animal is unique among primates. Bachmann and Kummer (1980) have shown experimentally that adult males observe neck-biting interactions and thereafter respect the bond between the male and his female; observers do not try to take the female over themselves as long as the male takes an interest, whereas strange females are coopted immediately. Thus, the stability of the harem group depends ultimately on a "transaction" between males. The harem group forms a foraging unit during the day range. Kummer (1968) and Abbeglen (1976) have stressed the high level of cooperation between related males. Indeed, the interaction between males proved so fascinating that relatively little information was collected about female interactions before the field study was brought to an end by the Ethiopian revolution; it seems that female hamadryas baboons interact little among themselves when compared with female olive baboons *(Papio cynocephalus)* and do not form such obvious hierarchies (Sigg 1980). Is it possible that transactions between the males largely free the females from competition with each other, allowing them to concentrate on extracting nourishment from a rather unproductive environment in which baboons could not otherwise survive? In that case one could propose that the transactions between the males have a primarily economic function to which the resulting mating system is incidental.

## MATING SYSTEMS OF GUENONS

Many species of monkey cannot be kept in captivity in groups which include more than one adult male with females and young. One male will hunt and harass another until he is removed or dies. In the wild, such species are also found in one-male groups, and other adult males live in small male groups or apparently alone. The patas monkey *(Erythrocebus patas)* is a classic example, and the one-male group pattern of organization has also been described for many members of the African genus *Cercopithecus* to which *Erythrocebus* is extremely closely allied in a group of species commonly called guenons. Most guenons inhabit closed-canopy tropical forests, although the patas lives in open country. It has generally been assumed that the one-male group is a harem mating system, the single adult male siring all infants born to females in the group.

We have studied the patas (Chism, Rowell, and Olson 1984; Chism and Rowell 1986) and two sympatric species of forest guenon, the redtail *(Cercopithecus acanius;* Cords 1984a) and the blue monkey *(Cercopithecus mitis stuhlmanni;* T singalia and Rowell 1984; Cords 1984b; Cords et al. 1986). Each species had an annual birth season. Most patas females gave birth each year within a four-week period. Redtail females gave birth at intervals of two to five years, most births occurring within three months each year. Blue females also had two- to five-year intervals between successive births (Cords and Rowell in press), and each year most births occurred within four months. For all three species, then, there were long periods when no female conceived, and there was a distinction between mating and nonmating periods.

Redtail and blue females defended territories with the aid of their juveniles; adult males accompanying them did not usually participate in boundary fights. The much larger home ranges of the patas female groups overlapped: troop encounters were not infrequent and often included aggression between the females, occasionally between the males. Adult males resident in groups of all three species spent much time scanning their environment for other adult males and vigorously chasing them away from their group.

In all three species, female groups were accompanied by a single male during the long intervals when no females were sexually receptive. If a single blue female became receptive she mated with the resident male, but even a single receptive patas female attracted extra males to the group. When several females became receptive at about the same time, other males approached and began to move with the group. The resident male blue monkey was always deferred to by the incoming males, but he was unable to keep them away simply because he couldn't be everywhere at once. Several males mated with each of the females, in general promiscuity. The appearance of receptive behavior and the arrival of the males in the group have happened so close together that we are not sure which precedes, and so might be causal, to the other. During mating periods the males of all three species fought with each other, and hierarchies could be recognized among blues and redtails. Among the redtails there was a correlation between agonistic rank of the males and several measures of sexual activity within some sections of the mating period but not in others; length of stay in the group was also correlated with mating success. In a group of blue monkeys there was no correlation between agonistic rank and mating in 1981, while in 1983 copulation frequency could be correlated with rank and length of stay in the group only if the resident males of the study group and of the neighboring group were excluded. The most surprising finding of both years was that the resident male, who was highly visible, active in attacking other males, and clearly deferred to by all incoming males, was seen to copulate only rarely in 1981 and not at all in 1983.

Adjacent blue groups were less habituated and less observed, but some of them were also seen to have more than one male in the mating period, and again the male who was most active in challenging, fighting, and chasing other males was not necessarily the one seen to copulate most frequently. Males attending the main study group would enter adjacent groups, court and mate with the females there, and become involved in fights with other males there. In other years there was no influx of male blue monkeys into the main study groups during the mating period, but receptive females were seen to leave their group surreptitiously to meet and copulate with males who lurked nearby. Male patas also moved from group to group and mated with females in more than one group, even within their extremely short mating period.

It is clear that the one-male group of guenons cannot be equated with a harem mating system where we have studied them. Most of the time, indeed, there was no mating in a one-male group. Most conceptions occurred during synchronized bursts of female receptivity which may be directed toward several males at a time.

While we have been working toward a more accurate, if more complicated, description of the mating system of these monkeys, two lessons have already been learned. The first concerns a redefinition of the *deme*, and the realization that it will not be sufficient to look at a single group of females to understand a mating system. The deme includes, minimally, several adjacent groups of females and the males who move between them. The same point has become clear in several long-term studies of monkeys in which males have been recognized and followed for several years, including Japanese macaques (*Macaca fuscata;* Sugiyama 1976) and olive baboons (*Papio cynocephalus;* Strum 1982b). The roving, opportunistic behavior of adult males of all these species is, I think, impossible to replicate under conditions of captivity, even in free-range facilities, so that mating systems can probably only be fully understood through the inconveniences and inadequacies of long-term field studies. Conclusions drawn from captive animals about relative mating success of males in natural habitats should be treated with great caution.

The second lesson we learned concerned the impossibility of one animal controlling another in a visually dense environment. Even though a blue monkey male's ability to detect another male approaching far exceeds ours, we have several times watched a male sit quietly and unobserved while another passed within a few yards. Females who are accosted by a male have a choice of "betraying" him by calling a resident male who will chase him, or of quietly responding to his courtship and moving with him to an inconspicuous site for copulation. Thus, any exclusive mating can only be by mutual consent of male and female; it cannot be imposed on females by interactions between males. This is even more true if two or more females are receptive together and do not stay close to each other. Even in the "open" habitat of patas monkeys, the grass is long relative to the height of a monkey, and there are anthills, bushes, and rocks; at our study site, patas foraged mainly in patches of acacia woodland. Patas frequently scan bipedally, and it is clear that maintaining contact with the rest of the group can be a problem for them (Rowell and Olson 1983). As with forest monkeys, it was rare to be able to see more than a few members of the group at a time or to follow a moving interaction for long without losing sight of participants behind some obstacle. In spite of the intense vigilance of the resident male, other males can approach and interact with females if they cooperate, and cooperation seems the more likely since the approaching male is frequently well-known to the females from previous stays in the group.

The question is, why do they do it? Why do males reside in female groups and spend much time watching for other males and much energy challenging and chasing them, making themselves conspicuous and so more vulnerable to predators (certainly to human hunters)? Blue male residents increase their conspicuousness still further by making loud "rallying calls" as well as alarm calls in response to predators, and they will approach and threaten some predators. Resident adult males are probably not closely related to the females of the group or even to many of the infants and juveniles: the longest known tenure of a patas male was less than a year; some blue males have been resident in a single troop for more than four years, longer than many birth intervals, but most have stayed for shorter terms. Thus they cannot be seen to be protecting a group of their close kin. Residency does not guarantee exclusive access to receptive females, unless perhaps a single female becomes receptive out of synchrony with the rest and can be closely attended. It may be this occasional circumstance which gives a reproductive advantage to offset the resident males' greater energy expenditure and risks.

Most adult male guenons of our three species spend most of their time away from female groups. Sometimes they are clearly in male groups; at other times they appear to be solitary, although since nonresident males are very quiet and inconspicuous we have found it is easy to miss male companions, who may not be very close and are unlikely to interact in any overt way. Such companions, however, observe and follow each other. Although we know little yet about the behavior of males outside female groups, it is reasonable to suppose that their interactions, however subtle, have some function and may in some way enhance their survival. Survival, especially in species which breed in several mating seasons, is an important component of reproductive success. Is it possible that, in concentrating on males during mating periods and in female groups, we are missing the point of their interactions? Is it possible that the exciting and noisy interactions of males during the mating period are simply extensions, magnifications, expressions, or assertions of their long-term relationships, and that their pattern can only be understood in terms of those long-term relationships?

Very few copulations result in conceptions, yet we assume that male monkeys are trying to cause conceptions when they mate. Subjectively, however, it sometimes looks as if a blue monkey male is more interested in the effect his copulation is having on a neighboring male than he is in the copulation itself. Is it possible that the vast majority of copulations which are infertile do have a function in male relationships, as well as in male-female relationships, so that conception becomes an almost incidental, unpredictable side effect of copulation? We should at least keep an open mind until we know more about the system; it is possible that even here we have an important system of male transactions whose economic function can be more important than the mating which it accompanies.

Comparing guenons with elephant seals, we find in each gregarious females, but the origin and function of the group and the way in which its size is determined are different. Guenon female groups are based on kinship, while female elephant seals are attracted to the breeding beach and don't seem to recognize adult kin. Groups of both species probably serve, in different ways, for avoiding predators: the guenons by early warning and defense, the seals by being in a safe place—the presence of other seals is probably no additional protection. Primate groups may be limited in size by the amount of food available in the area that can be covered in a day's foraging; since seal breeding groups are only for breeding, they do not have such limitations, and their size seems to be controlled by the available space on the beach.

In neither case is there any evidence of males being able to control the behavior of females, nor is herding necessary to males since females stay together anyway. In both cases male competitive behavior is striking and has been assumed to determine a high degree of differential mating success among males. Among guenons, great variance in lifetime reproductive success has not been substantiated so far, and more work is needed on these long-lived animals. Among elephant seals, differential male mating success is documented, but it seems that much of the dramatic competition between them is ritual, in that the outcome of fights is largely predetermined by interactions of males with their environment in other contexts. For both animals, the possibility remains that transactions between males outside the mating situation may be more important than has been thought.

## CONCLUSIONS

Most mammals live in habitats with poor visibility, and it is exceptional to live in bare, open habitats in which it is possible for one animal to monitor the behavior of several others continuously. Only in these latter places is it possible for one animal even to attempt to control the behavior of others. A harem is an extreme example of a system of control, by a male, of the behavior of other males and of females. Male animals fighting, and females staying in groups while mating is going on, are most easily observed in an open habitat. Such observations are likely to be interpreted as attempts by males to control females, or access to females by other males, and to be described as a harem mating system. Closer study may show that, as with elephant seals, the analogy to the human marriage system is not very close. Among mammals, a harem, or some approximation of it, might be seen as what happens when too much information is available to a system of interaction developed to function in cryptic conditions. Although obvious and easy to study, the behavior of animals in unusually open habitats should be extrapolated with caution. The guenons that we expected to be living in harem groups turned out to be doing no such thing.

Both human and animal harems are expected to confer exclusive mating rights on a male who successfully sequesters a group of females and excludes other males, giving a harem-owning male a large reproductive advantage—that is, making him highly successful in biological terms. Whereas exclusive mating rights are probably unrealistic in either human or animal harems, at least a relatively large contribution of offspring to the next generation is expected of harem males as compared with their unsuccessful rivals. In this context, I reiterate that we rarely know about paternity, and where we do the results are unexpected; that is, they do not conform to the assumption that males with high agonistic rank are always the most successful sires. Let us assume for a moment that this is general and that apparent control of the behavior of other animals does not in itself confer reproductive success. We would then be left with an enormous queston: why do males fight, interfere with copulations, and generally act, with enormous energy, in ways that have been interpreted as competing directly for copulations? Why do they act as if it were indeed their aim to maintain a harem?

Some explanations fall into the "it can't be true" category: even if such behavior does not confer immediate advantage here and now, it does so under other conditions (in the wild rather than in captivity, for example); or it has done so in the past, or does so very occasionally, but with such effect that the selective advantage of the behavior is maintained. By their nature, such explanations cannot be refuted: they may appear more or less likely as more information becomes available.

One suitable response to an apparent paradox is to look more carefully at the data on which it is based, and that is what I have been trying to do throughout this essay. It seems, for example, that control of females by males is difficult to substantiate; the hamadryas baboon seems to offer the only satisfactory example. This is not unexpected, since the survival of her offspring (and its father's reproductive success!) depends on a female mammal's finely balanced interaction with her environment. Any behavior by the male which effectively disrupted that interaction could hardly be to his long-term advantage. Control of other males—preventing their mating by winning fights with them—seems more obvious and general. It does seem to work on the open breeding beaches of elephant seals, for example. A problem of interpretation arises, however, because the outcome of most fights is probably predetermined by the combatants' individual interactions with their environment elsewhere. Fights are thus more a form of communication than competition, and so their interpretation is more problematical, and more interesting, than that of crude contests would be.

Human marriage systems have social, political, and economic functions independent of the biological paternity question. Harem polygamy is the outcome of transactions between men, or families, and an expression of the power relationships between them; it has to do with success measured in economic or political terms. Biological success is measured strictly in the currency of surviving offspring, not the condition of the parent. We have seen, however, that lifetime reproductive success may be strongly correlated with lengthy survival, and the wherewithal for an animal's survival might be more easily measured in the human currency of economic success. I suggest that male interactions may be important in determining male survival. These interactions could be competitive, but it is important to remember that in many species males establish generally friendly relationships in the absence of females. The guenons provide good examples. Males spend most of their lives outside female groups, interacting with other males, and it is reasonable to think that male groups, even if widely dispersed and with low rates of interaction, may provide some protection from predators. When males enter a group of females, the rules for male interaction apparently come under great stress and break down or are replaced by a less sophisticated system based on aggression. Hamadryas baboons seem to be exceptional in their ability to maintain a mainly cooperative male organization while living permanently with females; their cooperation is necessary for their individual "ownership" of females to be possible. Here, at least, is a harem system which does seem somewhat comparable to its human namesake, and it depends on cooperation between related males and the respect of possession by other males, and not primarily on aggressive competition between males. Hamadryas baboons are also exceptional in that they are one of the very few species in which interactions between males have been intensively studied. I predict that, when we know more about them, other species will show, at least in rudimentary form, the pattern of alliances between males that de Waal (1982) has described as essentially political in chimpanzees.

# 4

# *Redefining the Social Link*
# *From Baboons to Humans*

Shirley S. Strum and Bruno Latour

In the last decade, a wealth of data on human and nonhuman societies has been collected that contains a hidden challenge to existing ideas about the nature of society and the social link. The ambiguities and discrepancies in these data have completely swamped earlier attempts to define society in simple terms. Are these incongruities and inconsistencies merely the result of "practical difficulties" that will be eliminated with more data, better methodology, and better insulation of scientific endeavors from ideology and amateurism? In this paper we will not take this conventional position but rather offer a different way to approach the problem.

What if the discrepancies are real and the frame of reference is wrong? In order to explore the implications of such a shift in framework, we will first consider alternative paradigms of society and then take a specific case: the history of ideas about baboon society. Next we will investigate the consequences of adopting a different meaning of *social* for our ideas about the evolution of the social link. We conclude by suggesting the usefulness of our new framework in resolving several existing problems in human and nonhuman sociology, including the evolution of "politics."

REDEFINING THE NOTION OF SOCIAL

Sciences of society currently subscribe to a paradigm in which "society," although difficult to probe and to encompass, is something that can be the

This paper was presented at the interdisciplinary symposium "Political Behaviour as a Primate Social Strategy," organized by Glendon Schubert and Shirley Strum at the Tenth Congress of the International Primatological Society in Nairobi, Kenya, 24 July 1984. It was originally published in *Social Science Information*, 26: 783–802; reprinted by permission.

object of an ostensive definition. The actors of society, even if the degree of activity granted them varies from one school of sociology to the next, are *inside* this larger society. Thus, social scientists recognize a difference of scale: the microlevel—that of the actors, members, participants—and a macrolevel—that of society as a whole (Knorr and Cicourel 1981). In the last two decades this ostensive definition of society has been challenged by ethnomethodology (Garfinkel 1967) and by the sociology of science (Knorr and Mulkay 1983), especially of the social sciences (Law 1986) and the sociology of technology (Latour 1986a). In the light of these studies, the conventional distinctions between micro- and macrolevels have become less clear-cut, and it is more difficult to accept a traditional definition of society. Instead, society is more compellingly seen as continually constructed or "performed" by active social beings who violate "levels" in the process of their "work."

The two positions, the ostensive and the performative model, differ in principle and in practice, with crucial consequences for how the social link is characterized. These two views can be summarized as follows.

*Ostensive Definition of the Social Link*

1. It is *in principle* possible to discover the typical properties that hold a society together, properties which could explain the social link and its evolution, although *in practice* it may be difficult to detect them.

2. These properties or elements are social. If other properties are included, then the explanation of society is economic, biological, psychological, etc.

3. Social actors (whatever their size—micro or macro) are *in* the society as defined in point 1. To the extent that they are active, their activity is restricted because they are only part of a larger society.

4. Because actors are in the society, they can be useful informants for scientists interested in discovering the principles of society. But because they are only *part* of society, even if they are "aware," they can never see or know the whole picture.

5. With the proper methodology, social scientists can discover the principles that hold society together, distinguishing between actors' beliefs and behavior. The picture of society as a whole, thus devised, is unavailable to the individual social actors who are within it.

According to the traditional paradigm, society exists, and actors enter it adhering to rules and a structure that are already determined. The overall nature of the society is unknown and unknowable to the actors. Only scientists, standing outside of society, have the capacity to understand it and see it in its entirety.

*"Performative" Definition of the Social Link*

1. It is impossible *in principle* to establish properties which would be peculiar to life in society, although *in practice* it is possible to do so.

2. A variety of elements or properties contribute to the social link as defined by social actors. These are not restricted to the purely social and can include economic, biological, psychological, etc.

3. *In practice*, actors (no matter what their size—macro or micro) define, for themselves and for others, what society is, both its whole and its parts.

4. Actors "performing" society know what is necessary for their success. This may include a knowledge of the parts and of the whole and of the difference between beliefs and behavior.

5. Social scientists raise the same questions as any other social actor and are themselves "performing" society, no more and no less than nonscientists. They may, however, have different practical ways of enforcing their definition of what society is.

According to the performative view, society is constructed through the many efforts to define it; it is something achieved in practice by all actors, including scientists who themselves strive to define what society is. To use Garfinkel's expression (1967), social actors are transformed, in this view, from "cultural dopes" to active achievers of society. This shifts the emphasis from looking for the social link in the *relations between actors* to focusing on how actors achieve this link in their search for what society is.

Going from the traditional to the performative framework creates two sets of inverse relationships, one that reveals a strange symmetry among all actors and another that points out a new asymmetry. The first inverse relationship is the following: the more active the actors, the less they differ from one another. This shift in definition is tantamount to saying that actors are fully fledged social scientists researching what the society is, what holds it together, and how it can be altered. The second inverse relationship is this: the more actors are seen to be equal *in principle*, the more the *practical* differences between them become apparent in the means available to them to achieve society. Let us now see how we can apply these principles in the case of baboon societies.

## BABOONS: HISTORY OF IDEAS

When Darwin wrote that we could learn more from baboons than from many of the Western philosophers, he knew very little, in fact, about baboons (Darwin 1977). It was the Darwinian revolution that initiated the modern scientific study of the behavior and society of other animals.

Prescientific folk ideas about baboons claimed that they were a disorderly gang of brutes, entirely without social organization, roaming around at random (Morris and Morris 1966). A picture of an orderly society emerged with the first "scientific" studies. The early laboratory studies of monkeys (Kempf 1917) and studies of captive baboons (Zuckerman 1932) incorporated only a very small amount of knowledge about the behavior of the animals in the wild (Marais 1956, 1969; Zuckerman 1932). Despite this, the studies did demonstrate that baboons had a society, albeit very simply organized. Sex and dominance were the primary factors at work (Maslow 1936; Zuckerman 1932). Sex held society together, or rather the desire of males for sexual access to females. Baboons were thus both the earliest and most classic representatives of the orderly and simple society of primates.

The modern baboon field studies initiated in the 1950s (DeVore 1965a, b; DeVore and Hall 1965; K. Hall 1963; Washburn and DeVore 1961) were among the pioneering attempts to understand primate behavior in its natural, hence evolutionary, setting (Washburn and Hamburg 1965; Washburn et al 1965). The data suggested that society was not based on sex; the social structure was, instead provided by the effects of male aggression and the dominance hierarchy it created. Social not sexual bonds held the group together. Comparing their results, Washburn, DeVore, and Hall (DeVore and Hall 1965; Hall and DeVore 1965; Washburn and DeVore 1961) were impressed by the similarity of their baboons, although three species were involved and the different populations lived from a hundred to thousands of miles apart. Not only were baboons paragons of orderly social life, but they persisted in that same society regardless of geography or even species distinctions.

As primate field studies proliferated in the 1960s and 1970s, so did studies of baboons (e.g., Altmann and Altmann 1971; Ransom 1984; Rowell 1966, 1969; Stoltz and Saayman 1970). Some observations of baboons in a variety of habitats challenged accepted ideas about baboon society. Forest-living baboons in Uganda (Rowell 1966, 1969) lacked a stable male dominance hierarchy and a variety of "adaptive" male behaviors documented earlier. Kinship and friendship, rather than the male dominance order, appeared to be the basis of baboon society (Ransom 1984; Ransom and Ransom 1971; Strum 1975a, 1982b). These new discoveries were made possible by new methods which included following individually recognized animals over long periods of time. Soon, each baboon troop under observation diverged from the norm, and variations in its behavior undermined both the nice species pattern and its evolutionary interpretation.

One way out of the dilemma of intraspecies variability, a way to eliminate the accumulating discrepancies (and, by implication, the increasing unpredictability of baboon behavior), was to reject data and the views of the observers. A common position was this: other baboons did not behave differently; they were just inaccurately studied. Baboon social structure did exist in a stable way underneath the variety of observations.

Yet the amount of variation documented among baboons (and for other primate species) eventually subdued, to a degree, the methodological argument. Scientists accepted the idea that both behavior and society were flexible (e.g., Crook 1970a, b; Crook and Gartlan 1966; Eisenberg et al 1972; Gartlan 1968; Jay 1968; Struhsaker

1969). The difficulty was to find principles that governed the variability. The best candidates at that time were ecology and phylogeny, but only the sociobiological approach of the mid-1970s (Wilson 1975) provided a new synthesis. This revamped evolutionary framework supplied a compelling solution to the question of the principles of society. Stable properties were not in the social structure itself but rather in individual genotypes. Groups were not selected, as earlier evolutionary formulations had implied; instead, individuals were. The society itself was a stable but "accidental" result of individual decisions—an Evolutionary Stable Strategy (ESS)—and ESSs varied with circumstances (Maynard Smith 1976; Maynard Smith and Parker 1976; Maynard Smith and Price 1973).

The sociobiological solution left moot the question of the proximate means by which society could be achieved. Smart gene calculators might be appropriate actors in an "ultimate" scenario, but whole individuals coexisted, competed or cooperated as real participants in society. It is the most recent stage of baboon (and primate) research which had addressed this proximate level. The information comes primarily from long-term studies of baboons in the wild (field sites: Kenya—Amboseli, Gilgil/Laikipia, Mara; Tanzania—Gombe, Mukumi; Botswana—Okavango).

The recent research is of great interest to our argument. The trend has been in the direction of granting baboons more social skill and more social awareness (Griffin 1981, 1984) than the sociobiological "smart biology" argument allowed. These skills involve negotiating, testing, assessing, and manipulating (Strum 1975a, b, 1981, 1982a, 1983a, b, c, in press; Western and Strum 1983). A male baboon, motivated by his genes to maximize his reproductive success, cannot simply rely on his size, strength, or dominance rank to get him what he wants. Even if dominance was sufficient, we are still left with the question: how do baboons know who is dominant or not? Is dominance a fact or an artifact? If it is an artifact, whose artifact is it? Is it the observer's, who is searching for a society into which he or she can put the baboons? (Even in the classic dominance study, the investigator had to intervene by pairing males in contests over food in order to "discover" the dominance hierarchy.) Or is it a universal problem, one that both observer and baboon have to solve?

If, as recent evidence suggests, baboons are constantly testing, trying to see who is allied with whom, who is leading whom, and which strategies can further their goals, then both baboons and scientists are asking the same questions. And to the extent that baboons are constantly negotiating, the social link is transformed into a process of acquiring knowledge about "what the society is." To put it in a slightly different way, if we grant that baboons are not *entering into a stable structure* but rather negotiating what that structure will be, and monitoring and testing and pushing all other such negotiations, the variety of baboon society and its ill fit to a simple structure can be seen to be a result of the "performative" question. The evidence is more striking in reverse. If there was a structure to be entered, why all this behavior geared to testing, negotiating, and monitoring (e.g., Strum 1975a, b, 1981, 1982a, 1983a, b, c; Boese 1975; Busse and Hamilton 1981; Cheney 1977; Dunbar 1983; Gilmore 1980; Hamilton et al. 1975; Hausfater 1975; Kummer 1967, 1973, 1978; Kummer et al. 1974; Nash 1976; Packer 1979, 1980; Popp 1978; Post et al. 1980; Rasmussen 1979; Rhine 1975; Rhine and Owens 1972; Rhine and Westlund 1978; Sapolsky 198, 1983; Seyfarth 1976; Smuts 1982; Stein 1984; Walters 1980, 1981; Wasser 1981)? And baboons are not alone among the nonhuman primates (e.g., Bernstein and Ehardt 1985; Chepko-Sade 1974; Chepko-Sade and Olivier 1979; Chepko-Sade and Sade 1979; de Waal 1982; Drickamer 1974; Gouzoules 1984; Kaplan 1978; Kleiman 1979; Parker and MacNair 1978; Seyfarth 1977, 1980; Silk 1980).

We can summarize the baboon data and argument as follows: first, the traditional, ostensive definition of baboon society has been unable to accommodate the variety of data on baboon social life. As a result, some information has been treated as "data" and other information as discrepancies to be ignored or explained away. Second, more recent studies demonstrate that baboons invest a great deal of time in negotiating, testing, monitoring, and interfering with each other.

A performative definition of society allows us to integrate both sets of "facts." Under this definition, baboons would not be seen as being *in* a group. Instead, they would be seen as striving to define the society and the groups in which they exist, the structure and the boundaries. They would not be seen as being *in* a hierarchy; rather, they would be ordering their social world by their very activity. In such a view, shifting or stable hierarchies might develop not as one of the principles of an overarching society into which baboons must fit, but as the provisional outcome of their search for some basis of predictable interactions. Rather than entering an alliance system, baboons performing society would be testing the availability and solidity of alliances without knowing for certain, in advance, which relationships will hold and which will break. In short, performative baboons are social players actively negotiating and renegotiating what their society is and what it will be.

The performative version of society seems better able to account for the longitudinal data from one baboon site than can the traditional model. This is true when examining predatory behavior (Strum 1975b, 1981, 1983c), male interactions (Strum 1982b, 1983a, b), agonistic buffering (Strum 1982a, b), social strategies (Strum 1982a, 1983a, b, in press), the evolution of social manipulation (Western and Strum 1983), and the fission of the main study troop (Strum in press). Baboons "performing" society might also allow a more consistent interpretation of the cross-population data and data from other species of monkeys and apes.


## SOCIAL COMPLEXITY AND SOCIAL COMPLICATION

When we transform baboons into active performers of their society, does this put them on a par with humans? The performative paradigm suggests an important distinction. What differs is the *practical* means that actors have to enforce their version of society or to organize others on a larger scale, thereby putting into practice their own individual version of what society is.

If actors have only themselves, only their bodies, as resources, the task of building stable societies will be difficult. This is probably the case with baboons. They try to decide who is a member of the group, what are the relevant units of the group that have to be considered, what is the nature of the interaction of these other units, and so on, but they have no simple or simplifying means to decide these issues or to separate out one at a time to focus upon. Age, sex, and perhaps kinship can be taken as givens in most interactions. To the extent that dominance systems are linked to kinship, dominance rank may also be a given (Chapais and Schulman 1980; Hausfater et al. 1982). But even age, kinship, and kinship-linked dominance may be the object of negotiation at critical points (J. Altmann 1980; Cheney 1977; Chepko-Sade and Sade 1979; Popp and DeVore 1979; Trivers 1972; Walters 1981; Wasser 1982; Wasser and Barash 1981). A profusion of other variables impinge simultaneously. This is the definition of *complexity*, "to simultaneously embrace a multitude of objects." As far as baboons are concerned, they assimilate a variety of factors all at once.

For the rest of our discussion we will consider that baboons live in *complex* societies and have complex sociality. When they construct and repair their social order, they do so only with limited resources: their bodies, their social skills, and whatever social strategies they can construct. A baboon is, in our view, the ideal case of the *competent member* portrayed by ethnomethodologists, a social actor having difficulty negotiating one factor at a time, constantly subject to the interference of others and similar problems. These limited resources make possible only limited social stability.

Greater stability is acquired only with additional resources; something besides what is encoded in bodies and attainable through social skills is needed. Material resources and symbols can be used to enforce or reinforce a particular view of "what society is" and permit social life to shift away from complexity to what we will call *complication*. Something is "complicated" when it is made of a succession of simple operations. Computers are the archetype of a complicated structure where tasks are achieved by the machine doing a series of simple steps. We suggest that the shift from complexity to complication is the crucial *practical* distinction between types of social life.

To understand this point better, we might look at what baboon-watchers do in order to understand baboon social life. First, individuals are identified and named, and the composition of the group is determined by age, sex, kinship, and perhaps also dominance rankings. Items of behavior are identified, defined, and coded. Then attention is consciously focused on a subset of individuals, times, and activities among the variety of interactions that occur simultaneously. Of course we could interpret this procedure as merely a rigorous way of getting at the social structure that exists and informs baboon societies. This interpretation of the

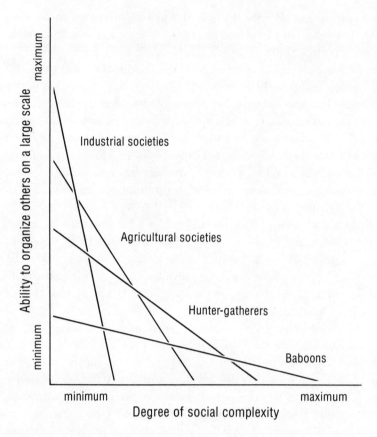

Figure 4-1. Complexity versus complication: the trade off.

scientific work fits nicely with the ostensive definition of society. In our view, however, the work that human observers do in order to understand baboon societies is the very same process that makes human societies different from baboon ones. Modern scientific observers replace a complexity of shifting, often fuzzy, and continuous behaviors, relationships, and meanings with a complicated array of simple, symbolic, clear-cut items. It is an enormous task of simplification.

How does the shift from social complexity to social complication happen? Figure 4-1 illustrates how we imagine this progression. The first line represents a baboon-like society in which socialness is complex, by our use of that term, and society is complex but not complicated because individuals are unable to organize others on a large scale. The intensity of their social negotiation reflects their relative powerlessness to enforce their version of society on others or to make it stick as a stable, lasting version.

The second line represents hypothetical hunter-gatherers who are rich in material and symbolic means to use in constructing society compared to baboons, although impoverished by comparison with modern industrial societies. Here language, symbols, and material objects can be used to simplify the task of ascertaining and negotiating the nature of the social order. Bodies continue their social strategies in the performance of society, but on a larger, more durable, less complex scale. Material resources and the symbolic innovations related to language allow individuals to influence and have more power over others, thereby determining the nature of the social order.

The third line represents agricultural societies, where even more resources can be brought to bear in creating the social bond. In fact, the social bond can be maintained in the relative absence of the individuals. These societies are more complicated and more powerful than hunter-gatherer groups, and the performation of society is possible on a large scale because negotiations at each step are much less complex.

Modern industrial societies are depicted by the fourth line on the diagram. Here individuals are able to organize and "mobilize" others on a grand scale. According to our scheme, the skills in an industrial society are those of simplification, making social tasks *less complex* rather than more complex by comparison with other human and animal societies. By holding a variety of factors constant and sequentially negotiating one variable at a time, a stable *complicated* structure is created. Through extrasomatic resources employed in the process of social complication, units such as multinational corporations, states, and nations can be constituted (Latour 1987). As we have sketched it, the trend is from complex sociality, as found among baboons, to complicated sociality as found among humans. Starting with individuals who have little power to affect others, to enforce their version of society, or to make a lasting social order, we encounter a situation where individuals employ more and more material and "extrasocial" means to simplify social negotiations. This gives them the ability to organize others on a large scale, even when those others are not physically present. By using additional new resources, social actors can make weak and renegotiable associations, such as alliances between male baboons, into strong and unbreakable units (Callon and Latour 1981; Latour 1986a).

## THE EVOLUTION OF THE PERFORMATIVE SOCIAL BOND

Our use of a performative framework produces two important permutations. First, it grants full activity to all social participants. Individually and together they create society and, in theory, they are all equal. But second, new asymmetries are introduced when we consider what practical means actors have to enforce their own definition of the social bond and to organize others according to individual views of what society is.

This suggests a novel way to examine the evolution of the social bond. What follows is really a classification of meanings of "social" which may have implications for an evolutionary scenario.

We can begin with the common definition of "social" — "to associate." But how does an actor make the social link hold? Some associations are weaker while some are stronger and longer lasting. Our comparison of complexity and complication, from baboons to humans, suggests that resources play a role in the construction of society and in social stability.

The etymology of the word "social" is also instructive. The root is *seq-*, *sequi*, and the first meaning is thus "following." The Latin *socius* is a fellow sharer, partner, comrade, companion, associate. *Socio* means to unite together, to associate, to do or to hold in common. From the different languages, the historical genealogy of the word "social" is construed first as following someone, then enrolling and allying, and last as having something in common. These three meanings are quite appropriate for baboons. The next meaning of "social" is to have a share in a commercial undertaking. "Social" as in the social contract is Rousseau's invention. "Social" as in social problems, the social question, is a nineteenth-century innovation. Parallel words like "sociable" refer to skills enabling individuals to live politely in society. As is clear from the drift of the word, the meaning of social shrinks as time passes. Starting with a definition which is coextensive with all associations, we now have, in common parlance, a usage that is limited to what is left after politics, biology, economics, law, psychology, management, technology, and so on have taken their own parts of the associations.

The performative framework we are advocating, in effect, gives back to the word "social" its original meaning of association. Using this definition we can compare the *practical* ways in which organisms achieve societies. Figure 4-2 summarizes our views about the possible evolution of the performative social bond. We focus on the types of resources that actors have with which to create society and to associate, but we do not restrict the idea of "resources" in any sense.

Aggregations of conspecifics is the first meaning of "social" in various accounts of the origin of society (see Latour and Strum 1986 and references included there). However, most accounts fail to distinguish between this aggregation and the origin of social skills. Once aggregation occurs, whatever its cause (e.g., Alcock 1975; Hamilton 1971), two different strategies are possible in our model. The first is for the actor to depart, fleeing others as soon as possible. This option generates asocial animals who exist alone except for brief reproductive interludes and temporary associations.

The second option is of greater interest. If the aggregated individual is not going to flee, he or she must adapt to a new environment of conspecifics. This is the meaning of "social" most common in the animal behavior literature: to modify one's behavior in order to live in close proximity to others of the same species. Acquiring the skill to create society and hold it together is then a *secondary* adaptation to an environment made up, in large part, of conspecifics. In order not to be exploited by their new social environment, individuals must become smarter at manipulating and maneuvering around each other.

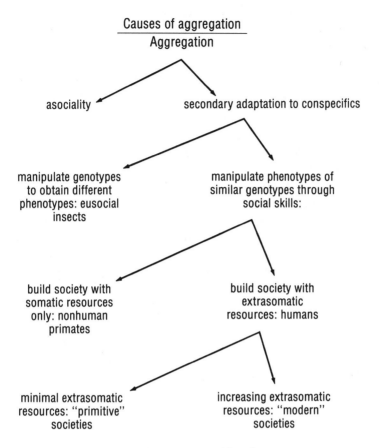

Figure 4-2. The evolution of the performative social bond.

Once the social option has been chosen, two other possibilities appear. In the first, it is the genotypes that are modified until they are socially distinct. Insect societies are an example where the actors' own bodies are irreversibly molded. In the second possibility we find a different meaning of "social." In this case the genotypes produce similar phenotypes. These phenotypes are then manipulated by the ever-increasing social skills of individuals. This option also branches into two alternatives.

Baboons provide an example of the first. Social skills are necessary to enroll others in the actor's definition of what society is. But baboons have only "soft tools" and can build only "soft" societies. They have nothing more to convince and enlist others in their definition than their bodies, their intelligence, and a history of interactions built up over time. This is a *complex* task and only socially "smart" and skillful individuals may hope to be successful in baboon society.

The second possibility is to acquire additional means of defining and strengthening the social bond. Here we have the human case where the creation of society uses material resources and symbols to simplify the task. Social interactions become more *complicated* but not more complex. Much of the skill necessary to achieve society in the other, baboon-like option now resides in the creation of symbolic and material bonds. The result is that actors, rather than appearing to create society, now appear to be inserted into a material society that overpowers them (the traditional paradigm discussed earlier).

For human societies there is an additional branching: "primitive" societies are created with a minimal amount of material resources; increasing such resources produces "modern" societies. Thus technology becomes one way of solving the problem of building society on a larger scale. In this sense even modern technology is social. It represents a further resource in the mobilization of individuals in the performation of society.

To summarize our theoretical model, once individuals are aggregated and choose not to avoid each other, there must be a secondary adaptation to a new competitive environment of conspecifics. Two strategies are possible: manipulate the genotypes to obtain different phenotypes (eusocial insects) or manipulate the phenotypes of similar genotypes through increasing social skills. Similar bodies adapting to social life have, themselves, two possibilities: build the society using only social skills (nonhuman primates) or utilize additional material resources and symbols, as necessary to define the social bond (human societies). In the human step different types of societies are created depending upon the extent of new resources that are used.

## POLITICS

What relevance does our exploration of the meanings of "social" have for politics? The answer depends, of course, on how politics is defined (Mackenzie 1967). At the simplest and broadest level, "politics" is simply that which is characterized by policy, of "sagacious, prudent, shrewd persons" or of "expedient, skillfully contrived actions" (*Oxford English Dictionary*). G. Schubert (1986b) proposes a definition of politics that would allow cross-species, evolutionary comparisons. For him, politics is the manner in which individuals seek to influence and control others who are not closely related to them but live together in large social groups. In these groups there are subgroups that cooperate or compete for control over the policy that determines the group's cultural rules.[1]

Both our approach and Schubert's suggest that the ability to influence and control conspecifics is an important aspect of political behavior. In shifting to a performative definition of social, we conceive of the social link as an *active* exercise in negotiation and control. What is different, between different species

---

1. Until recently, "cultural rules" might have excluded nonhuman animals a priori. Now the evidence is striking for animal "mental models" (e.g., Griffin 1981, 1984).

and between different human groups, is the scale on which others can be organized, mobilized, and influenced. In our model, material resources and symbols play a significant role in creating the difference between a "soft" society with limited stability, where individuals have minimal power to influence others, and a "hard" and stable society, where others can be influenced without even being present.

Can we identify the beginnings of political behavior in the beginnings of socialness, as we have redefined it and traced its development through our version of the evolution of the social bond? Certainly the traditional view that individuals are relatively passive and enter into a society that overpowers them would lead us to believe that political action begins when individuals become "actors," taking the initiative in determining "what society is." In this view such initiative comes very late in the evolutionary time-scale. But if all social actors "perform" society to some degree, are active participants from the *beginning*, probing and investigating, negotiating and renegotiating, where would we comfortably place the beginnings of political behavior? Should we exclude the eusocial insects because the major negotiations occur before the phenotypes appear? Should we exclude nonhuman primates because their sphere of influence is limited by the extent of their material and symbolic resources?

While the thrust of Schubert's "biopolitical behavioralist" definition is to urge caution when attributing political behavior to nonhuman primates, at least as some recent animal studies have done (e.g., de Waal 1982), the thrust of our argument is to draw a closer parallel between what we call "social" and what has been defined as political. These efforts do not erase the significant differences between ants, baboons, and, for instance, the technocrats of the Pentagon. Rather, they highlight the source of those differences in a new way: the resources used and the practical work required in mobilizing them. In our definition of resources, genes, power, language, capital, and technology, for instance, are all seen as strategic means of enhancing one's influence over others in increasingly more durable ways. Politics is not one realm of action separated from the others. Politics, in our view, is what allows many heterogenous resources to be woven together into a social link that becomes increasingly harder and harder to break.

# PART II

*Chimpanzees*

# Introduction
## The Missing Political Link?

Glendon Schubert

In his popular book on the chimpanzees of Kibale forest, Michael Ghiglieri (1988, 4; for his scientific report see his 1984) presents an excellent map of East Africa and especially of the western Great Rift valley, which extends a thousand miles from the Sudan to the head of Lake Nyassa in Malawi. The western valley should not be confused with the eastern Great Rift valley, which extends much further—four thousand miles—from southern Turkey through the Dead Sea and the Red Sea, through Ethiopia, Kenya, Tanzania, into Lake Nyassa, and Malawi, and at last through Mozambique into the Indian Ocean. Lucy and the manifold discoveries of the Leakey family (plus Shirley Strum's baboons) all were or are found in the eastern valley, which drains Ethiopia's Omo River through central Kenya into Tanzania, bearing almost due south. The northern half of the western valley arcs to the north by north-northeast from Lake Tanganyika through a chain of three other lakes to the outlet of the Albert Nile River. Arrayed along the eastern side of that arc are the chimpanzees studied by Nishida at Mahale, Goodall at Gombe, and Ghiglieri at Budongo (less than 250 miles from Mahale), with the mountain gorillas studied by George Schaller and Dian Fossey only a hundred miles south of Budongo, on the slopes of the volcanic mountains that tower above the western Great Rift valley floor. Thus, the eastern valley defines the heartland of African paleoanthropology into human origins; while the western valley contains, within a span of barely three hundred miles, most of the major field research sites for the study of human-kind's sibling species, chimpanzees and gorillas (see Strum 1987, 74). For two maps as excellent as Ghiglieri's, but of the eastern valley and all of the principal hominid paleoanthropological sites dating back to three to four million years ago, see the seminal paper by the late Glynn Isaac (1978a, 93), who worked at several of these locations, and see Leakey (1984, 10) for what the map captions as "Mary Leakey's Africa."

The two chapters of part II discuss the two most important research projects, which have generated the most extensive and intensive studies, on and of chimpanzee behavior. The longer-established, larger, and best-known chimpanzee project ever is that of the Kasakela group ("community") in Kakombe Valley of Gombe National Park, on the central eastern shore of Lake Tanganyika in Tanzania. Over the nineteen-year period 1965 to 1983, the core Kasakela chimpanzee community varied in size between thirty-eight and sixty individuals, with an average of fifty. For a similar but somewhat shorter period for Arnhem, from 1971 to 1980 (i.e., from the project's inception until de Waal cut off data for his book), the Burgers' Zoo group never exceeded nineteen (i.e., about 40 percent of the size of the Gombe study core group). Of course, the Arnhem group was completely isolated from all other mammals (including other chimpanzees), except for human keepers and observers, whereas the Gombe group lived both in association with—not kept by—one or more resident humans (Goodall's group) and in association always with other contiguous chimpanzee groups, one to the immediate north and another to the immediate south (along the shore of Lake Tanganyika, and hemmed in by that lake on the west and by the top of the rift escarpment about two miles to the east). Gombe National Park extends over about forty-two square kilometers (Goodall gives the figure as thirty-two, but cf. the map in Goodall 1986, 46) and includes about a dozen and a half major valleys and a chimpanzee population estimated in 1985 to be about 160 individuals. The Kasakela chimpanzee group's range varied during the decade 1973 to 1983 (1986, 505, 515) from a maximum of about 9.5 square kilometers to a minimum of about 7 square kilometers, with a core area of about a third of that range. In comparison, the outside (moated) area for the Arnhem group is .008 square kilometers—about ⅟₁₀₀₀th of the average range of the Kasakela group—and the Arnhem inner range is .0004 square kilometers, about ⅟₇₀₀₀th of the average core area of the Kasakela group. The Arnhem chimpanzees are in a *zoo*. The zoo is managed by a director; and he (Anton van Hooff) is the brother of Jan A. R. A. M. van Hooff, professor of psychology at the University of Utrecht, who with his students (including Frans B. M. de Waal) has studied the zoo's chimpanzees consequent to the establishment of the Arnhem chimpanzee population in 1971.

## 1. CHIMPANZEES IN PARADISE LOST AND IN CAPTIVITY

Jane Goodall's chapter 5 has four major parts: (1) "Chimpanzees in a State of Nature"; (2) "Foraging Nature"; (3) "Community Politics"; and (4) "Community Warfare." These sections demonstrate the following points:

1. The juvenile and adult Gombe chimpanzees exercise considerable individual freedom in roaming in diverse patterns, sometimes alone and otherwise with shifting companionship.

2. They are forced to roam to find enough food to sustain life.

3. Their community contains a substantial number of male as well as of female adults, ranging from an average of 13 males to 9 females in the earliest period of observation (1965 to 1968); with equal numbers of males and females (10–11 each) for the next three years until it split into two groups; and with an average of 5.5 males to twice that many females for the third period of 1972 to 1983 (Goodall 1986, 82). The overall averages of 7.8 adult males and 11.2 adult females indicate that modally about 19 mature adults formed the social core of the Gombe community; in addition, there was on average one older male and one older female in the group, plus several late adolescent males and several late adolescent females (and also 20 to 30 early adolescents, juveniles, and infants). The range of social diversity, and of choice among voluntary social contacts, was considerable.

4. The Kasakela "community" was sufficiently flexible to include both marginal and peripheralized individuals (typically females) and small groups (typically females with offspring), plus males as well as females who emigrated to or immigrated from neighboring social groups. In addition, both voluntary and involuntary contact—almost invariably hostile—was experienced by Kasakela group "members" in relation to chimpanzees associated with neighboring communities to either the north or the south.

The captive chimpanzees of Arnhem can be compared point by point:

1. The Arnhem chimpanzees are in a situation similar to that of mental patients in a ward of a 1950s-style American psychiatric hospital, with a few "normal" individuals (who are hearing impaired, autistic, or just unlucky) mixed in with schizoids, paranoids, and others who are merely mildly neurotic. The chimpanzees are periodically forced into often unwanted social contact, and their behavior is monitored by caretakers and researchers.

2. Like the mental institution inmates, the Arnhem inmate chimpanzees are sequestered for the purpose of being fed, but otherwise have an immense amount of time on their hands with nothing to do but socialize. Socialization for the Gombe chimpanzees is a function (in the strict biological sense) of getting enough to eat and otherwise of staying alive; the Arnhem chimpanzees are the property of a large human institution (Burgers' Zoo) whose *caretakers* try to protect the chimpanzees from each other, thereby safeguarding the zoo's investment in them. The limited feeding of bananas to many of the Kasakela group of chimpanzees, however serendipitous in its inception, accomplished the positive goal of making it easier for the researchers to make observations, but entailed the negative consequence of escalating the habituation of the Kasakela group of chimpanzees generally. But the feeding experiment at Gombe was minor in its impact on the social behavior of Kasakela chimpanzees as compared to the fundamental difference that *total* feeding of the Arnhem chimpanzees makes for their social behavior. As Goodall clearly recognizes, even limited feeding reinforced observational contact to convert the habituated

Kasakela chimpanzees into animals somewhat different from the *un*habituated wild chimpanzees in both the northern and southern extremes of even the Gombe reservation (i.e., the Mitumba and the Kalande community groups). In this sense, it is the habituated Kasakela community that constitutes a "halfway house" between captive chimpanzees on the one hand and wild chimpanzees on the other.

3. With regard to social structure, the Kasakela and Arnhem groups differ in two principal respects. First, the larger the number of adult males in the group, the more difficult it is to establish a linear hierarchy among them (except for the denotation of the alpha). Over a period of twenty-one years (1963 to 1983), there were five alpha males for Kasakela (of whom two had discontinuous tenure in the role), with an average of four years in the role; three others competed but never succeeded, and two of them emigrated after having been defeated. In chapter 6 of the present volume, de Waal indicates three different alpha males—Yeroen, 1973–1976; Luit, 1976–1980; and Nikkie, 1980–1984—for the Arnhem group over a period of a dozen years, so the average alpha tenure is the same for both the Arnhem and the Kasakela groups. But de Waal denoted a stable and consistent female hierarchy based on affection ("respect") rather than intimidation. Goodall notes that there was considerable aggression among adult females when the colony was first established at Arnhem, to such an extent that it was deemed necessary to remove both of the two most dominant females from the group for an extended period of time in order to enable one of the two adult males (who were also dominated by the females when the males joined the group in 1973) to assume the alpha role. At that time the older male, Yeroen, was about 23 years of age; Luit, about 18; and Nikkie, an early adolescent male also introduced to the colony in 1973, was 10. A male at age 23 is in "prime" maturity (according to Goodall 1986, 81); one of 18 is a "young adult"; and males of age 13 to 15 are in "late adolescence."

4. The Kasakela chimpanzee community lives in a condition that probably comes somewhat closer to Rousseau's description of the state of nature in the *Second Discourse* (Rousseau 1964, 145, 150–51, 195, 222) than to the "war of all against all" of Hobbes's *Leviathan*. In addition to the persistent violence within the local population, different groups are engaged in intermittent small-scale internecine homicidal conflict with neighboring groups; they are also occasionally involved in larger-scale intergroup conflict (e.g., when the Kasakela group divided in 1972) similar to what Chagnon describes as normal for the Yanomamö when population densities exceed tolerable limits. The Arnhem chimpanzees have no one to fight with except themselves, apart from occasional targets of opportunity that are presented by human visitors (de Waal 1982, 82).

The unhabituated Gombe chimpanzee communities appear to have represented a good sample of a natural East African chimpanzee population, at least in 1960 when Jane Goodall began her work there (but compare the degree of environmental deterioration that had occurred twenty-five years later [Goodall

1986, 49]; see also section 3 below). The Arnhem aggregation, to the contrary, was purchased from other European zoos, animal dealers, and circuses. Prior to their induction into the Arnhem colony, all of the chimpanzees had experienced varying degrees of what for them was most unnatural treatment (from diverse human owners): de Waal notes, for instance, that the two oldest (and subsequently the initial succession of alpha) males "both came from the zoo in Copenhagen [where] they had [probably] spent two years together in the same cage" (1982, 61).

## 2. "POWER AND SEX" AMONG CHIMPANZEES

De Waal raised many explicit researchable questions about what the subtitle of his book (1982) refers to as "power and sex" in the Arnhem group, although by five years later, he had become somewhat more skeptical about the first attribute, stating (de Waal 1987a, 429) that "the concept of power in primate societies is still poorly developed" (cf. de Waal 1989). His essay in this volume (chapter 6) attempts to answer these questions:

1. Which does more to improve an adult chimpanzee's inclusive fitness: competition or cooperation?

2. Why do adult males cooperate: to improve their individual chances of becoming dominant or to protect their friends and relatives? What about adult females: is their reason the same or different?

3. De Waal classifies the Arnhem chimpanzees into sex-by-age subcategories. In what kinds of conflicts do all such subgroups tend to intervene the most: those between adult males or those between adult females?

4. Are the decisions of adult male chimpanzees to intervene in conflicts between others more or less consistent than those of females and/or juveniles?

5. Is social bonding among individual members a condition precedent to the establishment of coalitions among adult males? What about among adult females? If so in either case, is this due to the frequency or the intensity of dyadic bonding?

6. How does instability in adult male predominance affect bonding and coalitions among adult males?

7. Why is adult female dominance hierarchy so much more stable than that among adult males?

8. Is the adult male intervention behavior unstable (1) because of the opportunistic base of adult male coalitions or (2) because of the adult female bonding base of adult female coalitions; or both?

9. What is the principal cause of instability in the adult male dominance hierarchy?

10.  When do chimpanzees intervene in support of probable *winners* when conflict occurs? In support of probable losers?

11.  Why does "winner" support increase under conditions of crowding?

12.  In terms of their individual behavior as members of coalitions, do chimpanzees act as though they believe that adult female hierarchies will react as a group, whereas adult males will react as indviduals?

Chapter 6 raises a number of other provocative theoretical questions, of which the most important is probably the matter of level of analysis, which he does not attempt to answer. In chapter 2, Glendon Schubert emphasizes the problems raised in philosophy of science when small, face-to-face social groups of less than a hundred individuals are analogized behaviorally to large, purely artificial "groups." This is due to fundamental differences in the constraints upon and opportunities for dyadic (not to mention more complex) behavioral transactions when humans confront each other in face-to-face settings as distinguished from their attributed—never observable—relationships in sociological constructs. This has nothing to do with anthropomorphism, but it does have something to do with similarities and differences between chimpanzees and humans. Chimpanzees in the present and past have NEVER, naturally or otherwise, congregated in groups of even, say, a *thousand* individuals. Attempts to congregate even natural-sized chimpanzee groups under conditions of captivity have led to disastrous consequences (see de Waal 1982, 23; Goodall 1986, 417). Needless to add, such congregations will be even less likely to occur in the future as the chimpanzee population continues to decline due to human competition (i.e., further destruction of their diminishing natural habitats; see section 3, below). So it should be perfectly clear that human warfare between, say, the United States and the Soviet Union—which is the level of analysis in the passage from Martin Wight cited by de Waal—is methodologically difficult to equate with the within-group conflict observed among chimpanzees, and even with the between-group chimpanzee violence closer to the definition of human war as "armed conflict between groups" (Goodall 1986, 530). But from the same point of view, Goodall's speculations about the possible homological bases for comparing the "war" of attrition and annihilation carried on by the Kasakela group against the splinter Kamaha group in Gombe with feuds or intergroup warfare between human gathering-hunting bands (e.g., Chagnon 1968; Durham 1976) is unobjectionable on the grounds of level of analysis.

In many species of mammals besides chimpanzees and humans (e.g., lions), conspecifics often violently attack one another; most ethologists and psychologists believe that these attacks are the result of stress (Davies 1980), xenophobia (Flohr 1986), and/or resource competition (Durham 1976). It would certainly be an orthodox use of evolutionary theory to interpret all of the many chimpanzee killings discussed by Goodall (1986), both those *within* the Kasakela group (i.e., her chapter 12 on "Aggression") and those *on* members of the Kasakela group (chapter 17 on "territoriality"), in terms of other factors that Goodall also discusses—including those mentioned above—instead of homologizing the intergroup killings as akin to human warfare (cf. Shaw, Wong, Goldstein, and Kitcher 1987). De Waal's subsequent book (1989) on reconciliation among human and nonhuman primates alike analyzes the transactional relationships among competition, cooperation, and rapprochement as functions of international peacemaking among humans, which he analogizes (e.g., 66–69) to his own and other primatological studies of the social behaviors of groups of apes or monkeys.

In chapter 6, de Waal mentions that the original Arnhem group came from diverse origins (mostly European zoos), and so far as was known none of them were kin. He does concede that females (as well as males) might use coalitions for dominance purposes, although the female hierarchy of the Arnhem group is much more stable than the male hierarchy (i.e., coalitions). The maturation of female juveniles does not destabilize the female hierarchy; but for adult females under crowded conditions (i.e., locked in the indoor cages during the winter months), stress may be as important as "inclusive fitness" in influencing their behavior. But his major thesis is that "coalitions of adult male chimpanzees are part of dominance strategies, whereas those of females serve to protect friends and relatives. The first indications of this difference were provided by de Waal (1978)" (but cf. Wrangham 1975). He characterizes the male hierarchy as vertical but argues that the females live "in a horizontal world of social connections. Their coalitions are more or less permanently linked to particular individuals, whose well-being is their goal." De Waal closes his discussion of sex differences in the coalitional behavior of chimpanzees by a comparison with humans, among whom males are said to be exploitive, wanting to win and form beneficial coalitions (see Nishida and Hiraiwa-Hasegawa 1987), while females are accommodative, wanting to play a pleasant game. De Waal offers the "plausible hypothesis" that for both chimpanzees and humans "both sexes may have the same mental abilities and social tactics available but do not use them in the same way because the kind of outcomes they try to achieve are different. This might mean that the resemblance between human and chimpanzee coalition patterns is due to similar social goals in the lives of women and female chimpanzees on the one hand, and in the lives of men and male chimpanzees on the other. If so, the two species would share a personality difference between the sexes that is very profound indeed." Goodall likewise emphasizes the strong behavioral homology between chimpanzees and humans, particularly with regard to the bellicose behavior of males (1986, 531; chapter 6; cf. de Waal 1989), stating that many leading evolutionary theorists believe that

> the powerful pressure that warfare almost certainly exerted on the development of the human brain . . . [has] been the *principal evolutionary pressure* that created the huge gap between the human brain and that of our closest living relatives, the anthropoid apes. . . . Another basic preadaptation would have been an inherent fear of, or aversion to,

strangers, expressed by aggressive attack (Eibl-Eibesfeldt 1979a). Early hominid groups possessing these behavioral characteristics would theoretically have been capable of the kind of organized intergroup conflict that could have led to destructive warfare. Chimpanzees not only possess, to a greater or lesser extent, the above preadaptations, but they show other inherent characteristics that would have been helpful to the dawn warriors in their primitive battles.

Nancy Tanner's book *On Becoming Human* (1981) advocates comparing the social behavior of modern chimpanzee females and human women to help reconstruct the "stem ape" *Sivapithecus* that was their common ancestor; Tanner emphasizes the crucial importance of female hierarchies and behavior to the successful adaptation and survival both of chimpanzees, as they dwelt in central Africa a century ago, and, say, of San women living at the same time in the same continent although in a more southern locale. William McGrew's paper "The Female Chimpanzee as a Human Evolutionary Prototype" (1981) discusses at length Tanner's hypothesis; but neither Goodall nor de Waal cites Tanner or mentions her model, which was widely cited and discussed by feminist primatologists and feminist philosophers of science (cf. sections 3 and 4 of chapter 1) throughout the early and middle 1980s. Goodall (1986) does list McGrew's paper as a reference (together with seven other papers that McGrew either authored or coauthored: he undertook important postdoctoral research as one of Goodall's resident visitors at Gombe), but she cites it only once, in support of the observation that "Gombe females also ate more termites and weavers, and possibly more driver ants, than did males"—not in regard to the social behavior of female chimpanzees as a prototype for the behavior of women in gathering-hunting bands. In chapter 6, de Waal confines his discussion of analogies to human politics to table 6-3 and the concluding two paragraphs of his essay, which would not necessarily imply a reference to human political behavior except in the context of and in relation to his book, which (as he explicitly says in the chapter) is the way it should be read. Reading it that way, it is clear from his book that another question is raised by de Waal's posture in regard to chimpanzee intentionality. "Mentalism" and "dualism" remain respectable postures in human psychobiology, but clearly not in cognitive ethology (Terrace 1979; Sebeok and Umiker-Sebeok 1980). There are important cortical differences between the structures of chimpanzee and human brains; chimpanzees do not *speak* any language, human or otherwise; and human language is inextricably involved both in the lateralization of the human brain and in human thinking and consciousness (G. Schubert 1983e). Any claim that Arnhem chimpanzees demonstrate self-consciousness in their development—as de Waal seems to suggest (1982, 1987, 421)—must certainly be challenged as unwarranted in the absence of scientifically acceptable evidence. Of course, scientists should distinguish between their speculations and what they assert to be scientific findings; and de Waal does precisely that in chapter 6, where he refers to his *Chimpanzee Politics* (1982) as having been written "for a general public." However, he immediately adds that "the present publication may be regarded as a quantitative supplement to the book," which implies that he is prepared to stand behind the book and defend it on the basis of his scientific restraint in chapter 6. But the claims made in the book in behalf of chimpanzee self-consciousness are clearly *not* supported by the scientific evidence reported in chapter 6.

Potts (1988, 282–83, 288, 284) describes and analyzes in detail how two different populations of West African wild chimpanzees habitually use tools to crack nuts too hard for them to bite open (a behavior analogous to that of sea-otters swimming on their backs while cracking mollusc shells with stones, which many readers doubtless will have seen on television nature programs):

> At Bossou, Guinea, and in the Tai Forest, Ivory Coast, researchers have observed common chimpanzees (*Pan troglodytes versus*) to carry pieces of stone or large sticks that are then used as hammers and anvils to crack open nuts. At Bossou, pairs of loose stones are left at certain nut trees. Individual chimpanzees or small groups independently visit these trees, collect the nuts, and crack them for a period of time at the food source itself. . . . The cracking stones are left behind with associated nutshells. The nut trees are visited repeatedly when nuts are available, and the hammer and anvil stones are reused, apparently over many years. The Bossou chimpanzees engage in this activity only at trees where stones have been left; all nuts processed at a nut-cracking station come from that particular tree. . . .
>
> In Tai National Park, 200 km away, chimpanzees appear to take a slightly different approach toward the transport of nut-cracking tools. Either exposed tree roots or outcrops of granite or laterite situated near the nut tree are used as anvils. While the anvils are immobile, hammers of wood (sticks or broken roots) and stone (granite or laterite) are frequently carried from one anvil/nut tree location to another and are sometimes carried considerable distances. Like at Bossou, individuals or pairs of chimpanzees collect nuts in a tree (coala nuts) or on the ground (panda nuts). They then either crack the nuts at an anvil located within the area of the tree (ca. 10 m diameter) or carry the nuts up to about 30 m away to better anvils (often rock outcrops) than are available right at the tree. Hammers are brought to the anvils usually over a short distance (5–20 m). Yet out of 603 observations of hammer transport, 21 (3.5%) involved distances of 200–500 m (stones weighing up to 9 kg), and 3 cases (0.5%) involved movement of hammer stones (weighing up to 3 kg) over 500 m. . . . Unlike the Bossou example, the Tai chimpanzees do not always leave hammers at the nut-cracking sites; rather they often transport them from one anvil/nut tree spot to another. Since panda trees are widely scattered in the Tai Forest, the distance hammers are transported between panda nut–cracking sites (preferentially granite hammer stones) may be especially long.
>
> Interestingly, the Tai chimpanzees will collect nuts at an anvil only if a hammer is already present. When chimpanzees require a stone hammer at a cracking site (usually ascertained by visiting the site first), they will take one from a site where a hammer is available. This latter site tends to be the nut-cracking site (with a hammer) nearest to the site previously visited by the chimpanzees, thus minimizing the distance of hammerstone transport. The researchers who have analyzed the nut-cracking activities at Tai suggest that these chimpanzees remember where nut-processing stones are located in their foraging range and transport stones between nut trees based on past experience, or a "mental map" [cf. the discussion of "cognitive mapping" by hominids and carnivores in savanna predation; G. Schubert 1983d]. . . . [But] it must be realized that these two examples are not

analogous to inferences about the role of hominids at the Olduvai sites. Chimp nut-
cracking sites and the Olduvai artifact sites differ in ways that probably signify important
evolutionary differences between chimpanzees and early tool-using hominids, at least
those at Olduvai. . . . [The Tai chimps] illustrate the end of the range of variation in
foraging among living nonhuman primates closest to that inferred for hominids at Olduvai. . . . However, the degree of transport at Olduvai is of a different order from that
exhibited by chimpanzees. This greater reliance on transporting implements and food
implies a considerably greater delay in the use of stone and consumption of food than is the
case in chimpanzee nut-cracking activities. . . . [And this amplifies] only slightly two
features exhibited by chimpanzee nut-cracking activities: (1) anticipation based on past
experience in foraging, and (2) the fact that tool availability guides the concentration
(production) of food debris.

Potts (1988, 281, 284) disputes the suggestions of other commentators that
stone caches at Olduvai are evidence of the self-conscious foresight of Bed I
hominids of 1.85 Mya:

> The creation of stone caches would have involved moving flaked tools and raw materials
> from their sources to convenient locations in the foraging range. Over a period of time, food
> that required processing with stone tools would be brought to these "stockpiles" of stone.
> On the surface, this activity would appear to involve an extensive degree of forethought
> and planning—"thinking ahead." . . . In fact, the cache idea is claimed to imply a degree
> of strategic anticipation that is known only among complex logistically organized groups of
> modern hunter-gatherers—a behavioral characteristic unlikely to have occurred in early
> hominids. . . .
> The stone cache interpretation proposed here for Olduvai suggests that early hominids
> anticipated finding food that required processing with stone tools. Anticipation, though,
> largely entails remembering the past in some detail, not necessarily complex planning
> ahead. . . . The formation of stone caches would have required memory of past experi-
> ence, particularly precise spatial locations and areas of successful foraging. This kind of
> memory appears to be represented in the behavioral repertoires of chimpanzees and of a
> wide range of animals observed in the light of optimal foraging theory. The assertion that
> stone caches would have required cognitive and strategic skills known only among
> logistically organized, future-thinking modern humans inappropriately extrapolates behav-
> iors of modern people onto the ancient context at Olduvai.

As pointed out above (chapter 1), *supra*, Potts likewise rejects (1988, 287, 290,
294–96, 304) the interpretation of Olduvai hominid Bed I stone caches as "home
bases":

> Analysis of the Olduvai sites indicates that recurrent visiting of, and transport of
> resources to, fixed points were already aspects of hominid behavior by 1.8 Mya. [But the]
> development of home bases required that this pattern of occasional visits to processing
> sites (to which stones and animal tissues were brought) became integrated with, and
> transformed by, a social pattern of return every day by independent foragers to a specific
> place . . . [whereas] stone caches . . . preceded [the] social developments associated
> with home bases [e.g., food being brought there for redistribution and the expectation of
> reciprocation of food-sharing in the future, although it] made them possible at some later
> point in time. . . . Undoubtedly, the presumed importance of home bases for the earliest

hominids is fueled by the [mistaken] view that archaelogists have [already] *demonstrated* that home bases were a well-developed phenomenon by 2 Mya. . . . [Nevertheless,] research on Olduvai indicates that the existence of such home bases has not yet been demonstrated archeologically. . . .

[Notwithstanding the great popularity of San studies, leading to the view that] the Pleistocene evolutionary past shared by all humans is largely that of a hunter-gatherer, a way of life that has shaped our sociality and our anatomical, physiological, mental, and emotional makeup . . . [my] proposal that home bases, as a fundamental component of hunter-gatherer adaptation, developed later in human evolution than originally believed opens these ideas about human evolution to question. . . . [The] behavioral, social, and reproductive features that appear to typify humans probably do not represent a coherent package ingrained in our biology by virtue of *millions* of years of natural selection. Rather, they would reflect a mosaic pattern of change, similar to the varying rates of evolution in different aspects of hominid anatomy, that is, a series of changes laid on top of one another through time, under varied conditions of survival and reproduction. . . .

The conclusion reached here . . . is that home base social behaviors were not focused at the particular sites we have examined. Moreover, the apparent absence of evidence for a home base (resource transport and social activities focused in the same place) suggests that key ingredients in the socioecology of modern hunter-gatherers did not exist. In no way does this imply that the socioecology of chimpanzees or other nonhuman primates better portrays these hominids of Bed I Olduvai.

Chapter 2 (section 1) points out that in de Waal's book, Arnhem chimpanzee females frequently "are described as being *content* to accept their respective statuses, as distinct from sexually mature males, who are said to '*strive* for higher status'"; compare his later (and therefore more considered) defense of "status striving" as a function of the chimpanzee male "dominance drive" (de Waal 1987, 425). That raises the question of the great nonexperiment, when the Arnhem project directors refused in 1973 to let nature take its course by tolerating the well-established matriarchal dominance structure in an endeavor to ascertain how long it would take for the female the experimenters jovially called "Big Mama" to get so old and feeble that some male might have superseded her.

She really *was* tough on the boys (although de Waal does not call them that: he calls a spade a spade; males he calls males, including early adolescent Nikkie when he was ten or eleven; and nonparous adolescent females he calls "girls" [de Waal 1982, 52–53]). As for "Mama," "Not only did she bite frequently, but she drew blood and sometimes ripped the victim's skin." She even "would perform intimidation displays just like a male [, walking] about stamping and with her hair on end. Her specialty was giving a tremendous kick against one of the metal doors" (de Waal 1982, 59). Yet in darkest Africa, near Kakombe stream on the shore of Lake Tanganyika, females acted much more brutally than that, and not even in leadership roles. For instance, the female aptly named "Passion" and her adolescent daughter had a penchant for cannibalizing the infants of other young chimpanzee females by biting the neonates in the head, a technique that the same mother-daughter team had perfected in attacks on bushbuck fawns (Goodall 1986, 296–97, 351). Hence it is impossible to infer from the fact that female apes typically form hierarchies in a different manner than do males that "Big Mama" was *content* to lose her dominant status in the Arnhem zoo or that some other female would have been incapable of following her.

Why, then, was the experiment not allowed to occur? Perhaps the project directors were really afraid (cf. G. Schubert 1978) that another female (Mama's sidekick "Gorilla") might (as the "beta" female) have succeeded and thus perpetuated the first known chimpanzee matriarchy in history. De Waal relates (1982, 58) that "when I tell this story [of Big Mama's putdown] to a group of visitors among whom are some feminists, there are always questions. Why did we so want to see the males in control? Was Mama not good enough?" In reply, he suggests a number of putatively prima facie justifications for deposing Mama ("It is known that in the wild the adult males are dominant"); but the bottom line is zoo economics: valuable *male* (as opposed to female) chimpanzees might have been injured (veterinary costs) or even killed (replacement costs) in the power struggle to succeed the initial matriarch.

Another question of zoo policy concerns its getting in the way of scientific behavior, in this case timely scientific reporting of important information about the otherwise best-publicized captive chimpanzee group in the world. Although it was published two years after the event, de Waal's book does not mention that the alpha male (Luit) was killed by the other two adult males during the night of 12 September 1980. The custodian did not securely fasten the cage doors, and the other two adult males in the group ganged up and succeeded in killing the alpha, an obviously opportunistic killing that de Waal subsequently described as "murder"—and as a "political murder" at that! The subsequent death by drowning of the successor alpha, Nikkie, some three and one-half years later was likewise made possible by an improperly fastened door—this time the main one leading outside from the winter quarters where Nikkie and the other chimpanzees had been locked up for the preceding six months. Computer-monitored videotaping, with an electronically triggered alarm system to alert custodians in crisis situations, was available in the Netherlands before 1980 and would not have been *that* expensive—at least not compared to the cost of buying and raising a replacement adult male chimpanzee at even 1980 market prices, not to mention today's. Maybe zoo economics should evince as much concern for the quality of the human custodianship as it does for the behaviors of the chimpanzees themselves.

CHIMPANZEES AND GORILLAS IN A STATE OF
INCREASINGLY RAVISHED NATURE: EPILOGUE OR EPITAPH?

Like the book on which it is based (Goodall 1986), chapter 5 looks back over the remarkable and unequaled quarter century of field primatological research by

Jane Goodall, beginning in the summer of 1960. A female journalist (Fichtner 1988) claims that Goodall "seems destined—like Izak Dinesen or Beryl Markham before her—to become one of those transplanted women whose heart-sprung associations with Africa eventually spin themselves into legend." At this time, only four years have elapsed since her book went to press; nevertheless, it is time to look into the future that already has become imminent during even that short a period of time. Dr. Goodall closes her book on an upbeat note; the final sentence of her text reads (1986, 594), "At least during their ['the chimpanzees'] lives, Gombe—in conservation-minded Tanzania—will still be safe." But in 1975, the year after her second marriage (to Derek Bryceson, the head of Tanzanian national parks, including of course Gombe National Park) armed rebels from Zaire crossed Lake Tanganyika in small boats and kidnapped for ransom four Stanford students; that was the beginning of Paradise Lost, at least from the point of view of political ecology. After that the Tanzanian government refused to allow even Goodall herself to live full-time in Gombe, which since 1975 it has considered to be a politically sensitive area.

A journalist who interviewed Goodall in Gombe, apparently in early 1988, reported (McRae 1988, 49, 85) that "the [Gombe] park is hemmed in by settlements. Just outside it, the land is denuded—the trees cut for firewood, grasses burned off or clipped down to stubble by goats—and the thin soil has eroded away. Gombe is an island unto itself, and the chimps' access to the gene pool of nearby chimpanzee populations is blocked. Human encroachment also keeps the chimps from feeding outside the park." Furthermore, "Hundreds of fishermen camp along the beach—four times as many as a decade ago, Goodall says, and far more than government regulations allow. The men don't live in the park, but they walk through it every day to reach their villages. The permanent [human] population at Gombe . . . has swollen to 50"—about a third of the Gombe park chimpanzee population. Primatologist Geza Teleki, who worked at Gombe for two years during the 1960s, is quoted as being "appalled" by the contrast between then and now and to have described the situation at Gombe, which he visited during the summer of 1987, as "chaotic."

Now there are also the tourists (McRae 1988, 45): "For the last three years, [the Tanzanian government] has encouraged the growth of tourism at Gombe but has done little to control it." There still was no reservation system, although only a single ten-bed hostel was available for tourists to stay overnight at the Gombe park headquarters. Habituated chimpanzees are potentially dangerous to tourists; even Goodall was attacked in October 1987 by the dominant male of the chimpanzee population resident in the area of the park where Goodall stays when she comes to visit. She thought the attack occurred because the chimpanzees get tense and irritated (stressed) by the presence of tourists—too many strangers in groups coming too close to the animals. The dominant male in 1987 was Goblin; born into the group four years after Goodall had begun her work, he therefore knew and recognized her on the basis of twenty-three years of continuous interaction and acquaintance. Nevertheless, on this occasion he kept on pushing her all the way down a steep slope and pulled her violently away from a tree that she had grabbed onto to halt her slide; then, seizing her with one hand around her neck, he stomped furiously on her back. She avoided screaming or seeming to fight back, but in retrospect she wondered, "What on earth would happen if Goblin were to attack a tourist? If they screamed or panicked, I think they might be killed."

The following winter, a potentially greater problem was posed by an eleven-year-old adolescent male, Frodo, a sexual harasser who liked to run from behind past women on the trails (including Goodall herself and the journalist's wife) and slap or kick them as he whizzed past; Goodall is reported to have said (McRae 1988, 87), "Now I'm just someone for him to take his aggressions out on." The beautiful color photograph on the dust jacket of her book must have been taken early in 1972 by Goodall's first husband, Hugo van Lawick. I found no credit line or legend, but evidently it is of Flo and her daughter Fifi, with Fifi's first infant (a male, Freud) resting his hand affectionately on Flo's knee. The bulbous-nosed Flo's estimated life span was forty-three years: extraordinary for a chimpanzee not in captivity. Most of that time she was the reigning matriarch of the Kasakela group. She was also deeply loved, not only by Goodall, but also by many others, according to the chimpanzee's obituary published in the London *Sunday Times*. Flo died of old age later in 1972; Goodall and van Lawick were divorced the following year; and Frodo, Fifi's next infant, was born in 1976, after the usual five-year spacing.

Chimpanzees may no longer be imported into the United States and many West European countries for exhibition in zoos and circuses or even for nonmedical primatological research; but they are imported for medical purposes, serving as alternates for human subjects for research on AIDS and hepatitis B. It now seems probable that AIDS is a mutant form of the "Green Monkey" disease that even in the 1960s occasionally escaped out of central Africa (see Crook 1970b, vii); but humans as disease carriers are much more dangerous to chimpanzees than vice versa. A 1966 polio epidemic in Kigoma, the village nearest Gombe, infected a dozen members (of whom half died) of the Kasakela-Kamaha community of about sixty chimpanzees; evidently it spread through contact between the chimpanzees and natives passing through or working in the park. Eleven years later, in June 1987, nine chimps died in a pneumonia epidemic, this time probably imported from Kigoma by tourists; by then tourists and chimpanzees not infrequently touched each other in nonaggressive nonverbal communication. Obviously, one of the biggest threats raised by increasing tourism in Gombe is of human diseases for the chimpanzees. Poaching per se had not become a major problem in Gombe, but it clearly was in the Kibale Forest region of Uganda, where human predation on chimpanzees is illegal: more than 10 percent of the resident population of about a hundred chimpanzees had been mutilated by poachers' snares (putatively intended for ungulates, which are better to eat and legal game), while almost half that many were killed by poachers; other chimpanzee victims of human encroachment were fed to dogs, or were captured infants used as pets (Ghiglieri 1984, 62–63). In a move to get chimpanzees declared an endangered species, early in 1989 Jane Goodall and the World Wildlife Fund filed with the United States Fish and Wildlife Service a petition in which it is estimated that the global (i.e., African) population of "wild" (not yet dead or caged) chimpanzees has declined in the past half-century by more than 80 percent—from at least a million to about 175,000.

Tourism is much better organized (and exploited) by the importation of tourists from throughout the relatively affluent industrialized "first" world nations, who come to an even less accessible and a demonstrably much more dangerous locale, right in the heart of central Africa, to ogle the gorillas that Dian Fossey—with extraordinary post hoc publicity—died trying to protect on 27 December 1985 (see also McRae 1986). Fossey's problem was the Rwandan government itself, as well as poachers; today the African Wildlife Foundation (AWF), which administers access to the mountain gorillas in the Parc National des Volcans, portrays tourists as the saviors, not the enemies, of the four "families" of gorillas that are used for purposes of tourist observation (other gorillas are earmarked for research observation). Fossey's study has been widely and recently publicized (e.g., Fossey, *Gorillas in the Mist*, 1983; Mowat, *Woman in the Mists*, 1987; and the movie with the same title as the Fossey book, 1988, with Sigourney Weaver portraying a romanticized version of Fossey). In January 1989 the California Academy of Sciences in Golden State Park in San Francisco presented a remarkable photographic exhibition on Fossey's gorillas in their historical and ecological setting, with detailed information about the tourism and research programs of the AWF. The exhibition is scheduled to tour the country for a year beginning in May 1989, arriving at the Smithsonian Institute's National Museum of Natural History adjacent to the Mall in Washington, D.C.

Gorilla viewing in the Parc National des Volcans proffers a potential gross income of one and one-half million dollars a year, based on a maximum of 8,500 tourists annually, viewing in four groups of six persons daily throughout the year, each group spending all day getting up and down the mountain with only an hour of rapprochement with a gorilla family. Although to Americans that may seem like small potatoes, "Tourism has now become Rwanda's second-largest foreign-exchange earner, after coffee and tea" (Perlez 1988). The incumbent Rwandan "president," Major General Juvenal Habyarimana, is said to be an enthusiast for gorilla preservation, and he is credited with having so far "kept the lid" on tourism (at the 8,500 level that thus far has not yet been empirically achieved). Officials of the African Wildlife Foundation are credited with having encouraged controlled tourism throughout the 1980s "as a way of preserving the gorillas," and certainly the posters at the exhibition of Michael Nichols's work in Golden Gate Park, *supra* (see also Stack, 1989), argued strongly for such a policy.

The AWF is a major supporter of the work of Craig R. Sholley, who directs the Mountain Gorilla Project in cooperation with the Rwandan government, and who claims (Perlez 1988) that "conservation today is a world of compromise so we're making compromises that will insure the survival of the gorillas into the 21st century" (but see Haraway 1989, 265–67). Otherwise, poachers would continue their work—already well-advanced during Fossey's last two or three years—of eliminating the survivors foot by foot and head by head; the actual bodies are large and cumbrous and the market for complete gorilla skins as throw rugs is much smaller. Then, according to Sholley and the AWF, once the poachers had removed the animals, farmers would continue denuding and terracing the mountain for agricultural purposes. On the other hand, five of the 150 gorillas in the park died in 1988 of pneumonia and another one from measles, all presumably from contact with tourists or natives: that is only 4 percent but "the scientists say they don't know if disease has affected the [remaining] gorillas still in the wild state. Next year [i.e., during 1989], they will take a census to find out."

According to McRae (1988, 85–86), Goodall approached the AWF in 1986 for help in restructuring tourism in Gombe on a better organized and more systematic basis, by having them write a management plan for Gombe based on their seven years of experience working with the Rwandan government; Fossey fought against that prototype program as long as she lived. But Goodall now says that "if we're going to conserve some of these forest habitats in West and Central Africa, the only possible way is by allowing tourism, so that the government can have some foreign exchange coming in. You compromise a piece of the park, habituate the animals there, and create trails so people can walk to see these shy forest creatures." At Gombe, "Her plan is to partially habituate the now wild chimps in the northern and southern valleys and redirect tourists there." A frontispiece to McRae's article (1988, 3), showing Jane Goodall sitting and taking notes beside a forest trail, is captioned: "Last Stand at Gombe." Goodall herself is quoted (McRae 1988, 46) as having said that "Soon . . . there will be no more chimpanzees in the wild."

# 5

## Gombe Chimpanzee Politics

### Jane Goodall

#### 1. CHIMPANZEE NATURE

*Chapter 5 begins with Jane Goodall's description of the extraordinary individualism and mobility of chimpanzees who are born—and lucky enough to remain—free. Goodall compares their cognitive abilities to those of humans, with whom chimpanzees have much in common, with the critical difference that the development of modern chimpanzees is perhaps more similar to that of hominids five to six million years ago. But even then our immediate primate forbears were uniquely bipedal with vertical posture (Kinzey 1987, 11, 205; M. Leakey and Harris 1987, chap. 13; Reader 1981, chap. 12), so that their spatial orientation and perception (Laponce 1987; Chevalier-Skolnikoff 1977; S. Parker and Gibson 1979) must have been very different from that of modern wild chimpanzees.*

*The contemporary chimpanzees who epigenetically have more in common with humans are the display or experimental animals housed in cages in zoos and medical laboratories, and in the enclosures of primate research centers. These captives have the freedom, and the social choice and mobility, of committed human felons in penitentiaries—or of committed patients in mental storage facilities in the USSR today or the United States a generation ago. Somewhere in between (and in Jane Goodall's opinion much closer to their wild conspecifics) are the habituated—to humans—chimpanzees of Gombe, whom she contrasts with the Arnhem consortium inmates that comprise the subject of chapter 7.—Eds.*

---

This chapter appeared in revised form in *The Chimpanzees of Gombe: Patterns of Behavior* (Cambridge: Harvard University Press, 1986); reprinted by permission.

*The Chimpanzee State of Nature*

Fusion and fission in chimpanzee society are carried to the limits of flexibility; individuals of either sex have almost complete freedom to come and go as they wish. The membership of temporary parties is constantly changing. Adults and adolescents can and do forage, travel, and sleep quite on their own, sometimes for days at a time. This unique organization means, for one thing, that the day-to-day social experiences of a chimpanzee are far more variable than those of almost any other primate.

A chimpanzee rarely sees all the members of his community on the same day and probably never sees them two days in succession. He may travel one day in a large, noisy, excitable gathering; the next day, completely by himself. He may feed peacefully with a small, compatible party in the morning, then join fifteen other chimpanzees, after a successful hunt, in the late afternoon. He may be one of six males competing for the same female one week and associate with one female, far from any other males, the next. He may spend one day at the very center of his core area and move out to a far-flung boundary on a patrol the next.

We know that there are exceptionally gifted chimpanzees in the wild and that the higher cognitive abilities of the chimpanzees *are* called upon in their natural habitat, even though some are brought into play much more frequently than others. Thus we are now in a position to superimpose two portraits of the chimpanzee: the one that is emerging from studies in captivity, and another that is gradually being constructed from observation in the natural habitat.

One striking finding from all studies of the chimpanzee—in laboratory, home, and forest—is the sometimes uncanny similarity between certain aspects of chimpanzee and human behavior: the long period of childhood dependency, the postures and gestures of the nonverbal communication system, the expression of emotion, the importance of learning, the beginning of dependency on cultural tradition, and the startling resemblance of basic cognitive mechanisms. Our own success as a species has been due entirely to the explosive development of the human brain.

We must not forget that even if we do differ from the apes not in kind, but only in degree, that degree is still overwhelmingly large. Knowledge of the ways in which our behavior is *similar* to that of the chimpanzee, combined with knowledge of how it is *different*, helps us to pinpoint what it is that makes humans unique. First, we have developed a complex symbolic language. Second, we are able, as no other creature is, to overcome by conscious choice our biological heritage (e.g., our acts of altruism are *not* always selfish; and by the same token our acts of violence are *not* always inevitable). And third, while our basic aggressive patterns are not so different from those of a chimpanzee, our comprehension of the suffering we may inflict on our victims typically is of an entirely different order of magnitude.

Certainly the conditions for observation are superior when the subjects are in an enclosure. They can be watched continuously, day after day, with little to obstruct the view; events that are crucial to the understanding of changing relationships are likely to be recorded; and subtle changes in these relationships can be documented on a daily basis. And the more complete the history of complex events, the more complex the behavior of the various actors is likely to appear. Nevertheless, I suspect that the difference between the Arnhem and Gombe chimpanzees is real, and that it is largely the result of a captive versus a wild group. The large field enclosure is, in a sense, a halfway house between the laboratory and the field. In the controlled conditions of the laboratory, it is the *investigator* who, by skillful manipulation of testing procedures, can encourage the chimpanzees to perform at high levels and thereby obtain evidence of cognitive sophistication. In the field enclosure, it is the *conditions of captivity* that, by their pressure on the existing repertoire of social skills, encourage the chimpanzees to develop increasingly elaborate performances.

There are three ways in which the captivity of the Arnhem chimpanzees may have affected their social interactions. First, confined primates have considerably more time available for social pursuits. In the African forest, chimpanzees cannot afford to devote the whole of their considerable intellectual abilities to competing with rivals or improving relations with friends. They must expend a good deal of energy, particularly during the dry season, in finding and processing food. Life in the wild carries with it at all times an element of uncertainty, often of excitement. At any moment the chimpanzees may encounter a party of hostile, potentially dangerous neighboring males. There may be a strenuous hunt, a stimulating encounter with baboons, and so on. In other words, much of the chimpanzees' mental skill is occupied with day-to-day living. In marked contrast, captive chimpanzees are provided with food and shelter and their ills are attended to. They do not have to seek food and spend long hours in its preparation, nor do they sit for hours hunched and shivering in the rain. They have no complex decisions to make about the direction in which to travel or the company to keep. By the same token, they miss out on the excitement and tension of patrols and hunting and the like. There is no element of danger to spice their lives. And so they can devote themselves almost entirely to their position in the hierarchy and their relations with others. This freedom from survival pressures may lead to novel social behaviors in other primates (Kummer and Goodall 1985). Kummer and Kurt (1965) recorded nine communicative signals in a troop of zoo hamadryas baboons — signals that had not been observed in any wild group. In addition, the protected threat sequence was more sophisticated and effective in the zoo group than the version observed in the wild.

Furthermore, the conditions of captivity result in *stability of the social environment*. At Gombe, individuals are relatively free to associate with whomever they choose, and the number and identity of their companions change continually. Captive chimpanzees have no such freedom of choice, and they do not have to cope with the complexities inherent in the comings and goings of their wild counterparts.

### Chimpanzees: Wild, Habituated, and Captive

De Waal (1982, 186) found that in the Arnhem colony the female hierarchy was stable and was based on "respect from below rather than intimidation and a show of strength from above." He ascertained that most pant-grunts (which he referred to as "greetings") were "spontaneous" and felt that, for the female, the *acceptance* of dominance was probably more important than the *proving* of dominance. He therefore suggested that Rowell's (1974) "subordinance hierarchy" might be applied meaningfully to female chimpanzees.

However, de Waal was not present when the Arnhem colony was first formed. It is possible that the "respect from below" was in fact based on the outcome of aggressive interactions at the time of first acquaintance. Yerkes (1943) found that when adult females were placed together, they went through the same process of settling their relative status as did the adult males.

Since all members of their group are always present, they are far more familiar with one another than are most adults at Gombe and thus are better able to predict one another's behavior. Allies are continually at hand, and social strategies that rely on cooperative support can be developed into polished performances that are not readily attainable in the natural habitat.

Finally, the conditions of captivity may actually create a *need* for more sophistication in the social sphere. At Gombe, when levels of aggression become too high, a chimpanzee is able to leave the group and move off with a companion of his choice or by himself. We can imagine the male who has lost a dominance conflict inwardly fuming as he stalks through the forest, and we know he may vent his frustration on a lower-ranking individual unfortunate enough to cross his path. But with the passing of time his tension will lessen. Admittedly, he will not forget his grudge, and when he next meets his rival there may be a renewed outbreak of aggression; but this time he may have an ally with him, or the rival may *not* have his ally. The female at Gombe is even more likely to slip off by herself, or with her family, and thus avoid the tempestuous conflicts of rival males.

The Arnhem chimpanzees have no such freedom. They are captives not only in the literal sense, but figuratively, in the web of their society. They can move to the other side of their enclosure, but a male cannot lead a female away from his rivals and in a distant place mate with her in peace; he cannot avoid the persistent persecution of a powerful rival. Nor does he have the benefit of the occasional cooperative foray into hostile territory, where fear of a common enemy will create temporary solidarity among community males. Thus, for the captive male there is a new need for improved social maneuvering, particularly when this involves the concealment of intention, the maintenance of close bonds with allies, and, above all, reconciliation after conflict.

It seems that the behavior of female chimpanzees may be affected by confinement even more than that of the males. Captive females, unlike those at Gombe, form close and enduring friendships (Köhler 1925; de Waal 1982). And, perhaps because they cannot leave when their situation becomes too demanding, they are apt to play a more active role in the ordering of their society. Their alliances with the males often swing the outcome of dominance conflicts in favor of the males of their choice. Their mediation between unreconciled rival males restores peace to the group, a harmony that Gombe females can find by moving off and leaving the males to their own devices.

It is fascinating to contemplate the changes that would occur if the Gombe chimpanzees were deprived of their freedom—or if the Arnhem chimpanzees were given theirs.

## 2. FORAGING NATURE

*Feral male chimpanzees spend most of their waking time foraging for either food or conspecific strangers who might compete for the resources available within the residents' customary habitat. Resources for males include fixed and known flora such as the fruit trees, nuts, and leaves of tropical forests; certain insects and/or their products, in stable or relatively predictable locations; and infant (mostly mammalian) prey that are hunted and/or encountered. At least equally important as a male resource is the community's supply of resident adult females.*

*The second part of this chapter discusses the ranging, feeding, and hunting behaviors of Gombe chimpanzees: these define the repertoire of customary social activities that constrain and make possible the protopolitical chimpanzee (1) individual and group behaviors of aggression and (2) social organizational relationships of dominance and submission—Eds.*

### Ranging

Within the home range of the community, each adult chimpanzee is free to choose where he will go and the routes he will follow to get there. To some extent, however, his choice will be influenced by the movements of the other community members. Some chimpanzees, more than others, have the ability to affect the travel patterns of their companions. Because of the fluid nature of chimpanzee society, there is no single overall leader. Almost any adult, or even adolescent, may at one time or another lead a small party and determine the direction of travel.

A number of factors influence the distance traveled in a day: (a) seasonal distribution of foods, distance between major crops being particularly important; (b) health: sick individuals do not travel far; (c) weather: travel is curtailed when it pours rain; (d) consortships: a male-female pair travel very short distances once they have established their consort range; (e) the activity of the previous day: after a long excursion there is a tendency to travel a much shorter distance the following day.

Males typically travel farther in a day than do females (a mean distance of 4.9 kilometers versus a mean of about 3.0 kilometers). Males also range more widely than do females, tending to visit each of the boundary areas of the home range once every four days or so, whereas females, at least when anestrous, spend a great deal of time in their core areas. The distance traveled by a female will be affected by her reproductive state: she ranges farther than usual when in estrus and associating with the adult males, less during late pregnancy and for the first few weeks after giving birth. Her movements may also be influenced by the age and sex of her offspring.

The community range must be large enough to support the males and the females and young. It is not sharply delineated from that of neighboring communities, although to the north and south, streams often serve as rough boundary lines. The chimpanzees sometimes cross these boundaries into the range of an adjacent community, but usually show signs of apprehension when they do so. Thus an area the equivalent of at least one valley can be referred to as an overlap zone, utilized at different times by members of neighboring communities. In general this arrangement is not a friendly one. In some other areas chimpanzees travel much more widely than they do at Gombe.

The movements of chimpanzees within their community range are dictated by a variety of environmental and social factors that may differ from one locality to another: the distribution of food and water; the availability of females in estrus; the size and movement of neighboring communities; the presence of predators or other dangers. Traditional travel routes are passed on by mothers to their offspring, by adult to adolescent males, and by residents to immigrants. Community members may wander over a huge range, as in the Senegal, curtailed only by shortage of water in the driest months, or they may be restricted to a tiny area by the encroachment of human cultivation, as is the case with a small remnant population north of Gombe.

*Feeding*

The introduction of large-scale banana feeding at Gombe had profound effects on many aspects of chimpanzee behavior, including party size in the feeding area (Wrangham 1975). To summarize, the number of chimpanzees in the camp area gradually increased, from 1963 on, as more and more chimpanzees discovered the new food source and tended to congregate there for longer and longer periods in hopes of another handout. It was not unusual, at the height of the banana feeding, for parties of over twenty individuals to be waiting around in camp. By 1970 the size of parties in camp had decreased. Although, as Wrangham and Smuts (1980) have shown, the party size of target males and females tends to increase during the time they visit camp, this does not appear to have any significant effect on party size outside the camp area.

When two or more chimpanzees are feeding together there may be competition either for actual food objects or for feeding sites. Wrangham (1975) found that *overt* competition (one individual displacing another or showing threat or attack behavior) was not common. He observed approximately one such incident every twenty hours. However, he inferred competition from instances like the following: (a) individual B sat, not feeding, until more dominant chimpanzee A left his feeding site, at which point B took over; (b) A sat in a site surrounded by food in abundance, which he could obtain simply by reaching out; B, on the other hand, had to move all over the tree, picking the few available fruits from various branches; or (c) B, in a large party, did not feed at all, and it appeared that all the feeding sites were occupied. Competition over plant food is, in fact, one of the two most common causes of aggression in adult females. Only twice during the time period was an adult male seen to threaten (mildly) a female, and only once another adult male. Fifteen straightforward displacements were described in which one individual approached another, who promptly left the feeding place. Probably this is the most common overt competitive behavior, but it is less likely to be recorded than the more obvious aggressive patterns.

When bananas were provided daily at camp in large amounts, there was a dramatic rise in the frequency and the severity of food competition as well as in the numbers of chimpanzees visiting the camp at any one time. When we changed the feeding system, aggression and party size in camp both dropped. During the ten-month period in 1979 there were only three fights in camp over bananas—twice between two females, and once between a mother and her juvenile son. On five occasions adult males charged after adult females and took their bananas; the females dropped them before physical contact had been made, and the incidents did not lead to fighting.

*Honey, Galls, and Termite Clay.*   Often larvae and a few workers are eaten along with the honey when the chimpanzees seize and chew the actual honeycomb. The grubs are a delicacy for the people of many tribes, and although the chimpanzees probably seek the honey for its own sake, they undoubtedly appreciate the grubs also. When chimpanzees eat galls, they inevitably eat the insects that have formed them, but almost certainly are seeking the gall substance itself. Typically, during gall formation additional tannins are produced, but at the same time starches are turned to sugar by the actions of the insect (Frost 1959). Some galls are eaten by humans (for example, the "gall of sahe" produced by a species of *Aulax* in the Near East).

About once a day, as they pass termite mounds (usually of *Pseudacanthotermes militaris*), chimpanzees pause to pick off and eat small amounts—not more than would fill a walnut. Analysis of samples of termite clay collected by R. Wrangham revealed substantial quantities of potassium, magnesium, and calcium and traces of copper, manganese, zinc, and sodium. There was wide variation in the amounts of the different minerals present in samples taken from different termite mounds. These minerals are present, often in larger amounts, in some plant foods and it is not yet clear exactly why chimpanzees (and other primates) feed on termite clay. It may be to neutralize tannins and other poisons present in plant foods (Hladik 1977). The clay is eaten by humans in rural areas in many parts of the world (M. Latham pers. comm.). Sold in markets in most parts of Tanzania, it is eaten by the Waha people of the Kigoma region, particularly by pregnant women from the fourth month on.

*Cultural Differences.*   Most of the differences in food selection, however, are probably due to tradition. An infant chimpanzee, from the age of about five months, tends to watch closely when his mother is feeding; he may put his face very close to hers and sniff the food she is eating. Once he begins to eat small pieces of solid food (at about four to six months), he usually chews the food on which his mother is feeding, taking some from her hand or mouth or from nearby food clusters. He also samples food eaten by siblings, peers, or other individuals who happen to be in the group. Infants do sometimes pick and chew plant materials that adults have not been seen to feed on, but such experiments, at least sometimes, are discouraged by their mothers or other individuals. But it does seem that youngsters, with their more flexible behavior and their predilection for exploration, are the most likely age class to introduce a new feeding tradition.

### Hunting

The hunting, killing, and eating of medium-sized mammals is probably a characteristic behavior of chimpanzees throughout their range though more common in some areas than others. Meat eating has been recorded at three study sites in western Tanzania, in Uganda, and in the Senegal and Ivory Coast. Two groups of chimpanzees that have been rehabilitated into the wild, in the Gambia and in Gabon, have also been seen hunting, killing, and eating prey. The observed prey range in size from mice, rats, and small birds to a more than half-grown bushpig estimated to weigh not less than twenty kilograms. A variety of primates, *including human infants*, account for about half the prey species. Cannibalism has been reported at two sites in Tanzania—Gombe and Mahale— and also in Uganda.

Red colobus monkeys are by far the most frequently eaten prey. The impact of chimpanzee predation on the red colobus monkey population at Gombe is obviously significant, and these monkeys certainly suffer severe annual loss from chimpanzee predation.

Chimpanzees encounter baboons more frequently than any other primate species. Nevertheless, with the notable exception of 1968, baboons were preyed upon much less frequently than colobus and during some years were probably not caught at all. Similar numbers of young bushpigs and bushbucks were observed to be eaten per year; many of the fawns were taken over from baboons and not captured by the chimpanzees themselves.

To some extent all hunting may be opportunistic and happen only after the sighting of suitable prey. Nevertheless, there is a difference between a capture that occurs when a chimpanzee simply happens upon and seizes a certain prey (such as a bushbuck he presses to the ground) and a capture that follows an extended period (up to two hours) of watching, following, and chasing intended prey. On several occasions chimpanzees saw monkeys across a valley, perhaps half a kilometer distant, and at once set off to hunt them. Sometimes, after a kill has been made, an individual who has been unable to acquire a share moves away from the prey and starts hunting again.

A single chimpanzee may hunt successfully on his or her own; often, however, hunting is group activity. A lone chimpanzee who has made a kill usually keeps silent, whereas loud (and distinctive) calls typically break out at the climax of a successful group hunt. Thus the latter are far more likely to be detected (both by nearby chimpanzees and by human observers). During some hunts there is clear evidence of cooperation between two or more individuals, but the methods differ depending on the kind of prey.

*Arboreal Monkeys.* Wrangham (1975) observed that chimpanzees seldom hunted when they encountered monkeys moving through unbroken canopy, but usually did so when the canopy was broken, particularly when the monkeys were feeding in tall, emergent trees from which escape was difficult. Sometimes monkeys fall during hunts. They may be knocked to the ground by chimpanzees trying to capture them (or their infants), or they may fall when a branch breaks, or when making too large a leap—particularly after a long pursuit when they are probably tired. Many of those killed were seized by arboreal hunters who hurled themselves down after their prey, but the others (almost half) were captured by chimpanzees already on the ground, watching the progress of the hunt from below. Individuals who remain on the ground during a hunt may well be anticipating the fall of a monkey.

Adult male colobus monkeys, on many occasions, actively defend troop members from the predatory attacks of one or more chimpanzees. Busse (1976) found that half of the successful predations recorded in the 1973–74 period occurred within seven minutes of the initial encounter, and he suggests that the reason may have been that the monkeys were still widely dispersed and potential victims often far from the protection of the adult males. As a hunt progresses, adult males quickly move toward the chimpanzees and usually threaten them vigorously, shaking branches and bobbing up and down, uttering their alto threat calls. In the face of colobus male aggression, chimpanzees almost always retreat, often whimpering or screaming, and climb rapidly (sometimes precipitously) to the ground. On nineteen different occasions male colobus actually attacked chimpanzees as they hunted, leaping onto them and biting at their backs or around their scrota. When this happened, the hunters almost always retreated.

*Bushpigs.* Bushpigs are nocturnal and lie in dense thickets during the day. Very rarely, when it is gray and damp, they move about in the daytime. Over the entire twenty-two years sixty-six piglets were seen being consumed by the chimpanzees on forty-five different occasions—1.5 piglets per successful hunt. When chimpanzees see or hear pigs in the undergrowth, they almost always stop to investigate. If one or more adults run off, the chimpanzees check the undergrowth carefully; six times they found and seized piglets. Pig hunts are almost always very difficult to observe. For one thing, they usually take place in thick undergrowth. For another, human observers are normally not very close.

*Bushbuck Fawns.* A total of forty-nine fawns are known to have been wholly or partially consumed by chimpanzees since 1960. Only a few, however, were seen to be actually captured by chimpanzee hunters. Many were known or suspected to have been stolen from baboon predators.

*Baboons.* A total of twenty-five young baboons are known to have been eaten by the habituated chimpanzees (and two by unhabituated individuals in the south) since the beginning of the study. One other infant was captured and killed, but retrieved by its mother before being eaten. Of the twenty-two prey whose ages were known *precisely* (eight) or *approximately* (fourteen), 77.3 percent were black infants (those under six months old). Victims were seized sometimes from the midst of their troops, sometimes from a smaller subgroup, and sometimes when they were on their own or with just one caretaker. Fifty hunts, of which eighteen were successful, were well observed. In many of these instances the attention of the chimpanzees was first aroused by various distress calls made by infant baboons. Sometimes this was during weaning incidents, sometimes when the infants were being carried by adult males, who often handled them roughly.

The tactics employed by male chimpanzees when hunting baboons have been described in detail by Teleki (1973). Sometimes two or more (occasionally just one) male chimpanzees rushed toward an intended victim and seized or tried to seize it on the run. At other times several males approached their prey slowly, and there was often a high level of coordination and cooperation among them. As soon as an intended victim, its mother, or another nearby individual became alert to the possibility of danger, there were loud calls of fear (from infant or mother) or threat (from adult males). These sounds often attracted other baboons, who ran to the defense of the endangered youngster. Sometimes the ensuing interspecific aggression resulted in absolute pandemonium, with chimpanzees and baboons (often including females) screaming, roaring, barking, and lunging. During skirmishes of this sort the combatants sometimes engaged in physical conflict, standing up and hitting out at one another. On six occasions male baboons leaped onto chimpanzees and appeared to be slashing with their canines at the chimpanzees' backs.

After such incidents human observers always looked for signs of injury in the chimpanzees, but only once was an open wound seen (Wrangham 1975). Baboon males have large and powerful canines; in other areas they have been known to mortally wound leopards caught attacking troop members (Goodall 1975), and it is puzzling that they almost never hurt chimpanzee hunters. Nevertheless, many times chimpanzees were clearly prevented from seizing their intended prey by intensive mobbing and harassment from adult male baboons.

Baboon hunts tend to be much shorter in duration than predatory attacks on colobus monkeys. When attempts to seize baboon victims fail, the hunters usually give up quickly; presumably, once a troop has been alerted, it is not worthwhile for the hunters to continue. Ransom, who studied the baboons during the 1968–69 period, suggests that their increased vigilance may have played a considerable part in the reduction in numbers of hunts. He comments that during the first few occasions when he watched predatory incidents, the target mother-infant pairs and the associated adult male baboons seemed oblivious to the chimpanzees' intentions. Then, as more kills were recorded, the baboons became increasingly alert to signs of danger. During 1969 the ratio of successful to unsuccessful hunts dropped sharply, and it was after this that baboon hunting decreased in frequency and finally appeared to come to a halt.

Why, then, the sudden renewal of interest in 1979? Perhaps it was not until there had been a fortuitous, opportunistic kill that baboons were once more perceived by the chimpanzees as a possible source of food. It may be significant that all seven of the successful kills between 1979 and 1981 were from *unhabituated* troops. Habituated baboons, during encounters with hunting chimpanzees, are not distracted by the presence of human observers and so can concentrate their efforts on repelling the predators. Unhabituated baboons are typically nervous and usually run away. But after a few relatively easy captures the chimpanzees once more began to hunt habituated baboons; during 1980 and 1981 eleven such attempts were observed. These elicited extremely aggressive and rapid defensive action from the adult male baboons, and the chimpanzee hunters were routed.

*Human Infants.*    Prior to my arrival at Gombe there were two reports of chimpanzee attacks on human infants in the area. One of these took place outside the national park (near the Manyovu Road, to the east). An African woman was gathering firewood when a male chimpanzee suddenly appeared, leaped at her, and seized the infant from her back. The woman was injured; the infant was dead when recovered and had been partially eaten (Thomas 1961). The second incident took place in the park (a game reserve at the time) near Nyasange Beach. A six-year-old boy was minding his baby brother when a male chimpanzee rushed at him and seized the baby. The child gave chase, whereupon the chimpanzee dropped the baby (which survived) and pulled the older child to the ground and began biting at his face. The screaming alerted his mother who, along with other women, ran at the chimpanzee, which fled. This child also survived, but with a badly mutilated face. No further predatory attacks on human infants have been reported since.

*Cannibalism.*   Between 1971 and 1984 six infant chimpanzees were seen to be killed and/or eaten by members of the study community. Three times the victims were infants of "stranger" females, estimated as being one and one-half to two and one-half years old. Whereas the killing of infants by the adult males seemed to be a *consequence of the attacks on their mothers* (similar equally brutal attacks on stranger females were seen on many other occasions), one adult female and her late-adolescent daughter attacked the mothers of their victims *only in order to acquire the infants* as meat. Once they had possession of the babies, no further aggression was directed toward the mothers.

*Female Strangers.*   The following case provides the best example of the persistence with which chimpanzees may *hunt* a stranger female. A large party of Kasakela chimpanzees, including one adolescent and nine adult males, suddenly heard a single chimpanzee call. Instant pandemonium broke out and, with pant-hoots, waa-barks, and screams, they raced toward the sound. Presently they fell silent and traveled in a fairly compact group toward the place where the call had originated. There they sat for fifteen minutes. They traveled on a short distance, stopped again, and sat in silence for half an hour. Afterward they moved on, still silently, penetrating the home range of the northern Mitumba community. They began smelling the ground and tree trunks, but then seemed to give up and began to feed. Suddenly, three hours and twenty minutes after the original call had been made, they raced to the east (retracing their steps); a few minutes later there was a tremendous outburst of calling. When the observers caught up, they saw Humphrey, Evered, and Satan jointly attacking an old anestrous female, who was crouched to the ground and screaming. She managed to escape and ran off with the Kasakela party in hot pursuit; the observers were quickly left behind. The quantity of blood at the site of the attack suggested that the victim had been badly hurt.

*Cooperation in the Hunt.*   There have been many observations of cooperation between nonrelated males. Although chimpanzees can and do hunt some prey very successfully on their own, the presence of other hunters is often beneficial and in some cases, particularly during hunts of baboons and large bushpig young, may even be essential to the success of the hunt.

*The Kill.*  Chimpanzees kill their prey by (1) biting into the head or neck, (2) flailing the body so that the head is smashed against branches, rocks, or the ground, (3) disemboweling it, or (4) simply holding it and tearing off pieces of flesh (or entire limbs) until it dies. When several chimpanzees converge upon a small animal, it may be literally torn to pieces within moments of capture. Small prey, such as infant or juvenile colobus, black infant baboons, and striped piglets, are usually killed by eating. Since the brains of such victims are almost always consumed first, death is very quick. The chimpanzee, often holding the victim by its neck, bites into the head, crushing the frontal bones. Thirty-one of the thirty-four infant or juvenile colobus whose capture was well observed were killed in this way (two were flailed and one was disemboweled).

Prey such as an adult monkey or large bushpig youngster sometimes present problems. The chimpanzee is not equipped with the teeth of a carnivore and often has trouble tearing open the skin of the victim. However, a combination of smashing against tree trunks or rocks and tearing at limbs (sometimes breaking them) usually ensures that large victims are rendered fairly immobile within five to ten minutes, although they may not actually die until later.

*Scavenging.*  On twenty-seven separate occasions chimpanzees have been seen feeding on bushbuck fawns which they were known or suspected to have seized from baboons. Only once has a baboon been seen to succeed in snatching meat from a chimpanzee. And only ten times in the history of the research at Gombe have we observed the chimpanzees feeding on meat that they found on the ground. Four times this was remnants of previous chimpanzee kills.

*Distributing Meat.*  A chimpanzee traveling by himself or herself can, as we have seen, hunt successfully. In that case he or she quietly consumes the meat alone—unless another individual happens to pass by and notices the hunter, when he will almost certainly approach and try to obtain a share. However, when a capture is made during a group hunt, especially when this involves a number of adult males, intense excitement usually breaks out as those present converge on the successful hunter. An adolescent or low-ranking male captor, or a female, is likely to lose possession of the carcass within moments of capture.

During the first few minutes after a kill has been made, before the excitement has died away, those who are present (at least the males) often manage to obtain quite large portions. They rush up to the successful hunter, seize hold of the prey, and pull. Sometimes competitors tear off and move away with large portions of viscera or entire limbs; at other times they start to feed on the carcass along with the captor. During this initial division the forest is filled with screams, barks, waa-barks, and pant-hoots—sounds that alert other chimpanzees in the area, most of whom hurry to join the meat eating.

Meat is a highly coveted food and often there is intense aggressive competition around a kill. This aggression comprises (1) attacks on possessors of meat by those who have none, (2) attacks or, more usually, displays or threats by possessors toward individuals trying to share their prey, and (3) attacks or threats directed by those who have not managed to acquire portions toward lower-ranking individuals who are also trying to get some meat.

*Adult Females.* While it is certainly true that adult males hunt far more frequently than do females, recent observations show that females at Gombe hunt more often, and eat much more meat, than was previously supposed. A female traveling in a family unit with her dependent young, or in a small female party, is more likely to be successful in obtaining and retaining prey than when she hunts in a mixed party. Much of the observed female predatory behavior (including unsuccessful hunting) was, however, in the context of mixed-party hunts. During colobus hunts female chimpanzees, like males, were often chased by male monkeys. Females were often present during baboon hunts, but were never observed to participate in events leading up to a capture.

Females, like males, differ in their abilities to acquire meat at group meat-eating sessions. They beg much more frequently from males than from other females. This is mainly, of course, because males are more often in possession of large portions of meat, but also because, if females do beg from other females, they are seldom rewarded.


### 3. COMMUNITY POLITICS

*Like many other primates, chimpanzees are exceptionally emotional mammals, easily aroused and not quite so easily pacified. In that regard, humans differ from chimpanzees primarily in their use of language for thinking and communication alike as well as in the self-consciousness of their thinking. Chimpanzees display in their behavior the emotions that move them; humans have more choice in how, when, and indeed whether they will communicate their feelings.*

*The third part of this chapter focuses on the circumstances under which the feral chimpanzees of Gombe behave aggressively, and with what consequences (both personal and social); and upon the social structures of dominant/submissive relationships, which function as a major (although only partial) biosocial constraint upon the expression of violent aggressive behaviors among the conspecifics that constitute the community.*

*This dominance structure is the initial stage of a prototype for the emergence of political behavior among the community of Gombe chimpanzees, establishing experientially based and habitually patterned limits upon all individuals in the group. And, as we shall see in the next part of this chapter, the same structure denotes the aggregation of adult males as the chimpanzees most likely to become involved in cooperative group aggression against individuals identified as nonparticipants in the recognized dominance structure of the local community.* — Eds.

*Aggression*

Chimpanzees can easily be roused to sudden violence, particularly during social excitement. While most fights do not lead to wounding, some certainly do—particularly those directed at individuals of neighboring social groups.

*Contagion.* Sometimes an individual may suddenly charge over and take part in a fight that, as far as the observer can tell, has nothing to do with him. Or for no apparent reason he may, after watching an aggressive episode, initiate a parallel incident with an innocent bystander. Aggression of this sort can lead to serious fighting because more than one other individual may join in.

In some incidents involving more than one male aggressor, it is possible that each, given such environmental stimulations as the arrival of a female in estrus and heavy rain, might have attacked independently of the others; if so, the first attacks merely served to focus attention on suitable victims. There are other occasions, however, when a second aggressor, who was sitting quite calmly before, gets up and charges over to join a nearby attack. Fortunately for the victims, such multiple-aggressor attacks are rare. During a five-year period there were only three observations of fights in which more than two aggressors converged on a single individual. In each case three males attacked a single female.

It is possible that the observation of fighting may in itself stimulate aggressive behavior in the onlooker through the mechanism of social facilitation. If this is so, a chimpanzee, his level of arousal raised, may join a fight simply for the sake of fighting—we might almost say "for the fun of it." It is known that in some situations aggression is attractive. But chimpanzees are unlikely to attack an animal that remains quite calm and does not run.

*Submission and Reassurance.* Submissive behaviors comprise a variety of nonaggressive postures, gestures, and calls that are directed up the hierarchy, from a low-ranking to a higher-ranking chimpanzee. They occur not only when the subordinate has been threatened or attacked by the other, but even when he or she approaches or is approached by, or passes or is passed by, a higher-ranking individual who has *not* shown overt signs of aggression toward the gesturer.

The higher-ranking individual, although he or she may ignore submissive behaviors of this sort or may even threaten or attack the subordinate, is most likely to respond by touching, patting, kissing, embracing, or grooming the other. Any of these friendly responses tends to calm and relax the subordinate and thus serve to reestablish harmonious relations between the individuals concerned.

*Factors Affecting Level of Arousal.* Most of the aggression at Gombe takes place in the following behavioral contexts: reunion, social excitement, competition for food, sexual competition, protection, and "no obvious context." There is a significant sex difference in the frequency with which males and females show aggressive behavior in these major contexts.

A relaxed and calm chimpanzee is less likely to threaten a subordinate who approaches to feed nearby than one who is tense and socially aroused. Hair erection is a useful indicator of the state of arousal: a chimpanzee whose hair bristles all over the body is far more likely to show intense forms of aggressive and/or fearful behavior than one with sleek hair.

There are a number of ecological and social factors which, in general terms, affect the state of arousal and thus the likelihood that a chimpanzee will behave aggressively in a given situation. An important ecological factor is the nature and abundance of the *food supply*, which to a large extent is determined by the season of the year. Probably the most significant effect of seasonal variation is on the size of the foraging party. When food is relatively scarce, particularly if the sources are widely scattered, chimpanzees usually travel in small parties of two or three compatible individuals; in this situation aggression is rare. When food is abundant in large stands of fruiting trees, many individuals forage together and aggressive incidents are relatively frequent. And when a highly prized item (such as meat) is in short supply, aggressive competition will be at its height.

The *weather* and *temperature*, again largely determined by the time of year, can also affect the expression of aggressive behavior. Very heavy rain, typical of the last three months of the wet season, tends to depress all activity; the chimpanzees sit huddled, waiting for it to end. However, at the onset of heavy rain there may be much wild displaying among the males, during which aggressive incidents often take place. Similar displaying occurs when a sudden very strong wind springs up.

When chimpanzees are sick, they sometimes seem to be especially irritable and often direct mild forms of threat, such as the arm raise or head tip, at individuals who approach them too closely or annoy them in other ways. Pain can elicit an immediate aggressive response (Plotnik 1974). It tends to increase irritability: a mature male who had a broken toe repeatedly threatened noisy youngsters who played nearby.

There are two major social factors that affect the frequency and intensity of observed aggressive behavior. The first of these is *party size*. An increase in the number of associating chimpanzees correlates positively with increased rate of aggression per individual (Wrangham 1975; Bygott 1979). This is partly because in a large group two or more relatively incompatible individuals are apt to be present, and partly because large aggregations so often form in response to situations likely to increase the level of arousal (after a successful hunt, for instance, or because of the presence of one or more females in estrus). In situations of this sort, when the threshold for aggressive behavior is lower, aggression is more likely to be triggered by seemingly trivial causes—such as an adolescent male passing too close to a grooming senior.

The second social factor is the current state of the *male dominance hierarchy*. During periods when the rank order of the adult males is relatively stable, there is less fighting than at times of change. During two years when the current alpha male was being challenged, there was much tension among the adult males. It often erupted into charging displays and fighting during times of social excitement—as when a large party arrived at a rich food source, when two parties met, or when a resting party got up and started to move on. The males typically redirected their aggression onto adolescent male and female scapegoats. Many of the aggressive acts performed by males during other forms of intense social excitement can be interpreted as status rivalry.

*Fear of the Unfamiliar.* In a few rare instances we have observed aggressive acts that are directed toward victims who, by their abnormal behavior, appear to frighten the aggressors. The most notable examples took place during the 1966 polio epidemic, when three individuals became partially paralyzed and as a result developed bizarre movements. When the other chimpanzees saw these cripples for the first time, they reacted with extreme fear; as their fear decreased, their behavior became increasingly aggressive, and many of them displayed toward and even hit the victims.

Other aggressive responses may also stem from feelings of aversion following fear, such as those directed toward some creatures of different species (pythons, for examples). The sight of "stranger" conspecifics from neighboring communities may elicit feelings of fear, particularly when the strangers are adult males. Chimpanzees typically show fearful behavior when they travel in the unsafe peripheral zones of their community range, startling at the sound of a twig breaking or at a sudden rustle in the undergrowth. Obviously they are well aware of the danger inherent in a surprise encounter with a strong group of hostile neighboring males. When patrolling individuals return to the "safe" area of the home range after a long period of stealthy travel, they sometimes engage in a series of vigorous charging displays, hurling rocks and branches and sometimes attacking subordinate scapegoats (Goodall et al. 1979). Such performances may well serve as outlets for tensions built up during travel in the danger zone.

It takes some time, usually, for chimpanzees to overcome an inherent dislike or "hatred" of strangers. At Gombe resident females may show quite severe aggression toward young immigrants for some months after they have joined the new community.

It may be significant that the worst assaults on members of neighboring communities at Gombe were perpetrated on individuals who were not completely strange to the aggressors. The Kahama chimpanzees had associated with the Kasakela males for years before the community division and had only become estranged a few years before the attacks. A compounding factor here perhaps is that when a chimpanzee rejoins his or her companions after a long separation, levels of arousal are apt to be high. In the case of family members or other individuals with close, supportive bonds, this excitement is expressed by embracing, holding, patting, screaming, and so on. But when there is any kind of competitive dominance relationship between the returning individual and one or more of those whom he meets, it seems that the same high level of arousal is likely to be expressed in violent hostility.

Greeting behavior, made up as it is of elements of submissive, aggressive, reassurance, and sexual behavior, serves to reestablish the nature of existing relationships, in that the subordinate typically indicates with clear-cut submissive signals his recognition of the higher rank of the other. Tension generated by reunion with a social competitor (unless of an extremely hostile nature) is decreased by reassurance contact, and further relaxation is made possible by the long sessions of social grooming that may follow reunion of adult males.

*Interspecific Aggression.*   Various aggressive patterns, ranging from threat to fierce attack, may be directed toward animals of other species. Often this aggression occurs in the context of hunting. The behavior surrounding the actual killing of a prey animal may or may not include aggressive feelings. (Indeed, both chimpanzees and humans often do not actually kill prey that cannot escape and poses no immediate threat.) But when the prey fights back, as does an adult colobus monkey, particularly if the chimpanzee hunter is bitten, his subsequent actions may well be prompted by retaliatory aggression.

Play between young chimpanzees and young baboons is common at Gombe. Quite often it becomes highly aggressive. Sometimes the chimpanzee has the upper hand and chases off his playmates with much stamping, slapping, and hurling of rocks and sticks; at other times it is he who is routed by the baboons. These incidents occasionally end in actual attacks, during which the opponents, screaming loudly, may hit or grapple with one another. Females of both species are then likely to intervene aggressively in defense of their young, and nearby adult males may act protectively.

A few encounters between chimpanzees and large predators (lions and leopards) have been observed at both Gombe and Mahale: the chimpanzees sometimes brandished branches, hurled rocks and sticks, and performed intimidation displays. A variety of aggressive behaviors, such as swaying of branches, hitting with sticks, and throwing, may be directed at creatures such as pythons and monitor lizards.

*Juvenile Aggression.*   The young chimpanzee gradually acquires the aggressive patterns of the adult, partly as a result of the maturation of species-specific behaviors, partly from actual experience of aggressive action, and partly as a result of observational learning. Adult females, particularly the mothers of the infants concerned, provide important models of agonistic patterns for small infants of both sexes. An elder sibling may also be important. Adult males become increasingly important as models for juvenile and adolescent males. From the age of about nine years, when a young male begins to leave his mother, he may select one particular adult male and associate with him very frequently (Pusey 1977). A follower relationship of this sort involved young Goblin and the alpha male Figan; Goblin learned a number of Figan's display and attack techniques, which he used to good advantage.

The personality of the mother (especially whether she is sociable or relatively solitary) and her dominance rank have an effect on the aggressive behavior of an infant. If she is sociable, the infant will spend more time with other chimpanzees and have more opportunities both to watch and to experience aggression. The infants of high-ranking females tend to be more assertive than those of low-ranking ones, presumably because they learn early that their mothers will not only come to their help, but are likely to protect them successfully. Older siblings will protect them in the same way. Aggression may thus be repeatedly rewarded with success, and both sons and daughters of high-ranking mothers are likely to rank high when they become adults. Of course, infants of low-ranking females are sometimes assertive too—but with less rewarding results.

*Differences in Male and Female Behavior.*     Male aggression in the framework of reunion, social excitement, and "no obvious context" is often triggered by dominance rivalry. The picture for the adult females is very different. Two major contexts elicited aggressive behavior—feeding (on plant foods) and protection. (In fact, about a quarter of their overall aggression was directed toward their own offspring of various ages.) Many (66.7 percent) of the observed female *attacks* were directed against other adult females.

*Political Socialization.*     Aggression compels attention, and youngsters watch fights and displays with interest. Perhaps to some extent this underlies the fascination shown by young males in the behavior of adult males (Goodall 1971). When these youngsters first leave their mothers, it is the big males with whom they choose to associate, despite the inevitable risk that they will become the targets of male aggression. An early-adolescent male, on occasion, will actually leave his mother to travel with a male who has just attacked him severely.

The child assimilates a great deal about aggression (and social dominance) during play sessions. As he or she gets older, play is increasingly likely to become very rough and, in fact, often ends in aggression. The child thus not only learns facts about the strengths and weaknesses of his playmates and the dominance position of his own mother in relation to theirs, but he also develops skills in fighting, bluffing, and forming alliances. These skills, once mastered, will enable him to compete in a society in which the ability to defend his "rights" and raise his status by fighting may be important. For the young male, successful domination of a female, which is accomplished by means of displays and fighting, functions at least sometimes to ensure that she will follow him in consortships. And if she refuses, he will display at her and sometimes attack her severely until she does.

*Social Structure, Aggression, and Dominance.*   Aggression serves to reduce the distance between individuals. The pair may then remain together, with no further aggression, for periods of several weeks. Mild fights and displays directed toward young cycling females from other communities function to recruit them into the male's own social group.

Male-male aggression, at least as it operates within the community, functions primarily to establish and maintain a dominance hierarchy. But once a reasonably stable ranking order has been worked out, the benefits are obvious—not only to the more dominant but also, as Lack (1966) has pointed out, to the subordinate. Knowing that it is useless for him to compete for resources with those who rank higher, the lower-ranking individual does not waste time and effort, or run the risk of injury, but goes off to try his luck elsewhere. Chimpanzees are highly excitable, and especially when a number are together, trivial disputes may erupt into aggressive interactions and displaying; but as long as the hierarchy is stable, serious fighting seldom occurs. The minor attacks and the wild charging displays with all their elements of aggression function to relieve social tensions and thus to minimize the physiologically undesirable components of stress.

Often the role played by aggression is not immediately obvious, simply because it operates at second hand through the dominance hierarchy it helped to create. Thus, when many individuals climb into a large fruiting tree, there may be no overt aggression, yet the dominant individuals will be seen to occupy the best feeding sites, while subordinates move about picking one fruit here and another there or simply waiting on the ground (Wrangham 1979).

And so, gradually, the complex functions of aggression are disclosed. But they reveal only half the picture. We cannot hope to understand the role played by aggression in the ordering of chimpanzee society without consideration of the equally powerful forces of social attraction. It is the interplay between those two opposing forces, aggressive hostility and punishment on the one side and close and enduring friendly bonds on the other, which has led to the unique social organization that we label a community.

### Dominance

In the natural habitat the hierarchy, the patterning of all the different relationships within the chimpanzee society, is never static. Changes occur as youngsters compete during play sessions, learning the strengths and weaknesses of their companions; as games become aggressive; as allies step in to help on both sides, and win or lose; as young males challenge first the females of the community and then, one by one, the senior males; as young immigrant females go into estrus; as each individual watches the interactions among all the others. Nevertheless, for weeks or months at a time the ordering of relationships may be relatively stable, at least among the older individuals. When it is at its most stable, overall levels of aggression are likely to be low; each individual, in a manner of speaking, "knows his place" relative to each other. Threats in many contexts take the place of attacks. Thus a hierarchy, while it cannot be said to develop in order to control aggression within a society, often functions in exactly this way. We need only observe the escalation of levels of fighting during times of instability. But there are also occasions when aggression toward a subordinate is inappropriate—when the dominant chimpanzee, in order to get his way, must resort to persuasion.

A chimpanzee, during intense social excitement, particularly when in the presence of an ally, may display toward or hit a superior (to whom he would normally pant-grunt); but the latter will not pant-grunt to him. Presenting and crouching are also indicators of relative status, particularly among adult males. The soft bark of mild threat, uttered by confident individuals, is a call that is directed only *down* the hierarchy.

In chimpanzee society in the wild, males are the dominant sex. A normally healthy adult male is able to dominate all the females of his community, even when a number of them are together. In some captive situations, coalitions of females can put fully grown males to flight (de Waal 1982) but this almost never happens in the wild, either at Gombe or at Mahale (Nishida 1979).

*The Male Hierarchy.*　When Bygott (1974) studied male dominance at Gombe between 1970 and 1972, there were fifteen socially mature males, and there was no precise linear hierarchy. For example, although Humphrey at that time certainly dominated more individuals than did Charlie, Humphrey was very wary of Charlie and avoided him whenever possible. Some of the males interacted so infrequently that meaningful conclusions could not be drawn about their relevant social rank. Bygott (133) thus proposed a "hierarchy of levels." There was a clear-cut *alpha*—Mike; three *high-ranking* males—Humphrey, Hugh, and Charlie; six *middle-ranking* males—Figan, Evered, Hugo, Leakey, Faben, and De; and five *low-ranking* males—Godi, Goliath, Willy Wally, Jomeo, and Satan. After the community division in 1972, when there were fewer males in the Kasakela community, they could most of the time be ranked in a linear hierarchy (Riss and Goodall 1977).

Factors other than age which determine the position of a male in the dominance hierarchy include physical fitness, aggressiveness, skill at fighting, ability to form coalitions, intelligence, and a number of personality factors such as boldness and determination. At Gombe some males strive with much energy to better their social status over a period of years; others work hard for a short while, but give up if they encounter a serious setback; a few seem remarkably unconcerned about their social rank.

Although the hierarchy of the adult males may be relatively stable for months, even years, at a time, there will always be some young, low-ranking males on the lookout for opportunities to better their status, ready to take advantage of a senior should he show signs of ill health or aging, or if he loses an ally. For the most part a reversal of dominance between two males takes place over an extended period of time during which it is difficult to ascertain which of the two holds the higher rank. Other changes occur more quickly as the result of one or a few severe, decisive fights.

Our long-term study has emphasized the fact that while threats (among which the charging display is particularly effective) serve, for the most part, to *maintain* or challenge the existing social order, *reversals* in rank among the males have, in almost all cases, been the result of fights. As Scott (1958) pointed out, fear is quickly learned and hard to extinguish, so that a single decisive loss can have a long-lasting effect. Moreover, fighting ability itself may be diminished by failure, just as it may be enhanced by success (Kuo 1967).

Dominance conflicts involve two kinds of fighting. First the "hit-and-run" variety, as when a young male displays past a rival, slapping or stamping on him briefly as he does so, or when he seizes the opportunity offered by an ongoing fight to pound quickly on one (or even both) of the contestants, then hastens away. A combination of repeated attacks of this sort, during which the aggressor is seldom hurt, together with avoidance responses to his vigorous charging displays, gradually increases the confidence of a young male to the point where he will either dare to initiate a more severe attack or will stand firm and retaliate in the face of aggression directed toward him by his rival. This is the second and far more serious kind of dominance fighting—the kind that may lead to a permanent reversal of rank between two males. Sometimes it takes the form of a single decisive attack, but more often, rank reversals occur after a series of significant fights.

*Coalitions.*    The ability of a male chimpanzee to enlist support during conflicts is perhaps the most crucial factor in attaining and maintaining high rank. At Gombe there are *stable coalitions*, based on long-term mutually supportive relationships or friendships (often involving siblings), and *opportunistic coalitions*, when two or more males (whatever their relationship) temporarily join forces against a common rival. Senior males often form opportunistic coalitions against a young male who is striving for high rank.

Stable coalitions are characterized by high levels of association between the partners. This means that when one of the pair is in trouble, his ally often happens to be present and thus *able* to help. Moreover, the very fact that they are together often inhibits aggression from other males. Bygott (1974) noted that the only time he ever saw Humphrey direct aggression toward Faben was when Figan was not present. Typically, when one member of a stable coalition displays (whether against a rival or not), his partner joins him and the two display in unison.

*Motivation and Alpha Status.* The alpha is the highest-ranking male of the community. This does not mean that he is able to control *all* situations, but instances when he is intimidated by other males (including coalitions) are rare. Some males devote much more time and energy than do others to the improvement or maintenance of their social status. And some males begin to drop in the hierarchy at a much younger age than others; some show a gradual loss of rank and others lose status rapidly. The response of a male to his loss of rank— whether because of ill health, defeat by another male, loss of an ally, or any other factor—will be determined in large part by his age at the time. Thus, when an old male (over thirty years of age) suffers a serious setback, he is likely to drop precipitously through the hierarchy.

*Female Dominance.* One factor that is of overwhelming significance for the rank of a female at Gombe, outweighing all other variables except extreme sickness or extreme old age, is the nature of her family—and which family members are with her when she encounters another female.

For the young female, the rank of her mother is of crucial importance, for a high-ranking, aggressive female will almost always support her daughter during agonistic interactions with other females. While coalitions between mothers and members of their immediate families are the most usual, adult females who are not closely related do join forces from time to time on an opportunistic basis. Quite often two females will form a temporary alliance against an adolescent male when he persists in challenging one or both.

*Conclusion.* The immediate advantage of high rank in the female hierarchy lies mainly in increased ability to appropriate desirable food. Many aggressive interactions that take place between females are in the context of feeding. Theoretically, increased food intake produces healthier females, who give birth more often and raise offspring who are also fitter since they too have more food. In some parts of Africa, though, where the environment is more harsh than it is at Gombe, the ability to compete successfully for food may be critical. We do know that the offspring of high-ranking females tend to become high-ranking themselves. If, therefore, it can be shown that a high-ranking female has a reproductive advantage, it will clearly be significant to her overall genetic fitness. It means that her daughters will, in their turn, be more productive and successful as mothers, and her sons will probably have a reproductive advantage also.

But the benefits of high rank—reproductive advantage and priority of access to desired resources—seem, for the most part, less significant for chimpanzee males than for the males of many other primate species. When food is short, the chimpanzees tend to fragment and the alpha male will have no greater advantage than the top-ranked individual in each of the small groups. In competition for meat, the *older* males are often more successful than those who have highest rank. A high-ranking male has less reason to fear aggression from other males, and he is the frequent recipient of deferential behavior from many subordinates. These benefits will increase as he works his way up the hierarchy; but, at the same time, he will have to work harder to maintain his position.

## 4. COMMUNITY WARFARE

*The concluding part of this chapter emphasizes the extent to which no viable community of wild chimpanzees exists in isolation from other similar chimpanzee communities. Each such group maintains its own dynamic adaptation to the local ecology, including such diverse components as climatic change (and consequent effects upon the availability of water, food, other animals, and shelter); the group's own collective social ontogeny, with expanding, stable, or diminishing quantities and proportions of adult males, adult females, juveniles of either sex, and of infants. And probably most important of all—for such groups generally, even if not for Gombe—the effects of contacts with humans, whether benevolently—as in the case of observer-habituators—or malevolently—as in the most usual case of farmers and traders.*

*The focus here is upon the cross-boundaries contacts between the Gombe community and its neighboring chimpanzee groups and upon the dynamics of boundary change during the quarter century of continuous observation and study on which are based this discussion of the Gombe group's territory and territoriality—Eds.*

### Territoriality

We should consider as the basic unit of political organization not a single group, but rather a *system of social groups* interacting in a given area. It has become clear, from the pattern of intercommunity interactions that has emerged at Gombe over the years, that this approach would be very meaningful. Unfortunately, until very recently we have been able to habituate only one social group of chimpanzees (although it divided, so that for a while there were two groups: the Mitumba community to the north and the Kalande community to the south). The unhabituated chimpanzees from these groups usually flee whenever they see humans. When females have transferred into our study group, we have known nothing of their background; when our known females left, we were unable to follow their subsequent careers. Nevertheless, it has been possible to piece together an overall picture of the relations of Gombe chimpanzees with members of neighboring communities, a picture that accords well with the description of intercommunity (or interunit-group) interactions at Mahale (Nishida 1979; Nishida et al. 1985).

Three facets of chimpanzee social organization are crucial to the understanding of interactions between neighboring communities. First, chimpanzees neither travel in stable groupings nor follow predictable travel routes from day to day. A lone male may suddenly encounter several males of a neighboring community, a party of males may surprise a single female, and so on. This random pattern contrasts with intertroop encounters in many other primate species. The baboons at Gombe, for example, can anticipate where they are likely to encounter neighbors. And when they do meet them, they know that even if the whole troop is not visible, the other members are unlikely to be far away. Second, male chimpanzees remain in their natal community, whereas females may transfer out. Third, female chimpanzees are so distributed throughout the community range that some will travel relatively often in the overlap zones between neighboring communities. Keeping these facts in mind, we can now examine the role played by adult male chimpanzees in maintaining, defending, or enlarging the range they share.

*Are Chimpanzees Territorial?*   In a number of respects chimpanzees comply with classical territoriality:

1. Conspecifics from neighboring social groups who intrude into the home range are aggressively expelled (except for those females who are recruited).
2. Boundaries are visited frequently and monitored.
3. Parties traveling to peripheral areas show tense, nervous behavior and are much less confident than when in their core area.
4. Auditory displays, loud pant-hoots, and drumming may be exchanged between parties of adult males of neighboring communities, followed by ritualized aggressive display, and members of both sides may retreat without conflict.
5. Boundaries may be respected over a number of years. For two years after the community split, Kasakela males recognized Mkenke Stream as a boundary between themselves and the Kahama community; at Mahale, members of the powerful M group, over a seven-year period, seldom moved into the exclusive area of the smaller K group.

In three important ways, however, chimpanzee behavior does *not* comply with classical territoriality.

1. Both at Gombe and Mahale it is the relative size and composition of the two neighboring parties that determine the outcome of an encounter, rather than the geographic location. A small patrol will turn and flee if it meets a larger party, or one with more males, even *within* its own range, whereas if a large party, traveling *out* of its range, meets a smaller party of neighbors, it is likely to chase or attack. When parties are approximately the same size, with similar numbers of adult males, visual and auditory display exchanges without conflict typically result.

The social structure of hyenas is similar in many ways to that of chimpanzees. The fact that in both species individuals of the community (or clan) travel around

in parties of *variable* size and composition means that there will be opportunities for intimidating neighbors seldom vouchsafed to other species. Because
hyenas and chimpanzees are intelligent, as well as being hostile to neighbors,
they can and do take advantage of such opportunities when they arise.

2. Chimpanzees have a large home range with *considerable overlap* between
neighboring communities. Chimpanzees actually expend considerable energy
in *creating* opportunities to encounter intruders at close range. The adult males
move out to peripheral areas, on average, once every four days.

3. It is perhaps in the *violence* of their hostility toward neighbors that
chimpanzees, like hyenas and lions, differ most from the traditional territory
owners of the animal kingdom. Their victims are not simply chased out of the
owners' territory if they are found trespassing; they are assaulted and left,
perhaps to die. Moreover, chimpanzees not only attack trespassers but may
make aggressive raids into the very heart of the core area of neighboring groups.
Admittedly, boundaries may be respected for some of the time, but during the
long-term studies at Gombe and Mahale there have been three major "invasions": Kasakela males took over Kahama range, Kalande males pushed deep
into Kasakela range, and M group moved into K-group range. During all these
invasions adult males (and some females) were killed or disappeared. Even if it is
argued that the Kasakela males were merely trying to *reclaim* an area to which
they previously had free access, the assertion does not explain the northward
thrust of the Kalande community or the takeover by the M group at Mahale.

Chimpanzee territoriality has shifted away from the relatively peaceful,
ritualized maintenance of territory typical for many nonhuman animals toward a
more aggressive type of behavior. In the chimpanzee, territoriality functions
not only to repel intruders from the home range, but sometimes to injure or
eliminate them; not only to defend the existing home range and its resources,
but to enlarge it opportunistically at the expense of weaker neighbors; not only
to protect the female resources of a community, but to recruit actively and
aggressively new sexual partners from neighboring social groups.

*Excursions and Patrols.* A patrol is typified by cautious, silent travel during
which the members of the party tend to move in a compact group. There are
many pauses as the chimpanzees gaze around and listen. Sometimes they climb
tall trees and sit quietly for an hour or more, gazing out over the area of a
neighboring community. They are very tense and at a sudden sound (a twig
cracking in the undergrowth or the rustling of leaves) may grin and reach out to
touch or embrace one another.

Perhaps the most striking aspect of patrolling behavior is the silence of those
taking part. They avoid treading on dry leaves and rustling the vegetation. On
one occasion vocal silence was maintained for more than three hours. By
contrast, when patrolling chimpanzees return once more to familiar areas, there
is often an outburst of loud calling, drumming displays, hurling of rocks, and

even some chasing and mild aggression between individuals. Particularly spectacular are displays along streambeds or around waterfalls, which may last as long as ten minutes.

During excursions or patrols to peripheral areas the chimpanzees often hear, smell, or actually see individuals of the neighboring community. Responses vary from quiet avoidance or flight to aggressive chasing or fighting and depend to a large extent on the relative size and age-sex composition of the two parties.

*Contacts Between Males of Neighboring Communities.* When males hear pant-hoots and drumming from an obviously *larger* number of unhabituated adult males, they sometimes stare toward the sounds in silence, then hastily retreat. When the number of males in the two parties appears to be similar, members of both sides usually engage in vigorous displays with much drumming and throwing, interspersed with pant-hoots, roar pant-hooting, and waa-barks. After a wild outburst the participants stand or sit in silence, apparently waiting to see if the other party will reciprocate. If it does, another outburst ensues. Vocal challenges of this sort are common and usually end with one or both parties withdrawing, noisily, to the core areas of their respective home ranges.

There have been very few occasions when encounters between males of neighboring communities have been relatively well observed—when, that is, at least some of the strangers were actually *seen* by field observers. And even these are incomplete, because the unhabituated individuals invariably flee once they see the humans. The most complete observations include the following encounter that took place at the end of 1974, between the three surviving Kahama males (Charlie, Sniff, and Willy Wally) and males of the Kalande community to the south (see also Goodall et al. 1979):

> November 1974. The three Kahama males Charlie, Sniff, and Willy Wally have captured a piglet. As they feed, another adult male appears on the far side of a narrow ravine. The observer has never seen him before; he is obviously a member of the large Kalande community that ranges over the hills to the south. Charlie, upon seeing the stranger, drops his meat and runs northward, closely followed by Sniff and Willy Wally. The observer hastens after them and presently finds Charlie in a tree, screaming loudly. Other chimpanzees are calling up ahead, so the observer leaves Charlie and runs on. A few minutes later he catches up with Sniff. Hair bristling, the young male is performing a spectacular display along a trail partway down a steep-sided ravine. Charlie is still screaming back in the forest, but Sniff is uttering deep, fierce-sounding roar pant-hoots. Below, hidden in the vegetation, other chimpanzees are heard calling loudly and charging through the undergrowth. Sniff, as he displays, repeatedly picks up large rocks and hurls them into the ravine so that they land near the strangers beneath. He hurls at least thirteen before he moves out of sight. The chimpanzees below are throwing too; every so often a rock or stick flies up from the undergrowth but, falling far short of Sniff, the missiles roll back harmlessly into the ravine. The observer determines that at least three of the strangers are adult males. They see him and retreat southward. (Observer: H. Matama.)

It is clear that interactions between males of neighboring communities are typically hostile, a finding that has emerged also from the study at Mahale (Nishida 1979).

*Interactions Between Habituated Males and Unhabituated Females.*   The response of adult males to a "stranger" female—that is, a female unknown to the human observers and presumed to be from a neighboring community—depends to a large extent on her age and reproductive state.

*Young Nulliparous Females.*   Usually well tolerated by neighboring males, females of this category may move freely between natal and neighboring communities, although they may encounter aggression from resident females of the new community. When adult males encounter one of these young visitors, the greeting may be relatively calm, or the female may flee—in which case she is likely to be chased and mildly attacked. When they are in estrus, mothers with infants can probably be considered as part of this category.

*Anestrous Mothers and Infants.*   The response of Kasakela males to strangers of this category is very different. During the eight-year period 1975 to 1982 Kasakela males were observed when they encountered such females on twenty-five occasions. Seventy-six percent of these encounters were aggressive in nature, involving chases or attacks. Moreover, in contrast to the brief attacks on young nulliparous females, all but one of the fifteen actual attacks on the older females were extremely severe.

*Interactions Between Habituated and Unhabituated Females.*   Females of the Kasakela community have sometimes taken part in chases that preceded male attacks on unhabituated females. Once, after a large party had raced noisily in the direction of a single call, the unhabituated female (Harmony) who was found was attacked by only one member of the Kasakela party: adult female Fifi kicked the stranger some thirty meters to the ground after chasing her through the branches. In fact, young immigrant females (Harmony was already transferring at that time) face a good deal of hostility from resident females.

### Border Skirmishing

By the beginning of 1973 two separate communities were recognized, the northern or Kasakela community, based on Kakombe and Kasakela valleys, and the southern or Kahama community, based on Kahama Valley. Wrangham (1975), when he analyzed ranging data for 1973, confirmed that the areas used by males of the two communities were geographically separate, with only one significant overlap zone. Although a few nonaggressive interactions were observed that year between males of the two new communities, they involved only the three oldest members: Mike and Hugo of Kasakela, and Goliath of Kahama. All had associated closely for many years. Indeed, Goliath and Mike had become very friendly from 1967 until the community division and Goliath's move to the south.

Early 1974 saw the first of the series of violently aggressive episodes that led to the complete annihilation of the Kahama community. The Kasakela males began a southward movement that culminated in 1977 with annexation of the Kahama community range. By the end of 1974, the estimated range of the Kasakela community was 15 square kilometers; the range of the Kahama community, estimated at about 10 square kilometers in early 1973, had shrunk to about 3.8 square kilometers. During the 1974–75 wet season, the four Kahama males who remained seldom left an area that was only 1.8 square kilometers, and even this was sometimes entered by parties of Kasakela individuals. Moreover, the large, unhabituated Kalande community to the south was also encroaching on the small remnant of the Kahama community range (Pierce, 1978). By the end of 1977, the last Kahama male had vanished. The Kasakela males, along with their females and young, began feeding and nesting in the southern part of their community range. This led to a marked increase of the Kasakela core area. The total range at this time was estimated at approximately 17 square kilometers. The attacks on the members of the Kahama community that took place between 1974 and 1977 were all consistently brutal and protracted, and each one has been described in some detail in an earlier publication (Goodall 1986, 506–14).

*Individual Participation.* Without doubt most adult male chimpanzees, particularly young prime individuals, are strongly motivated to travel to peripheral areas of their home range. In many instances their responses to the sight or sound of presumed strangers (especially the frenzied rush toward females), as well as the long periods spent in stealthy stalking of victims, suggests that these encounters are highly attractive to the participants. To some extent all adult males show a keenness to participate in these exciting incidents, although old males take part less often as it becomes harder for them to travel long distances. Even among the prime males, however, there are distinct individual differences.

*Other Populations.* The evidence that has been gradually accumulating at Mahale, the only other long-term study site, points to a similar aggressive relationship between males of different communities or different unit-groups (Nishida 1979; Nishida et al. 1985). More recently, all the adult Kasakela-group males over six years old have disappeared, one after the other. Nishida and his colleagues (1985) speculate that intercommunity conflict may have been responsible for at least some of these disappearances. The larger Kahale group is now in the process of taking over the Kasakela-group females.

Brewer (1978) has described a series of nighttime raids made by wild chimpanzees of Niokolo-Koba National Park (in Senegal) on a group of chimpanzees being rehabilitated there. Why these violent incidents after several relatively peaceful years? The rehabilitant group was located in part of the home range of the wild chimpanzee community. The year of the raids there was a drought, and at the height of the dry season the only known source of running water was that close to Brewer's camp. This, moreover, was one of the few locations where tabbo trees produced fruit that year, a particularly important resource because many fruit crops had failed or yielded poorly. Finally, the wild chimpanzees were the focus of a study initiated by W. McGrew and C. Tutin in mid-1976 (McGrew, Baldwin, and Tutin 1981) and by 1977 had begun to lose some of the fear of humans that previously would probably have kept them away from Brewer's camp.

As a result of the aggression the rehabilitant group was relocated elsewhere. In some ways the situation is comparable to that at Gombe where, as a result of their repeated attacks on Kahama individuals, Kasakela community members regained access to an area which, before the community division, had been an integral part of their home range.

*Assaults on Stranger Females.*   The attacks on unhabituated females at Gombe led on four occasions to the death of their infants; three times those infants were eaten or partially eaten. And twice at Mahale adult males are thought to have seized and then eaten the infants of females of a neighboring unit-group. But in the cases at Gombe the aggression was clearly directed against the *mothers*, not the infants.

At Gombe, there is no evidence to suggest that any of the four mothers who were attacked, and whose infants were killed (or died), subsequently became available to the Kasakela males for mating; they were, if anything, more likely to have died themselves of their injuries. Moreover, one of these mothers and her family actively avoided the presumed location of their attack by Kalande males and stopped using part of what had been their preferred area.

If, then, the assaults are not directed at infanticide and subsequent recruitment of the female victims, why are they perpetrated? Probably we do not need to search for any causal explanation beyond the fact that the victims were all members of neighboring communities: chimpanzees have an inherent aversion to strangers. The female victims at Gombe and Mahale were strangers, although they might have been encountered by their attackers previously (perhaps several times) during patrols and excursions to peripheral areas. They may even have visited the aggressor males as late adolescents during periods of estrus. But they were still highly unfamiliar, and their social bonds were with members of another community—which, of course, included dangerous (to the aggressor males) males. Furthermore, these females were for the most part encountered in overlap zones where the chimpanzees, fearful of neighboring males, are more nervous. The tension that builds up during travel in these unsafe areas may lead to wild displays and occasional attacks on scapegoats within the party once the males have returned to their own safe core area. Thus, when patrolling males encounter an anestrous female (who poses no threat and who is not at the time sexually desirable), she is likely to be attacked. And because of the heightened level of arousal the aggression is apt to be fierce.

Perhaps the recruitment of new females into the community at Gombe is facilitated by repeated brutal attacks on their mothers, which serve to weaken the mother-daughter bond or to break it altogether.

*Chimpanzee Protowarfare?*

Granted that destructive warfare in its typical human form (*organized, armed* conflict between groups) is a cultural development, it nevertheless required preadaptations to permit its emergence in the first place. The most crucial of these were probably cooperative group living, group territoriality, cooperative hunting skills, weapon use, and the intellectual ability to make cooperative plans. Another basic preadaptation would have been an inherent fear of, or aversion to, strangers, expressed by aggressive attack (Eibl-Eibesfeldt 1979a). Early hominid groups possessing these behavioral characteristics would theoretically have been capable of the kind of organized intergroup conflict that could have led to destructive warfare.

Chimpanzees not only possess, to a greater or less extent, the above preadaptations, but they show other inherent characteristics that would have been helpful to the dawn warriors in their primitive battles.

1. The killing of adult conspecifics is not common among mammals, for such conflicts can be dangerous for aggressors and victims alike. It is often emphasized that it has been necessary to train or shape human warriors by cultural methods: glorifying their role, condemning cowardice, offering high rewards for bravery and skill on the battlefield, and emphasizing the worthiness of practicing "manly" sports during childhood (see, for example, Tinbergen 1968; Pitt 1978; Eibl-Eibesfeldt 1979b). But if the early hominid males were *inherently* disposed to find aggression attractive, particularly aggression directed against neighbors, this trait would have provided a biological basis for the cultural training of warriors. I describe in this chapter how a young male chimpanzee is often strongly attracted to intergroup encounters, even to the extent of approaching a number of potentially dangerous neighbors on his own. This characteristic is shown by young males of other nonhuman primate species.

2. In our own species cultural evolution permits *pseudospeciation* (Erikson 1966)—the transmission of individually acquired behavior from generation to generation within a particular group, leading to the customs and traditions of that group. This process is analogous to the formation of species through genetic inheritance. Pseudospeciation in humans means, among other things, that the members of one group may not only see themselves as different from members of another, but also behave in different ways to group and nongroup individuals.

In its extreme form pseudospeciation leads to the "dehumanizing" of other groups, so that they may be regarded almost as members of a different species (LeVine and Campbell 1971). This process, along with the ability to use weapons for hurting or killing *at a distance*, frees group members from the inhibitions and social sanctions that operate within the group and enables acts that would not be tolerated within the group to be directed toward "those others." As Eibl-Eibesfeldt (1979a) stresses, this lack of inhibitions is a prime factor underlying the development of destructive warfare.

Thus it is of considerable interest to find that the chimpanzees show behaviors that may be precursors to pseudospeciation in humans. First, their sense of group indentity is strong; they clearly differentiate between individuals who "belong" and those who do not. Infants and females who are part of the group are protected even if the infants were sired by males from other communities. Infants of females who do not belong may be killed. This sense of group identity is far more sophisticated than mere xenophobia. The members of the Kahama community had, before the split, enjoyed close and friendly relations with their aggressors. By separating themselves, it is as though they forfeited their "right" to be treated as group members; instead, they were treated as strangers. Second, nongroup members may not only be violently attacked, but the patterns of attack may actually differ from those utilized in typical intracommunity aggression. The victims are treated more as though they were prey animals: they are "dechimpized."

These are two further aspects of chimpanzee behavior that are of interest in relation to the evolution of behavior associated with human intergroup conflict.

1. Cannibalism, in humans, has been reported from almost all parts of the world, and evidence from paleoanthropology suggests that it dates back at least to the mid-Pleistocene. Many fossil skulls from that time on are characterized by a "careful and symmetric incising of the periphery of the foramen magnum," which on the basis of comparative evidence is assumed to have been made for the purpose of extracting the brain for eating (Blanc 1961, 131). The motives behind the eating of enemies have varied historically: a preference for the taste of human flesh; revenge: by eating an enemy he is completely destroyed; a magical belief that the victor can acquire some of his enemy's qualities of courage or strength from the flesh (Eibl-Eibesfeldt 1979b). Until comparatively recently, cannibalism was thought to be another behavior "by which human animal may be sharply distinguished from other primates" (Freeman 1964, 122). In the chimpanzee, we have seen that cannibalism may follow intergroup conflict with neighboring females. The bizarre behavior directed at the corpse by some adult males could well, with a little more intellectual sophistication, evolve into ritual.

2. Warfare, in humans, almost always leads to acts of great cruelty (by no means, of course, confined to warfare). Freeman (1964, 121), writes that "the extreme nature of human destructiveness and cruelty is one of the principal

characteristics which marks off man, behaviorally, from other animals." Implicit in the Oxford dictionary definition of cruelty as "delight in or indifference to another's pain" is a certain level of cognitive sophistication. In order to be cruel, one must have the capability (1) to understand that, for example, the detaching of an arm from a living creature will cause pain and (2) to empathize with the victim. It is because we humans unquestionably have these abilities that we are able to be cruel. Both human and chimpanzee children may mutilate insects or small animals; human children, at least in most Western cultures, are taught that this is cruel. If a group of humans behaved in the same way as the gangs of Kasakela males when they attacked their Kahama victims, the behavior would be described as cruel; so would the slow killing of large prey animals. Of course, chimpanzees are intellectually incapable of creating the horrifying tortures that human ingenuity has devised for the deliberate infliction of suffering. Nevertheless, they are capable to some extent of imputing desires and feelings to others (Woodruff and Premack 1979), and they are almost certainly capable of feelings akin to sympathy. The Premacks' Sarah consistently chose photographs of her "enemy" strewn with cement blocks, suggesting that she may possess some precursor of sadism. On the other hand, her motivation may have been nothing more than mischief making.

"War among primitives," writes Eibl-Eibesfeldt (1979c, 171), "is often limited to raids in which they stalk or creep up to the enemy, using tactics reminiscent of hunting." However "primitive," raids of this sort are the result of careful planning; and if the enemies somehow find out about these plans, they will counter with a plan of their own. This, of course, is the major difference between primitive warfare and the stealthy, cooperative raids of the Kasakela males into Kahama territory, which sometimes culminated in brutal assault. While fully admitting the major role that warfare has probably played in shaping our uniquely human brain, I submit that until our remote ancestors acquired language, they would not have been able to engage in the kind of planned intergroup conflicts that could develop into warfare—into organized, armed conflict.

The chimpanzee, as a result of a unique combination of strong affiliative bonds between adult males on the one hand and an unusually hostile and violently aggressive attitude toward nongroup individuals on the other, has clearly reached a stage where he stands at the very threshold of human achievement in destruction, cruelty, and planned intergroup conflict.

# 6

## Sex Differences in the Formation of Coalitions among Chimpanzees

Frans B. M. de Waal

### INTRODUCTION

Chimpanzees have a strong tendency to interfere with aggressive interactions among others. If they do so by supporting one of the two conflicting parties we speak of a coalition. In an observational study of five years on a zoo colony of twenty-three chimpanzees my students and I have recorded several thousand instances of coalition formation.

Coalitions often create extremely tense situations because of the inevitable ambivalence between competition and cooperation. Before two individuals are able to jointly outcompete a third one they have to overcome their own antagonistic tendencies, and they rarely seem to solve this problem completely. Study of these tense interactions is important for two reasons. The first is because of the growing interest in animal mental abilities. Coalitions may exist over a long time, being used day in and day out in a variety of competitive contexts. To establish such a supportive relationship with a particular partner is making a choice, the consequences of which are not all necessarily visible in the short run. The study of these choices may provide insight into the role of

I am indebted to the students who helped to collect data, to Dr. J. van Hooff for encouragement and discussion, and to Dr. R. Weigel for comments on the manuscript. I also thank the directorate of the Arnhem Zoo for offering the opportunity to observe the colony. Finally, I am grateful to Mary Schatz for typing the manuscript, and to Janet Ballweg and Linda Endlich for the drafting of illustrations.

The study was financially supported by the Research Pool of the University of Utrecht (1975–79) and the Dutch Organization for the Advancement of Pure Research, Z.W.O. (1979–81). Writing of the manuscript was supported by NIH grant RR-00167 to the Wisconsin Regional Primate Research Center. Reprinted by permission of the publisher from "Sex Differences in the Formation of Coalitions among Chimpanzees" by Frans B. M. de Waal, *Ethology and Sociobiology* vol. 5, pp. 239–68. Copyright 1984 by Elsevier Science Publishing Co., Inc.

experience, calculation, and planning in the spontaneous social behavior of animals. Second, the study focus is important because the capacity to form effective coalitions may contribute to an individual's reproductive success either through an increase in inclusive fitness or through beneficial "transactions" with nonkin. The relative importance of kin selection and reciprocal altruism in the evolution of the behavior is still hardly understood (see Packer and Pusey [1982] for similar problems concerning coalitions among lions). Thus the study of coalition formation unites two main issues of the modern approach to animal social behavior: the role of cognition and the evolution of apparent altruism.

The present analysis concentrates on some remarkable differences between the sexes. Globally, the interpretation of the data is that coalitions of adult male chimpanzees are part of dominance strategies, whereas those of females serve to protect friends and relatives. The first indications of this difference were provided by de Waal (1978). The much larger amount of data and some new analytical techniques developed in this study confirm and refine the distinction. Since this is a stepwise analysis with logical connections between the different parts, each presentation of results will be preceded by an introduction or followed by a brief conclusion to prepare the reader for the next step.

The complicated pattern of dominance reversals and related changes in collaboration and social isolation within our colony has recently been described for a general public (de Waal 1982). The present publication may be regarded as a quantitative supplement to that book. The reader is referred elsewhere for a more extensive description of the methods (de Waal 1978; de Waal and van Hooff 1981).

## METHODS

### The Group

During this study the chimpanzee colony of Arnhem Zoo (Netherlands) was composed of four adult males, nine adult females, four adolescent females, six juveniles and infants ranging between two and five years of age (five males, one female), and some younger infants not considered here. The animals lived on an island of nearly one hectare. During the winters, from the end of November until mid-April, the group lived indoors in a large heated hall. If not stated otherwise, the data presented stem from outdoor periods, that is, the summers of 1976 through 1979 and the first half of the summer of 1980.

Due to the chimpanzee's slow maturation there existed few kinship relationships in this group, which was founded in 1971. The only kinship ties were those of the six juveniles and infants with their four mothers, and two juvenile sibling relationships. The older group members, coming from different European zoos,

**Table 6-1.** Name, sex, estimated age by the end of the study (1980), and zoo of origin of seventeen adult and adolescent group members[a]

| Name | Sex | Est. Age | Origin | Rank | Offspring |
|------|-----|----------|--------|------|-----------|
| Yeroen | M | >25 | Copenhagen | Alpha 1973–76 | |
| Luit | M | >25 | Copenhagen | Alpha 1976–77 | |
| Nikkie | M | 17 | Ice Revue | Alpha 1978– | |
| Dandy | M | 15 | Arnhem | | |
| Mama | F | >25 | Leipzig | Class I | 1 |
| Gorilla | F | >25 | Leipzig | Class II | 1 |
| Puist | F | >25 | Paris | Class II | |
| Franje[b] | F | >25 | Leipzig | Class III | 1 |
| Jimmie | F | >20 | Arnhem | Class III | 2 |
| Tepel | F | >20 | Frankfurt | Class III | 3 |
| Krom | F | 20 | Arnhem | Class IV | |
| Spin | F | 20 | Czechoslovakia | Class IV | |
| Bruin[c] | F | (16) | Emmen | Class IV | |
| Amber | F | 11 | Animal dealer | Class V | |
| Oor | F | 10 | Animal dealer | Class V | |
| Zwart | F | 9 | Animal dealer | Class V | |
| Henny | F | 8 | Animal dealer | Class V | |

[a]All individuals are presumably feral born. For males the period of alpha rank has been indicated; for females the rank class (five classes) and number of own or adopted offspring living with them during the study period.
[b]Died in 1979.
[c]Died in 1977.

were almost certainly unrelated. Table 6-1 provides details on the group composition. Rank has been determined by the direction of submissive greeting behavior, or "rapid ohoh" (Noë et al. 1980). Females did not show a clear-cut rank order, but could be divided into rank classes. Between these classes the relationships were better defined than within them. This female class-order was extremely stable. For further description of the colony and an indication of the personality differences between the individuals, see de Waal (1982).

*Observations*

Together with a changing team of doctoral students of about four per year the author recorded agonistic interventions. All instances observed were noted down in special lists in the tripartite form: C supports A against B. This routine was followed by all observers present at any time, regardless of whether they worked on their own project or ate their lunch while witnessing an intervention. In this way we were able to collect about five instances per observation day, giving a total of 4834 for the five years, of which 2983 occurred during outdoor periods.

We followed a very strict definition of a supportive intervention, described by de Waal (1978), requiring the occurrence of particular agonistic behavior patterns (e.g., screaming, full-speed chasing) and an interval of less than thirty seconds between the initial agonistic dyad and intervention by a third individual.

In addition, a standardized observation procedure was followed during all these years for an average of three hours per week, giving a total of 334 hours for the five summers. During one hour two simultaneous observers with tape recorders scored all instances of aggressive, submissive, and sexual interaction. They also took five-minute time samples on "state" behaviors, such as grooming, proximity, and play.

RESULTS

*Direction of Interventions*

*Introduction.* We may distinguish between "intervention directions" and "support choices" (de Waal 1978, 274). The first term refers to the initial agonistic dyad at which the intervention is aimed, regardless of which individual receives support. The second term refers to the side actually taken by the intervener. Obviously, coalition studies usually restrict themselves to the latter aspect, that is, the relationship between the intervener and the party receiving support. This means reduction of a triad to a dyad, however. The following analysis tries to do some justice to the triadic aspect by investigating intervention directions between age and sex classes. This is done by means of a comparison of the total observed number of interventions in particular conflicts with the frequency of these conflicts, as recorded with the standard procedure.

*Analysis.* We can distinguish four classes of group members: adult males, adult females, adolescent females, and juveniles or infants (which are called juveniles from now on). This means that there are ten different class combinations in which agonistic interaction can occur. We recorded 2508 agonistic interactions, or conflicts, during the same summer periods as those from which the intervention data will be used. The distribution of conflicts over the ten class combinations is known, and, according to a null hypothesis of random intervention, it is to be expected that the number of interventions in a particular category of conflicts is proportional to the relative conflict frequency. For example, from adult female Puist we recorded 221 interventions, of which 10.4 percent were aimed at female–female conflicts. Our matrix with conflict frequencies shows that conflicts among females constitute only 2.4 percent of the total (that is, if we exclude all conflicts involving Puist herself from the matrix). The difference between the two percentages indicates that Puist had a relatively high tendency to intervene in conflicts among other adult females.

This example shows how we can calculate for each individual the expected number of interventions in the ten possible directions. Then we sum these

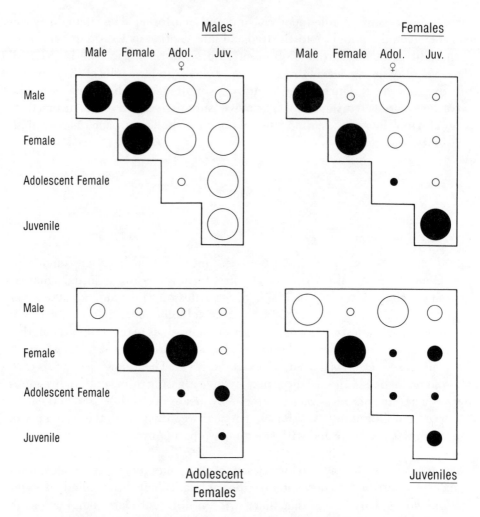

Figure 6-1. Data for males as intervenors are presented in the upper left diagram, females upper right, adolescent females lower left, and juveniles lower right. For each of these four classes the ten possible intervention directions are presented as a matrix. A black dot in the matrix represents a high tendency to intervene in a particular category of conflicts (e.g., females often intervene in conflicts among juveniles) and open circles represent a relatively low tendency. For further explanation see text.

expected frequencies *(e)* for the individuals of each age and sex class and compare them with the observed frequencies *(o)* for their class, expressing the difference as a standardized residual, s.r. $= (o-e)/\sqrt{e}$ (Everitt 1977). Figure 6-1shows the results, with black dots for positive s.r. values and open circles for negative ones. The biggest dots represent s.r. values of 4 or more ($p<0.0001$), the medium sized dots are for values between 2 and 4 ($p<0.05$), and the smallest dots reflect nonsignificant differences between *o* and *e*. Pooling of data per class was done after individual trends were found to be generally similar within the classes.

When interpreting these results we have to bear in mind one important restriction: the underlying assumption here is that the sample of interventions is about as representative as the independently and much more systematically collected (two observers, fixed observation schedule) data on agonistic interactions. This assumption is debatable, because the ad lib sample of interventions may be biased toward relatively conspicuous interaction types (J. Altmann 1974). Yet at least some of the results cannot easily be ascribed to this possible bias. The noisiest and longest lasting conflicts are those among adult males, whereas the least noticeable conflicts are those among juveniles, but these two extremes do not receive respectively high and low numbers of interventions from all classes. Some classes show highly significant tendencies to the contrary.

*Conclusion.* Figure 6-1 shows that each age and sex class has its own field of interference in the group. Males restrict their interventions mainly to conflicts among adult group members. Females mainly intervene between members of the same class, thus differing from the males by their frequent interventions in

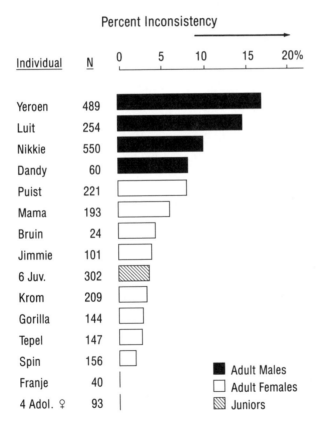

Figure 6-2. The number of inconsistent support choices expressed as a percentage of the total number of choices (*n*) per individual.

conflicts among juveniles and their lower tendency to intervene in male–female conflicts. Their high involvement in male–male encounters is in line with the picture sketched in de Waal (1982) of considerable female influence on the male hierarchy in our colony. The younger group members, on the other hand, seem to avoid agonistic interactions involving adult males. All this is relative, however; that is, small infants of two years of age have been seen to support one adult male against another by grabbing and biting his opponent, but usually they stay away from such interactions or are quickly picked up and carried away from the scene by their mother.

The four age and sex classes have one point in common: they all have a relatively high tendency to intervene in conflicts among adult females. This result corresponds with our impression that female conflicts, which are relatively rare, very easily escalate into major group incidents.

### Inconsistencies

*Analysis.* If an individual A intervenes ten times in conflicts between B and C, supporting B eight times and C two times, the latter two support choices are called "inconsistencies." If the ratio had been 5:5 we would speak of five inconsistencies. The parameter used in Figure 6-2 is the sum of an individual's inconsistencies in all its intervention directions expressed as a percentage of the total number of interventions $(n)$ by this individual. The data have been lumped for the six juveniles and the four adolescent females.

It should be noted that the percentage of inconsistency is not completely independent from $n$. Individuals who show few interventions will have many directions with 1:0 ratios. Therefore, I have done another analysis comparing observed inconsistency frequencies with those expected on the basis of random support choices. The results of this much more elaborate statistical procedure were essentially the same as those of the straightforward analysis presented in Figure 6-2.

*Conclusion.* The adult males show less consistent support-choices than the females and juniors (Mann-Whitney $U$ test comparing four males and nine females, $U = 0$, $p < 0.01$, two-tailed). The inconsistency is especially high for the oldest two males, that is, Yeroen and Luit. This result should not be taken to mean that adult males are simply less predictable. Inspection of the data shows that their support choices are fairly consistent per period, but not over the whole series of five summers taken together here. This means that males, rather than changing their support preferences from one incident to the next, change some of them slowly but radically over time. These changes are much like dominance reversals; that is, the pattern is well established for a certain length of time, then gradually becomes less predictable until a new consistent pattern is established. A good example is Luit's support reversal from pro to contra Nikkie, for which the data have been presented by de Waal (1978, table 8).

In the course of the years we have observed many volte-faces in the coalitions of adult males. It seems more appropriate, therefore, to call male coalitions flexible than inconsistent. Also, adult females have shown support reversals, but in fewer intervention directions. It is noteworthy that most reversals by females concerned their coalitions with adult males. Of the fifty-six statistically significant reversals in the support attitude of one individual towards another, more than 80 percent concerned relationships involving adult males.

*Influence of Social Bonds*

There are two possible mechanisms underlying the male flexibility demonstrated above: (1) coalitions are part of social bonds and male bonds are unstable,

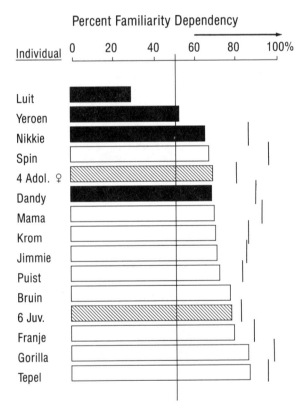

Figure 6-3. The proportion of support choices in favor of the more familiar party per individual. If familiarity had no effect on intervention behavior the expectation would be 50 percent. The small black lines give the results of a more "severe" analysis (see text).

or (2) their bonds are not unstable, but coalitions do not depend on them. The question here then is to what extent interventions depend on social bonds.

*Analysis 1.*   In this study, social bonds were defined in terms of the percentage of time samples two individuals spent in proximity (i.e., within arm's reach) or contact (including grooming) with each other. This percentage is called the familiarity index. The degree to which support choices correspond with familiarity is assessed in the way developed by de Waal (1978): if individual A supports B against C and has a higher familiarity index with B than with C the intervention is said to be in line with A's familiarity relationships. If we assume random support choice, independent from familiarity, we expect 50 percent of the interventions to be that way. To test this, the intervention data of each summer are compared with the familiarity indices for the same period, and then the outcomes per individual are summed over the five summers. This procedure means that there is a correction for changes in familiarity relationships over the years. The resulting parameter, expressing the number of familiarity-linked interventions as a percentage of the total number of an individual's interventions, is called familiarity dependency.

The support choices of twenty-two of the twenty-three individuals score over the 50 percent mark. Figure 6-3 gives the results, again lumping the data for the two younger age classes. The two oldest males, Yeroen and Luit, have the lowest familiarity-dependency scores. Luit's behavior is very strange, because he often intervenes against his most familiar partners; that is, he scores far below 50 percent. The two young adult males, Nikkie and Dandy, fall within the range of the other group members, but are positioned at the lower end of the scale. According to a Mann-Whitney $U$ test the four males scored significantly different from the nine females: $U = 1$, $p < 0.01$, two-tailed.

*Analysis 2.*   A possible objection against the previous analysis is that it measures responses to sometimes minor differences in familiarity. Perhaps adult males have less pronounced social bonds but do support the few closely bonded partners they have. In this second analysis, therefore, a much more severe criterion for the difference in familiarity is used.

The analysis is restricted to interventions between parties, of which (1) the familiarity indices with the intervener differ with a factor of at least 2, and (2) the party with the higher index has in addition been groomed more often by the intervener. The number of interventions that could be considered is necessarily lower in its analysis, and adult female Bruin has been dropped from analysis because of lack of data, as she died in the second year of the study.

The vertical black lines in figure 6-3 show the results. As could be expected the link between interventions and familiarity is stronger with the more severe criterion, with three adult females even scoring over 95 percent. However, most importantly, for the two oldest males there is no difference from the previous results.

*Conclusion.* The results indicate that for the two oldest adult males there is a disconnection between familiarity relationships and intervention behavior. My interpretation is that their coalitions, instead of being linked to social bonds, are part of strategies aimed at status improvement. These males are opportunistic. There is no room for sympathy or antipathy in their strategies. Perhaps the more mature a male, the greater his capacity for distancing himself from his social preferences when dealing with intragroup conflicts.

It should be noted that Luit's remarkably low score on the familiarity-dependency scale (Fig. 6-3) is presumably related to interventions that led to his being separated from others. Every time Luit sat with Yeroen or with the alpha female, Mama, the new leader, Nikkie, would display until the contact was broken off. This reduced Luit's familiarity indices with these two group members, whom he usually supported in conflicts. In other words, Luit's interventions were perhaps not so much against his social preferences, but the affiliative expression of some of his preferences was obstructed during the years of rivalry between Nikkie and himself. A result in line with this explanation is that Luit's highest familiarity-dependency score of unstable periods occurred during the winter of Nikkie's absence (see next analysis, fig. 6-4).

Finally, fortunately we can base at least one clear and testable prediction on the strategical interpretation given above. If the lack of correlation between male coalitions and social bonds has anything to do with dominance struggles, we would predict the disparity to be most pronounced during periods of hierarchical instability.

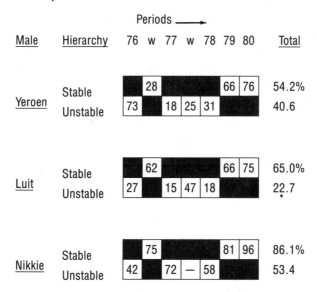

Figure 6-4. Seven periods are categorized as either stable or unstable. The figures within the boxes give a male's percentage of familiarity dependent support for each period. On the right one finds the percentage for the combined stable and unstable periods, respectively.

*Male Coalitions and Hierarchical Instability*

*Analysis.*   This analysis will be restricted to the three big adult males, because the youngest male, Dandy, did not perform enough interventions and was not involved in dominance reversals. The five years have been divided into seven periods, two of which are winter periods spent indoors. Subsequent winters could not be included because we did not collect data on familiarity relationships during these periods.

Each period was designated as either stable or unstable. Stability means (1) that one male, the alpha male, receives submissive greeting behavior from both other adult males, and (2) that these males greet him more frequently than they undertake actions against him (i.e., initiate agonistic interactions or perform bluff displays directed at the alpha male). Periods in which these requirements were not fulfilled are called unstable. During the second winter (1977–78) the new alpha male, Nikkie, was temporarily removed from the group. This caused a high frequency of conflicts and bluff displays between the remaining two males. This period was therefore categorized as unstable.

The sequence of dominance reversals has been described in detail elsewhere (de Waal 1982). Yeroen lost his top position during the summer of 1976. Luit became alpha male, while Nikkie, his coalition partner, reached dominance over the adult females and Yeroen. During the summer of 1977 Nikkie and Yeroen formed a coalition against Luit, and Nikkie acquired the alpha position at the end of that period. After his removal during the winter Nikkie was returned to the group in the spring of 1978. Although he quickly became dominant over Luit again, Yeroen did not submit to Nikkie and initiated many actions against him until the middle of summer 1978.

For the adult males taken together there were nine stable and eleven unstable periods (fig. 6-4). Comparison between these two sets of periods shows a significant difference in the familiarity-dependency of interventions (Mann-Whitney *U* test, $U = 12$, $p<0.01$, one-tailed). This trend was representative for all three individuals. Figure 6-4 shows that for both Nikkie and Luit the highest percentages reached occurred during stable periods. Yeroen showed two exceptions to the pattern (a high percentage during the period in which he defended and lost his alpha position and a low percentage during the next winter in which Luit was leader), but his overall trend was the same as that of the other two males.

*Conclusion.*   The males showed the predicted pattern. I regard this as strong support for the idea that our adult males use coalitions as an instrument to improve or defend status and give coalitions, during those periods, priority over their social bonds.

It is entirely possible, even likely, that females are also capable of using coalitions as status instruments. Great stability in the female rank-order, however, precludes a similar analysis of their coalitions. It might be argued that it is precisely this difference in hierarchical stability which is responsible for the observed sex differences in intervention behavior. Yet the opposite causal connection is equally plausible: namely, the dynamic nature of the male hierarchy may be a product of their opportunistic mechanisms of coalition formation, whereas the female pattern of familiarity-linked support may have a stabilizing effect on their dominance relationships.

Long-term field studies on chimpanzees have reported on lasting reversals in the male but not in the female hierarchy (Goodall 1971; Riss and Goodall 1977; Nishida 1979, 1983). The principal factors involved in upsetting the status quo among males seem to be the joining of the adult cluster by maturing young males and the formation of new coalitions between pairs of males. Also in the Arnhem colony destabilization of the hierarchy followed the final growth spurt of a young adult male, Nikkie. After conclusion of the present study, maturation of the second adolescent male, Dandy, had similar far-reaching effects (Otto Adang pers. comm.). In contrast, the four adolescent females reaching adulthood in Arnhem have not in the least disturbed the female hierarchy.

This striking sex difference in impact of young individuals upon the adult structure suggests that there might be greater room for maneuvering within the male structure, where ambitions seem constantly alive and where, as shown above, the connection between coalitions and social bonds can be temporarily loosened.

*Winner Support, Loser Support, and Control Role*

*Introduction.*   One obvious distinction in intervention behavior is between support for the aggressive party and support for the recipient of aggression. These types of intervention were labeled actor and reactor alliances by de Waal et al. (1976). The ratio between the frequencies with which the two types are performed seems highly variable. There are studies indicating that captive Java macaques and feral vervet monkeys direct their interventions mainly down the hierarchy (de Waal 1977; Cheney 1983), whereas other studies on macaques report equally high, or even much higher, frequencies of protective interventions as compared to interventions on behalf of aggressors (Massey 1977; J. Kaplan 1978; Watanabe 1979; Datta 1983). In this chimpanzee study a similar classification is used, namely that of winner and loser support. De Waal (1978) gives the definition, which is based on whether an intervention is in favor of the party that usually wins dyadic agonistic encounters or in favor of the usual loser of such relatively uninfluenced encounters.

One possible proximate function of winner support is tension reduction and bond strengthening between the parties forming the aggressive alliance. Confrontations between high-ranking group members may cause frictions, which are not always expressed in conflicts among themselves, but jointly redirected at subordinates who serve as scapegoats. In this view, based on a previous macaque study, one of the functions of winner-support may be to maintain or restore peace among high-ranking individuals (deWaal 1975; 1977). A qualitative indication that this mechanism may also operate in chimpanzees is that dominant group members regularly join in a brief alliance against a low-ranking individual just before or after their reconciliation. (Reconciliation refers to positive contact behavior between former opponents not long after their conflict; de Waal and van Roosmalen 1979.) These situations give the impression that a common enemy is temporarily "created" for the sake of peace.

Loser support serves very different functions. It may play a role in rank reversals, if a subordinate party receives systematic support against a particular dominant. Usually, however, it is used for the protection of close friends and relatives against aggression. In addition, for adult males, loser support can be part of their so-called control role.

Control activities form a very special category of protectiveness. Since their performance is usually restricted to a single high-ranking individual, these activities are often regarded as being part of a "role" pattern (e.g., Bernstein and Sharpe 1966). Elsewhere, I have argued that this control role may be an integral component of male dominance strategies (de Waal 1982). The suggestion is that males show two main types of strategies: (1) in order to *rise* in rank males form flexible coalitions with other potential social climbers, and (2) in order to *stabilize* a high rank, males break up fights and support weaker group members, who may pay back by collective support in case their protector's position should be threatened. The one is an offensive, the other a defensive strategy, and males may at times also show mixtures of the two. Both strategies involve loser support, but the last one especially does so.

This view of the control role as a male's way to secure "grassroots" support within the group is still mainly theoretical. It is based on the following observations. Yeroen played the role for several years, and received massive support when his position was challenged in summer 1976. After Yeroen's fall, the new leader, Luit, turned from a winner supporter into a loser supporter. A few months later the adult females started to support Luit instead of the old leader (for data see de Waal 1978). Nikkie became the next leader, but his coalition partner, Yeroen, aggressively prevented Nikkie from interference in female fights and thus seemed to *claim* this role for himself. From then on it was Yeroen, not the new alpha male, who received the most support from the group. All of the 110 interventions over 1978–80 by females and juniors in conflicts between Yeroen and Nikkie were in favor of Yeroen.

Interventions in interventions, reflecting competition among adult males about the "right" to break up intragroup disputes, were fairly common during periods of unstable leadership in our colony. Such competition is to be expected if fulfillment of this role would bring strategical advantages. Also in macaques the central male seems to actively inhibit control activities by other males (Watanabe 1979; personal observations on rhesus monkeys).

Two questions concern us here, both regarding the ratio between winner and loser support:

1. If winner-support reflects tensions among high-ranking group members, its frequency might be affected by the amount of space available to a group, as suggested for macaques by de Waal (1977, 276). Our chimpanzee colony spends the winters indoors in an area about one-twentieth of that of the outdoor enclosure. Is the relative frequency of winner support increased during the winter periods? Note that the question is not whether the mere frequency of this intervention type is increased, which would not be surprising in view of the general aggression increase under the crowded condition (Nieuwenhuijsen and de Waal 1982), but whether the *ratio* between winner and loser support changes.

2. Both the control role, as expressed in loser support, and the reduced influence of social bonds (see the section "Influence of Social Bonds") have been suggested here to be aspects of male dominance strategies. Are these two aspects correlated?

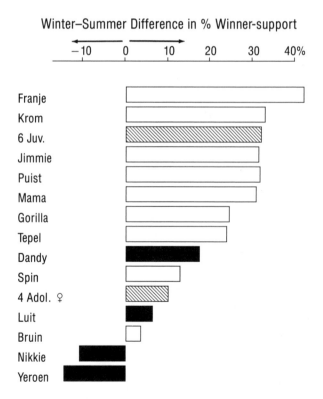

Figure 6-5. The percentage winner support during winter periods minus such percentage during summer periods, per individual.

*Analysis 1.* Each individual's intervention data was divided into that shown in summers or winters. The frequency of winner support was expressed as a percentage of all interventions by the individual, resulting in a winter and a summer percentage. The index used in Figure 6-5 is the difference between these two percentages of winner support. A positive difference means that the individual tended more to winner than to loser support during winter periods as compared with summers. Negative differences, on the other hand, reflect increased tendencies to support losers during the winter.

The data reveal that, in general, winner support is more common during winter periods. Females show this trend very clearly, but adult males do not: for two of them the trend is weaker than for most females and the other two males even show the opposite trend. In addition, females showed the same difference during both of the winters considered here, their percentages going up, down, up, and down again over the seasons. For adult males there was no such regularity. To some extent the winter–summer differences of the females showed the expected correlation with rank: that is, Krom, Spin, Bruin, and the four adolescent females rank at the bottom of the hierarchy, and all of them, except Krom, show smaller differences than the dominant females (fig. 6-5).

*Analysis 2.* For each adult male and each of the seven periods we compared the percentage of loser support to the percentage of familiarity-dependent support (as persented in fig. 6-4 for the latter). Due to lack of data, Dandy was not included in this analysis. The Spearman rank correlation coefficient over the periods were $-0.29$ (Yeroen), $-0.71$ (Luit), and $-0.49$ (Nikkie). Luit's coefficient was significant ($p<0.05$). If we rank all indices, irrespective of from which male they came, we arrive at a correlation coefficient of $-0.69$, $n = 20$, $p<0.001$. Loser support usually is of a protective nature (i.e., a defense against aggression rather than a joint challenge of a dominant). Therefore, this outcome indicates that the more protective a male is, the less his interventions correspond to his social preferences.

*Conclusion.* Winner support is shown both by adult males and females, but whereas females do so more often during crowded periods, males show no such difference. If we accept tension as the underlying mechanism, it follows that a decrease in interindividual distances has a stronger effect on female than on male tensions. This would not be surprising in view of the more dispersed way of life of feral female chimpanzees, as compared with adult males (Bygott 1974; Wrangham 1979; Nishida 1979).

This raises a theoretical point. Tension reduction among dominants as a possible major function of aggressive alliances that are directed down the hierarchy is bound to complicate current evolutionary explanations in terms of reciprocity or inclusive fitness theory. Instead of each and every supportive act being a form of "altruism," which sometimes seems an assumption underlying these analyses, many of these acts may be self-serving attempts at dyadic conflict resolution at the cost of subordinate outsiders.

Under the more natural living conditions during summers a remarkably high proportion of female interventions was of a protective nature, that is, almost 80 percent. For males this proportion was less than 50 percent but they showed enormous individual fluctuations over the years, related to their position in the male hierarchy. The above data suggest that their protectiveness was very different from that of females: loser support by males goes hand in hand with a decreased influence of social bonds. When fulfilling the role of intragroup protector males seem to place themselves *above* the conflicting parties.

Since the decreased influence of social bonds is especially marked during unstable periods (see the section "Male Coalitions and Hierarchical Instability"), loser support by males is also expected to occur more often during unstable periods. This is indeed the case. Yeroen showed his highest percentage of loser support in the period when he lost his alpha rank and in the subsequent period. Also, Luit showed his highest percentages when he lost his position and in the subsequent summer period. Maybe a male's control activities are intensified when his position becomes threatened by a rival. Partly, this may be due to the rival's behavior, because a common method of testing a leader's power seems to be to attack his protegées (de Waal 1982).

However, rather than trying to solve these problems on the basis of the present data, which at the same time gave rise to the hypotheses, we need an experimental approach to find out whether male protectiveness can indeed be regarded as a defensive dominance strategy. This possibility is of considerable theoretical importance in connection with the controversial concept of "role" in primate research (Crook and Goss-Custard 1972; Hinde 1978). If the stability of a male's status depends on the group's evaluation of his abilities as arbitrator in disputes and on his own success in keeping others from performing this type of intervention, the concept of control role would be broadened to include "norms," "expectations," and in the end even "responsibilities." Since these mechanisms presuppose influence of subordinates, especially adult females, on the outcome of male status competition, it is to be expected that the intragroup control role will be more pronounced in primate species in which subordinates are known to exert such influence than in species in which it is restricted or absent.

### Support "Forks"

*Analysis.* Having addressed the question of the degree to which coalitions depend on social bonds, the question here is to what extent coalitions depend on other coalitions. Does an individual, while intervening in a conflict, take the coalitions of the two combatants with others into account? Does he or she "generalize" in the sense that support to A implies support to A's coalition partners as well? If chimpanzees would do so their group life would be divided into camps, that is, subunits of supporters. If not, each individual should select its coalition partners independent from what others do.

One approach to this problem is a "fork" analysis. We first determine which individuals have formed coalitions. This is done on the basis of their support scores. The calculation of this score is explained by de Waal (1978, 278–79). The support score of an individual A toward B is defined as the number of different group members against which A usually supported B minus the number of different group members which A usually supported against B. In a group of 23 individuals support scores can range between $+21$ and $-21$.

If two individuals, measured over the whole period (including winter data), both have positive scores toward each other they are called *mutual friends*, and if they both have negative scores, *mutual enemies*. In this analysis these are the "original relationships." For simplicity, non–mutually supportive relationships are not considered here. Also, original relationships involving juveniles are excluded because the strongest mutual supporters in this category are mother–offspring and sibling relationships. By excluding these the results may indicate the existence of camps other than the obvious kinship camps. We are considering here twenty-five mutual friend and thirty-eight mutual enemy relationships.

The next step is to determine each individual's (including juveniles) support scores toward the two partners in an original relationship. These are the "forks" illustrated in figure 6-6. There are six possibilities. In symmetrical forks an individual shows positive support scores toward both partners or negative scores toward both. If an individual usually supports one of the two but shows a negative score toward the other, we speak of a nonsymmetrical fork. In some directions the support score was 0, and these incomplete forks are not considered here. The 869 support forks were comprised of 745 positive and 993 negative support scores, making the chance to find symmetrical forks under the assumption of randomness equal to 51.0 percent. The percentage of symmetrical forks observed was 49.2 percent. This means that there is no general tendency to form either symmetrical or nonsymmetrical forks, the chances being 50–50, as expected.

The question underlying this analysis is whether support forks depend on the nature of the original relationship. One might expect that coalition partners, that is, mutual friends, are treated on the same basis, resulting in a relatively high number of symmetrical forks. Similarly, one might expect that support attitudes toward mutual enemies often differ from each other, resulting in a relatively high number of nonsymmetrical forks. In fact, the latter situation is well known from international politics: "My enemy's enemy is my friend."

When doing the analysis for the group as a whole the results fit the above expectations, but the differences are not striking. This is due to forks toward

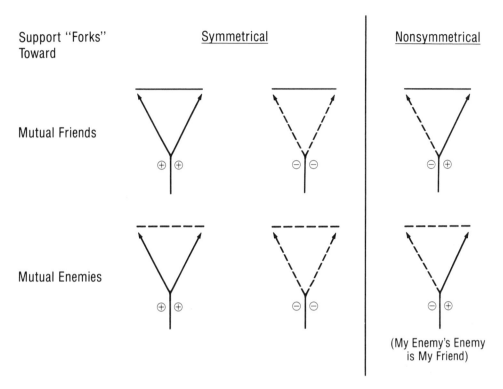

Figure 6-6. Illustration of support "forks." Horizontal bars represent the original supportive relationships, which can be mutually positive (solid bars) or mutually negative (dotted bars). The support "forks" are formed by third individuals and can be either symmetrical ($+$ $+$ and $-$ $-$) or nonsymmetrical ($+$ $-$).

original relationships involving one or two adult males. Figure 6-7 shows that there is no significant difference in symmetry toward mutual friends or enemies for these 399 forks. The remaining 470 forks toward original relationships involving only adult and adolescent females show the expected pattern very clearly, however ($\chi^2\sqrt{}$ = 17.2, $p<0.001$).

An additional analysis showed that, as far as forks toward female relationships are concerned, the 50 percent symmetry limit is exceeded by significantly more individuals toward mutual friends than toward mutual enemies. This means that the difference in the lower half of figure 6-7 is representative for the large majority of individuals. As far as forks toward male relationships are concerned, a nonsignificant opposite trend was found in the individual data. Also, the adult males themselves failed to show significant differences in their forks toward the relationships of other males.

*Conclusion.* The interpretation of these results is that an individual's support attitude toward a particular female depends partly on her position in the female

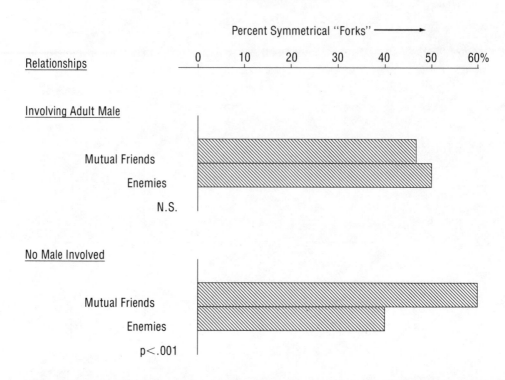

Figure 6-7. The number of symmetrical support "forks" as a percentage of all "forks" toward either mutual friends or mutual enemies. Original relationships involving one or two adult males are presented separately from those without a male, that is, those among adult and adolescent females.

coalition network. It matters who her supporters and enemies are. Since this network strongly overlaps with female social bonds (see the section "Influence of Social Bonds"), this means that females are treated on the basis of the subgroup in the community to which they belong. Further inspection of the data indicates that this attitude is also shown toward juveniles, which belong to the mother's subgroup.

Adult males, in contrast, are treated on an individual basis. Group members may fervently support a particular male and at the same time have a negative attitude toward his closest ally. Also, support to females is independent of the female's coalitions with males. It seems that the adult males in our colony do not belong to any of the existing camps and are treated as individual strategists.

DISCUSSION

Table 6-2 provides a summary of the sex differences in coalition formation. The bottom line of the table summarizes the functional interpretation of the differ-

**Table 6-2.** Summary of sex differences in coalition behavior observed in the Arnhem colony

| *Adult Males Are* | *Females and Juniors Are* |
| --- | --- |
| 1. Flexible | 1. Stable |
| 2. Less influenced by social bonds (especially when their ranks are changing) | 2. Strongly influenced by social bonds |
| 3. Treated on an individual basis | 3. Treated on the basis of their connections |
| Vertical, Strategists | Horizontal, Protectors |

ences as given throughout the present paper and by de Waal (1978). Adult males give the impression of living in a vertical world of hierarchical positions and related dominance strategies. It appears that their coalitions are not linked to particular individuals but, rather, to particular social goals. Adult females, on the other hand, live in a horizontal world of social connections. Their coalitions are more or less permanently linked to particular individuals, whose well-being is their goal.

Whereas few objections will be raised against the supposed female strategy, the supposed male strategy may not be readily accepted. It might be argued that my interpretations are acceptable only after it is proven that males purposefully strive for status. I realize that it is nearly impossible to prove this beyond any doubt. But is it necessary? Although many students of animal behavior are now turning their attention from one mechanistic animal model (the "black box") to the next (the "survival machine"), there remains room for a *proximate* approach to social behavior that simply *assumes* that subjective states, rationality, and purposefulness are not restricted to our own species. Fortunately, the taboos surrounding this topic have now lost most of their power (e.g., *The Behavioral and Brain Sciences*, vol. 4, 1981; Griffin 1982). Obviously, the shortcomings of mechanistic models are felt more strongly in behavioral studies on chimpanzees than on species that are more distantly related to us. On the other hand, there is no reason to treat the chimpanzee as a unique case (Beck 1982; Fox 1982; de Waal and Yoshihara 1983). The new perspective may be fruitfully applied to a wide variety of animal species.

The way male coalitions, and their flexibility, are related to dominance struggles is clear from the detailed account of the group processes, given by de Waal (1982). By regarding male coalitions as part of political maneuvers with a certain cognitive component it is possible to make sense of what one sees. There is no alternative, simpler point of view from which to draw equally plausible connections between the observed phenomena. For example, the numerous separating interventions by the alpha male, preventing contact between his coalition partner and his main rival, fit easily in the same strategic explanation as used here for coalition behavior. These separating interventions, however, would presumably demand an entirely separate hypothesis if one were not to accept the assumption of calculation and status-striving.

When ascribing the many striking differences between male and female coalitions to a single difference in proximate social goals, one automatically raises the question whether these goals are congruent with plausible ultimate goals. In other words, how might the sex differences have evolved?

Kinship does not yet play an important role in our chimpanzee colony. It is conceivable though, that the proximate mechanisms demonstrated here for females and junior group members have evolved by kin selection, because familiarity and matrilineal relatedness usually correlate. Stable, protective coalitions with closely associated individuals may in the natural habitat benefit a female's relatives. In addition, females may increase offspring survival probabilities by reducing agonistic tensions and maintaining group integrity. As yet there are no indications that females play an important role in the power politics of wild chimpanzee communities, but in the Arnhem colony we observed stabilizing female strategies, such as massive support for alpha males whose position was challenged and "mediation" during reconciliations following intermale conflicts (de Waal 1982).

Dominance status presumably is not an important factor for the survival and reproduction of female chimpanzees, due to their dispersed foraging habits (Wrangham 1979). Both in the natural habitat and under the more confined conditions in Arnhem Zoo females appear to lack the clearly defined dominance relationships and assertiveness that are so characteristic of male chimpanzees (Bygott 1974; Nishida 1979; de Waal 1982). For males the road to reproductive success is different. The primary aim of their coalition strategy seems high status and, once this has been achieved, maintenance of that status, together with protection of lower-ranking individuals. There is some evidence that high-ranking male chimpanzees copulate more frequently than low-ranking ones, both in the wild (Nishida 1979) and in the Arnhem colony (de Waal 1982). We do not know to what extent mating frequency correlates with reproduction, but it is at least likely that males who do *not* play this game have to follow other, perhaps more difficult, strategies in order to reproduce.

Whereas the evolution of the female intervention strategy is mainly regarded here in terms of kin selection and generalized reciprocity, the male strategy must be based, at least partly, on balanced reciprocity, which depends less on kinship and social bonds (see de Waal [1978] for a discussion of these two forms of reciprocity, derived from Sahlins [1965]). It should be repeated, though, that our males did show familiarity-linked support during stable periods. And among freeliving males one coalition between known siblings has been observed (Riss and Goodall 1977). We do not know whether coalitions between brothers are the rule or the exception in the natural habitat, but if it were the rule there might remain a strong transactional element in these associations. Riss and Goodall's (1977) account does not convey the impression that Figan's power takeover was the product of automatic "brotherly" collaboration. After Figan had actively challenged and subdued his elder brother, Faben, who had lost the use of one arm, years had followed without a close relationship between the two brothers, during which period "Faben was still uncommitted in his support to Figan" (140). Only a few months before the most important confrontation between Figan and his rival, Evered, a closed coalition formed, and the two brothers became inseparable. The tightening of their bond may have occurred in anticipation of the dominance struggle.

To explain the collaboration between these two males on the basis of kinship alone seems a simplification. It is more reasonable to assume that male chimpanzees take many different factors into account before reaching full establishment of a coalition with another male. Familiarity and kinship may be one factor, but if the chances to win and the possible payoffs are expected to be considerably greater in a coalition with a less familiar partner, feral males may, just like the males in Arnhem, ignore existing social bonds and try out some new combinations. See Wasser (1982) for a theoretical discussion of the relevance of "associate quality."

Recently, Nishida (1983) described a process of coalition formation among three apparently unrelated feral male chimpanzees. One male, named Kamemanfu, showed a pattern similar to that described for Yeroen following his drop in rank (de Waal 1982, 175–76). Kamemanfu manipulated the relationship between two dominant males, making them dependent upon himself by regularly changing sides in their disputes, especially in periods of sexual rivalry. Like Yeroen, Kamemanfu seemed to increase his mating success in this way. Nishida (1983) speaks of "allegiance fickleness" and suggests that this strategy may be especially pronounced in postprime males. The two independent observations of this kind of social manipulation illustrate the degree to which coalition patterns of adult male chimpanzees can be flexible and opportunistic.

The generality of the sex differences reported here is difficult to estimate. Constant and intensive observation over many years cannot alter the fact that the present comparison concerns only four male and nine female chimpanzees kept under special conditions. And in spite of a fair number of studies on coalition formation, comparable information on social dynamics is still scarce for other primates (but see, e.g., Chance et al. [1977] and Dunbar [1975] for indications of a similar degree of complexity during dominance reversals or harem takeovers among monkeys). In fact, the only comparable data come from investigations of our own species. A remarkably similar sex difference has been found by social psychologists in experimental games that test human coalition behavior. According to Bond and Vinacke (1961) men are "exploitative" and women are "accommodative" in their alliance strategies. In another study, Nacci and Tedeschi (1976) found that men, when predicting coalitions, are more sensitive to the power distribution in the game, whereas women predict coalitions mainly on the basis of interpersonal attraction. Other experimental

**Table 6-3.** Hypothesis of Hominoid Sex Differences in Coalition Strategies, Based on Observation of the Arnhem Chimpanzee Colony and Experiments on Human Subjects Living in Western Cultures

|  | *Males* | *Females* |
|---|---|---|
| Chimpanzees | *Vertical, Strategists* <br> Interventions seem to serve dominance positions | *Horizontal, Protectors* <br> Interventions seem to serve the well being of friends and relatives |
| Humans | *Exploitative* <br> Want to win and form beneficial coalitions | *Accommodative* <br> Want a pleasant game and support persons they like |

studies confirm that men and women show different modes of cooperation (van de Sande [1973] gives a review). Here again generalizability is a problem, however, because all studies so far concern human subjects living in Western cultures. It may be too early for conclusions, but we can at least speak of a plausible hypothesis of coalition formation in human and nonhuman primates. Table 6-3 summarizes the comparison.

Generally, the social psychological literature does not pay too much attention to the above-mentioned sex differences. Their models explain typical male coalition patterns only, assuming that players are rational in that they attempt to maximize their outcomes (see Murnighan [1978] for a review). This is not to say, however, that the cause of the sex difference is that women are incapable of calculating winning moves. Winning may simply not always be their highest priority. Also in the case of chimpanzees, priority differences may explain most of the discussed sex differences. In other words, both sexes may have the same mental abilities and social tactics available but do not use them in the same way because the kind of outcomes they try to achieve are different. This might mean that the resemblance between human and chimpanzee coalition patterns is due to similar social goals in the lives of women and female chimpanzees, on the one hand, and in the lives of men and male chimpanzees, on the other. If so, the two species would share a personality difference between the sexes that is very profound indeed.

# PART III

*Humans*

# Introduction
## Human Politics

### Roger D. Masters

Throughout the social sciences there is a division between descriptive or holistic approaches in the tradition of sociology or history, and formal or deductive models like those in economics or game theory (Mills 1959; Barry 1970). Similarly, two characteristically different methodologies have played an essential role in the study of animal behavior over the last decade: while some scientists excel at observation and description, working in a tradition that has developed from "natural history," others prefer to formulate and test theoretical models or hypotheses, using cost-benefit approaches derived from economics to analyze strategies for optimizing reproductive success. The first of these perspectives has dominated classical "ethology" (Lorenz 1966; Hinde 1982; chap. 5), whereas the second is epitomized by research in "sociobiology" (Hamilton 1964; Wilson 1975; Maynard-Smith 1978).

It would, of course, be an error to exaggerate these methodological differences. Ethologists often perform experiments or quasi experiments and undertake careful statistical analysis of observational data (e.g., chapter 6; Lorenz 1970–71; Hinde 1982), whereas sociobiologists use field observations to test predictions derived from calculations of inclusive fitness (Barash 1982); in recent approaches to behavioral ecology, the two approaches are often effectively integrated (Dunbar 1988). It is nonetheless convenient to distinguish between descriptive or empirical studies which begin from observed phenomena, and research which originates in the formulation of cost-benefit models: in the latter case, hypotheses are deduced from general theoretical principles in order to predict responses to ecological or social situations, whereas the former or more inductive approach seeks to explain how each species' behavioral repertoire functions in observed social interactions.

163

As we turn to the study of *Homo sapiens*, each of these methods sheds valuable light on the foundations of politics. On the theoretical level, deductive cost-benefit models can lead to a reconsideration of such basic concepts as social cooperation, competition, and selfishness. Under what circumstances is social behavior actually described as "cooperation" or "altruism"? In many cases, animals can improve their reproductive success—whether measured as the individual's direct offspring or in terms of "inclusive fitness" (Hamilton 1964; Wilson 1975)—by sharing resources with some (but not all) conspecifics. The identification of cooperation and competition is not always easy, however; as Rowell has shown for nonhuman primates (chapter 3), what appears to the casual observer as competitive exclusion of sexual access by other males may actually be a very different form of interaction. It is critical to introduce greater caution in the definition and specification of the basic terms we habitually use when discussing "human nature."

Nicholas Blurton Jones's analysis of food sharing (chapter 7) provides an excellent illustration of the benefits of the deductive approach in the study of primate politics and its extension to humans. Ever since Kropotkin (1902) challenged the radically individualistic misinterpretation of evolutionary theory, it has been apparent that human competition is not as ubiquitous or pervasive as some social Darwinists had implied. One of the social practices that has often been used as evidence of the central role of "altruism" and "cooperation" in human society is the virtually universal practice of food sharing. In the light of contemporary studies of primate behavior, the question arises: how should these practices be defined? What are the consequences for the individuals who share food resources, and to what extent can these behaviors legitimately be attributed to cooperative or self-sacrificial motivations?

From the perspective of evolutionary theory, this issue is situated in the broader context of assessing alternative behavioral "strategies" (Slobodkin 1964; Maynard-Smith 1978). For each individual organism, differences in social response can be predicted to have effects on rates of survival and reproduction; from the theoretical perspective, true "altruism" must be defined as a behavior which lowers the reproductive success of the individual compared to genetic rivals. As Hamilton (1964) showed, however, reproductive competition with other members of the species depends on the extent of genetic relatedness between those who interact.

In many circumstances, an organism can increase the net proportion of its genes in future generations by assisting close kin as well as—and sometimes in preference to—reproducing more offspring itself. While this phenomenon has been confused by popularizations of sociobiology that treat "altruism" and "selfishness" as universal abstractions (Dawkins 1976), behavioral ecologists approach the question of sharing and competition as a variable depending on the environment and social structure of each species.

Blurton Jones's analysis in chapter 7 can be viewed as an exploration of the strategic rationale underlying food sharing as a behavioral norm in hominid groups. Like an economist, he defines the costs and benefits of consuming food resources in different ways, suggesting that observed behavior is likely to optimize the net benefits to the individual. But unlike most of those utilizing economic or game theoretical models, Blurton Jones includes such factors as the social situation in which the individual is found (e.g., whether other members of the group are within sight or likely to see the actor) and the size or quality of the resource in question.

In economics textbooks, one is sometimes taught that cost-benefit theory concerns the trade-off of "guns versus butter." Blurton Jones suggests that the size of a resource package might be a fundamental factor in such an analysis, particularly because some individuals will adopt quite different resource acquisition strategies than others and will find competitive defense of large food sources to be excessively costly. As applied to hominid evolution, the trade-off that may have been of particular evolutionary significance could thus be restated as "cows (or beef) versus butter."

In suggesting that much food sharing be defined as "tolerated theft" rather than altruism, Blurton Jones contributes fundamentally to the precision of our descriptive assessments of human social behavior. At the broadest level, his analysis suggests that social scientists and philosophers have often been too hasty in presuming they know what it means to describe a particular behavior as either cooperative or competitive. More specifically, Blurton Jones's approach indicates that one needs to specify many factors before qualifying a behavior as "altruistic." Among these factors, some concern ecology and the environmental setting (what is the size, distribution, storage life, and energy value of alternative food sources?), some the social structure of the group (how dispersed is the group, how are members genetically related, and what patterns of reciprocity have been established?), and some the individual's own behavior strategy (is the actor highly competitive or socially cooperative, does such a strategy differ for males and females, etc.?)

As a way of defining "human nature," such an approach poses more questions than it answers. Unlike the introduction of reductionist versions of sociobiology to the study of human behavior (e.g., Beckstrom 1985), Blurton Jones's analysis of food sharing does not imply that there is a single answer to the origins and causes of human cooperation, regardless of the social and ecological setting. Although his account of "tolerated theft" provides a plausible hypothesis for the explanation of increased food sharing during hominid evolution, his approach cannot therefore be viewed as solving the question of whether cooperation or competition is more "natural" to humans: instead, this type of behavioral ecology shows that, on theoretical grounds, the typical "either/or" formulation is essentially meaningless.

Turning to the descriptive or inductive approach popularized by ethological observation, human social behavior can be characterized by the signals or cues that have evolved as mechanisms of coping with the environment. With each of their five senses, humans perceive social signals from conspecifics. Because these senses are active over different interpersonal distances, from an evolutionary perspective it should hardly be surprising that each sense has a different functional significance for social behavior. Taste and touch normally communicate over what Edward Hall (1959) calls "intimate" social distances: these signals are most likely to be relevant to wrestling, grooming, sexuality, and close interpersonal relations. Smell can be sensed over somewhat larger distances: while campfires and other cues of social behavior may communicate over significant distances, pheromones and other bodily odors of group members are most likely to serve as social cues within the range of "personal" space. Sight and sound, in contrast, can be used to transmit and receive complex and rapidly modulated messages across what Hall describes as "social" and "public" spaces — i.e., the contexts in which what we call "politics" usually occurs.

It should therefore not be surprising that the cues of greatest relevance to human politics are transmitted, at least within face-to-face groups, by the sensory modalities of sound and sight. The vocal channel, of course, transmits not only verbal messages in human languages for which there is no precise analogue among nonhuman primates (Masters 1970; G. Schubert 1981a), but also paravocal cues of emotion and arousal which seem parallel to the vocalizations of monkeys and apes (van Hooff 1969; Montagner et al. 1988). The visual channel permits us, among other things, to decode the "body language," facial displays, and other nonverbal cues associated with dominance and subordination among nonhuman and well as human primates. Like sound, sight is of course also used for distinguishing one individual from another as well as for identifying strangers, enemies, and environmental cues that vary as behavior is adapted to time, place, and need.

The social signals associated with nonverbal behavior have long been a focus of study: even before Darwin in 1872 (1965) showed the enormous evolutionary significance of facial expression, traditional teachers of rhetoric emphasized the need to communicate emotion through the appropriate displays, movements, and rhythms (e.g., Scott 1820). In recent years, social psychologists have elaborated an entire subfield of their discipline devoted to this area, complete with journals, textbooks, and courses.

Although ethology is not a necessary prerequisite for the study of vocal and visual signals, the approach of primate ethology is particularly important if one is to integrate the paravocal cues and facial displays into the study of politics. Indeed, the methods that have been presented in parts I and II of this volume provide a way to correct some important weaknesses in the study of nonverbal communication as it relates to political behavior.

In social psychology, much research has focused on nonverbal displays as *expressions of emotion* (e.g., Osgood 1966; Ekman and Friesen 1975; Ekman and Oster 1979; Izard 1979; Plutchik 1980). While consistent with the title of Darwin's own work in the area, this approach has viewed nonverbal cues as an outward manifestation of the inner state (or, to use the ethological term, the "mood" or behavioral "tendency") of an individual. Where the display does not correspond with the "actual" emotion or mood of the actor, one speaks of "deception"—as if the only purpose or meaning of nonverbal cues were an accurate presentation of inner feelings.

There is every reason to question this view as an assumption or theory of social communication among animals. While Rousseau in his *Dialogues* imagined a "transparent" world in which social individuals could always perceive the inner intentions of each other with complete accuracy (Rousseau 1990, 9–12), evolution often seems to generate contrary pressures; among social animals, if perfectly accurate signal detection should arise, deception can easily become selectively advantageous (Lockard 1980; Frank 1988). Nonverbal cues are social signals—and as such, their relationship to the inner state of an individual may often be less important than their function as mechanisms of interaction and social regulation.

While the approach to human politics in terms of social processes like those observed in nonhuman primates necessarily emphasizes nonverbal communication, this is far from a reductionist endeavor. Were facial displays or paravocal cues merely outer signs of individual emotions and feelings, perhaps social interactions could be reduced to the motives or behavior of the individual participants. As primate ethology teaches us, such an understanding of nonverbal communication does violence to the facts: we should not forget that, as children, we were taught to smile when shaking hands with strangers.

In chapter 8, Sullivan, Masters, Lanzetta, McHugo, Plate, and Englis show the importance of facial displays and demonstrate the error of reducing social signals to expressions of individual emotion. In chapter 9, James Schubert considers the vocal channel, showing how the paravocal cues typically associated with emotion play a central role in the decision making of important political groups.

Each of these chapters presents significant methodological and analytical contributions to contemporary political science. Sullivan and his colleagues use the approach of controlled experimentation, long dismissed as impossible in political science, as a means of exploring how viewers respond to videotapes of leaders. By way of contrast, James Schubert shows how observation of political decision making need not be limited to the printed record of the deliberations or result; on the contrary, the actual process of discussion and decision is itself a vital source of information about the political process.

The approach of James Schubert permits us to convert observation into a process akin to the field research of primatologists. The behavior of known and named participants can be recorded in its natural site, related to the dynamic processes of actual decision-making groups, and studied systematically to determine the relationships between process and outcome. Ironically enough, after a generation of political science that used the concept of "behaviorism" as its shibboleth, the perspective of primate politics thus leads toward a more scientific focus on the active *behaviors* that really occur in political settings.

The approach of Sullivan and his colleagues provides a complementary perspective on the political process, allowing one to disentangle the contributions of seeing and hearing a leader to producing the impressions formed by citizens. Moreover, this technique makes it possible to assess the effect of the attitudes and opinions of the viewer—as well as such attributes as the viewer's gender, the social context of the display, and even the political environment—in the way identical nonverbal cues are processed.

Now that virtually everyone in industrial societies uses sound and video technologies for recreational purposes, it is time for scholars to supplement reading printed texts with tape recorders and VCRs. It is ironic that the perspective of human evolution implicit in the study of primate social behavior should be one of the principal incentives for bringing new methods and technologies to the study of politics. Perhaps, however, this is only logical: if television has created the face-to-face communicative environment of McLuhan's "global village," could it have been long before the approach to face-to-face communication in our primate relatives and ancestors was suggested as an explanation for the transformations of contemporary political life?

Such speculations to one side, the chapters in part III should be seen as a step toward broadening the study of human politics through the introduction of ethological theories and modes of analysis while deepening primate ethology by revealing dimensions of social interaction that have often been oversimplified. If the communicative significance of a tense human voice, furrowed brow, or smiling face depend in part on the people concerned and the context in which they interact, similar caution is required in assessing the social behavior of nonhuman primates.

In political science as elsewhere in the social sciences, one of the critical questions concerns individual variations in the way that social behaviors are *performed*. Here the methodological perspective outlined by Strum and Latour has a direct application to the study of human politics. Different leaders and rivals have quite distinct styles of public behavior. Nowadays, candidates take lessons to improve their performances. Clearly it is time for political scientists to catch up with the media consultants and leadership training specialists.

James Schubert shows us how these differences can play a role in the patterns of influence within a decision-making group, while Sullivan and his colleagues focus on the performance styles of leaders as they appear on the media, influencing electoral outcomes and public attitudes more broadly. In each case, however, the results complement and enrich our understanding of human behavior. Primate politics is not only more "naturalistic" than conventional approaches to the study of politics; it is also more varied, more realistic, and of greater potential value as a predictive science.

A final word. The first chapter in part III shows how behavior can be predicted to vary under different circumstances, whereas the next two chapters utilize complex statistical analyses of empirical data. Different disciplines have quite diverse conventions with regard to the sometimes obscure decisions concerning types of regression coefficients, analysis of variance, and measures of statistical significance. At this stage in the development of primatological studies and their application to human behavior, it is fitting that no such orthodoxies have yet emerged. For the present, it is quite enough to show that "primate politics" is as feasible an approach to behavior in human social groups as it is to the patterns of social interaction among chimpanzees considered in part II.

# 7

## Tolerated Theft
### Suggestions about the Ecology and Evolution of Sharing, Hoarding, and Scrounging

Nicholas G. Blurton Jones

### INTRODUCTION

Sharing food and information about food have been held to be crucial features of human evolution (e.g., Isaac 1978a; Feinman 1979; Kurland and Beckerman 1985) and of human societies in general (Mauss 1962). It is thus worth examining the ecological conditions which would favor such traits. Elucidating the costs and benefits that accrue to individuals from sharing or not sharing food may help us understand both the origins of sharing and its contemporary variation between individuals, cultures, and species.

The theory of food sharing presented here is based on the theory of contests over resources that has been developed in animal behavioral ecology. The concept of "sharing" is turned on its head and examined as "tolerated theft." A brief account of the theory was published previously (Blurton Jones 1984). The theory begins from two principles:

1. Contests over resources tend to be won by the individual for whom the resource is most valuable.

2. The curve of value of resource against amount of resource held is a diminishing returns curve for food, but may take other shapes for other resources.

I argue that theft will be tolerated when the resources follow a diminishing returns curve of benefit gained from the resource against amount of the resource

This paper was presented at the Tenth Congress of the International Primatological Society in Nairobi, Kenya, 24 July 1984. It was originally published in *Social Science Information* 26 (1987): 31–54; reprinted by permission.

held, and when the resource is found unpredictably, seldom, and in large packages.

The model is particularly relevant to some issues in the hunter-gatherer literature. In this literature it is sometimes claimed that people cannot refuse to share nor avoid scroungers, that they resist accumulating wealth, that disruption and hostility is caused by wealth; some forager populations have leisurely work schedules and many men who do not hunt. Two implications will be discussed at some length. These are:

1. The conditions under which hoarding may become possible in a population of foraging theft tolerators. Testart (1982) and Woodburn (1982) argued that storage or delayed consumption is the basis for a major dichotomy among hunter-gatherer societies. The material conditions favoring hoarding are thus an important key to understanding variation in hunter-gatherer societies and indeed may be a neglected aspect of the study of the origin of agriculture.

2. Implications of the model about the easy work schedule of some foragers, specifically for the mixture of foragers and full-time scroungers that we expect in a group. The low work rates of some forager cultures provide a challenge to all the materialist approaches in anthropology that has yet to be satisfactorily met (Smith 1987; Hawkes et al. 1985). Suggestions arise from the model about ecological reasons for "the Zen road to affluence" (Sahlins 1972) that rely only on individual interests and not on long-range benefits to the group.

Major theories about the origin and ecology of food sharing have been kin selection (Hamilton 1964; Feinman 1979), reciprocal altruism (Trivers 1971), "tit for tat" (Axelrod and Hamilton 1981), and variance reduction (H. Kaplan 1983).

Several authors have emphasized the variance reduction benefit of sharing: leveling out day-to-day variation in the food supply, when catches/finds are large but rare (e.g., Woodburn 1972). Woodburn and earlier authors have also pointed to the negligible cost of giving away portions of the enormous prey taken by some contemporary foragers. The variance hypothesis has been explicitly and systematically modeled by Winterhalder (1985) and data presented that demonstrates its effectiveness by H. Kaplan et al. (1983, 1984, 1985). Kaplan showed that sharing reduced day-to-day variance in food intake among Ache hunters and that their pattern of sharing did not fit with expectations from kin selection. Reducing variation in food intake makes considerable intuitive sense and need not be restricted to meat caught rather than found. Obviously it is to the advantage of an individual to receive food from another when he cannot find any. But the evolutionary theorist must ask whether the individual who found the food and refused to share, while continuing to accept food from others, would do better than the others, with selfishness thus spreading through the population. We cannot take for granted the existence of a tendency to reciprocate in the way it is implicit in some early accounts of sharing. We must ask ourselves whether the variance reduction advantage that Woodburn and others describe (and that H. Kaplan [1983] demonstrated) relies on an existing tendency to reciprocity whose origin we cannot explain.

The theory of sharing presented here in no way denies the effect of sharing on variance of food intake. It attempts to tackle issues of the initial invasion of a population by "sharers." It fails to account for some observations that the variance reduction theory addresses, but it directs attention to a wider range of behavior and readily suggests links between behavior and circumstances, thus offering to explain variation in sharing and related behavior.

In the anthropological literature sharing has sometimes been linked to cooperative hunting. Permitting each other a share might be seen as a necessary inducement to combine in the hunt. The advantages of cooperative hunting might seem fairly clear; returns may be greater for all participants (though attempts to demonstrate this suggest that the matter is not so simple; e.g., Boorman and Levitt [1980]; Hill and Hawkes [1983]; Smith [1981, 1985]; but see Sibly [1983] for reasons why we may expect this to be difficult). If sharing evolved as an inducement for cooperation we would be compelled to regard the origin of food sharing as dependent on hunting rather than scavenging. The model proposed here does not link the origin of sharing to hunting rather than to scavenging. It only links the origin to food that arrives in large packages.

The two other well-known mechanisms for the evolution of sharing are kin selection (Hamilton 1964) and reciprocal altruism (Trivers 1971; see also Feinman 1979). Boorman and Levitt (1973) argued that reciprocal altruism was frequency dependent and therefore difficult to get started. The possibility of kin selection does not absolve us from thinking about the actual costs and benefits of actual behavior in real circumstances. Although kin selection is undoubtedly at work in any small, related population, I propose that "tolerated theft" is a simpler explanation for the evolution of food exchange and has the advantage that it draws attention to some ecological factors and thus to the variation of behavior with circumstances. This model may also explain how exchange could begin and spread to a frequency where reciprocal altruism could take off.

## BACKGROUND TO THE APPROACH

Behavioral ecologists tend increasingly to regard all species as opportunistic and efficient in adaptation (Krebs and Davies 1981). Thus, ecologists are little concerned about the developmental mechanisms that produce adaptive responses. These mechanisms may be strongly environment-resistant genetic effects or learning, imitation, or conscious thought. To the behavioral ecologist those are questions of developmental and proximal causal mechanisms ("motivations," in Harris's terminology [1968]) and are irrelevant to the task of assessing the costs and benefits of behavior and calculating what would be an adaptive response to particular circumstances (long range "causes," in Harris's terminology). Thinking out the costs and benefits of a range of actions under specified circumstances allows us to predict the outcomes of the adaptive decisions of an opportunistic species.

The definition of adaptiveness as maximization of reproductive success has been much treated in the literature. For the purposes of this paper we need to remember that the behavioral ecologist's usage is closer to "selfish interest" and the economist Marshall's dictum "men labor and save chiefly for the sake of their families and not for themselves" (Marshall 1920; cited by Becker 1976) than it is to the archaic biologism of "for the good of the species." Indeed, in many places in this paper it would be possible to substitute without detriment the word "utility" for the word "fitness." Of course equally important is that thinking in terms of maximization of reproductive success gives us a way to assess the expected balance between differently measured outcomes like calories and injury.

Behavioral ecologists have changed the study of animal behavior from being mostly inductive to being mostly deductive. They aim to derive testable hypotheses from a few first principles. Often the models are intentionally over-simplified at first. This is because great importance is given to trying to set out the assumptions and show how they are manipulated to reach predictions. This can be a long and difficult process. Thus, while some of the ideas in this paper can be found already in the anthropological literature, they have only very recently been made explicit. One of my aims is thus to try to make the assumptions and arguments more explicit. It is also worth noting that while in this paper some curves of value against amount of resource are given shapes familiar to any economist, their significance for determining the outcome of contests over resources seems not to have been stated explicitly by economists.

This approach adopts the target not of being able to explain all observations that have already been made, but of moving from the fewest possible first principles toward expectations about variation of behavior with circumstances and thence to predictions about observables that can be tested.

## THE TOLERATED THEFT MODEL OF FOOD SHARING

Despite Isaac's (1978a, b) deprecating (but very stimulating) comment about chimpanzee sharing as merely "tolerated scrounging," I propose that we turn the idea of sharing on its head and think more about "tolerated theft." It is important to remember that food, unlike other forms of help such as rescue, can be taken by force. But it is equally important to remember that contests over resources can often be resolved without fights and with a minimum of threat and display. The tolerated theft theory of sharing is not a theory of incessant squabbling!

I argue that the assumptions used by G. Parker (1974) to discuss fighting over resources and their subsequent tests and elaborations (e.g., Maynard-Smith and Parker 1976; G. Parker and Rubenstein 1981; Hammerstein and Parker 1982) suggest a form of sharing, or tolerated theft, which could spread and remain in a population under particular conditions. According to Parker's "fitness budget" argument (1974), natural selection may be expected to have favored individuals that fight only for a fitness gain. A fight may gain a fitness-enhancing resource but it may cost time, energy, and fitness-decreasing injury. The greater the potential fitness benefit from the resource, the greater the costs that can be incurred while still coming out with a net gain in fitness at the end. Thus, between otherwise matched contestants one would expect the fitness benefit of the resource to determine the outcome. The one to whose fitness the resource is most valuable should be expected to profit, and usually to win, even if that means bearing greater costs and fighting hardest or longest.

The literature on animal contests seems unanimous that the outcome of a contest will be determined by such an asymmetry in resource value, or, if resource value is equal, by asymmetry in strength and fighting ability (resource holding potential [RHP], Hammerstein and Parker 1982). There has been relatively little exploration of the outcome when these two asymmetries are in opposite directions or of the way in which we should consider them to interact. For the purposes of this paper we will proceed simply to examine asymmetries in resource value. The model proceeds on the assumption that the contestants are of near enough equal RHP. It seems reasonable to assume that ability to inflict costly injury will be very high in creatures that are able to dismember and perhaps kill sizable prey and thus that strength and fighting ability (RHP) will be roughly equal in both contestants (i.e., differences in overkill capacity are assumed to be unimportant). It is also important to realize that this animal literature has mostly considered contests in the framework of a "war of attrition" game, judging this to be the most appropriate for the conditions under which animals contest resources.

In the case of a group of individuals that find food rather seldom but in large packages, a series of asymmetric contests can easily arise. They will arise if the fitness gained from food follows a diminishing returns curve and if food items are large enough. Consider an individual that acquires a large food item. Because this will happen very seldom, then most probably other individuals will have found nothing. Recall that food can be broken into pieces. Some portions represent a large fitness gain for the finder (e.g., Y1 on figure 7-1B). Other portions represent a much smaller gain (portion 2 represents, say, Y2 fitness units on figure 7-1B). But for a latecomer who found nothing that day, any one portion of size X that he or she can get will represent a gain of Y1 fitness units. Thus for a contest over portion 2 we have an asymmetry in resource value. Its value to the finder is only Y2 fitness units; to the latecomer it is worth more, Y1 fitness units. Thus the latecomer will be expected to win easily in a contest over portion 2. The finder should relinquish this portion without a fight.

For purposes of illustration one can think of this process either in temporal sequence or spatially. One can think of the two contestants positioned at opposite ends of a carcass (vultures may squabble with their neighbors, but what

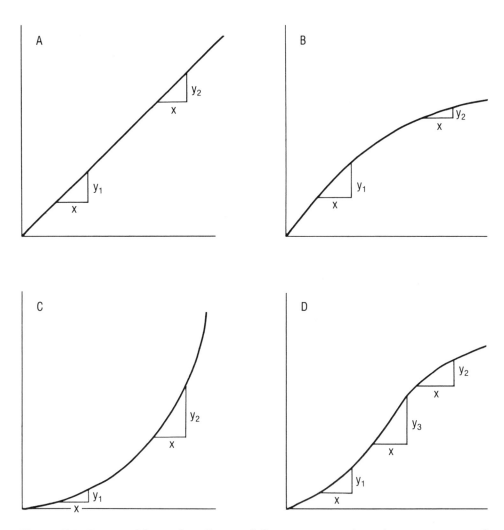

Figure 7-1. Curves of fitness benefit gained from a resource (*y*-axis) against amount of resource held (*x*-axis).

is the chance of defending the whole carcass?), portion 1 being a part near the finder, portion 2 being a part far from the finder. Or one can think of the finder having a headstart at the meal, becoming gradually satiated and then being joined by a hungry latecomer. But these figurative, or motivational, versions of the argument could be misleading. The argument does not depend on the end of the carcass being out of reach, nor on the finder having time to fill his belly before a latecomer arrives. And it is important to emphasize that it does not imply endless squabbles. Ability to assess the costs and benefits will be strongly favored by natural selection (G. Parker 1974; Maynard-Smith and Parker 1976;

G. Parker and Rubenstein 1981; Hammerstein and Parker 1982) and will be expected to be a well-developed ability in many animals.

If we consider the process of tolerated theft continuing among a group of individuals who frequently meet, there is another interesting outcome. An individual who is one day a finder will also often be a latecomer on other days and will steal from the others who previously stole from him or her. Although all are merely following their selfish cost-benefit equations (fitness budgets) and avoiding costs of injury, the effect is a good deal of reciprocal transfer of resources. The amount occurring will presumably depend largely on the frequency of catches of large prey.

There are two interesting things about this. One is that the day-to-day variance in food intake will be greatly lowered, just as H. Kaplan (1983) has argued from the other premises and has demonstrated to be the case for Ache foragers. The other is that if large prey is a frequent or relatively abundant part of the diet, the group consists of, in effect, good altruists and reciprocators. Thus, the condition that Boorman and Levitt (1973) argued was necessary for the evolution of reciprocal altruism (Trivers 1971) is fulfilled: reciprocation is already occurring at a high frequency, just because the contestants do better to avoid injury.

Not only will reciprocation be at high frequency but it will also be hard to avoid. Cheating will be immediately dealt with, because the very condition that gives rise to the "sharing" is the condition that provokes contests and fights. Sharing happens because it avoids a costly fight; refusal to share provides a situation in which it is worthwhile for the latecomer to fight to gain a share, not because the system needs safeguards against cheaters, but just because that is the condition under which attack offers a net gain.

A further interesting point is that the basic propositions about the contest imply that the "shares" be almost equal. The implication is not that they be exactly equal in amount of food but that the shares endow equal fitness value to the contestants, perhaps offset to the extent of differences in strength or fighting ability. There is, of course, no guarantee that the shares be adequate. This equality is predicted not necessarily by endowing the individuals with a sense of fairness, but by assuming each to be maximizing its fitness budget. Nor is there any implication that such selfish maximization must have an equable outcome under every circumstance. We will briefly discuss some such other circumstances (curves that are not diminishing returns curves) later in the paper.

Many hunter-gatherer societies have complex rules about sharing food. Yet this model predicts very even sharing of food. Despite the existence of many rules of sharing, it appears that equal sharing is the eventual consequence of these rules in most hunter-gatherer cultures (according to the literature review by Hayden [1981]). However, the only quantified direct-observation study of sharing in hunter-gatherer society is that by H. Kaplan (1983; H. Kaplan and Hill 1985). Kaplan's study shows that the individual who catches an animal keeps less of the animal than was expected. Kaplan shows that successful hunters receive better treatment from others in many respects, and he favors a trade or exchange theory of sharing.

It remains for me to argue that food can be a resource that follows a diminishing returns curve of fitness against amount. The concept of a dietary requirement is in essence an extreme form of a diminishing returns curve. We could set the model in the context of an individual attempting to fill his daily dietary requirement. A sizeable prey item would take it well beyond the requirement; many portions of the prey would be of no fitness benefit and would therefore not be worth defending. But daily dietary requirements may be neither realistic nor strictly relevant to such a model, especially for a creature that can provision mates and offspring. If we are concerned with fitness it is relevant that more offspring are likely to survive if well fed than adequately fed; more offspring can be raised if more food is available for them. Fitness benefits of food therefore increase beyond an individual's "daily requirement." In addition, nutritionists seem unable (perhaps ultimately for this very reason) to agree on precise daily requirements (e.g., Durnin et al. 1973). However, it is very likely that fitness returns for food nonetheless follow a diminishing returns curve. At any one moment there is only a finite number of offspring to be fed, only so much increased probability of their mother becoming profitably pregnant, and so on. If there *are* diminishing returns our propositions will hold. Only if the line is straight or concave will this condition for tolerated theft not be met.

Another important component of my argument is the size of the items of food. I took the example of large items, found unpredictably and seldom, and therefore on different occasions by different individuals. Let us consider the case where all the individuals are on average about equally satiated; that is, they are all at about the same point on the $x$-axis of my graphs. Then a large item of food will have the effects described. There will be large differences in the value of portions of that item to the finder and to a latecomer. If the finder kept all the food he would move well up the $x$-axis and along the diminishing returns portion of the curve. But if food comes in small packages, the finder who keeps the item will not move much further up the $x$-axis than the latecomer. The very small asymmetry that would result from keeping all of this small item may be negligible and frequently overwhelmed by small differences in strength or fighting ability. Thus we might not expect theft of small items to be so often tolerated. We should expect more even contests or more contests settled by individual differences in strength of fighting ability.

The argument about tolerated theft is simple and adds only the individual selection argument of avoidance of injury to the traditional anthropological view of sharing meat, but it seems to be both somewhat counterintuitive and very productive. Several commonsense objections are often raised which, although the theory deals with them easily, raise other stimulating issues. Three interesting objections are as follows:

1. *Storage and hoarding.* The model may be fine for a situation where the food rots quickly and there is no technology for preserving the food. But once the technology was available, surely an individual that kept and stored more of his find would do better. And if not, under what conditions would we expect hoarding to pay?

2. *Scrounging.* Would not the tolerated theft situation simply lead to all individuals becoming thieves and the gains from foraging getting so low that individuals all stopped foraging and became full-time scroungers?

3. *Different resources and different curves.* Food may follow a diminishing returns curve, but what about resources that might give increasing returns or straight-line or sigmoid curves?

## STORAGE AND HOARDING

If an individual could preserve food, would it pay to defend more food so that it would have food for the next day?

Under the conditions of the model there will still be an asymmetry in resource value on the second day. The value of the resource will increase by virtue of storage, but it will increase even more for the now starving latecomers. Only when the gains to contestants become nearly equal—for instance, if the curve nears a straight line—will the condition for tolerated theft disappear. Thus, knowledge of storage or preservation techniques seems unlikely to be the critical factor determining whether food is stored.

In animals, storage of food is most often found in species which defend a territory during the season when food is stored. So what are the conditions under which hoarding is to be expected in a species that does not defend a territory? First, it seems clear that hoarding can begin under conditions of synchronized catches. If individuals make catches on the same day as each other, then the conditions for theft disappear. We no longer have the situation in which one individual has an enormous package of food and another individual has none, which makes the enormous package not defendable. Each individual will be left with the beginning of a hoard and in a population of equally well endowed individuals. Supposing that they use up their hoards at about the same rate, then conditions for theft still do not arise. Thus, one obvious context in which hoarding meat can begin and will be expected is under conditions of a seasonal glut.

A second condition which would favor accumulation of resources, and yet allow them to be defendable, is when the curve of fitness value of the resource against amount of resource held follows an increasing returns curve (fig. 7-1C). In this case, an individual that has more of the resource will gain more from adding a unit of resource than will an individual that has less. It is possible that at some levels land and livestock perform this way, but the only obvious example would seem to be financial capital.

Common sense, and the ethnographic record, suggest that hoarding pays when there is a season of scarcity such as a cold and snowbound winter. It is clear that the effect of such a seasonal scarcity on my model is to steepen and straighten the curve of fitness returns for food. But it is not clear whether this is a sufficient condition to make it profitable to defend the hoard. If other individuals do not have a hoard, then the hoarders' hoard will be as valuable or more valuable to them and theft will be expected. In practice many of the environments with severe winters also have seasonal gluts such as a salmon run, caribou migration, or pinyon nut season. Careful analysis of a large number of ethnographic cases might allow this issue to be resolved.

While predictions about hoarding meat may fit well with the hunter-gatherers of the Pacific Northwest and Anaktuvuk Pass, I have no predictions about hoarding plant foods. I cannot say why the Shoshone should hoard whereas the !Kung (assuming the end of the !Kung dry season to be a season of scarcity) should not hoard. Further refinement of the hoarding model is obviously desirable.

There are several interesting anthropological implications about sharing and hoarding from the tolerated theft model. The difficulty of escaping the necessity of sharing and thus the difficulty of beginning to hoard and store food in a population of food exchangers (forager thieves) is familiar in the field. It is commonly reported that accumulation of wealth (e.g., cattle, money, stored food) is resisted when hunter-gatherers are becoming settled. Explanations have ranged from a tradition of fecklessness to the ease and reliability of foraging. The tolerated theft model emphasizes the potential for violence that arises from a minority of individuals beginning to accumulate wealth, a proposition remarked on and implied but not emphasized in the hunter-gatherer literature (e.g., Lee 1969).

The model does imply that hoarding is not dependent on knowledge of techniques of food preservation. This is consonant with the ethnographic data. !Kung know how to dry and preserve meat, but they often do not do this. Indeed, my model might predict that they are more likely to preserve meat in the wet season (when in small groups and despite greater abundance in that season) than in the larger dry season groups, when any prey species will be shared, leaving little that cannot be quickly eaten up. Of course in the unlikely event that two or more large catches were made on one day, one might see meat being dried in a dry season camp.

Another form of sharply synchronized glut (besides a salmon run or a confined and intense ungulate migration) is an agricultural harvest (so long as many people planted a crop). It should be easy for agriculturalists to hoard their harvest (unless their crops yield asynchronously) so long as all of the population are farmers. A harvest from agricultural crops can be regarded as a synchronized "catch" and would clearly be defendable. But the model may predict that nonsynchronized crops (not nonseasonal) might be hard to defend and worth raiding. This should provide easily falsifiable predictions. One such prediction might be that nowhere in simple societies do individuals plant briefly high-yielding crops at different times of year from their neighbors.

Moore (1984b, and pers. comm.) pointed out that one implication of compulsory food sharing is that it will be extremely difficult for theft-tolerating foragers to begin to farm. An individual who begins to farm in a population of theft-tolerant thieves will lose his harvest. The model would suggest that farming and hoarding can only begin if tolerated theft conditions have disappeared (unless the remaining share of the harvest is more valuable to the first individual who plants a crop than are the gains of foraging). Agriculture might begin in a society that already hoards much more easily than it would begin in a theft-tolerant society. High dependence on a synchronized, seasonal plant food (which does not present the conditions for tolerated theft) might be one such context. A harvest that coincides with some other synchronous glut might also be defendable. But a culture that no longer catches large prey might have also lost the context for tolerated theft. These theoretical issues should be explored at greater length and more rigorously before attempting to match them to the ethnographic or archaeological data.

## SCROUNGING

Will some individuals give up hunting and be pure scroungers? Models have been devised to account for the mix of foragers and scroungers in animal groups (e.g., Barnard and Sibly 1981; Barnard 1984). These contrast pure foragers and pure scroungers, but the present discussion is concerned with pure scroungers and forager-scroungers.

The tolerated theft model implies that food will be shared roughly equally. If we take this conclusion as our starting point a number of arguments can be made about scrounging. If an active forager sometimes misses the opportunity to scrounge a share from other foragers, then full-time scrounging becomes a more attractive proposition and an interesting mixed strategy can easily result. An example of such a situation is as follows. It is, like all models, rather simplified; real life may combine features of several possible models.

To begin, with let us suppose the following:

1. Each active forager misses the chance to take a share of the catches of 25 percent of the other active foragers. Perhaps the forager is still out foraging when those 25 percent come home with their catches.

2. Full-time scroungers have the chance to take a share of 100 percent of the catches.

3. Any catch must be shared equally among all those present (other models of sharing might predict a different distribution).

4. A missed opportunity to join a share-out cannot be compensated by scrounging smaller portions from the recipients of the original shares (an

assumption that follows from the tolerated theft model since they are unlikely after a share-out to have such large amounts that the entire package is not worth defending).

Since foragers miss some of the share-outs—each forager is only there for 75 percent—we reduce the amount of food that they join in sharing in proportion to this. Each forager gets 75 percent of the total catch, divided among the number of people who are in camp when the average forager is in camp (all the scroungers, plus the 75 percent of foragers who are already at home).

The share that a scrounger gets is the total catch divided among all the scroungers plus the 75 percent of foragers who are present at each share-out.

These calculations are presented in table 7-1 for a group of ten individuals, using estimates of hunters' returns within the range reported by Lee (1979). It can be seen from Table 7-1 that under these conditions foragers always do worse than scroungers. We can also see the bigger the proportion of foragers there is in the group, the better everyone does. But if we consider the outcome for an individual deciding whether to become a forager (and as a result change the composition of the group), we see that only at a quite low frequency of foragers is there a gain for a scrounger in becoming a forager (row 3 to row 4). At high frequencies of foragers we see that there is a gain for a forager in becoming a scrounger (row 5 to row 4). Consequently there is an equilibrium mixture of forager-thieves and full-time scroungers.

We can also see from table 7-1 that the gains from remaining one of a reduced number of scroungers are much greater than the gains from switching to foraging. Thus there is great advantage in persuading another individual to become a forager, much more than there is advantage for that other individual. Even in this possibly primeval context, the gift of prestige to the active forager

**Table 7-1.** Returns for foraging and scrounging when foragers miss 25 percent of opportunities for theft, in a group of ten individuals (total catch is based on returns of 2000 grams of food per forager day)

| Scroungers (n) | Foragers (n) | Total catch | Each scrounger's share | Each forager's share |
|---|---|---|---|---|
| 9 | 1 | 2,000 | 205.1 | 153.8 |
| 8 | 2 | 4,000 | 421.0 | 315.7 |
| 7 | 3 | 6,000 | 648.6 | 486.5 |
| 6 | 4 | 8,000 | 888.9 | 666.7 |
| 5 | 5 | 10,000 | 1142.8 | 857.1 |
| 4 | 6 | 12,000 | 1411.7 | 1058.8 |
| 3 | 7 | 14,000 | 1696.9 | 1272.7 |
| 2 | 8 | 16,000 | 2000.0 | 1500.0 |
| 1 | 9 | 18,000 | 2322.6 | 1741.9 |
| 0 | 10 | 20,000 | — | 2000.0 |

would be a self-serving deceit by the scrounger. The model describes a mixed strategy, with an equilibrium point above which it pays a forager-thief to become a pure scrounger, and below which it pays a pure scrounger to become a forager-thief, but would pay him even better to *remain a scrounger while persuading another individual to resume foraging.* We thus have the prospect of defining a situation in which there is strong selection pressure for persuasion. At low frequencies of foragers there is an advantage in being persuaded, but at all frequencies there is more advantage in joining the persuaders.

The calculations were repeated for differently sized groups of individuals and for different proportions of missed opportunities to join in a share-out. The results of these calculations are shown in figure 7-2. The equilibrium point

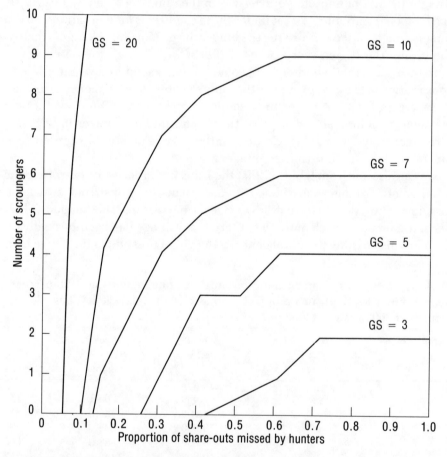

Figure 7-2. Results of repeated calculation of scrounger model. GS = group size. In a large group, even missing quite a small proportion of share-outs leads to many individuals becoming full-time scroungers. In small groups all forage unless a very high proportion of share-outs is missed. For a group of ten individuals, when 0.15 (15 percent) of share-outs are missed, four individuals will be scroungers. When 0.3 (30 percent) of share-outs are missed, then seven will be scroungers.

occurs at different proportions of foragers and scroungers depending upon the size of the group and the proportion of share-outs missed by the forager. These repeated calculatons show that in largish groups full-time scrounging begins to pay even when there are very small losses of opportunity to join in a share-out. But in small groups (five or fewer foragers) it only pays to become a scrounger in the very unlikely event that nearly half the share-outs are missed by foragers. Thus, this model of scrounging predicts that full-time scrounging is more likely to occur in larger groups and that it is very unlikely indeed to occur in small groups.

The tolerated theft model thus can imply that some individuals will give up foraging. To this extent it could explain the low "productivity" of forager cultures. How many give up and become full-time scroungers will depend on size of group and on other costs of foraging, such as missing share-outs, risks of being in the bush, reproductive costs of leaving wife and offspring unattended, and so on. The same arguments should apply to individual mixed strategies, in which individuals forage more or less often according to these same considerations. It could be that individuals are able to assess the probable payoffs each morning, in accordance with the number of individuals who have gone hunting or who say they are going, and decide whether to go hunting or to stay in camp.

One may wonder whether tolerated theft penalizes good hunters to the extent that they should attempt to leave the group. H. Kaplan (1983) and Vehrencamp (1983) consider this issue more extensively, using other models with many interesting consequences. Scroungers are presumably always at liberty to follow the successful hunter. In the tolerated theft model, although good hunters will not receive the advantage that may appear due to them, they will nonetheless gain from their efforts. They are likely to gain more from their efforts than from the efforts of less good hunters—an equal share of their own greater returns will be greater than an equal share of a poor hunter's lesser returns. Under most conditions poor hunters will be the ones to opt first for a pure scrounging strategy, or a less active mixed hunting-resting strategy. Good hunters should persist despite the drain of "spongers." We should expect that "Some people like to hunt, other people just like to eat," as a !Kung informant said to Konner and Blurton Jones.

Alternative explanations in the literature for the low work rates of some foragers are (1) they conserve resources ("prudent predators"); (2) the population is kept at a level that requires high work rates only in times of exceptional scarcity; (3) "the Zen road to affluence," the claim that forager behavior is guided by an ideology that values leisure and security, avoiding overproduction with its attendant overreproduction. Thus, the most significant aspect of the tolerated theft-scrounging model for anthropological theory is that it gives one possible, indeed plausible, answer to the challenge: how can individual economic or reproductive interests lead to low work rates and the toleration of scroungers? This may provide a route to an ecological explanation of the influential concept of the "Zen road to affluence" (Sahlins 1972), an explanation which does not rely on the unrealistic "prudent predator" proposition. We have here a mechanism by which individuals maximizing their selfish interests come to underproduce. Thus there is no need to postulate long-range planning, adaptation to a seldom observed "worst year," a group survival strategy such as altruistic restraint to conserve the environment, or a nonmaterialist cause for lowered work rates.

The differences between this model and one that views behavior as maximizing the benefit and endurance of the group are striking. If foragers forage for the group, they should all forage, unless the alternative explanations mentioned above operate. When one pays attention to the interests of the individual, the "underproducing" societies become easier to understand than if one attends only to the group outcome. Such an explanation may also enable us to understand why the members of such societies profess to believe not that eating is bad but that generosity is good, and that eager and successful hunting is good.

## DIFFERENT RESOURCES, DIFFERENT CURVES

Parker's "fitness budget" argument of contests over resources, from which I derived tolerated theft, can be applied to other curves of resource value against amount of resource (Blurton Jones 1986). If contests are won by the individual that will gain most from the contested resource we can conclude that in figure 7-1B the individual that has most will relinquish a contested item to an individual that has less (the tolerated theft model). In figure 7-1C, the individual that has most will be able to defend an added item from an individual that has less ($Y1 < Y2$). In figure 7-1D, the outcome will depend on the exact positions; compare $Y1$, $Y2$, $Y3$. In figure 7-1A, wherever an individual lies on the $x$-axis, he or she stands to gain the same amount from an added item. For such a resource, contests will not be predictably resolved by asymmetry in resource value.

Outcomes of repeated contests may lead to even distribution of resources (curve 1B), accumulation of resources by few individuals (curve 1C), and a population of resource holders alongside a population of nonholders (curve 1D). Repeated contests over a resource that follows curve 1A must lead to allocation of resources according to differences in strength and fighting ability. These being relatively constant features of an individual, the result will be a ranking of individuals. The most interesting feature of these outcomes is the difference between the rank order arising from curve A (or as argued in the section on tolerated theft, a rank order arising from contests over food that is found in small packages) and the "stratification" arising from curves C and D. The latter may be more important in human society and its evolution than the rank order. Rank orders are common in animal societies but would appear likely to have a different ecological basis from stratification in human society.

The increasing returns curve will lead to individuals that have more, being able to acquire and defend more. This curve is in effect a curve which demonstrates economies of scale. Among many good theories about stratification is the view that it arises particularly when there are economies of scale in some subsistence activities (A. Garfinkel 1981). If this is correct, then the difference between stratification of human societies and the dominance hierarchies of nonhuman primates may be at least as profound as anthropologists have always felt. One can argue that monkey hierarchies can be explained adequately by the straight-line curve (or by the use of food that comes in small packages). A straight-line curve will lead to less easily resolved contests. Differences in strength and fighting ability will be the only sources of asymmetry, and if present are most likely to determine the outcome. Differences in strength and fighting ability do not change rapidly, so the outcome will be a ranking of individuals according to their ability to win resources from each other. A sigmoid curve may lead to a population of owners and a population of "dispossessed." Arguments for these conclusions and possible examples of resources that follow each curve are described in Blurton Jones (1986). This "ecological determinist" view may be contrasted with the view that a common primate tendency toward rank ordering displays itself in our species in social inequality or class systems. However, I do not claim that my argument necessarily applies to phenomena such as leadership in small experimental or informal groups. It might be worth examining the extent to which it applies to the groups of nursery school children in which rank orders have so often been described.

I have discussed no applications of the tolerated theft model within stratified societies. There are some important inconsistencies. I have described a condition in which it pays the poor to threaten the rich, and in which it does not pay the rich to resist. In the increasing returns curve we have a condition where this is reversed. But in real societies factors such as control of access to weaponry may be just as important a factor as the resource value curves. Nonetheless, aspects of the resource value curve idea are implicit in the anthropological literature. An incomplete irrigation system is not much use. The whole intact system gives enormous returns. It seems clear that the principles of this "fitness budget" approach to conflict over resources offer an explanation for an encouragingly wide range of social phenomena.

## DISCUSSION

I have taken a robust finding of Parker and others about contests over resources and tried to show how we could relate it to actual ecological circumstances. My main aim was to argue that the models could account for a form of passive reciprocal exchange of food, "tolerated theft." The proposed mechanism might increase exchange of food to a frequency at which reciprocal altruism could begin to evolve. The circumstances under which this would operate are: food is found in large packages, infrequently, by different individuals on different occasions, and the individuals find each other with the food. These circumstances could have been present over long stretches of the evolutionary history of our species, they could arise from scavenging as much as from hunting large animals, and they are present in many contemporary and recent hunter-gatherer societies. The model implies that gathering plant food would be a highly unlikely origin for sharing, unless plant foods that could fulfill the required conditions were involved (e.g., truly enormous tubers that were very hard to find).

A number of alternative models of the evolution of altruism already exist and were mentioned in the Introduction. I claim that my model has the advantage that it draws attention more directly to circumstances than do the other models. Alternative theories of the origin of food sharing give little lead into the examination of the circumstances that favor sharing. When so much variation exists in contemporary societies, it seems more hopeful to attend to environmental or materialistic differences than to hope that a model unlinked to the environment can explain both origins and variation. Kin selection, as it is normally used, is one of these alternative theories. All higher primate groups consist of closely related individuals, and kin selection seems to be the key to understanding many features of their social behaviour. But kin selection unlinked to environmental variation cannot tell us why some species or cultures habitually share food and others do not, or why some are conspicuously hierarchical and others are more variable in this. Kin selection theory really gives us only a coefficient by which to adjust measurable costs and benefits. Thus it is neither in conflict with nor a substitute for other theories that attend to the costs and benefits.

It seems to be difficult to choose between tolerated theft (injury avoidance) and variance reduction as prime movers for evolution of food sharing. An important consequence of real-life food sharing is the reduced day-to-day variance in an individual's food intake, as demonstrated from data on the Ache by H. Kaplan (1983 and subsequently). The same consequence follows from the tolerated theft model, and the same circumstances lead to advantages from both tolerated theft and variance reduction. One potential disagreement concerns whether, if variance reduction were the only advantage, the system could be exploited by individuals who decided to receive but not give. This is exactly the same question as arises with reciprocal altruism. Why could not an individual raise his mean intake and keep his variance low by defending his own catches and stealing from others? The tolerated theft model overcomes this problem.

The use of a central site is better explained by variance reduction benefits. The tolerated theft model leads to variance reduction, and I do not wish to underrate the importance of variance reduction. Given that cheating is impossible because of the costs and benefits of contests, then if variance reduction is advantageous we should expect individuals to do whatever achieves this. I have assumed that variance reduction had to be a by-product of a process that can evolve by selection acting on individuals.

If we remove the variance reduction advantage from consideration, we get a scenario in which an individual that makes a catch will do better to avoid others and hide the catch (if he or she can hide it from other species as well!), and an individual that makes no catch will do well to follow other individuals. The implications of this unlikely model may be worth pursuing.

Besides continuing to try to pin down the rationale of each model, we may be able to derive contrasting predictions from reciprocal altruism, tolerated theft, kin selection, and so forth, to test against real data. Thus, tolerated theft may predict more even sharing than reciprocal altruism, in which individuals may be expected to favor good reciprocators. H. Kaplan (1983) usefully contrasts variance reduction with kin selection predictions. Many other topics deserve further exploration, including the economics of alliances of thieves or owners.

It has been my aim in this paper to outline the model and illustrate some of its implications, not to relate the model in detail to the ethnographic literature. But the model, the discussion of hoarding, and the analysis of scrounging impinge on existing data or theory at several points and these deserve emphasis; the model makes us less puzzled by

1. the undercurrent of potential hostility associated with sharing;
2. the near impossibility of avoiding scroungers;
3. the challenge to find materialist explanations for the "Zen road to affluence";
4. the difficulty of persuading hunter-gatherers to hoard;
5. the possible association of hoarding and seasonal gluts;
6. the self-serving nature of some ideology; and
7. differences between primate rank orders and human social stratification.

Closer examination of these issues would be rewarding. For example, the model may help make more explicit the links between seasonality and hoarding discussed by Testart (1982), who argues that hoarding is the key distinction between types of hunter-gatherer social organization. The model suggests we look again at sharing in simple societies. Is it really so altruistic? Or really so reciprocal? Although hunter-gatherers all appear to support the sharing ethic, is there really an undercurrent of threat, appeasement, and personal power behind it?

# 8

## Facial Displays and Political Leadership
### Some Experimental Findings

Denis G. Sullivan and Roger D. Masters,
with the collaboration of John T. Lanzetta,
Gregory J. McHugo, Basil G. Englis, and Elise F. Plate

We report on the first stage of a research project that draws on ethological and social psychological perspectives to explore the ways in which facial displays of political leaders combine with other verbal and nonverbal cues to influence viewers through the medium of television.

Many citizens receive their information about politics from television and frequently see images of political leaders as well as hear their messages. Television is an emotionally involving medium, and recent research in political science and social psychology demonstrates the importance of the emotional responses elicited by candidates in shaping attitudes toward them (Kinder and Abelson 1981). Moreover, as Abelson and Roseman (1984) point out, candidates elicit feelings in different ways — by distinctive rhetorical styles, through being held responsible by citizens for positive or negative policy outcomes, and by nonverbal gestures communicated over television. Although television is implicated as a source of each of these effects, it may be especially important in exposing viewers to facial gestures of candidates that research in social psychology and ethology show to be emotionally evocative and significant as social signals.

After presenting a model of emotion and nonverbal display behavior (section 1), we describe these selected facial displays that should elicit theoretically predicted descriptive and emotional responses (section 2). Sections 3 and 4 present the results of experiments designed to assess the validity of the stimulus selection procedures. Section 3 demonstrates that viewers' descriptions of a political leader's displays are congruent with the objective criteria defined in terms of research in ethology and social psychology. Section 4 describes the distinct patterns of psychophysiological and self-report measures of emotional response to the three kinds of facial displays as well as the relationship between these measures and prior attitude toward the leader.

## 1. AN APPROACH TO THE STUDY OF FACIAL DISPLAYS

Ethologists since Darwin (1965 [1872]) have emphasized the social signaling role of nonverbal gestures among nonhuman primates. While body postures and vocalizations are means of communication for many animals, facial gestures are particularly central to the process by which primates establish and maintain social dominance (Chance 1976a; de Waal 1982; van Hooff 1969). For ethologists, a single element of an expressive display, such as raised eyebrows or a smile, can acquire multiple functional significance in communicating reassurance, dominance, and/or subordination (Eibl-Eibesfeldt 1979b, 1989; van Hooff 1969).

Social psychological work on facial displays has proceeded in different but related directions. First, Ekman and his coworkers, after showing the expression of basic emotions to be universal (Ekman and Oster 1979), have turned more recently to a precise anatomical description of the muscle movements implicated in the expression, or masking, of different emotions (Ekman and Friesen 1975, 1976, 1978, 1982). Second, work stimulated in part by ethological considerations has focused directly on the signaling role of nonverbal gestures (Alexander and Babad 1981; Duncan, Brunner, and Fiske 1979; Ellsworth 1975; Englis, Vaughan, and Lanzetta 1982; Kraut and Johnston 1979; Lanzetta and Orr 1980).

While some of the studies just cited concern the social signaling role of facial displays, others examine their communicative significance in terms of the emotions they evoke in observers. For example, Englis, Vaughan, and Lanzetta (1982) used a conditioning paradigm to explore how a sender's "happy" face can come to evoke a "fear" emotional response in the receiver. Explanations of such results treat the facial display of the sender as a source of information for the receiver about expected pleasant or painful outcomes. The similarity of an "expectancy-based" explanation of facial display effects to ethological approaches suggests that a combined social psychological–ethological framework might be a useful way of incorporating expressive display variables in a theory of political leadership.

Despite differences in methodology, ethological and social psychological research converge on two basic propositions. First, humans decode accurately the emotion that a specific, expressive facial cue represents both within cultures and across cultures (Ekman and Oster 1979). Second, three dimensions relating to *attack, flight,* and *bonding or affiliation* seem to underlie many of the differences in responses to facial displays (Eibl-Eibesfeldt 1979b, 1989; Masters 1976b; D. Morris 1956; van Hooff 1973). From an evolutionary perspective, this should not be surprising; facial communication has played a critical role in organizing mammalian social behavior for millions of years.

The research discussed above suggests the usefulness of three levels of analysis in studying facial displays: (1) facial displays as *expressions* of a particular emotion; (2) the *meaning* or attributions to the expressor evoked by the display; and (3) the *impression*, which includes both the emotional response to the display and how that response combines with context and prior experience to affect bonding, submission, and dominance behaviors. In general, social psychologists and ethologists have concentrated primarily on only one of these levels of analysis. This creates the risk that findings on one level, such as the specific musculature involved in the displays, will be misinterpreted as referring to the entire process. Because similar words are often used for an expressive gesture, its meaning, and the functional behavior it elicits, it is easy to assume that a display of anger, for example, elicits anger in the observer that, in turn, evokes aggressive behavior. Such relationships must always be a matter of empirical analysis, since it is possible for an anger display to reassure observers or for a happy smile to be highly threatening.

The fact that a facial display's expressive significance, meaning, and impressive significance often diverge makes research difficult for two principal reasons. First, since the movements of the facial muscles and autonomic responses (e.g., heartbeat, galvanic skin response) operate somewhat independently, the outward and visible signs of a display may "impress" an observer even when an emotion is not being experienced by the sender. Observers may respond differently to subtle display differences that reflect whether the emitter is "pretending" an emotion not felt, "masking" a felt emotion, or "expressing" a felt emotion.

Second, it has proved difficult to isolate stimuli that have predictable functional relationships to the emotional states of *both* the sender *and* the receiver. In addition to the complex nature of the facial display stimulus itself, other determinants of responses to facial display behavior such as nonverbal and verbal cues, social context, as well as status and prior experiences of sender and receiver may produce different responses to the same display (Argyle and Cook 1976; Ellsworth 1975). For example, a facial expression associated with one affective state can come to be associated with quite diverse functional consequences, either in the actor or in the observer (Englis, Vaughan, and Lanzetta 1982).

## 2. THE SELECTION OF STIMULI

In order to explore the effects of facial displays experimentally, it is necessary to define them objectively in ways that do not prejudge their effects. To do so, we focus on the stimulus features of facial *expressions* of emotions, their social signal value *(meaning)*, and their *impressive* significance as elicitors of emotional responses (as distinct from the functional behaviors the emotional response may help mediate). Hence we speak of "happiness/reassurance" displays, for example, without assuming that they necessarily facilitate social bonding.

Social psychologists and ethologists have differed in the importance they place on each of these levels of analysis. These differences are evident when the analyses of four investigators are compared (Fridja 1973; Osgood 1966; Plutchik 1980; van Hooff 1973). Nevertheless, these investigators agree on the existence of three basic dimensions of emotional behavior that play a central role in social behavior: anger, threat, or aggression; fear, evasiveness, or flight; and happiness, affiliation, or reassurance (Masters et al. 1986). While other categories of emotion and behavior, such as sadness, may also be important, we focus on leaders' nonverbal displays in these three areas—the *agonic* displays of "anger/threat" and "fear/evasion" and the *hedonic* displays of "happiness/reassurance."

To assess the communicative significance of a facial display, one must consider, in addition to the precise facial display elements, the expressor's orientation to the target person in terms of head position, head movement, and gaze. In the following description of agonic and hedonic displays, we use the term "facial display" to include both the display elements *and* the expressor's orientation to the target person. Because televised images of political leaders with sufficient detail to be useful as stimuli are typically from the shoulders up, we will not discuss other important nonverbal cues such as hand gestures and lower body movement.

Using ethological and social psychological work, we describe in turn each kind of facial display's expressive and impressive significance. For description of facial expressions of emotions, we rely on the work of Ekman and his colleagues (Ekman 1979; Ekman and Friesen 1975, 1976, 1978) and Izard (1972, 1977). For descriptions of the communicative significance of facial displays, we rely on van Hooff (1969, 1973), Eibl-Eibesfeldt (1979b; 1989), Ellsworth (1975), Argyle and Cook (1976), D. Morris (1967, 1977), Lorenz (1970–71), Hinde (1982), and Zivin (1977).

After describing the hedonic displays, we turn to the emotions and behaviors associated with anger and fear, that is, the elements associated with competitive rivalry or what Chance (1976a) has called "agonic social interaction." This procedure leads to the specification of three distinct constellations of facial displays that underlie important dimensions of nonverbal communication relating to public perception of political leaders.

*Hedonic Displays: Happiness, Reassurance, and Bonding*

The facial display of happiness associated with the functional class of hedonic behavior is apparently universal among humans and is analogous, if not homologous, to an important class of nonverbal behavior in other primates. Displays expressing happiness are related to social facilitation as distinct from attack or flight.

According to Ekman and Friesen (1982), an important, but not sole, "marker" in emotional expressions of happiness is the smile in which the lip corners are pulled upward toward the cheekbones and crow's-feet wrinkles appear around the eyes. In the same paper, they hypothesize that other markers involve dynamic properties of the smile, including smoothness of onset-offset, symmetry, and period of time at apex. Although their research on these matters is just now being reported, their preliminary results suggest that, from an ethological perspective, emotional expressions of happiness and gestures of reassurance are imperfectly related.

Although social psychologists have not concentrated on the impressive significance of facial displays in social rituals such as greeting behavior, ethologists have analyzed how blends of different displays can be combined for communicative purposes. Eibl-Eibesfeldt (1979b) notes that the smile is associated with "elements of surprise," so that the entire display appears to signal " 'pleasant surprise' at seeing a friend." Yet in studies of human emotion, surprise is generally expressed by facial cues that are distinct from those of happiness. Thus, classifying a display element as hedonic or agonic depends on how it combines with elements from other expressive displays for communicative purposes.

From an ethological perspective, greeting displays marked by a smile are particularly likely to be associated with bonding and social facilitation. Among nonhuman primates, it is the greeting display used by strange animals, or those who have been separated for some time, to indicate the absence of hostile intent. This display should function to lower the probability of an aggressive or agonistic interaction. For instance, a smiling face may have both the property of inducing a similar gesture and mood in the observer and the property of cutting off aggressive or submissive responses by that observer. These properties of the smiling face were recently demonstrated in a psychology experiment (Orr and Lanzetta 1980) in which a fear response was more readily conditioned to a fearful than a happy face, presumably because humans are predisposed to associate a happy face with positive outcomes.

In describing the greeting display as an example of a reassurance display, one must consider the relationship between the sender and receiver as well as additional eyebrow movements that Ekman does not consider to be markers of emotional expressions of happiness. Ethologists assert that there is a universal greeting display when two individuals see each other at a distance (Eibl-Eibesfeldt 1979b; D. Morris 1977). In assessing this display, primacy apparently should be given to the movements of the eyebrows and head, not to the smile. For example, Eibl-Eibesfeldt describes this gesture as follows: "One universal pattern of distance greeting begins with eye contact, followed by a head toss combined with a rapid raising of the eyebrows for approximately one-sixth of a second. The greeting is terminated with one or a few nods. A smile is usually, *but not always,* superimposed upon the whole sequence after eye contact has been established" (Eibl-Eibesfeldt 1979b, 26; emphasis added).

According to Darwin's principle of antithesis, those features of the greeting display that are most opposite to threat are critical. Hence, raised eyebrows (antithetical to lowered brows of anger/threat displays), tilted or moving head (antithetical to lowered and fixed stare of the threat displays), and relaxed lips and mouth (antithetical to compressed lip and mouth positions of threat or anger) should be the most salient. Although eye contact forms part of these greeting displays, it must be cut off to avoid the prolonged stare associated with threat. The smile is itself an ambiguous signal because it can be present in gestures with a higher component of submission then is characteristic of the purest displays of happiness or reassurance.

In conclusion, at least five components of a greeting gesture or happy facial expression might be present, in more or less attenuated form, in human reassurance displays:

1. raised brows;
2. head tilted back, nodding, or tilted to the side;
3. a smile or at least a relaxed mouth position (absence of the tense mouth characteristic of threat);
4. eye contact followed by a cutoff (absence of either prolonged staring or averted gaze); and
5. smoothness of the display.

*Agonic Displays: Anger/Threat and Fear/Evasion*

Popularizations of ethology (Ardrey 1963; Lorenz 1966) have focused attention on displays of aggressiveness as a mechanism for establishing and maintaining dominance. This approach is now so well known that, to avoid misunderstanding, it is necessary to specify exactly which nonverbal displays are being analyzed and how they are related to social status. In so doing, we will focus on facial expressions of emotion (anger and fear) and the corresponding impressions they produce (threat and evasion).

Because Chance (1976a) claims that some primates signal dominance primarily through hedonic behavior, one cannot assume that displays of anger/threat are the only indications of social status. On the contrary, the relationship between each type of display and social status must necessarily be an empirical question; aggression in male groups, for example, may be more typical of a lower-status male than of the group leader (Masters 1981). Further, Montagner (1978) has shown that one typical behavior among human children involves frequent threat displays by a nondominant individual described as "dominated aggressive."

*Displays of Anger/Threat.* In emotional expressions of anger, the eyebrows are lowered and drawn together, which creates or deepens wrinkles between the brows. These brow actions are accompanied by raising the upper eyelids and tightening the lower ones; the lips are either pressed firmly together or squared and tightened (Ekman 1979). This anger display is one of the emotional expressions universally differentiated among humans in preliterate as well as literate cultures (Ekman and Oster 1979).

When shifting from the expression of anger to the *social signals* for threat, components of head orientation and movement become critical. For example, Eibl-Eibesfeldt defines a threat gesture in terms of the "fixed stare" as follows: "In man, as well as in some other primates, a fixating look (full gaze) is perceived as a threat, if not interrupted by periodic cut-offs and if not accompanied by other signals of friendly intent. Looking at a person is a behavior which signals readiness for contact and attentiveness. But the looking must not be prolonged or it is perceived as an attempt to dominate or even threaten" (Eibl-Eibesfeldt 1979b, 21). Hence the presence of widely opened eyes, fixed stare, and vertical head orientation, coupled with the absence of features of greeting, are distinguishing components of threat gestures, though they may not be present in anger displays (D. Morris 1967).

In summary, human displays of anger/threat would include

1.  raised upper, and tightened lower, eyelids;
2.  staring gaze at the target person;
3.  vertical head orientation;
4.  brows pulled down and drawn together;
5.  tense face and body; and
6.  body orientation facing target person.

*Displays of Fear/Evasion.* In emotional expressions of fear, the inner and outer corners of the eyebrows are raised, and the brows are brought together, resulting in a pattern of wrinkles in the middle of the forehead; the lips are stretched horizontally (Ekman 1979). Since the eyelid movements are similar to those of anger, the contrasts between anger and fear are primarily associated with the mouth and eyebrows. The brow configuration is distinctly different from either anger or happiness. (See Masters et al. [1986] for a discussion of these issues.)

Mouth positions are more variable than brow positions in fear and submission displays. The horizontal stretching of the lips may or may not reveal the teeth. There again, a variable feature is most significant for what is absent, namely, the relaxed mouth positions of happiness/reassurance displays. Ekman has shown that such facial expressions of fear are universally distinguished in literate cultures, but were confused with surprise in his preliterate sample (Ekman and Friesen 1976; Ekman and Oster 1979).

In describing the kind of fear display that communicates evasion or submission, it is necessary to add elements of head and gaze orientation, such as gaze aversion and lowering of the chin, that are absent from Ekman's specification of the fear expression. In research on pre-school children, for example, Zivin (1977) found a correlation between the functional consequence of losing the competitive encounter and a "minus" or submissive face in which the brows are gently furrowed, the eyes are dropped, eye contact is broken, and the chin is lowered. Here, the brow position that is unambiguously congruent with a fearful expression is combined with an evasive head orientation.

Thus, the dynamic components of human facial displays signaling fear, evasion of conflict, or flight would include

1. furrowed brows characteristic of a fear face;
2. gaze aversion;
3. head or body orientation away from direct confrontation with others;
4. brusque or rough transition movements, reinforcing avoidance of eye contact; and
5. overall indications of muscular tenseness, especially in such features as lips (tense against teeth, whether opened or not) and eyelids (upper lids raised, lower lids tightened against eyeball).

## 3. DESCRIPTION OF THE FACIAL DISPLAYS OF POLITICAL LEADERS

Many experiments on human emotion have used static stimuli from unknown actors whose social status was not a critical factor. Because of our theoretical interest in the impact of dynamic facial displays of powerful political leaders on viewers, we selected television excerpts of happiness/reassurance, anger/threat, and fear/evasion facial displays by President Reagan, according to the criteria discussed in section 2 (see table 8-1). The excerpts were taken from archival records of President Reagan's speeches, press conferences, and debates. Subsequent experiments (not reported here) extend this approach to other politicians and to actors posing as politicians.

The initial experiments using President Reagan were designed to answer two questions. First, do the kinds of facial displays identified by social psychologists and ethologists have the predicted meaning for viewers, and second, in what ways are the emotional responses to leaders influenced by the nonverbal facial displays, by the subject's prior attitude or affect, and/or by the social context in which the leader communicates with the public?

In one series of studies, nine videotape segments of President Reagan, providing three high-intensity, homogeneous instances of each of the three kinds of display specified in table 8-1, were selected. We used videotape segments of the full face that lasted between 20 and 120 seconds. Subjects performed two tasks after viewing each segment. First, they *described* the

**Table 8-1.** Criteria for classifying facial displays

|  | Anger/Threat | Fear/Evasion | Happiness/Reassurance |
|---|---|---|---|
| Eyelids | Open wide | Upper raised; lower tightened | Wide, normal, or slightly widened |
| Eyebrows | Lowered | Lowered and furrowed | Raised |
| Eye orientation | Staring | Averted | Focused, then cut off |
| Mouth corners | Forward or lowered | Retracted, normal | Retracted and/or raised |
| Teeth showing | Lower or none | Variable | Upper or both |
| Head Motion: |  |  |  |
| Lateral | None | Side-to-side | Side-to-side |
| Vertical | None | Down | Up-down |
| Head orientation: |  |  |  |
| To body | Forward from trunk | Turned from vertical | Normal to trunk |
| Angle to vertical | Down | Down | Up |

segment using nine scales, presented as triads of descriptive adjectives (strong, determined, self-confident; angry, threatening, aggressive; comforting, helpful, reassuring; evasive, insincere, untruthful; joyful, happy, amused; disgusted, disdainful, scornful; confused, puzzled, bewildered; fearful, anxious, worried; interested, eager, curious). Because decoding an expressive display is different from the emotional impressions it elicits, participants were asked to distinguish carefully between their descriptions and their emotional reactions. Therefore, they next reported their own *emotional response* to each segment using eight scales (the "strong" and "evasive" triads were not presented; the "supportive, sympathetic, inspired" triad was added).

Two groups of subjects were tested: 65 adults attending a continuing education program at Dartmouth College (experiment 1) and 145 Dartmouth undergraduates (experiment 2). To control for the distinct effects of facial gestures and verbal messages, subjects were randomly assigned to rooms in which the videotapes were presented simultaneously either without sound ("image-only" condition), without picture ("sound-only" condition), or with both channels ("sound-plus-image" condition). The second experiment included, additionally, a "filtered-sound-plus-image" condition (providing both the image and paravocal cues, but no understandable verbal message) and a "transcript" condition (printed verbal messages to be read silently). Since stimuli were chosen to be congruent in facial display, paravocal cues, and verbal affect, one can compare the effects of each channel of communication as well as measure their joint effects.

**Table 8-2.** Factor structure of the descriptions of President Reagan's happiness/reassurance, anger/threat, and fear/evasion displays for all media conditions combined*

| | Factor 1 Happiness/ reassurance | | Factor 2 Anger/threat | | Factor 3 Fear/evasion | | Communality | |
|---|---|---|---|---|---|---|---|---|
| Experiment | 1 | 2 | 1 | 2 | 1 | 2 | 1 | 2 |
| Strong | .59 | .46 | .37 | .32 | −.55 | −.69 | 79 | 78 |
| Joyful | .80 | .61 | −.04 | −.42 | .05 | −.28 | 64 | 62 |
| Comforting | .74 | .70 | −.12 | −.28 | −.35 | −.31 | 68 | 66 |
| Interested | .74 | .90 | −.07 | .04 | −.18 | −.12 | 59 | 82 |
| Angry | −.10 | −.05 | .90 | .92 | −.01 | −.13 | 83 | 86 |
| Disgusted | −.03 | −.17 | .83 | .88 | .25 | .08 | 75 | 80 |
| Fearful | −.32 | −.21 | .12 | .25 | .75 | .75 | 67 | 66 |
| Confused | −.21 | −.19 | −.03 | −.08 | .88 | .87 | 82 | 80 |
| Evasive | .05 | −.09 | .29 | .01 | .77 | .70 | 69 | 50 |
| Percent variance accounted for | 25 | 22 | 20 | 23 | 27 | 28 | | |

*Principal components analysis with Varimax rotation ($n = 65$ in experiment 1, and $n = 145$ in experiment 2). Italicized loadings were used to interpret the factors.

First, to assess the underlying dimensions of the viewers' descriptions, the correlation matrix of subjects' descriptive scale ratings of the nine videotaped displays were factor analyzed.[1] The results revealed a striking overall consistency in viewers' descriptions (table 8-2); for both groups of subjects, ratings were reducible to three easily identified factors: happiness/reassurance (factor 1), anger/threat (factor 2), and fear/evasion (factor 3). In each sample, the factors were robust, accounting for over 70 percent of the total variance; each factor was correlated with *only* the descriptive ratings predicted by these three dimensions of display behavior.

There was, no statistically significant correlation between viewers' descriptions of the displays and their prior attitude toward President Reagan (with an exception in one media condition found in reanalysis). In other words, even those individuals whose emotional responses to a political leader may be strongly influenced by their opinions and partisanship provided accurate descriptions of that leader's nonverbal expressions. Like previous studies on the

1. A traditional factor analysis, in which factors with eigen values greater than 1.0 are retained, yields two factors, each of which is bipolar. The first of these factors reflects reassurance (with its poles as descriptions of joyful versus angry); the second factor represents dominance (with poles of strong versus confused or weak); factor weights for these two factors are highly similar in France and the United States (Masters and Sullivan 1989b, table 1 and figure 1a–b). An additional factor analysis retaining factors with eigen values greater than .80 resulted in three more nearly monopolar factors, corresponding to joy, anger, and fear; these factors were also remarkably similar in composition not only in France and the United States but across media conditions. In this paper we report the three-factor solution.

recognition of facial expressions of emotion (e.g., Ekman 1972), the excerpts used here contained relatively homogeneous, high-intensity displays; it is possible that blends of lower-intensity expressions would produce different results.

Since table 8-2 pools data for subjects in the image-only condition and in the other four media conditions, the overall factor analyses do not distinguish descriptions of facial displays from attributions of emotional expression due to paravocal cues (such as tone and rhythm of voice) or to the verbal message. To separate the effects of the different nonverbal and verbal cues, we analyzed responses to each media condition using three distinct procedures: (1) a factor analysis to examine the structure of responses on all nine descriptive scales; (2) differences in profiles of standardized factor scores; and (3) a "centroid" cluster analysis to assess viewers' descriptive accuracy, on the assumption that our characterization of the display excerpts was correct. With only one exception, the factor analysis of two media conditions in experiment 2, there were no significant differences in descriptions of the nine excerpts in the eight subsamples (three in experiment 1, five in experiment 2).

First, the factor analyses for each media condition confirmed the general stability and robustness of the three factors defined above; despite small sample sizes, six of the eight analyses revealed the same happy/reassurance, anger/threat, and fear/evasion dimensions (table 8-3).

Although the factor analysis of the image-only condition of experiment 2 produced slightly different results, the differences concerned the factor loadings

**Table 8-3.** Factor structure of descriptions of President Reagan's happiness/reassurance, anger/threat, and fear/evasion displays for image-only (IO), sound-only (SO), and sound-plus-image (S + I) media conditions from experiment 1*

|  | Factor 1 Happiness/reassurance | | | Factor 2 Anger/threat | | | Factor 3 Fear/evasion | | |
|---|---|---|---|---|---|---|---|---|---|
|  | IO | SO | S + I | IO | SO | S + I | IO | SO | S + I |
| Strong | .58 | .52 | .60 | .43 | .32 | .32 | − .49 | − .64 | − .59 |
| Joyful | .81 | .84 | .82 | − .13 | .16 | − .09 | − .21 | .16 | .08 |
| Comforting | .83 | .64 | .70 | − .09 | − .26 | − .13 | − .18 | − .46 | − .43 |
| Interested | .82 | .55 | .75 | − .12 | − .16 | − .03 | − .03 | − .36 | − .18 |
| Angry | − .17 | − .04 | − .11 | .89 | .88 | .92 | .04 | .01 | − .10 |
| Disgusted | − .09 | − .01 | − .03 | .81 | .82 | .86 | .27 | .22 | .24 |
| Fearful | − .35 | − .08 | − .47 | .24 | .12 | .01 | .75 | .82 | .67 |
| Confused | − .23 | − .18 | − .21 | − .07 | .04 | − .04 | .88 | .87 | .90 |
| Evasive | .04 | .00 | .11 | .33 | .24 | .36 | .70 | .80 | .76 |
| Percent variance accounted for | 29 | 19 | 26 | 20 | 19 | 20 | 25 | 32 | 27 |

*Principal components analysis with Varimax rotation; $n = 65$. The results for experiment 2 (see Masters et al. 1986, table 5) were comparable. Commonalities are comparable in each media condition and are not reported here. Italicized loadings were used to interpret the factors.

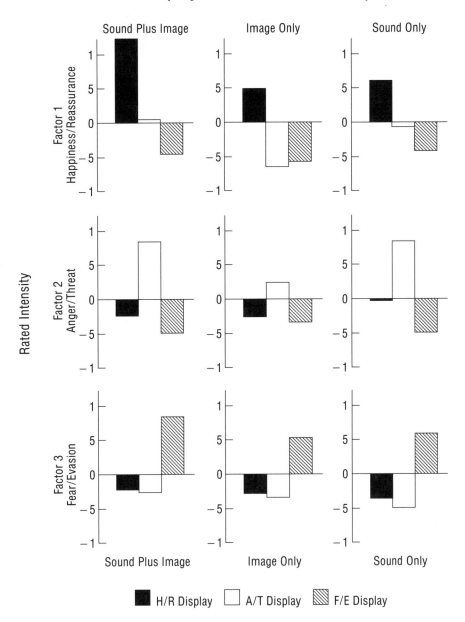

Figure 8-1. Subject descriptions (as factor scores) of President Reagan's happiness/reassurance (H/R), anger/threat (A/T) and fear/evasion (F/E) displays in sound-plus-image, image-only, and sound-only media conditions (experiment 1).

for relatively few descriptive scales. This anomaly does not seem due to differences in the way subjects perceived stimuli when they saw facial displays without sound. On the contrary, the second and third analytic tests indicated an extraordinary degree of redundancy in facial, verbal, and paravocal cues of emotion.

The second test used factor scores for subjects' responses to each kind of display (i.e., for each of the two experiments, raw scores on the nine descriptive scales were converted to three standardized scores based on the factor structure shown in table 8-3). If seeing the face without hearing the sound was a fundamentally different experience, subjects in the image-only condition, and perhaps filtered-sound-plus-image as well, should differ from those who heard (or read) the messages. Yet, as figure 8-1 shows, the factor score congruent with the expressive display was always significantly more positive than other factor scores regardless of media condition: within each media condition, it was the difference between descriptions of the three kinds of expressive displays that was significant.

Finally, an additional procedure comparing three of the media conditions in experiment 2 was used. A "centroid" cluster analysis was performed on the descriptive scale scores to test viewers' accuracy in decoding the three expressive displays (for details on this method, see McHugo, Smith, and Lanzetta 1982). This procedure determines the difference between the actual descriptive ratings and a set of idealized ratings that treat each display as if it were completely unblended. The cluster analysis showed that there were no significant differences between the image-only, sound-only, and sound-plus-image conditions for the descriptions of expressive displays (Masters et al. 1986). Taken together, these analyses of subject's descriptions support the theoretical distinctions between the three nonverbal displays identified above.

## 4. EMOTIONAL RESPONSES TO FACIAL DISPLAY BEHAVIOR

Many social psychologists describe "positive" and "negative" emotional responses that are parallel to the hedonic and agonic dimensions distinguished by Chance (1976a, b). For example, when voters were asked to recall their feelings toward presidential candidates, their emotional responses gave rise to two dimensions of affect, clearly characterized as positive and negative (Abelson et al. 1982). Hence we began with a two-factor analysis of the emotional responses in the experiments described above as well as in a third experiment (to be described below) in which psychophysiological responses were also recorded.

Table 8-4 shows that in responding to selected videotapes of President Reagan in the laboratory, subjects used emotional terms in much the same way voters did in a presidential preference survey (Abelson et al. 1982). Furthermore, when separate factor analyses were done for each media condition in experiments 1 and 2, the two-factor solution was remarkably stable across subsamples. We therefore conclude that viewers respond emotionally to televised displays of a political leader along the same positive (hedonic) and negative (agonic) dimensions identified by social psychologists and ethologists. Furthermore, these emotional responses, like descriptions of the same displays, are relatively invariant across different channels of communication.

**Table 8-4.** Factor structure of emotional responses to President Reagan's happiness/reassurance, anger/threat, and fear/evasion displays for all media conditions combined*

| | Experiment 1 (n = 65) | | Experiment 2 (n = 145) | |
|---|---|---|---|---|
| | Positive | Negative | Positive | Negative |
| Joyful | .70 | −.06 | .69 | −.34 |
| Comforted | .83 | −.26 | .83 | −.29 |
| Supportive | .83 | −.30 | .84 | −.25 |
| Interested | .71 | −.02 | .81 | .09 |
| Angry | −.05 | .87 | −.05 | .84 |
| Disgusted | −.21 | .81 | −.25 | .79 |
| Fearful | −.11 | .86 | −.17 | .81 |
| Confused | −.20 | .68 | −.15 | .58 |
| Percent variance accounted for | 31 | 35 | 33 | 33 |

*Principal components analysis with Varimax rotation. Italicized loadings were used to interpret the factors.

Unlike descriptions, however, the self-reported emotional responses were highly influenced by viewers' preexperimental attitudes. In figure 8-2, factor scores for positive and negative emotional responses to the three kinds of expressive displays are plotted as a function of prior attitude toward President Reagan; because media condition did not change the basic pattern of responses, the results from all groups were combined.

Clearly, emotional responses to exemplars of the three display types were influenced powerfully by prior attitude. Whereas happiness/reassurance excerpts generated very strong positive responses in the president's supporters and neutral reactions from his opponents, fear/evasion excerpts generated little positive affect from any viewers; anger/threat excerpts were intermediate, generating moderately positive responses from supporters but not from critics. Negative affect was roughly inverted: agonistic excerpts generated more negative responses in critics than in supporters, whereas happy/reassurance excerpts reduced negative emotional responses in critics and even more so in supporters.

These results show that viewers accurately describe and report different emotional responses to televised excerpts of three kinds of expressive behavior. Although emotional responses are somewhat weaker in the image-only condition, their direction is consistent with those for other media conditions. Yet the evidence of emotional responses in these two experiments is based on verbal self-reports, which could be unreliable as indicators of actual emotional arousal.

For this reason, a third experiment measured psychophysiological responses to videotape stimuli like these in experiments 1 and 2. Experiment 3, reported in detail elsewhere (McHugo et al. 1985), combined self-reported emotional

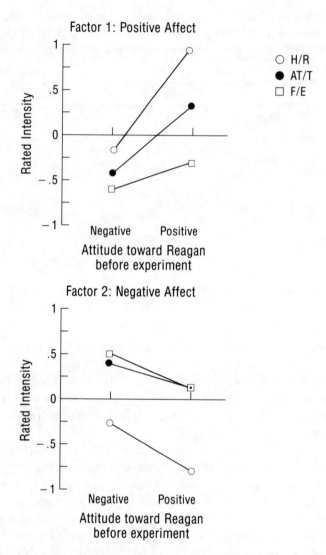

Figure 8-2. Positive and negative emotional responses (as factor scores) to President Reagan's happiness/reassurance (H/R), anger/threat (A/T), and fear/evasion (F/E) displays as a function of attitude toward Reagan before the experiment; (0–49 = negative and 51–100 = positive on a 100-point thermometer scale (experiment 2).

impressions with four psychophysiological measures: skin resistance, heart rate, and surface electromyographic (EMG) changes from two facial regions— corrugator supercilli (brow) and zygomaticus major (cheek/mouth). Since zygomatic activation is associated with positive emotional responses, whereas activation of the corrugator is reliably correlated with anger or tension, these two EMG measures are appropriate ways of testing the emotional responses at a physiological level (Cacioppo and Petty 1979; Fridlund and Izard 1983; G. Schwartz et al. 1976).

In Experiment 3, undergraduate subjects were presented with a randomized sequence of President Reagan's expressive displays in image-only and sound-plus-image media conditions. This experiment compared psychophysiological measures of the immediate emotional reaction with self-reports taken after a short time delay. Figure 8-3 presents the phasic amplitude (change from

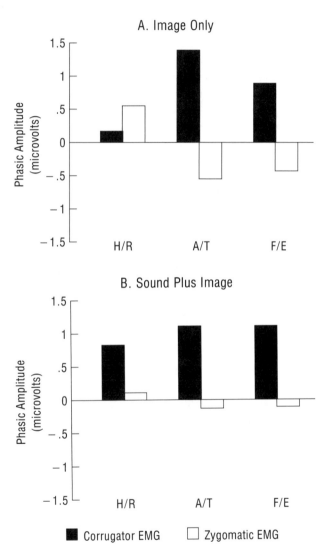

Figure 8-3. Corrugator and zygomatic EMG responses (as change from baseline) to President Reagan's displays of happiness/reassurance (H/R), anger/threat (A/T), and fear/evasion (F/E) in image-only (A) and sound-plus-image (B) media conditions (experiment 3).

baseline) of corrugator and zygomatic EMG to happiness/reassurance, anger/threat, and fear/evasion displays in both media conditions.

Four major results of this experiment are important to highlight. First, as figure 8-3 shows, for the image-only condition the three displays had different effects. All displays resulted in some degree of corrugator activation, reflecting the lowering of the brows associated with focusing visual attention. This activation was less pronounced in response to happiness/reassurance versus anger/threat displays. Our experiment thus confirms previous findings that corrugator activation is maximized in response to threat, consistent with the linkage between lowered brows and anger/threat responses discussed in section 2 above (G. Schwartz et al. 1976). In contrast, zygomatic muscles, associated with a smile, were activated by happiness/reassurance episodes, but relaxed by both anger/threat and fear/evasion displays.

Second, the physiological patterns of response were consistent with the results discussed earlier on self-reported emotional responses. In general, the pattern of EMG responses indicative of positive affect was present for the happiness/reassurance displays, which elicited self-reports of joy and comfort. In a similar manner, the anger response (relaxed zygomatic and activation of the corrugator) was strongest to anger/threat displays, which elicited self-reports of scorn and fear. Thus, the results indicate that there is an expressive substrate congruent with self-reported emotional responses to the expressive displays. Hence, our previous findings are unlikely to be artifacts of the use of self-report measures.

Third, the impact of a politician's nonverbal expressive behavior was greatly influenced by the presence or absence of a verbal message; psychophysiological responses were less marked when the viewer simultaneously processed verbal and nonverbal cues than when the facial displays were seen in the image-only condition. As figure 8-3 shows, the amplitude of happiness/reassurance responses (zygomatic activation, corrugator attenuation) to President Reagan's happiness/reassurance displays was greater in the image-only than in the sound-plus-image condition. In a similar manner, anger responses (corrugator activation and zygomatic relaxation) were more intense in the image-only than in the sound-plus-image condition. Fear/evasion displays seen without a verbal message produce intermediate activation of the corrugator and relaxation of the zygomatic. Anger/threat and fear/evasion display produced similar tensional patterns when the sound accompanied the image.

Fourth, the psychophysiological measures of facial expressions of emotion were not correlated with subjects' prior attitudes as were self-reported responses. Although the failure of attitude toward President Reagan to predict physiological responses to his expressive displays may be due to the fact that these responses were measured *while* the subject viewed the televised images, such effects have been found when viewers see rival leaders in a single study (McHugo, et al., in prep.).

Thus, in general, subjects' physiological responses differed by media condition and by expression condition, but were uncorrelated with preexperimental attitude toward President Reagan. Although these findings suggest that viewers' emotional responses to expressive gestures of political leaders may be an important factor in politics, the precise way that facial displays influence viewers is complex. The fact that prior attitude toward President Reagan affected viewers' postexperimental self-reported emotional responses, but not physiological responses measured during exposure to the displays, indicates that there are raw, unprocessed emotional responses to facial displays. Although the magnitude of such responses is not great, there are good theoretical reasons to expect these emotional responses to mediate the formation of, and changes in, impressions of political leaders. Moreover, the strong correlation between prior attitude and self-reported emotional responses indicates an important role for cognitive appraisal as well. Thus, a theory adequate to explain the effects of expressive displays of a known political leader on viewers must include both cognitive and emotional variables.

## 5. CONCLUSIONS

Our research program has begun outlining the dimensions of nonverbal display behavior in politics. We have demonstrated the feasibility of experimental analysis of the complex interactions between expressive behavior, the medium of communication, and prior attitudes, which can influence citizens' dispositions to support a political leader.

Subsequent work has extended our analysis of the effects of repeated exposure to televised coverage of actual political leaders. In one experimental design, images of President Reagan's facial displays were edited into the background of newscasts, so that the same story could be shown to different viewers accompanied by different facial displays; subjects exposed to sets of such stimuli had different emotional responses and judgments, depending on the mixture of displays to which they had been exposed (Sullivan et al. 1984b; Sullivan and Masters in press a). Another design used excerpts of all nine candidates in the 1984 and 1988 American presidential elections and revealed not only that candidates differed in their display behavior, but that seeing them elicited different patterns of emotional response and attitude change that might help to explain political outcomes (Sullivan and Masters 1988, in press b).

Replication of these studies in France showed that while leaders' facial displays have similar effects in another culture, anger/threat elicits more positive emotions in French than American viewers (Masters and Sullivan 1989 a, b). In another set of experiments, four actors posing as candidates gave the same standardized political speeches with different expressive displays; viewers' impressions of each actor were influenced by the display, the actor's gender, and the actor's personal style as well as by the gender and attitudes of the viewer (Plate 1984). Finally, in an experimental study, responses to the third

Ford-Carter debate in the 1976 presidential election were compared for viewers who saw a videotape of the debate with or without network "instant analysis"; after a pause, both groups saw a network newscast story about the debates. Here we found that both instant analysis and news coverage increased negative feelings and judgments of both candidates, but that these effects were greatest for viewers whose political opinions were not strongly developed (Newton et al. 1985).

The following conclusions can be drawn from our initial experiments:

1. Functionally important categories of facial display behavior can be defined *objectively*, based on research in ethology and social psychology.

2. When presented with videotape excerpts of a political leader exhibiting three different kinds of displays (happiness/reassurance, anger/threat, and fear/evasion), viewers *describe* the expression in terms consistent with the objective definitions. Moreover, these descriptions are relatively invariant regardless of media condition (image-only, filtered-sound-plus-image, sound-plus-image, sound-only or transcript) and are largely independent of viewers' preexperimental attitude.

3. Viewers also provide self-reports of *emotional response* that are different for each kind of facial display. Unlike descriptions, these emotional responses are influenced strongly by prior attitudes and, in general, show that facial displays have larger effects on the emotional responses of supporters than of critics.

4. *Prior attitudes* influence the quality as well as intensity of viewers' emotional responses: whereas supporters respond positively when presented with happiness/reassurance displays and (to a lesser degree) anger/threat displays, critics tend to be neutral after seing happiness/reassurance and negative after anger/threat. Agonic (anger/threat and fear/evasion) displays are more likely to generate negative emotional responses—or, for supporters, to produce weaker positive emotions—than do displays of happiness/reassurance.

5. *Psychophysiological measures* of emotion confirm the potency of these televised stimuli: each kind of expressive display generates EMG responses like those known to characterize emotional feelings. These effects, while evident when the sound accompanies the image, are considerably enhanced if the viewer sees only the visual image of the facial display.

These propositions indicate that the methods and approaches of ethology and social psychology can be combined to study political behavior. To go beyond the findings reported here, far more research is necessary. Expressive behavior of various political leaders differs in the frequency or character of its emotional impact on viewers. Prior attitude, social status, economic class, age, sex or gender, and partisan attachment influence viewers' emotional and political responses. On these and a host of related issues, we cannot foresee the conclusions of this line of research. But it should be clear that, by such an experimental exploration of the effects of nonverbal displays, we can contribute to a deeper understanding of the complex interactions between political leaders and their followers.

# 9

# Human Vocalizations
# in Agonistic Political Encounters

James N. Schubert

## RESEARCH PROBLEMS

An important category of human political behavior involves collective decision making in small groups. A variety of factors must be considered in the description and explanation of the decision-making process in political groups. One important facet of small-group decision making that has received scant attention in previous research in this area involves the social interaction process among group members engaged in decision making (Golembiewski 1978). Of particular concern are the impact of social relations in the group and individual behavioral strategies upon the structure and process of influence in collective decision making. This paper reports on one area of preliminary findings from a broader research project designed to explore the relationship between social dominance and political influence in small-group political decision making (J. Schubert 1984a, b).

Two research questions provided the central tasks of this paper. One question may be defined in terms of how humans use their voice in political interactions. The research task is to describe the paralinguistic properties of competitive verbal behavior of face-to-face encounters during the discussion or debate process preceding decision in small-group decision making.

This paper was presented at an Interdisciplinary Symposium on Political Behaviour organized by Glendon Schubert and Shirley Strum at the Tenth Congress of the International Primatological Society, which convened under the auspices of the Institute of Primate Research at the National Museum of Kenya in Nairobi, from 22 to 27 July 1984. The research upon which the paper is based is supported by a grant from the United States National Science Foundation (SES-8309643). It was originally published in *Social Science Information* 25, no. 2 (1986): 475–92; reprinted by permission.

A second research question involves the impact of social relationships within the group upon the structure of vocal behavior in group discussion and debate. Here, the research task is to explore the role of paralinguistic properties of speech in social dominance relations.

## METHODS

Data for this study are drawn from a year-long period of observation of decision making in a rural, small-town, municipal council in the United States. The group consists of an elected mayor and four council members. The group includes one woman, and ages range from approximately forty to sixty years.

All meetings of the council during the year-long period were observed by the author and recorded on audiotape; several were also recorded on videotape as well. The identity of the actors and targets of behaviors were coded live on an event recorder, which also provided data on time of occurrence.

Active consideration of issues is only one of the several group activities that occur at meetings. Data were developed for this paper only from those group discussions where substantive deliberation took place. Four general types of group interaction processes involving discussion among members may be distinguished. First is a category of "task-oriented" and technical problem-solving discussions where the group is in agreement on the general nature of the solution or decision. Second are noncompetitive consensus-building discussion processes where there is no fundamental disagreement among members but positions on issues are initially undetermined. Here, consensus formation occurs through the interaction process: the group achieves a common position but without major disagreement. A third category involves processes where competition over outcomes is manifest, but consensus is achieved. Thus, conflicts and disagreements are resolved in a process of consensus formation. In the group observed, all decisions in this category were based on unanimous votes, despite initial patterns of disagreement in the discussion. Finally, a fourth category involves "conflict" interaction processes in which competition over outcomes is present and disagreements are not resolved. In this category, dissenting votes are observed. Of these four types of interaction processes, only the latter two are considered competitive. Because this analysis focuses on patterns of competitive behavior to indicate social dominance relations, only behaviors in competitive interaction processes are addressed in this analysis. Data are developed on a total of eleven interaction processes: six competitive consensus processes and five competitive conflict processes.

For purposes of this analysis, data were only employed on the competitive properties of verbal behavior. A speaker's "turn"—the period in which a speaker held the floor—provided the primary unit of observation. The competitive properties of a turn were coded as a categorical variable. Turns were coded as primarily involving a competitive initiation, a competitive reaction, or as noncompetitive. A competitive initiation was coded if the turn initiated an attack on, or direct challenge to, the position of one or more other individuals. A competitive reaction was coded when an individual responded to a competitive initiation. Thus, initiations begin, or attempt to begin, an interaction process between two or more individuals where the initiator attempts to change, modify, or undermine the position in debate supported by the target or recipient(s).

Competitive reactions to competitive initiations were also coded in one of three categories. Offensive reactions were coded when individuals responded to an initiation by such strategies as answering a question with a question, responding with sarcasm or ridicule, providing a reciprocal attack on the challenger's position, or otherwise sidestepping the challenge. Defensive reactions were coded when individuals responded to an initiation by defending their position against the challenge. Questions are taken seriously and answered substantively, positions are reinforced with supporting arguments, and the individual generally acts to preserve his or her personal status and issue position before the group through defensive reactions. Submissive behavior was coded when individuals "backed down" or accepted the initiation directed against them. Statements such as "I guess I was wrong" or "that was a poor argument" are examples of submissive reactions where individuals effectively concede to their challenger.

Paralinguistic dimensions of vocal behavior include fundamental frequency or pitch, intensity or amplitude, variation in pitch and intensity, speech rate, and speech fluency. Paralinguistic aspects of speech play an important role in social communication, including cues to age, sex, ethnicity, socioeconomic status, as well as affective states (Scherer 1979). Paralinguistics may also be quite important as indicators of arousal (Scherer 1982). Vocal arousal may have causal effects on patterns of attention within a group (McGuinness and Pribram 1980), and paralinguistics provide important resources to actors performing social control functions and/or engaged in interpersonal competition (Edinger and Patterson 1983).

Data on paralinguistic aspects of vocal behavior in political debate were developed for the sample of behaviors and variables identified above. Speech rate was measured by counting words per turn and norming the result to yield a rate of words per minute. One dimension of fluency in speech involves smooth flow in delivery, as opposed to halting speech punctuated by frequent pauses. Pauses, fundamental frequency, intensity, and pitch and intensity variation in speech were measured through electro-acoustical analysis of audio recordings.

Audio recordings were made on a Sony TCM 5000 audiocassette tape recorder with a cardioid dynamic microphone and recording on TDK AD cassette tapes. The audio signal was input to a VisiPitch voice analysis instrument. The VisiPitch provides output voltages for fundamental frequency and intensity that were input to a chart recorder to provide continuous traces on a strip chart for these two variables. Continuous recordings were processed for an entire interaction or discussion process. As the strip chart recordings were made, the movement of the chart recorder pen on the chart was also recorded on videotape. The audio signal input to the VisiPitch was also copied on the audio track of the videotape. Thus, a permanent record was developed associating the traces on the strip chart with the voices they describe. The videotape was played back on a monitor to enable interpretation of the strip chart. Speaker turns, predefined on a typed transcript of proceedings, were marked off on the chart. A quarter-inch bar on the chart represents approximately three seconds in time. Within bars, high and low values of the traces were observed; means were calculated for all the bars in a turn on each variable. In addition, spikes or reversals in slope of significant magnitude were counted to measure variation in the trace. Finally, zero readings on the amplitude trace were counted to measure the frequency of pauses. Pen movements associated with coughs, extraneous noises, simultaneous speech by two or more actors, etc., were noted on the strip charts and these segments were skipped in quantification. Finally, because the measurement system was adjusted somewhat for each of the separate interaction processes, data on pitch and intensity were standardized for each interaction process and analysis was performed on $z$ scores.

## DATA AND FINDINGS

Data were first analyzed at the group level to describe general characteristics of competitive behavior and to explore with available data the construct validity of the typological classifications of behavior. Table 9-1 presents data on the characteristics of the two different types of competitive interaction processes. With respect to the type of behavior, there was 10 percent more competitive behavior in conflict than consensus processes—primarily more reactive behavior. The clearest differences between the two types of processes appear with respect to alternative types of reactive behavior. Processes in which conflict was not resolved reveal substantially more defensive behaviors, while consensus processes show greater offensive and submissive behavior. It might be expected that consensus will be achieved more readily when some individuals submit to others, rather than pursue and support conflicting positions. On the other hand, the greater frequency of defensive behavior in conflict processes may reflect greater effort to influence other members on the substantive issues. Defensive utterances respond directly to competitive initiations and tend to support a conflicting position in debate. Offensive reactions, by contrast, dodge the issues in contention and often respond to competitive initiations through social strategies.

In Table 9-1a, paralinguistic variables in vocal behavior are contrasted for the alternative types of competitive interaction processes. With regard to pitch,

**Table 9-1.** Competitive interaction processes

a. Frequency of competitive behavior

| | Type of interaction process | |
|---|---|---|
| *Type of behavior* | *Conflict %* | *Consensus %* |
| Reaction | 19.9 | 11.8 |
| Initiation | 15.1 | 13.5 |
| Non-competition | 65.1 | 74.7 |
| Total | 100.1 | 100 |
| *n* = | 186 | 178 |
| Type of reaction | | |
| Offensive | 40.0 | 57.1 |
| Defensive | 55.0 | 14.3 |
| Submissive | 5.0 | 28.6 |
| Total | 100 | 100 |
| *n* = | 60 | 21 |

b. Paralinguistic parameters of competitive interaction processes.

Type of interaction process*

| | *Conflict* | | *Consensus* | |
|---|---|---|---|---|
| Pitch (Z) | .022 | (1.06) | .007 | (1.00) |
| Pitch variation | 2.16 | (1.26) | 1.67 | (1.30) |
| Intensity (Z) | .098 | (1.02) | .009 | (1.01) |
| Intensity variation | 1.70 | (0.85) | 1.12 | (.75) |
| Pause rate | 4.11 | (5.45) | 5.36 | (9.11) |
| Speech rate | 156 | (65.6) | 167 | (100.2) |
| *n* = | 186 | | 178 | |

*Values are means with standard deviations in parentheses

pitch variation, intensity, and intensity variation, standard deviations are similar across the two types and conflict processes have higher values. That is, conflict processes were associated with somewhat higher pitch, intensity, and variation in pitch and intensity. Thus, vocal arousal appears greater in conflict than consensus interaction processes. Although pause and speech rates are somewhat lower in conflict processes, the standard deviations are so different that it might be unwise to take pause and speech rate differences too seriously. In general, it may be concluded that in this group, discussions that did not reach consensus were characterized by more competitive behavior and by verbal interactions at a somewhat higher level of vocal arousal. Table 9-2 presents data on paralinguistic characteristics of competitive behavior in the group as a whole. With the exception of pause rates, it is clear that competitive behavior is associated with higher levels of vocal arousal. Competitive verbal behavior is

**Table 9-2.** Paralinguistic properties of competitive political behavior*

| | Type of behavior | | | | | | Type of reaction | | | | | |
| | Reaction | | Initiation | | Non-competitive | | Offensive | | Defensive | | Submissive | |
|---|---|---|---|---|---|---|---|---|---|---|---|---|
| Pitch (z) | .42 | (1.1) | .03 | (.91) | −.08 | (.99) | .37 | (.87) | .62 | (1.6) | .00 | (.50) |
| Pitch variation | 2.46 | (1.4) | 1.92 | (1.3) | 1.79 | (1.3) | 2.35 | (1.07) | 2.95 | (1.6) | 1.29 | (.74) |
| Intensity (z) | .54 | (.91) | .08 | (.90) | −.06 | (1.0) | .68 | (.86) | .59 | (.87) | −.16 | (1.1) |
| Intensity variation | 1.72 | (.87) | 1.47 | (.71) | 1.33 | (.86) | 1.58 | (.64) | 2.21 | (.85) | .65 | (.52) |
| Pause rate | 4.15 | (4.9) | 5.07 | (5.5) | 4.78 | (8.3) | 3.48 | (4.5) | 4.89 | (5.7) | 4.37 | (4.2) |
| Speech rate | 187 | (67) | 165 | (48) | 154 | (92) | 182 | (45) | 199 | (92) | 171 | (35) |
| n = | 58 | | 52 | | 254 | | 28 | | 23 | | 7 | |

*Values are means with standard deviations in parentheses.

undertaken at higher levels of pitch, intensity, pitch and intensity variation, and at faster speech rates than noncompetitive behavior. While this finding lends support to the validity of the classification scheme for type of behavior, what is more interesting are the differences between reactive and initiating competitive behaviors. Thus, reactive behavior displays higher vocal arousal than initiating behavior across all the paralinguistic variables. Standard deviations and ns are quite similar between these two categories of competitive behavior. This difference between categories could reflect a cognitive situation in which the individual is free to launch a competitive initiation or to hold his or her peace. However, once individuals are the target of someone else's initiation, they are placed in a competitive context where they must respond: even silence is a response, albeit one that is likely to cost the individual in personal and group esteem. In other words, it may be hypothesized that arousal will be greater where behavioral choices are more constrained by the interactive situation.

Given that reactive behaviors appear more arousing, differences in arousal also appear with respect to type of reaction. Consistently least arousing is submissive behavior. That is, submissive utterances are associated with lower pitch, lower intensity, less variation in voice, and a slower rate of delivery.

Conversely, defensive reactions reveal higher pitch, greater variation in voice, and a faster speech rate. As a behavioral strategy, it may be proposed that a careful, deliberate defense of one's positions and argument requires greater risk and investment of personal resources than either a glib retort or an act of concession. In general, the data in table 9-2 show substantial and plausible differences between the paralinguistic characteristics of alternative forms of competitive behavior in small-group political debate.

Table 9-3 presents data on competitive behavior among individual group members. Individuals are ordered in these tables from left to right in terms of their rank in overall or total verbal participation and in behavior received from

**Table 9-3.** Individual involvement in competitive interactions

a. Type of process

|  | % Mayor | Member 1 | Member 3 | Member 4 | Member 2 |
|---|---|---|---|---|---|
| Conflict | 61.0 | 49.3 | 45.6 | 47.5 | 30.6 |
| Consensus | 39.0 | 50.7 | 54.4 | 52.5 | 69.4 |
| Total | 100 | 100 | 100 | 100 | 100 |
| n = | 141 | 69 | 57 | 61 | 36 |

b. Competitive participation

|  | % Mayor | Member 1 | Member 3 | Member 4 | Member 2 |
|---|---|---|---|---|---|
| Reaction | 14.9 | 24.6 | 15.8 | 13.1 | 8.3 |
| Initiation | 5.7 | 21.7 | 29.8 | 11.5 | 13.9 |
| Noncompetitive | 79.4 | 53.6 | 54.4 | 75.4 | 77.8 |
| Total | 100 | 99.9 | 100 | 100 | 100 |
| n = | 141 | 69 | 57 | 61 | 36 |

c. Competitive attention (behavior received)

|  | % Mayor | Member 1 | Member 3 | Member 4 | Member 2 |
|---|---|---|---|---|---|
| Reaction | 19.3 | 16.4 | 11.3 | 21.7 | 30.8 |
| Initiation | 21.6 | 18.0 | 9.4 | 6.5 | 0.0 |
| Noncompetitive | 59.1 | 65.6 | 79.2 | 71.7 | 69.2 |
| Total | 100 | 100 | 99.9 | 99.9 | 100 |
| n = | 88 | 61 | 53 | 46 | 26 |

d. Reactive participation

|  | % Mayor | Member 1 | Member 3 | Member 4 | Member 2 |
|---|---|---|---|---|---|
| Offensive | 38.0 | 64.7 | 44.4 | 25.0 | 100 |
| Defensive | 62.0 | 29.4 | 44.4 | 12.5 | 0 |
| Submissive | 0 | 5.9 | 11.1 | 62.5 | 0 |
| Total | 100 | 100 | 99.9 | 100 | 100 |
| n = | 21 | 17 | 9 | 8 | 3 |

e. Reactive attention (reactions received)

|  | % Mayor | Member 1 | Member 3 | Member 4 | Member 2 |
|---|---|---|---|---|---|
| Offensive | 35.3 | 30.0 | 83.3 | 50.0 | 0.0 |
| Defensive | 47.1 | 60.0 | 16.7 | 50.0 | 75.0 |
| Submissive | 17.6 | 10.0 | 0.0 | 0.0 | 25.0 |
| Total | 100 | 100 | 100 | 100 | 100 |
| n = | 17 | 10 | 6 | 10 | 8 |

other members in group meetings. The order also corresponds to the observer's impressions of social rank order based on fifteen months of observation of the group.

In table 9-3a the relative participation of members in different types of competitive interaction processes is contrasted. The mayor is substantially more likely to participate in conflict processes than are other members, while member 2 (as identified in all data files and live coding) is far more likely to participate in consensus processes. It may be noted that this is a successful mayor in the sense that he generally gets his way in the group. The inference could be drawn that he concentrates his participation upon debates where the outcome is in greater jeopardy and minimizes his role where the group may reach agreement without him. We may speculate that such a strategy allows a socially dominant leader to minimize the appearance of domination. It should also be observed that emphasis on consensus processes by member 2 may reflect a more general avoidance of conflict. On several occasions over the past fifteen months, this member has undertaken tension-releasing behavior for the group that promoted conflict management in heated exchanges between group members and various participants from the audience criticizing group decisions.

In table 9-3b it is interesting to observe that the mayor tends not to engage in competitive interactions with other group members. He has the lowest proportion of competitive initiations and the highest of noncompetitive behaviors. Taking the order of members in the table as the social rank within the group is consistent with the hypothesis of dominance literature (Bernstein 1981) that the middle-ranking individuals have the greatest proportions of competitive behavior.

Up to three recipients were coded for each behavioral event as targets. While the overwhelming majority of behaviors had a single target, a multiple-response procedure was employed to display the data in table 9-3c on competitive behavior received. Receipt of behavioral acts is one indicator of the attention paid by the group to other individual members. Competitive attention is especially important because it reveals which individuals are the objects of influence attempts by other members. The most striking pattern in table 9-3c is the perfect rank correlation between competitive initiations received and hypothesized social rank in the group. The mayor and member 1 received the highest percentages of initiations, while member 2 received none at all. Observing the total *n*s, it is also apparent that the amounts of all kinds of behaviors received is also strongly related with the percentage of initiations received and the hypothesized social rank of members.

Patterns of reactive behavior, displayed in table 9-3d, provide further data on the behavioral strategies of individuals. The mayor, once again, eschews more conflict-oriented behavior by emphasizing the substantive, defensive form of reaction. He tends to respond seriously to the competing positions of others. Member 1, on the other hand, appears far more likely to respond offensively to competing members in debate. It may be observed that member 4 is most likely to react submissively (primarily with respect to the mayor). Member 2 engages in so few reactions that his data on reactions should be ignored. Behavioral strategies differ substantially among group members. However, these differences may well be more a function of idiosyncratic factors than social order.

Two observations stand out with respect to reactive attention in table 9-3e. First, member 3 is the target of a highly disproportionate number of offensive reactions, while receiving the fewest total number of reactions. From table 9-3c it may be recalled that member 3 received the highest proportion of noncompetitive behaviors. In short, the group tends not to react competitively to this member, but when it does, the reactions do not respond substantively to the issues raised in member 3's positions. Member 3 is the only female in the group. It may also be noted that not only does member 2 not receive competitive initiations from the group, but he does not receive offensive reactions either. On those occasions, when member 2 is the subject of group attention, he is apparently taken seriously.

Table 9-4 presents data on the overall paralinguistic characteristics of individual participation in group discussions. In general, vocal arousal is correlated with the hypothesized social rank order in the group. This pattern is most pronounced with respect to intensity and variation in intensity. It does not appear to hold with respect to speech and pause rates. Member 1's very low pause rate is a function of his tendency to use "filled pauses" that are not captured with the measurement technique used for this variable.

More informative is the breakdown of paralinguistic properties for actors by type of competitive behavior. Here, attention should be directed toward both the order among members in variable values and the order across categories of behavior. The pattern is, again, strongest with respect to the intensity variables. Within categories, the higher the hypothesized rank, the greater the vocal intensity. For each member, competitive reactions have the highest vocal

**Table 9-4.** Paralinguistic parameters of individual participation

|  | % Mayor | Member 1 | Member 3 | Member 4 | Member 2 |
|---|---|---|---|---|---|
| Pitch $(z)$ | .22 | .51 | − .27 | − .54 | − .35 |
|  | (.87) | (1.1) | (.97) | (.90) | (.98) |
| Pitch variation | 2.26 | 2.30 | 1.55 | 1.29 | 1.46 |
|  | (1.3) | (1.3) | (1.4) | (.90) | (1.0) |
| Intensity $(z)$ | .48 | .42 | − .05 | − .72 | − .85 |
|  | (.93) | (.78) | (.99) | (.86) | (.54) |
| Intensity variation | 1.71 | 1.58 | 1.21 | 1.00 | .97 |
|  | (.80) | (.79) | (.76) | (.79) | (.87) |
| Pause rate | 5.52 | 2.79 | 4.44 | 5.07 | 5.18 |
|  | (9.9) | (4.8) | (5.6) | (6.7) | (4.8) |
| Speech rate | 164 | 186 | 136 | 141 | 176 |
|  | (112) | (55) | (54) | (56) | (68) |
| $n =$ | 114 | 69 | 57 | 61 | 36 |

**Table 9-5.** Paralinguistic properties of competitive individual behavior

|  | % Mayor | Member 1 | Member 3 | Member 4 | Member 2 |
|---|---|---|---|---|---|
| Intensity (z) |  |  |  |  |  |
| Reaction | .85 | .80 | .41 | −.46 | −.08 |
| Initiation | .47 | .16 | .14 | −.04 | −.81 |
| Noncompetitive | .42 | .35 | −.29 | −.87 | −.94 |
| Intensity variation |  |  |  |  |  |
| Reaction | 1.93 | 1.74 | 1.92 | 1.20 | .92 |
| Initiation | 1.71 | 1.75 | 1.36 | 1.14 | 1.10 |
| Noncompetitive | 1.67 | 1.43 | .92 | .94 | .95 |
| Pitch (z) |  |  |  |  |  |
| Reaction | .60 | 1.01 | −.13 | −.38 | −.26 |
| Initiation | −.09 | .62 | −.10 | −.29 | −.62 |
| Noncompetitive | .17 | .24 | −.39 | −.61 | −.31 |
| Pitch variation |  |  |  |  |  |
| Reaction | 2.87 | 2.46 | 2.33 | 1.83 | 1.55 |
| Initiation | 1.62 | 2.65 | 1.81 | 1.62 | 1.04 |
| Noncompetitive | 2.19 | 2.09 | 1.18 | 1.15 | 1.53 |
| Pause rate |  |  |  |  |  |
| Reaction | 4.58 | 1.72 | 4.07 | 6.42 | 9.09 |
| Initiation | 3.33 | 4.85 | 4.79 | 6.40 | 7.65 |
| Noncompetitive | 5.85 | 2.45 | 4.35 | 4.63 | 4.32 |
| Speech rate |  |  |  |  |  |
| Reaction | 197 | 185 | 170 | 200 | 151 |
| Initiation | 169 | 193 | 142 | 154 | 175 |
| Noncompetitive | 158 | 185 | 123 | 129 | 179 |

intensity and, with the exception of member 1, initiations have higher intensity than noncompetitive behaviors. In general, reactive comments are accompanied by higher vocal arousal and higher-ranking members show greater vocal arousal on all the paralinguistic variables except speech rate.

Figures 9-1 and 9-2 present dyadic data on behavioral patterns among individual members of the group. Competitive behavior as a proportion of total behavior provides the basis for the sociogram in figure 9-1. Because these data involve competitive behavior in competitive decision processes, they provide a model of the structure of influence attempts in the group. The mayor is the primary object of competitive behavior in the group. He receives more attention than he provides to all but member 2. The latter may reflect member 2's tendency to avoid competitive interactions as well as the seriousness attached to those interactions he does engage in. Member 1 receives more attention from members 3 and 2 than he provides. The competitive interactions between the three hypothesized lower-ranking members are so few in number that any generalizations about their interrelations would have questionable reliability. Overall, the structure of competitive attention quite clearly flows toward the two higher-ranking members.

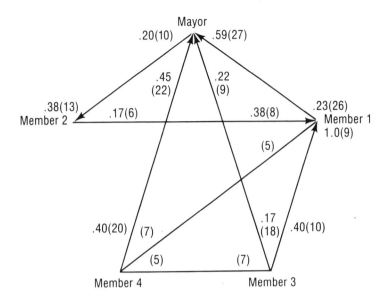

Figure 9-1. Dyadic relations of competitive attention. Data are competitive behaviors A–B as a proportion of total behaviors A–B. Totals are in parentheses. Dyads that are not tied are oriented toward the actor receiving greater proportional competitive attention.

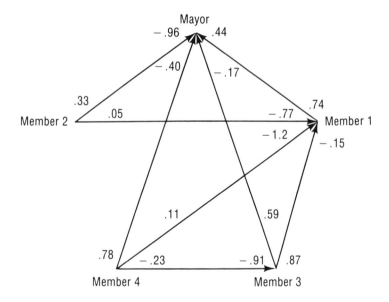

Figure 9-2. Dyadic relations of vocal intensity. Data are mean $z$ scores for intensity of comments. The value adjacent to an actor measures intensity in comments received by the actor from the opposite actor. Dyads are oriented toward the actor speaking with relatively greater vocal intensity.

Figure 9-2 presents data on dyadic relations with respect to vocal intensity in all interactions: The mayor speaks at higher intensity to all other members than they speak to him. Member 1 speaks at higher intensity to all members but the mayor, and member 3 speaks at higher intensity to member 4. In relation to the hypothesized social order in the group, these relations meet a criterion of transitivity. There is also a suggestion or partial pattern in these data that vocal intensity is varied by individuals in relation to social order: thus, members appear to speak at higher intensity to those nearest in terms of social rank position. Thus, for member 1, the order from high to low is member 3, the mayor, member 4, and member 2. For member 3 the order is member 1, the mayor, member 4, and member 2. A similar pattern holds for the mayor, with the exception of his comments to member 3 (that are lower than those to 4). For member 2, the order is members 3, 1, followed by the mayor. Member 4 does not fit the general pattern. While the relationship between vocal intensity and social position must be regarded as a tentative finding, it does suggest an intriguing hypothesis for further investigation.

## SUMMARY AND CONCLUSION

This paper has explored the paralinguistic dimensions of competitive verbal behavior in small-group political debate. A major concern involved the extent to which characteristics of voice in political speech vary across different types of competitive behavior or, in other words, whether or not vocal behavior is an important component of political behavior. A related concern involved the relationship between paralinguistic dimensions of competitive behavior and social structure in small political groups.

At least for the group observed, it may be reasonable to conclude that vocal behavior is very much a part of political behavior. Actors engaged in competitive political behavior—in influence attempts—speak at higher levels of vocal arousal. Arousal may play an important role in commanding attention from the group to the arguments presented and in promoting group confidence in them (J. Hall 1980). For the group as a whole and for the individual members, competitive behavior was accompanied by louder speech, at higher pitch, with greater variation, and generally at a faster rate of delivery.

This analysis described social structure in the group in terms of patterns of participation in the group and attention from the group in competitive interactions. Social dominance is assessed, by this approach, in terms of who attempts to influence whom (S. Altmann 1967). In general, members who more actively participated in the group interaction process were themselves more likely to be the subject of influence attempts. The rank order among members in terms of the total number of behaviors directed at them, as well as the proportion of competitive behaviors they received, were highly correlated with dyadic patterns of attention provided and received.

There is a clearly discernible social structure manifest in patterns of competitive behavior. The mayor is the primary focus of competitive interactions (even though he only votes to break ties). He took twice as many turns as any other member and was the target of a third more turns than any one else in the group. Member 1 also appears quite clearly in the data to be second in social rank. He was second highest in total behavior received, in competitive attention, and in total participation; in competitive participation, he was highest and most frequently engaged in competitive reactions, especially those in the offensive category. The third rank position is less clear cut. Member 3 earns this position on the basis of her competitive participation in these data (and total participation throughout all group activities) and total behavior received. However, she received less competitive attention than would be expected on the basis of the third rank; other members tended to concentrate their influence attempts on member 1 and the mayor to the exclusion of her, and she received the fewest number of competitive reactions. The social positions of members 2 and 4 are also somewhat ambiguous. This is partially a function of their relative lack of interactions. However, member 2 received less total behavior from the group. His tendency to avoid competitive interactions may be considered an adaptive strategy for a lower-ranking individual. It should be noted that while member 2 received less attention from the group, what attention he did receive was of the more substantive defensive variety. While it is impossible to assess the origins of social rank in a political group with only five members, it should also be noted that rank is correlated with experience on the council—tenure in office—and age. More dominant members are older and more experienced.

Paralinguistic behavior varies systematically with rank position as well as type of behavior. The higher the social rank of an individual the greater the vocal arousal—especially in competitive interactions. However, the association of vocal arousal with type of behavior holds across the rank positions.

The relationship between social position and voice characteristics is especially pronounced with respect to dyadic patterns of intensity in speech. Not only do dominants speak more loudly to subordinates, but also the possibility was observed that individuals may finely tune vocal intensity by increasing intensity with regard to those closer in rank and decreasing intensity toward those further above and below in rank position. As previously noted, these are tentative findings to be subjected to further testing, analysis, and replication within this group. All relevant data, such as that on interruptions and simultaneous speech, have not yet been included in the analysis.

The small group is a pervasive setting for collective decision making in human politics. When groups meet to make decisions and outcomes are not predetermined, understanding interactions among members may be crucial for understanding outcomes. In the group observed for this study, political debate did not occur when outcomes were not in question. For this group, description of the social structure of influence and the various dimensions of behavior in group interactions is a prerequisite for explaining decisional outcomes (a task addressed in another paper; see J. Schubert 1984b). Of course, the small group is a setting common to many primate species that quite likely has evolutionary significance (Omark 1980). Paralinguistic dimensions of verbal behavior are variables that appear to play an important role in collective political decision making and that are likely to require both ontogenetic and phylogenetic explanations. In short, this is an area in which biobehavioral and ethological approaches to behavioral analysis appear clearly relevant to the development of more comprehensive political behavior theory.

# 10

## *Conclusion*
## *Primate Politics and Political Theory*

Roger D. Masters

PRIMATE BEHAVIOR, HUMAN NATURE, AND POLITICS

Humans are fascinated by monkeys and apes. Primates, as our nearest relatives in the animal world, have long been seen as a mirror or image of human nature. But what do they tell us about ourselves?

A century before Darwin, Rousseau argued that humans originally were probably animals like monkeys or apes and wondered if orangutans or chimpanzees might be humans in the pure "state of nature" (Rousseau 1964, 104–15, 145, and esp. 203–13 n.j). These species, which resemble and differ from humans in such intriguing ways, still hold their fascination: witness the continued popular interest in the studies of chimpanzees by Jane Goodall and Frans de Waal, of gorillas by George Schaller and Dian Fossey, or of orangutans by Biruté Galdikàs.

Until recent years, information about primate behavior scarcely went beyond superficial anecdotes. Obviously, monkeys and apes lack verbal speech, traditionally the defining characteristic of human beings: on seeing a chimpanzee brought to France in the eighteenth century, the Archbishop of Paris supposedly asserted, "Parle, et je te baptise" ("Speak, and I'll baptize you!"). Also obvious, however, are similarities in physical conformation and behavior that make the monkey cage of most zoos such an attraction for adults and children alike. Are these similarities relevant to human behavior? Scientific developments in the last decade have made it possible to go beyond intuition and prejudice in answering this question. Research efforts in ethology and social science have begun to converge, showing the values—and limitations—of comparisons between human and nonhuman primates.

221

Humans are, as Darwin insisted, an animal species whose behavior is the product of the evolutionary process. While it is no longer reasonable to pretend that human social behavior is a unique phenomenon without parallels in the natural world, both the differences and the similarities between humans and nonhuman primates (let alone other mammals) are of the greatest importance to an accurate understanding of their social life as well as ours.

The similarities between human and nonhuman primates are especially central to the phenomena we call "politics." Dominance and subordination, cooperation and friendship, social cohesion and individual rivalries, even marked differences in the personality of members of the group: many of the things long taken as defining human political life have also been observed among primates. But equally evident among nonhuman primates is the *absence* of verbal communication, centralized authority, and the complex sociocultural as well as legal systems that characterize contemporary human societies.

Are the similarities truly fundamental, or are they merely epiphenomena? It has long been wondered what other primates can tell us about humans; just as important, however, is what knowledge of human politics can tell us about nonhuman social behavior. Given the considerable advances in research over the last generation, it is time to take a serious look at the scientific issues posed by "primate politics."

This volume is devoted to such an inquiry. By bringing together a series of essays by leading primatologists and political scientists, we hope to focus on these issues without the passions and the oversimplifications generated by hasty popularizations of ethology. But before discussing how the study of nonhuman primates can illuminate human politics, it will be valuable to describe the range of disagreement underlying theories in the discipline of political science.

## WHAT IS POLITICS?

In the natural sciences, it is usually assumed that the phenomena under consideration can be identified in a reliable way. Paradoxically, political scientists have had great difficulty agreeing on a definition of the subject of their research. Because the discipline of political science lacks generally accepted foundations, it has been hard to relate an understanding of politics to discoveries in such related fields as anthropology, social psychology, or evolutionary biology.

As conventionally understood, "politics" concerns social interactions between groups of humans; this "macrolevel" is distinguished from the physiological, developmental, emotional, or cognitive events within the human central nervous system, which constitute what can be called the "microlevel" of social behavior. To be sure, individual or microlevel phenomena are often extremely important in politics. But politics in its common meaning needs to be defined at the macro or social level before one can determine how it might be influenced by individual differences in physiology, development, hormonal functioning, or brain organization.

Beyond this, however, little is certain. The concepts usually used in political science provide a convenient outline of the persisting uncertainties at the foundations of political science. Each of these terms has been given different (and sometimes contradictory) meanings that can be associated with major theorists in the Western tradition. A survey of these divergent usages of the common vocabulary of political science shows quite abundantly the difficulty of reducing "politics" to a single definition which could claim to have general acceptance and suggests why the similarities and differences between the social behavior of nonhuman and human primates are of such broad interest.

*The Basic Concepts of Political Science*

1. *Society.* The arena within which politics occurs is a human "society," usually defined as an ongoing "group" or "community" that has been generated by the combination of cooperation and competition among nonkin. For example, when Aristotle used the word *polis*, from which the modern concept of "politics" is derived, he does not mean the "state" or some other institutionalized form of government; rather, he means the city as a social organization, localized in time and place, whose population attains self-sufficiency in both material and cultural life. As Aristotle's usage makes clear, a society or social community transcends the family or clan, yet is not merely a temporary "aggregation" or collection of people without a shared sense of membership. Between a nuclear family and a transitory, accidental group of nonkin, however, there is considerable disagreement about the origins, nature, and history of a "society."

For some (e.g., Machiavelli, Hobbes), a society in this sense is the product of a prior act of agreement or conquest, which is itself the political action of primary importance. For others (Hegel, Marx), societies evolve, and it is only in a mature phase of development that politics in a precise sense is possible. In recent times, the basic distinction between *gemeinschaft* and *gesellschaft* (Tönnies) has been used to differentiate between societies consisting of little more than a "market" or quasicontractual relationship between autonomous individuals and those in which the communal unity penetrates every dimension of behavior. However defined, moreover, societies are presumed to encompass diverse activities, only some of which are said to be "political." But which activities constitute human politics, and how does the political system relate to society more broadly?

2. *Power* and *influence* describe the control of some individuals over others— or deference to some individuals by others. The first of these terms typically designates formal or institutionalized relationships, whereas the latter is usually reserved for informal ones. However the concepts are used, "power" and "influence" refer to an asymmetry in the access to resources or status, whether attributed to nature (Plato's "philosophic king," Nietzsche's *übermensch*), to

personality (Machiavelli's "prince" coming to power through *virtù*), to popular choice (Locke's "executive" and "legislative" powers), or to history (Marx's "class"). As these examples suggest, power and influence can be attributes of individuals, of groups, or of social institutions. And while few would disagree that politics involves these relations, the most superficial consideration of economics or cultural anthropology demonstrates that not all instances of power and influence need be political.

3. *Social conflict* arises whenever there is open competition for power or influence within and between groups. In the tradition of political theory, such conflicts have been traced to "human nature" (Thucydides, Machiavelli, Hobbes), to historical change (Marx, Rousseau), or to God's will and human sin (St. Paul, Augustine). While it is usually assumed that political life arises from social conflict, rivalries for power and influence may be principally economic, cultural, or religious. Even when conflicts seem unambiguously political, they may be directly focused on the formal asymmetries of institutionalized status or more indirectly related to symbols of identity, reputation, and influence.

4. *Law* can be defined as the set of cultural rules or norms governing conflict, dispute resolution, or social cooperation. Since such laws or rules often differ in substance from one society to another, they have been distinguished from "laws of nature" by theorists as diverse as the pre-Socratics and Aquinas. As the rules or norms of a human community, however, laws need to be accepted as "legitimate" or authoritative by most if not all members of the society if they are to be effective — and the origins of law and legitimacy have been derived from a wide variety of sources. For some political theorists (the Sophists in ancient Greece, Hobbes, Locke, Rousseau), law is the result of a "social contract" between independent individuals; according to others, law emerges from an organic history or evolution of human society (Aristotle, Hegel, Marx), or from divine injunction that is merely carried out by humans (Exodus, Romans).

5. The *state* or centralized government is a formal institution with the power of exercising political control (behavioral coordination and dispute settlement), established by law and perceived as legitimate by the members of a society. Typically, the state presupposes the emergence of functionally specific roles for the individuals authorized to govern, a society with a population exceeding that of tribes, clans, or face-to-face village communities, and a productive surplus. The origins of the state have been diversely attributed to the consent of the governed (Locke, Plato), fear and conquest (Hobbes), creative leadership (Machiavelli), historical accident (Rousseau), historical necessity (Hegel, Marx), and divine plan (Augustine, Calvin). And forms of such an institution have varied widely in the past, including the feudal states of medieval Europe as well as the *polis* of ancient Greece and the empires of Mesopotamia, Egypt, and China (MacIver 1947; d'Entrèves 1967).

6. The *regime* or *political system* is the form of government or type of state established in a society, along with the political culture and social structures

necessary for its perpetuation. Traditionally, regimes have been classified in many ways: the five regimes of Plato's *Republic* (aristocracy/kingship, timocracy, oligarchy, democracy, tyranny); the six regimes of Aristotle's *Politics* (kingship, aristocracy, polity, tyranny, oligarchy, democracy); the two types of state in Machiavelli's *Prince* (principality and republic); or a single basic principle (as in Hobbes's *Leviathan*, which treats all commonwealths, whether by institution or by acquisition, as essentially similar). In contemporary terms, regimes are usually viewed as constitutional democracies or free governments versus totalitarian or dictatorial regimes (e.g., Friedrich 1963; Talmon 1961), as well as developed or industrialized versus developing or "backward" societies.

7. *Political history* is deemed to be the recorded changes over time in societies and governments or states. In modern times, patterns are often thought to represent linear "progress" or improvement (Thomas Paine, Kant, Hegel, Marx), although ancients often thought change was cyclical and not progressive (Thucydides, Plato), and some theorists have argued that change is primarily decay and decline rather than progressive improvement (Rousseau). If history is progressive, some argue that changes occur slowly (Social Darwinists, reformers, liberals, and social democrats) while others see violent change as necessary or at least typical (Marx, Nietzsche).

### Can the Study of Politics Be a Science?

The diverse interpretations given to the concepts outlined above raise the question of whether it is a misnomer to speak of political "science." At the theoretical level, this problem is reinforced by the lack of consensus on the relationships *between* concepts. In practice, many contemporary political scientists have focused on more or less descriptive empirical research, using techniques and concepts borrowed from the disciplines of history, sociology, or economics. Since such studies often seem to be atheoretical, other political scientists have begun to formulate models of rational choice, using concepts and methods borrowed from econometric game theory. Since supporters of competing approaches are highly critical of each other and different scholars typically use terms in an idiosyncratic way, political science appears to be in what Thomas Kuhn (1970) has called a "pre-paradigm" stage.

Even if one could speak of a common paradigm underlying political science, a further problem arises in claiming that the discipline has "scientific" status. In the study of human politics, a theory—or even an empirical study—is often not merely a neutral explanation of events, but also serves to legitimate a partisan preference. For some (relativists, deconstructionists) this danger is unavoidable, since all human thinking is a reflection of the subjective interests or desires of the thinker. Whatever the status of post modernism in literature or the philosophy of science, relativism in politics establishes a stance (cynicism and denial of meaning or legitimacy beyond mere power) that has political as well as artistic or epistemological consequences. While some philosophers of science have followed Nietzsche's charge that all natural science is essentially a subjective interpretation (e.g., Feyerabend 1975), the risk of ideological bias is thus especially likely to arise in the study of politics.

Empirical verification or falsification of hypotheses is, of course, the traditional means by which scientists respond to the charge of ideological bias. In political science, however, there is no agreed mode of falsification at the level of basic theories: doctrinaire Marxists assert that the use of cost-benefit models of behavior, whether derived from theories of market competition in economics or from the Lockean tradition in political philosophy, is inherently ideological; many liberals and conservatives consider the Marxist focus on history and socioeconomic determinants to be equally ideological. Insofar as such controversies lead political scientists to focus on descriptive empirical studies or very abstract models, the difficulty of generating a unified basis for any substantial portion of the discipline is only increased.

If the very concept of "primate politics" is to avoid becoming an ideological belief (cf. Caplan 1978), it must therefore be situated in terms of the key questions dominating the discipline of political science. To gain perspective on the nature of human politics, it is therefore useful to reconsider the competing answers that have been given to these theoretical questions in the Western tradition. Not only will this indicate the reasons for comparing the process of social behavior in nonhuman and human populations, but it should confirm how cross-species comparisons can serve as the foundation of empirically falsifiable statements about human nature and the varieties of political behavior.

1. *Why do societies arise?* (a) If competition or social conflict between individuals is "natural" (e.g., Machiavelli, Hobbes), self-interest seems to lead to defection rather than cooperation among nonkin, as in a Hobbesian war of all or the Prisoner's Dilemma. Kinship or reciprocal altruism might explain the human family or primitive "band," but not a large-scale society of millions of nonkin. From this perspective, societies seem to be the result of a convention or social contract—i.e., an artificial or human-made agreement in the "interest" of the individual. Such a view seems logical, but it is contested by all those whose theoretical perspective focuses on historical change or empirical evidence of the natural foundations of human sociability. In particular, explanations of human politics that derive all social cooperation from abstract models of conflicting self-interest need to be related to the understanding of hominid evolution in social groups over the last 5 million years or more. (b) If cooperation is "natural" (e.g., Marx, Plato), then there is a reason for the existence of human society—but no explanation for social conflict beyond either historical accident (Rousseau) or violence (property or "primitive accumulation" as theft—Marx). Here too the evidence of human evolution is necessary if one is to understand the origins and development of the social systems within which political life is observed. (c) If both cooperation and competition are natural (Aristotle), why do some commu-

nities develop beyond the primitive band and tribe whereas others do not? What are the transformations of "human nature" needed to sustain large-scale societies of nonkin? Is political development the "decrepitude of the species" (Rousseau) or an artificial "institution" imposed on the "tabula rasa" of animal drives for the selfish benefit of individuals (Hobbes)?

2. *Why do some individuals seek power?* (a) If human nature is basically selfish and competitive, then fear and conflict lead to the desire to control others (Thrasymachus, Machiavelli, Hobbes). But power requires consent or legitimacy—and since the assumption that humans are naturally competitive leads to a war of all, why should individuals or groups submit to the powerful? If obedience is merely due to fear or force (the negative self-interest of avoiding harm), then power is always fragile—and the powerful must devote more effort to insure successful maintenance of power than any possible benefit (Xenophon's *Hiero*). If obedience is due to gains from cooperation (positive self-interest), then the response of a free rider, appearing to obey while secretly "defecting," is always the best strategy and obedience will be deceptive (the ring of Gyges in Plato's *Republic*); again, power is always fragile. (b) In an alternative tradition, humans are seen as naturally unequal, giving rise to a different set of questions: Is submissiveness "natural" to some, and dominance to others (Aristotle's "natural slave"; Nietzsche's *übermensch*)? If so, how could the enormous differences in power found in states and empires arise, since power differences are so small in nonhuman primates or bands of human gatherer-hunters? Or is power an attribute of the *group*, such that the role of the leader is created by society and filled by one or another individual by accident? If so, what makes societies change over time: the socioeconomic basis (Marx) or the culture and norms of obedience (Hegel)?

3. *What is legitimacy?* (a) How do humans learn what to expect? It appears that human social behavior combines verbal information and symbols with nonverbal cues: culture is a system based on communication. Does this mean that politics is entirely "artificial" and completely divorced from "nature"? If so, then patterns of cultural expectation are the basis of legitimacy—and there is no "natural right" independent of time and place (Marx, Hegel, Nietzsche). If not, there is a natural foundation for obedience and legitimacy, and legitimacy is based on "consent" that cannot be deduced from culture (Hobbes, Locke, Rousseau). While this issue is best known in the context of philosophic debates, it also gives rise to empirical questions. (b) Why do people sometimes revolt against unpopular rulers—but often accept regimes even if they are *not* thought to be legitimate? If cultural norms provide a learned or social explanation for obedience, why does coercion sometimes succeed? For example, if humans have "natural rights" to self-preservation that are "inalienable" (Hobbes, Locke, Declaration of Independence), why should it be that violations of these rights are often accepted? The proposition that governments are legitimate except when they are disobeyed is a tautology rather than an empirically falsifiable scientific theory.

4. *Why do regimes change?* Are there "natural" reasons for different legal and political systems? Are laws and states adapted to the socioeconomic setting and physical environment—and if so, should political and cultural history be analyzed from the perspective of traditional Marxists, of materialist anthropology (Harris 1977), or of sociobiology (Wilson 1975; Chagnon and Irons 1979)? Is economic or political development a predictable process, or is change due to human nature and accident (Machiavelli)? And, at a more abstract level, are there broader analogies between human history and biological evolution, such as gradual processes of "random variation and selective retention" (D. Campbell 1965) or the pattern of "punctuated equilibria" (Gould and Eldredge 1977)? In contemporary political science, neither the existence of political societies and states nor the reasons for obedience are clearly understood as variables that can be predicted.

The mere listing of such questions reminds us of the absence of generally accepted theoretical *foundations* for the discipline of political science. If the study of politics is to be a science—or, indeed, if we are even to discover exactly what is meant by the concept of "political" behaviors and institutions—it is necessary to consider the foregoing concepts and questions. In so doing, the most persistent issues concern "human nature" and its relation to "nature" more broadly. Traditionally, philosophers have debated whether our species is the "political animal" described by Aristotle, and if not, whether states and governments are "artificial machines" created by convention and ingenuity as Hobbes proclaimed. In returning to such issues of human nature, clearly it is both reasonable and timely to consider what is now known about social behavior from the perspective of evolutionary biology.


## EVOLUTIONARY BIOLOGY AND POLITICS

While the relevance of natural science to the study of human life has sometimes been contested, the foregoing survey indicates that the tendency to isolate political science has led to persistent theoretical confusion. Perhaps the most important contribution of evolutionary biology to a theory of politics could be to clarify the primary concepts on which political science rests; even if theories that explain the behavior of other animals do not apply directly to humans, each new level of complexity in the natural world can at least be related conceptually to simpler phenomena from which it arose. Since it is now evident that biological events cannot be "reduced" to genes in any simplistic sense (Simpson 1969), the focus of attempts to relate biological science to the study of politics cannot be viewed as an attempt to destroy the specificity of human behavior, but rather to indicate more precisely how and why humans differ from other species (G. Schubert 1989a; Masters 1989a).

*Primate Behavior and the Foundations of Human Politics*

It is obvious that we cannot directly assess the foundations of political life merely by observing highly developed systems like the Soviet Union or France. In physics and biology, experiments on carefully controlled, "artificial" situations provide the grounds for clarifying broad theoretical questions. Despite this obvious lesson from the natural sciences, the study of politics has yet to develop an unambiguous way of approaching the foundations of human political behavior. In the Western philosophical tradition, this question took the form of considering the "state of nature" (Hobbes, Locke, Rousseau) or the origins of politics (Plato, Aristotle, Lucretius, Marx). Today, many of the philosophical debates about the origins of politics can be treated as scientific questions illuminated by evolutionary biology.

Hominids, great apes, and monkeys all evolved from a common lineage. While many details of hominid evolution are subject to continued debate, the broad outlines of our species' origins are as well established as any of the fundamental propositions in the natural sciences. On the one hand, this means that some traditional explanations of human life — such as the literal theological interpretation of "special creation" — no longer seem consistent with scientific knowledge. On the other, the specific characteristics of human origins lie within a narrower range of possibilities than was thought even a generation ago.

While paleontology and archeology provide direct evidence of the morphology of our hominid ancestors, such approaches permit only inferential studies of social behavior. In particular, observational or experimental studies of the dynamic processes of social interaction can be done only with living organisms. Thus modern ethology, the field and experimental study of animal behavior, can make a distinct contribution to the understanding of social processes. And within this field, primatology has a particular relevance to human behavior because it focuses on the living species that are our closest relatives.

*What Are the Differences Between Human and Nonhuman Primates?*

Common ancestry can be misleading: it is contrary to the principles of evolution to assume that related species are identical in all respects merely because of their evolutionary origins. Among the most obvious differences between humans and nonhuman primates, the following would probably be included by most specialists:

1. *Speech.* Humans have evolved the capacity to communicate using verbal languages that are not observed among nonhuman primates. While nonverbal communication has not been replaced by the emergence of speech, this new level of information processing has distinct features that make possible types and rates of cultural change not found in other mammalian species (cf. Gardner, Gardner, and van Cantfort 1989 with Sebeok and Umiker–Sebeok 1980).

2. *Size of possible groups of societies.* Humans sometimes form tribes, cities, and civilizations with populations that are orders of magnitude larger than the typical primate bands of 50 to 100. Even when such larger societies emerge, however, they are superimposed on family and face-to-face groups akin to those persisting among nonhuman primates or human gatherer-hunters.

3. *Cultural variation.* Humans have developed an extraordinary diversity of kinship systems and behavioral norms; even though these cultures have been elaborated by using elements of the primate social repertoire, the resulting systems of behavior are as different from each other as the social patterns of different animal species.

4. *Law.* Human speech has been used to create an elaborate system of rules about cultural norms — a second-order consciousness of consciousness — which permits us to organize social behavior in complicated ways. Other species may develop a form of culture or protoculture; only humans develop written rules governing social behavior.

5. *Agriculture, pastoralism, and industry.* In the last two millenia, complicated modes of producing food and material goods have generally replaced the gatherer-hunting mode of adaptation. As a result, recent history has permitted *Homo sapiens sapiens* to change somewhat its place in the global ecosystem, threatening the survival of our own species and the perpetuation of life.

6. *The centralized state or government.* In societies that have evolved beyond the gatherer-hunter structure, humans often have instituted functionally specialized roles of rule making and implementation. The resulting degree of social differentiation is unlike anything observed in a nonhuman primate.

Granted that no account of human politics would be acceptable without giving due attention to these distinct patterns of social behavior, it does not follow that the commonalities between nonhuman and human primates are irrelevant. To see whether an evolutionary approach is useful in the quest for a more scientific foundation for the study of politics, it is thus necessary to specify more precisely the similarities within the primate line which might form the basis of human nature.

*Similarities Between Nonhuman and Human Primates*

Humans retain behavioral patterns found in monkeys and apes even when we have elaborated more complex and distinctive social systems. Among the characteristic primate behaviors that persist in our species are the following;

1. *Nonverbal communication.* Like nonhuman primates, humans exhibit movements of the face and body that provide cues of emotional states and social intentions (Darwin 1965; Ekman and Oster 1979). These gestures, traditionally associated with the natural foundations of human social behavior (Rousseau, *Second Discourse*), have a direct relevance to the process of leader-follower interactions (chap. 8 and 9). Even if the cost-benefit calculus typical of eco-

nomics, game theory, and models of rational choice is used to study human behavior, a coherent explanation of human social behavior is impossible without reference to nonverbal cues of emotion and the nonverbal feelings they reflect (Frank 1988).

2. *The primate behavioral repertoire.* Both within face-to-face groups and between them, human patterns of cooperative and competitive behavior are built upon the basic primate repertoire or "biogrammar" (Konner 1983; Tiger and Fox 1971). Behaviors of greeting, reassurance, threat, and submission are ubiquitous in human society; these response patterns are phylogenetically derived from the primate social repertoire (chaps. 5 and 6), though they may be shaped differently from one culture to another (von Hooff 1969; Birdwhistell 1970; Masters and Sullivan 1989a, b).

3. *Sexual differences in maturation and social behavior.* Although there is much variation among primate species, parallel differences between males and females in patterns of development and social behavior are widely observed throughout the primate lineage. In particular, males tend to be somewhat more aggressive and competitive whereas females are more likely to engage in socially cohesive responses as a function of bonds with others in the group (chaps. 1, 5, and 6). Since variation in these traits, like many others observed in mammalian behavior, often takes the form of a normal or Gaussian distribution, it is prudent to view differences of sex or gender as overlapping distributions in a population (G. Schubert 1989a; Masters 1989b) rather than as the simple dichotomies implied by crude stereotypes. In particular, these differences in the average social behavior in no way preclude females from performing the roles associated with dominance or social coordination that have traditionally been associated with males in Western culture: quite the contrary, since there is ample evidence that females play a critical role in the social organization of nonhuman primate groups (Hrdy 1981; Goodall 1986) and that their patterns of assessing social situations complement those of males in ways that are particularly valuable in highly industrialized societies (chap. 1; G. Schubert 1985; Masters 1984).

4. *Face-to-face groups.* Even where the centralized state has emerged as the primary institutional form of political control, daily behavior is principally organized in stable face-to-face groups whose size is comparable to that of groups among nonhuman primates. Because the child first learns many cultural norms of social behavior in groups of peers that are not unlike the bands of nonhuman primates, political socialization is illuminated by the common attributes of the primate group (Barner-Barry 1981; Montagner et al. 1988). Even within formal political institutions, the social processes in many critical decision-making groups usually reflect patterns of interaction that can be compared to those of nonhuman primates (J. Schubert 1983, 1984a, b; chap. 9).

5. *Kinship and reciprocity.* While institutional forms of cooperation transcending the local community have emerged in civilized societies, most eco-

nomic and social activity is still focused on exchanges and cooperation among kin or reciprocating nonkin. As a result, even though most cultures have elaborated complex kinship systems, they are composed of structural elements which can be found in primate bands (R. Fox 1975). Similarly, while humans utilize many patterns of direct and indirect reciprocity, the underlying process is also found among nonhuman primates (chap. 7; R. Alexander 1987; de Waal 1982).

6. *Leadership and social differentiation.* Some elements of dominance and subordination are ubiquitous among nonhuman primates as well as in human societies. Social differences typically extend to some element of differentiation between the roles of males and females (chap. 3, 5, and 6; G. Schubert 1986b, 1989b; Masters 1984) as well as individuals of different ages (J. Schubert, Wiegele, and Hines 1986). To be sure, there is no fixed pattern of role differentiation common to all human societies, or, for that matter, to the behavior of all monkeys and apes: it is now evident that there is no simple formula for determining the characteristics of dominant members of a band or the roles associated with age and sex. But the existence of some form of social differentiation seems to be natural among primates generally, with the specific attributes associated with leadership, sex, and age depending in part on ecology and population structure as well as the history or culture of the society. Because the extent of role differentiation between males and females depends on ecology and the productive roles of the two sexes in primates, for example, it seems that similar factors may contribute to differing patterns of gender differentiation in human societies (e.g., Dickemann 1979).

As these similarities suggest, the elements underlying the more elaborate social and political systems found in contemporary societies can be found in the behavior of our primate relatives. Can the scientific study of this phylogenetic heritage illuminate politics? Is it now possible to study objectively the relationship between "human nature" and politics? And if so, can it be said that what humans identify as political behavior occurs in nonhuman primates as well? To turn to these questions, it is necessary to consider how these phenomena are studied from the perspective of evolutionary biology.

## WHAT IS PRIMATOLOGY?

### Ethology and the Science of Animal Behavior

Biology has many subfields: ethology is not identical to genetics or to abstract theories of evolution. There is a fundamental difference between an inductive science of behavior, based on observation (ethology), and deductive, theoretical models based on abstract concepts or mathematical relationships (sociobiology). Whereas the latter seeks to use general principles such as "inclusive fitness" and "reproductive success" to predict social behavior in varied environments (Wilson 1975; Dawkins 1976), the former is based on descriptive categories that cannot readily be reduced to universally observed theoretical concepts (Hinde 1982). As a result, ethologists have tended to insist on the independent role of social experience and individual development in explaining animal behavior. For example, some sociobiologists have been tempted to postulate genetic mechanisms such as the so-called "altruistic gene," but ethologists typically question whether mammalian social cooperation can be understood without careful classification and observation of the functionally diverse features of each species' behavioral repertoire.

While the approaches of ethologists and sociobiologists are in theory consistent, in practice they reflect different methods—and probably different scholarly temperaments as well (chaps. 1 and 2; Wilson 1975; R. Alexander 1979; Hinde 1982; Kitcher 1985). Within the conventional social sciences, a parallel difference has been noted between sociology or history, fields typically based on observation and description, and economics or rational choice theories using deductive methods (Mills 1959; Barry 1970). Since ethology and evolutionary theory are complementary but different approaches, it would be as erroneous to confuse ethological studies of primate behavior with genetic determinism as to impute the economist's assumptions of motivation to a sociologist's or historian's descriptive studies.

### Behavior as a Natural Phenomenon

An ethological study of social behavior begins from a careful description of the basic repertoire of individual and group behaviors (chapt. 2, 3, and 4). Such observational approaches require comparisons both within and between species. Precisely because individuals of a single primate species vary greatly in their behavior, categories of social interaction defined in functional terms can be used to contrast different species without assuming that identical "causes" have produced similarities in each instance (von Cranach 1976). For example, an ethologist can define locomotion as a similar functional process in different species without assuming that there is a common "gene" explaining brachiation in the orangutan, knuckle-walking in the chimpanzee, and human bipedal stature.

Ethological explanations of behavior view species-specific traits as well as individually learned behaviors as responses to the natural or social environment (chaps. 3, 5, 6, and 7). This approach has been described as the study of "proximate causes" or mechanisms responsible for observed behavior, as contrasted with the "ultimate causes" or phylogenetic adaptations studied by evolutionary theorists and systematists (Barash 1982). The methods used by ethologists range from field observation (Goodall 1986 and chap. 5) to studies of animals in enclosures large enough to permit the expression of substantial components of the behavioral repertoire (de Waal 1982 and chap. 6) to controlled experiments

(McGuire and Raleigh 1986; Raleigh and McGuire 1986). What then do we learn from primate ethology that might be of relevance to the study of politics?

### The Primate Behavioral Repertoire and the Elements of Politics

The study of primate social behavior from an ethological perspective has revealed microlevel phenomena that form the elements underlying more diversified and elaborate political processes. Social behavior can be understood as being "performed" by individuals who, to some extent, shape roles actively instead of responding passively to stimuli in the manner understood by early behaviorist psychology (chap. 4). What was traditionally called "human nature" can thus now be described in terms of the biogrammar of primate social behaviors which humans share with monkeys and apes (Tiger and Fox 1971). Among these common features underlying all political life are the following:

1. *Bonding.* For humans, as for nonhuman primates, individuals form lasting bonds with other members of their own species. Most notable in mother-infant bonding, reciprocal ties formed during development often last throughout life. In many cases, such bonds generalize to a persistent identification with a group and hostility toward outsiders (Goodall 1971, 1979, 1986, and chap. 6).

2. *Competition and aggression.* Although individuals engage in varied forms of rivalry with others, displays of threat typically do not lead to violence or physical damage; while exceptions, including occasional instances of intra-specific killing (Itani 1983; de Waal 1986), have attracted widespread attention, far more important is the process by which threat sequences lead to the strengthening of social bonds (chap. 6; Chance 1989). Where individuals engage in competitive interactions for social status within the group, aggressive behaviors are most likely to be exhibited by the challenger rather than by the dominant individual (Strayer 1981; Montagner et al. 1988).

3. *Dispute settlement, reassurance, and sharing.* Social processes in most primate groups are characterized by reassurance and dispute settlement. While easily divided resources are typically not shared, some degree of shared access to nondivisible resources of food or space is also generally evident (chap. 7). Particularly important are the responses of reassurance and social cohesion characteristic of the female behavioral repertoire: while long overshadowed by the focus on competition and dominance, female primatologists have convincingly shown the need to reconsider social processes from the perspective of both sexes (chaps. 1 and 3). Indeed, in free-ranging groups of nonhuman primates as in human societies, the agonistic or competitive behaviors long stressed in the literature often seem to characterize a minute proportion of total behavior: in Goodall's observations of the chimpanzees of Gombe over a twenty-five year period, for example, threat displays were initated during only 1.6 percent of observation hours of males, and during only during 0.6 percent of observation hours by females (Goodall 1986).

4. *Dominance and social control.* Asymmetrical relationships in the access to valued resources and in social interactions are evident, but the role of the leader or dominant member of the group is more complex than was thought a generation ago. While responding to challenges with counterthreat rather than fear, such a leader may also defend others against predators and limit the escalation of conflict by those of lower status (Kummer 1971; Montagner et al. 1988). In general, therefore, dominance hierarchies are characteristics of the group as a whole which cannot be reduced to a simplistic competition for food and mates (Chance 1989).

5. *Subordination and flight.* Since individual responses that cut off a competitive encounter are often mutually advantageous, behavior associated with subordinate or follower status is an adaptive strategy found throughout primate groups. In many species, for example, when bystanders observe a competitive interaction between a pair of individuals, the observer is likely to defer to the winner (Chase 1980). Indeed, the ability to adopt submissive postures is a necessary element in the developmental process rather than a sign of failure. Hence the interpretation of social interactions as if they reflected a Hobbesian conflict is contrary to the principles of evolutionary biology.

6. *Coalition formation and strategic behavior.* The social behaviors of nonhuman primates include instances of intentionality and deception that provide the basis for strategies of social behavior that are more consciously developed in humans (chaps. 6, 7, 8, and 9; Whiten and Byrne 1988; de Waal 1989, chap. 6). Building on reciprocities, for example, individual members of a primate group may form temporary or lasting coalitions which serve to increase the stability of the group.

7. *Individual "personality," social roles, and sex.* Individual primates differ in their responses to common social events. Obvious to anyone who has seen films of the chimpanzees of Gombe, the importance of individuality in primate social groups coincides with increasing evidence that stable individual patterns of social behavior are the product of inheritance and individual developmental experience (Kagan, Reznick, and Snidman 1988; Izard, Hembree, and Heubner 1987). Diverse social roles, particularly associated with sex and age, can of course be filled by individuals with differing "personalities" or response styles (chaps. 8 and 9). As a result, much of the diversity long presumed to be unique to human social behavior has now been observed throughout a wide range of primate species (Kummer 1971; DeVore 1965b).

### The Problem of Intentionality

When similarities between human and nonhuman primates are suggested, the principal objection has often been that no other species behaves with the intentionality and purpose shown by humans. Consider the fact that male and female social behaviors differ among chimpanzees in ways that seem to resemble human patterns of gender difference. De Waal (1982, 186) describes this comparison as follows:

> The female hierarchy in our chimpanzee group seems to be based on respect from below rather than intimidation and a show of strength from above. Females seldom display and 54 percent of the "greetings" among them are spontaneous, against as little as 13 percent among males. As among females of other great ape species, acceptance of dominance is probably more important than proving dominance. . . . Hence it is truer to speak of a *subordination hierarchy* among ape females than of a dominance hierarchy. The term "subordination hierarchy" was coined by the primatologist Thelma Rowell, who attributes the one-sided emphasis on studying dominance to the "unconscious anthropomorphism" of her male colleagues.

Granted that such a distinction can be inferred from statistical differences in male and female behavior, such as those presented by both Goodall and de Waal, it is not always clear that one can infer individual intentionality consistent with these differences (cf. Hrdy 1981). For chimpanzees, different patterns of hierarchy among males and females need not automatically be equated with an *intentional* process of "striving for higher status" among males that is totally absent in females. Since we generally assume that human behaviors are the product of individual purpose and intention, doesn't this difference override any similarities that may be found throughout the primate order?

Intentionality is one of the thorniest issues that can arise when discussing analogies between nonhuman primate behavior and human politics. Do other animals sometimes "intend" to act in the way they do? Even granting the existence of "consciousness" to a nonhuman animal (Griffin 1981, 1982, 1984), "self-consciousness" seems essential to human politics—and the mere existence of this phenomenon in species other than humans is subject to serious question. In no area, therefore, is it more important to avoid anthropocentrism than in the attributions of intention and self-consciousness (which are sometimes even given to inanimate objects, as in a newspaper report announcing that "the relentless lava threatened to cause even more damage last night as it filled in low points and appeared *intent* on advancing on"). But a failure to see intention where it exists could also be important (especially in the context of discussing primate "politics").

On the issue of "intentions" in nonhuman mammals generally, Vicki Hearne offers some interesting examples in *Adam's Task* (1987): perhaps because she is an animal trainer, Hearne presents many cases where it is hard to account for behavior without assuming a self-monitoring that is functionally similar to what we usually call "intentionality." On the other hand, as Sebeok has pointed out in his analysis of the celebrated "clever Hans" effect, many anecdoctal observations must be challenged as unwarranted in the absence of scientifically acceptable (i.e., replicable) evidence (Sebeok 1985, 1987). It is, of course, possible to define "intention" as the act of making a verbal statement of a future state and then modifying behavior in order to conform to that verbal statement; so defined, it would follow that insofar as nonhuman primates and other mammals lack verbal speech, only humans exhibit intentionality. But the verbal accounts of intention given by humans can be a means of deceiving others (or oneself)— and, indeed, some verbal statements of intentionality may represent attempts to produce consistency given contradictions between the unconscious or sub-conscious information processed by the parallel "modules" in the human brain (Gazzaniga 1985).

In what is one of the more detailed examinations of this problem, for example, Dennett (1988) has sought to define the philosophic justification for the "intentional stance"—that is, the observational stance of imputing intentionality to another actor. He defines three levels of imputing intentions, of which the third—an action by which one animal seeks to lead others to believe something that the first knows to be true (or false) but the others do not—is critical here. In so doing, Dennett used an example of vervet monkey behavior derived from the work of Cheney and Seyfarth, who in turn commented that while deceptions in most animals can be explained without attributing intentions to the actor, "an increasing number of anecdotes . . . suggests that nonhuman primates do sometimes falsify signals in a way that implies higher order intentionality" (Cheney and Seyfarth 1988, 507). They immediately add, however, that "closer scrutiny of the monkey's behavior just before or after the apparently deceptive behavior reveals just the sort of gaps and foggy places" that call into question the extent of the intention if not its existence.

This issue, central if one is to compare primate social behavior and human politics, has long been debated by philosophers and ethologists as well as by political scientists. It is therefore particularly useful to cite in detail the way Cheney and Seyfarth (1988, 507) analyze a highly relevant anecdote from primate behavior.

> Two vervet groups were involved in an aggressive skirmish on the boundary of their territories. A male member of the losing group suddenly ran up into a nearby tree and began to give leopard alarm calls, thus causing all participants to race for the trees. This ended the skirmish, restored the border to its former position and avoided a loss of territory by the male's group. Since then, we have observed a handful of similar instances (far outweighted by the frequency of "true" or reliable alarm calls), in which a male has given apparently false leopard alarm calls when a new male was attempting to transfer into his group. In the majority of the approximately ten occasions when this behavior has been observed in the last decade, the caller has been one perpetually low-ranking individual name Kitui, who could reasonably expect to be subordinate to the interloper if he transferred successfully into the group. Kitui has been second-ranking of two males, third-ranking of three males, and so on throughout his career. So far so good. The alarm calls appear deceitful because they signal danger which Kitui, but not the interloper, knows to be false, and they keep the interloper temporarily at bay.

Taken alone, therefore, the anecdote appears to represent a case of intentionality in a nonhuman primate—and one that is, interestingly enough, directly related to the questions of dominance, hierarchy, territory, and other behaviors usually called "politics" among humans.

The question does not, however, end here. Cheney and Seyfarth (1988, 507) go on to show that the observer can often be misled in such cases:

> As if to convince his rival of the full import of his calls, Kitui has on three occasions left his own tree, walked across the open plains, and entered a tree adjacent to the interloper's, alarm-calling all the while. These alarm calls couldn't be meant as threats, because alarm calls are not given in agonistic interactions and they are not accompanied by any other threat displays. Instead it is as if Kitui has got only half the story right: he knows that his alarm calls cause others to believe that there is a leopard nearby, but he doesn't seem to realize that other aspects of his behavior must be consistent with his calls. To leave the tree and to walk toward the other male simply betrays his own lack of belief in the leopard. He cannot keep up his end of the story. Numerous similar examples abound for the imperfectly rational (that is deceitful) minds of children. A child of three denies having been to the cookie jar when there are crumbs on his face; only at older ages does deception become sufficiently refined that the telltale crumbs are removed.

Attributing intentionality to the alarm-calling behavior may be reasonable; attributing a full and accurate *understanding* of the situation is clearly not.

Before assuming that Cheney and Seyfarth's second example of Kitui's behavior proves that this vervet was not self-conscious, the critical reader needs to be reminded of the distinction between intention and substantive rationality in human politics. Human leaders, like the three-year-old mentioned by Cheney and Seyfarth, often forget that observers are monitoring unexpected details in their behavior: one need only think of Nixon's decision to deliver the Watergate tapes on which eighteen minutes had been erased. In short, for nonhuman primates as for humans, it is often an error to assume that apparently intentional behavior is *fully* self-conscious or to equate the existence of an intention with a completely objective or rational knowledge of the relationship between the actor and the group. In each case, the observer needs to beware of erroneous attributions based on what seems to fit our preconceptions. But in so doing, there seems no *a priori* reason why one cannot accept the possibility of intentionality as long as it is viewed as a phenomenon distinct from the scientific accuracy of the actor's own understanding or predictions of the event. On the contrary, many definitions that would deny intentionality to any nonhuman primate have the inconvenience that they also deny intentionality or purpose to much—if not all—political behavior by humans.

It is probably reasonable, therefore, to admit that a form of intentionality can arise when an animal shows unmistakable signs of monitoring its own behavior as it relates to others *and* when that animal then modifies its behavior to conform to the way its own signals are apparently being perceived by those social partners. While the data concerning primate behavior presented in this book are not always accompanied by scientific evidence demonstrating the existence of intentionality in this sense, observers in the field often feel it is warranted to attribute something of this order to chimpanzees. In *Chimpanzee Politics* (1982), de Waal illustrates the difficulty by presenting a number of concrete instances of behavior which he first describes and then explicitly "interprets." Indeed, the section of *Chimpanzee Politics* entitled "Daring Interpretations" (46–50) is among the more careful attempts to justify the imputation of "intentionality" in a nonhuman mammal. While these cases often seem hard to explain without something like intention, critics might well disagree. Open dialogue on this point is clearly healthy if the study of nonhuman primates is not to degenerate into excessive anthropomorphism.

As the above suggests, the imputation of intentionality is probably best treated as an empirical matter of more and less rather than as an abstract question of theory — or, worse, of faith. Perhaps the most persuasive instance of self-monitoring followed by behavior shaped to alter the perceptions of others is the following example from the chimpanzees at Arnhem:

> The second change of leadership, unlike the first, was not brought about by a challenger who was physically stronger than the leader. I would say that Luit [leader at the time] and Nikkie were about equally matched as far as physical strength was concerned. . . . Both Luit and Nikkie did their best to show not the slightest trace of uncertainty in each other's presence — Luit with his characteristic hard thumps on the ground and Nikkie hooting and throwing carefully aimed stones. When they were out of each other's sight, however, they showed definite signs of fear. This was a case of *genuine bluffing*, in the sense that they each pretended to be braver and less frightened than they really were. During one of their confrontations, for example, I observed a remarkable series of signal disguises. After Luit and Nikkie had displayed in each other's proximity for over ten minutes a conflict broke out between them in which Luit was supported by Mama and Puist. Nikkie was driven into a tree, but a little later he began to hoot at the leader again while he was still perched in the tree. Luit was sitting at the bottom of the tree with his back to his challenger. When he heard the renewed sounds of provocation he bared his teeth [i.e., in the fear display that van Hooff (1969) has called the "silent-bare-teeth scream face"] but immediately put his hand to his mouth and pressed his lips together. . . . I saw the nervous grin appear on his face again and once more he used his fingers to press his lips together. The third time Luit finally succeeded in wiping the [fear] grin off his face; only then did he turn around. (de Waal 1982, 132–33)

It is hard to think of a case of nonverbal performance that is better suited to illustrate the *possibility* of intentionality in a nonhuman primate. That many instances of actual behavior do not fit the concept of intention, however, one must also agree. Among humans, in fact, the same problem can readily occur — as when a dyslexic child is sent to detention for *intentional* laziness in work containing errors due to a neurologically based learning deficit.

### What Can Primatology Teach Us about Politics?

This survey of similarities and differences between humans and other primates suggests some areas in which the scientific study of primates can illuminate the study of political behavior. The basic phenomena of political life—society, power, influence, social conflict, and history—all have direct analogues among nonhuman primates. In place of the traditional assumption that "human nature" consists of a set of fixed traits, the natural foundations of politics can thus be explored in terms of factors known to vary in predictable ways throughout the primate family. For example, if nonhuman primates generally engage in both cooperative and competitive behaviors, the nature of cooperation must be seen in terms of the relationship between the resources at issue and the needs of the species. Hence, from an ethological perspective, narrowly reductionist models of social interaction must be replaced by more dynamic and interactive theories of behavior.

More particularly, an ethological approach shows that the traditional nature-nurture dichotomy must be abandoned in favor of a subtler approach. Particularly among primates, not only will the same animals exhibit different behaviors depending on the natural setting, but social environment and individual experience are as much a factor as the species-typical repertoire or genetically transmitted behavioral propensities. If nonhuman primates cannot be understood in terms of such abstractions as a "gene for altruism," it makes even less sense to use simplistic concepts in studying human social and political life.

While primate ethology leads away from genetic or biological reductionism, however, it also challenges the prevailing view of sociocultural determinism. If chimpanzees in the Gombe show differences in rates of spontaneous aggression exhibited by males and females (Goodall 1986 and chap. 5), it is hardly acceptable to dismiss all forms of gender differentiation in human society as the product of culturally defined roles caused by "sexist" attitudes (G. Schubert 1987, 1989b). Granted that nonhuman primates, like most preliterate human gatherer-hunters, do not have the rigid dominance hierarchies found in the centralized state, all phenomena of leadership cannot be entirely reduced to sociocultural prejudice or economic power. In short, an ethological approach to primate social behavior teaches us that politics can only be understood in terms of dynamic interactions between the natural and cultural factors.

### What Primatology Cannot Teach Us about Politics

As the foregoing cautions should indicate, primate ethology can hardly "reduce" the study of human politics to the behavior of chimpanzees or rhesus monkeys (chaps. 1 and 2). No serious biologist would imply that the complexities of an ecosystem can be explained by the genetics or behavior of a single species. Emergent phenomena in hominid evolution distinguish many patterns of human politics from anything observed among nonhuman primates (chap. 4). While the building blocks of more diversified social structures may be found in simpler face-to-face primate groups, states and civilizations have properties that need to be studied on their own terms. While these caveats should be self-evident, they are reminders that no single theoretical approach is likely to exhaust the manifold phenomena usually studied under the rubric of political science.

### PRIMATE BEHAVIOR AND HUMAN POLITICS

To go beyond the foregoing generalities, three areas require careful analysis. First, what is the current status of ethological theory as it might apply to primate social and political behavior? Second, what is the evidence for—or against—the existence of meaningful parallels between human politics and the social life of nonhuman primates? And third, how do ethological perspectives illuminate the political behavior in contemporary industrial societies?

Each of these questions has been the focus of one part of *Primate Politics*. Each concerns major scientific issues that need further inquiry if we are to explore the links between evolutionary biology and the social sciences. To see why this is so, let us consider in more detail each of the three main areas approached in this volume.

#### Primatology and Political Theory

That it is necessary to integrate evolutionary biology and the study of human politics has been fully recognized by many scholars (G. Schubert 1981b, c, 1985, 1987, 1989a, b; Masters 1983, 1989a, b; E. White 1980, 1981; Lopreato 1984; Somit 1976; Rosenberg 1980). That it is dangerous to embark on this effort without adequate and precise information about contemporary biology is also more than evident (e.g., Caplan 1978; Masters 1979; G. Schubert 1983b, c; Kitcher 1985). Can we go beyond such generalities, shedding some light on the way recent findings point to a more precise understanding of the articulation between what is common to other primates and what is specifically human in our political behavior?

Despite the lip service paid to the proposition that Darwin's theory of evolution explains human origins, a precise understanding of evolutionary theory and hominid evolution is not as yet fully integrated into the theories and research of political science. In chapter 1, Glendon Schubert lays the groundwork for remedying this gap by placing political phenomena in the context of the scientific study of primates. Schubert's introduction to primatology not only shows some hidden implications of phrases often taken for granted in remarks about hominid evolution (e.g., "Man the Hunter"), but spells out the enormous gains in our understanding of primate social behavior and evolution that have been due to the work of female primatologists.

Among the theoretical problems Schubert stresses, anthropomorphism has long been noted as one of the principal dangers in extrapolations from nonhuman to human behavior. If one reads specifically "human" intentions or meanings into the responses of other animals, then of course the "humanized" animals become a prototype or model of human life itself. From Aesop to Beatrix Potter and Walt Disney, children have been enchanted and instructed by such an anthropomorphic view of birds and bees, bunnies, and mice. But science isn't a fairy tale: what is instructive as a children's bedtime story may make a poor basis for ethology and political theory.

Most discussions of this problem have focused on the danger of anthropomorphism in the work of the social scientists, philosophers, or literary writers who have been tempted to delve into ethological research. Although this danger remains important, it is sufficiently well known; there is no need to belabor the risks of a misinterpretation of technical information by nonspecialists.

More to the point is a different risk of anthropomorphism. Ethological descriptions of primates, even if presented with the appearance of scientific rigor, may rest on unconscious assumptions that reflect human concerns. Even without ideological intentions, political attitudes and expectations can color the language and conceptual apparatus of the student of primate behavior as easily as in any other field of the social sciences.

In chapter 2, Schubert explores this issue by looking carefully at the concept of politics implied in four contemporary writings by ethologists. As he shows, ethologists sometimes carry imprecise or misleading terminology from political science back into their study of the behavior of primates. What is supposedly "primate politics" may merely be a distorted and partial image of humans. By contrasting different degrees of this error, moreover, Schubert illuminates the way one can guard against anthropomorphism, moving toward a more precise and solid human ethology.

The conceptual problems of studying primate politics do not end here. Political life presupposes a social group. But is society a "thing," like a chair or a table? Or are there different modes of social interaction, depending on the actors (be they baboons or bureaucrats)? Are there definitional properties that permit us to distinguish, a priori, the nature of a society and a political system — or is this very approach, so traditional in political theory, a deformation of the behavior of both nonhuman and human primates?

Shirley Strum and Bruno Latour (chap. 4) consider this issue in a way that turns much of the prior debate on its head. Previous critics asserted that an ethological approach to human life was absurd because it would reduce politics to a matter of genetically controlled instinct (e.g., Montagu 1968). Strum and Latour suggest that intentionality and purpose are as critical for baboons as for humans: in this view, any primate society is "performed" by its members, not defined by nonparticipating observers. If so, the risk of what is usually described as anthropomorphism concerns a pattern of reification that has been as pernicious in political or sociological theory as in field studies of primates.

This danger of pretending that we know better than others what they are *really* doing has nowhere been more evident than in behavioral patterns that suggest sexuality and power. Thelma Rowell (chap. 3) provides a brilliant analysis of the dangers of misattributed function or intention in ethology by focusing on the concept of a "harem."

Among hamadryas baboons, as in other species such as elephant seals, we observe a single male who appears to herd a group of females and to exclude other males from approaching them. Although primate ethologists have typically used the word "harem" when describing these behaviors, it requires much analysis to see whether this unthinking reference to a human cultural practice is appropriate when discussing the behavior of baboons or elephant seals.

All four chapters of part I therefore lead us to inquire more carefully into the specificity of primate social behavior. Before we can say what is or is not "politics," whether in discussing chimpanzees or humans, some such assessment of the dangers of habitual metaphors and reification is necessary.

### Does Simian Politics Exist?

Once we are sensitized to the dangers of conceptual error, even in highly specialized work, it is possible to place the question of nonhuman primate behavior in a new light. Can we speak of "politics" among animals who do not use verbal language? Do the specifically political behaviors that have been attributed to nonhuman primates deserve to be considered as such? Part II considers this problem by examining the social behavior of the primate species most closely related to *Homo sapiens sapiens*. While chimpanzees provide some of the best-known examples of supposed politics among nonhuman primates, a comparison between findings based on different populations of chimpanzees shows the importance of such factors as group structure and ecological setting.

Jane Goodall's prolonged observation of the chimpanzees of Gombe has helped to transform our understanding of nonhuman primates. Like the extended fieldwork of Biruté Galdikàs, Dian Fossey, and Shirley Strum (and others—most often women—who have had the courage and patience to study the same population continuously over many years), Goodall's study has shown us the danger of assuming that a relatively brief period of observation could provide the basis of an accurate assessment of the totality of an animal's behavioral repertoire. As among humans, it is necessary to identify the members of a group individually, to watch their behavior develop throughout an entire lifetime, and to assess the development of responses among different lineages in many circumstances over many years. In chapter 5, with the permission of the author and Harvard University Press, the result of twenty-five years of observation at Gombe have been edited by Glendon Schubert from Goodall's magnificent work *The Chimpanzees of Gombe* (1986). The result provides us with a striking indication of the social behavior of chimps in the particular ecological and social context of the provisioned population that Goodall and her collaborators have so carefully studied.

Chapter 6 turns to a population of chimpanzees under rather different conditions. Frans de Waal's *Chimpanzee Politics* (1982) presents a picture of alliance behavior in the Arnhem colony and characterizes it as "political" in the fullest sense of the word. Is this accurate? In chapter 6 and a follow-up study, de Waal (1989) shows that some forms of social interaction observed among chimpanzees can be distinguished from responses to similar situations among other primates. As a result, it would appear that chimpanzees represent a stage in the emergence of strategies of retribution and coalition formation that is intermediate between fully articulated political processes and the social hierarchies of most groups of monkeys.

In both of these settings, considerations of reproductive success and survival are complex, particularly when including long-range consequences in changing environments. Chimpanzees are not identical in the Gombe reserve and at Arnhem; food sharing is not the same when populations rely on gathering and small game rather than on provisioned food. Evolutionary biology—as the study of the way mutation, natural selection, population structure, genetic drift, and other systemic factors shape the historical changes in living beings—deepens our understanding of such complexities among nonhuman primates. Do similar approaches illuminate human politics?

*Primatology and Human Politics*

The primate heritage shared by *Homo sapiens* includes many traits that make the social behavior of monkeys and apes instantly recognizable: doubtless this explains the fascination of children watching them in zoos. For the ethologist, however, such behavioral patterns must be defined precisely, observed empirically, and related systematically to biologically relevant outcomes.

In Part III, we turn to aspects of primate social behavior which have obvious implications for human politics. First Nicholas Blurton Jones (chap. 7) indicates the way conventional dichotomy between altruism or cooperation and self-interested competition needs to be qualified when human behavior is considered from an ethological perspective. Since food sharing has been viewed as a prototypical element of social cooperation in hominid evolution, the theoretical explanation of its origins and limits provides an excellent transition from the consideration of chimpanzees to humans.

In the tradition of political theory, cooperation and selfishness have often been viewed as alternative conceptions of "human nature." As Blurton Jones shows, however, what at first appears to be a species-typical trait of sharing or "altruism" may well be a response to the relationship between certain types of food resource and social organization. If food sharing is a response of "tolerated theft" of large edible objects whose defense or preservation would be more costly than beneficial, then cooperative behavior must be viewed more precisely as a variable that depends on ecological settings, on resource availability, and on social structure. Thus, the emergence and evolution of gathering, hunting, and agriculture—and the implications of these modes of subsistence for social interaction and politics—must be reconsidered from an evolutionary perspective (G. Schubert 1989a; Masters 1989a).

While many political phenomena depend on economic, sociological, and cultural variables, primate social behavior can also illuminate the processes of decision making and leadership at the center of human politics. Like monkeys and apes, we express feelings and communicate social intentions through nonverbal cues that are both visible and audible. While communication by olfaction (pheromones) and touch also probably play an important role for all primates, the group behaviors we call politics are most likely to be associated with gestural cues of face and body seen by others or with acoustic signals heard by members of the group.

Analysis of the political impact of facial displays and vocal sounds that accompany human speech provides a striking illustration of the benefits of extending ethological methods to our own species. Ever since Lorenz recognized how stereotyped actions of one animal can become a meaningful social cue (or "releaser") for conspecifics (Lorenz 1970–71; Lorenz and Leyhausen 1973), ethologists have studied the communicative significance of behavior and its phylogenetic as well as social transmission of adaptive responses. The last two chapters in part III suggest that humans are not exempt from evolutionary processes, although the integration of nonverbal and verbal communication produces a somewhat different form of politics than is observed among other primates.

In chapter 8, Sullivan, Masters, Lanzetta, McHugo, Plate, and Englis report on experimental studies of the effects of a leader's facial displays. Throughout the primate order there is a remarkable similarity in the types of gestural cues of the face and social cues they transmit (van Hooff 1969, 1973). In contemporary industrialized societies, most citizens frequently observe close-up images of political leaders and candidates on television; as a result, facial expressions that are typically seen in any face-to-face group of primates can have a direct effect on the emotional responses and judgments of the contemporary television viewer.

This research focuses on stereotyped facial displays studied as social cues and expressions of emotion in primate ethology and social psychology. By presenting carefully selected videotapes of a known and powerful leader exhibiting these nonverbal cues while controlling for the presence or absence of a spoken message, experimental studies can reveal the emotional and cognitive effects of primate signaling in the mass politics of an industrial society.

The results show that human politics is not exempt from the preverbal forms of social communication found among nonhuman primates. Leaders and decision makers have strong feelings about what they are doing and develop distinct styles of performing their roles. Communication of emotion, intention, and self-confidence by nonverbal cues is thus at the very center of the actual processes we call politics, even though most political scientists have abstained from serious study of these directly observable phenomena.

James Schubert has demonstrated, in chapter 9, how this ethological approach functions in the acoustic channel. Although speech at first seems to be merely a means of transmitting verbal or linguistic messages, sound is an important social signal among all primates. All primate vocal production carries paralinguistic cues of the initiator's arousal and emotion that influence listeners, so sound recordings of human decision-making groups are used to study the frequency and effects of the nonverbal dimension of acoustic behavior.

Once again, it becomes apparent that human politics is not a disembodied phenomenon. Schubert's work focuses on actual deliberations of city councils in the United States. In these face-to-face groups that actively make political decisions, the paralinguistic behaviors of leaders differ from those of followers. The cues associated with conflict differ from those eliciting consensus. And individual leaders have varied performance "styles" associated with differing degrees of effectiveness.

## CONCLUSIONS AND FUTURE RESEARCH

Human politics is, in part, influenced by the visual and auditory components of the primate social repertoire. Research like that in part III thus deepens our understanding of the complexity of political phenomena. In parts I and II, we found that a reinterpretation of research on nonhuman primates shows the risks of assuming we know what other animals are doing; in studying human politics as well, understanding is distorted by projecting our own intentions on the behavior of others.

As future research develops in primatology and human politics, we can expect to gain new insights into the reasons for otherwise puzzling phenomena. On the one hand, greater insights into the "proximate causes" of individual and group differences of human social organization and behavior are likely to result from new work in primatology as well as from rapid advances in such diverse areas as cognitive neuroscience, developmental psychology, and ecology. On the other, deeper understanding of hominid phylogeny along with research in ethology and anthropology will illuminate the way factors in the physical environment, social organization, and cultural practices of a human population function as "ultimate" causes influencing the evolution of authority and power.

If the life sciences continue to develop along the lines discussed in this volume, it seems highly likely that political science will come of age as a truly *scientific* discipline. The foundations of our understanding of human politics can only be deepened by understanding the extent to which similar phenomena arise among primates more generally as well as why the specific patterns observed in humans have occurred. Such developments would not, however, be as much of a radical break with the tradition as it might seem. While the insights and issues that will be contributed by the next generation of researchers cannot be predicted in detail, it should be evident that the study of primate politics will be an invaluable means of furthering the age-old quest for a better understanding of human nature.

*References*
*Notes on Contributors*
*Name Index*
*Subject Index*

# References

Abbeglen, J. J. 1976. *On socialization in hamadryas baboons.* Lewisburg, Penn.: Bucknell University Press.

Abelson, Robert P.; Kinder, Donald R.; Peters, M. D.; and Fiske, Susan T. 1982. Affective and semantic components in political person perception. *Journal of Personality and Social Psychology* 42:619–30.

Abelson, Robert P., and Roseman, I. 1984. Love appeals and anger appeals in political persuasion. Paper presented at the nineteenth annual Carnegie Symposium on Cognition, Carnegie-Mellon University, Pittsburgh.

Alcock, John. 1975. *Animal behavior: An evolutionary approach.* Sunderland, Mass.: Sinauer Associates.

Alexander, I. E., and Babad, E. W. 1981. Returning the smile of the stranger: within culture and cross-cultural comparisons of Israeli and American children. *Genetic Psychology Monographs* 103:31–77.

Alexander, Richard. 1979. *Darwinism and human affairs.* Seattle: University of Washington Press.

———. 1987. *The biology of moral systems.* New York: Aldine de Gruyter.

Altmann, Jeanne. 1974. Observation study of behavior: Sampling methods. *Behavior* 49:227–67.

———. 1980. *Baboon mothers and infants.* Cambridge: Harvard University Press.

Altmann, Stuart A. 1967. The structure of primate social communication. In S. A. Altmann, ed., *Social communication among primates.* Chicago: University of Chicago Press.

Altmann, Stuart A., and Altmann, Jeanne. 1971. *Baboon ecology.* Chicago: University of Chicago Press.

Andrew, R. J. 1963. The origin and evolution of the calls and facial expressions of the primates. *Behavior* 20:1–109.

Andrews, Peter, and Cronin, J. F. 1982. The relationships of sivapithecus and ramapithecus and the evolution of the orangutan. *Nature* 297:541–46.

Ardrey, Robert. 1963. *African genesis.* New York: Atheneum.

Argyle, Michael, and Cook, M. 1976. *Gaze and mutual gaze*. Cambridge: Cambridge University Press.

Aubert, Vilhelm. 1959. Chance in social affairs. *Inquiry* 2:1–24.

Avery, M. I. 1984. Lekking in birds: Choice, competition, and reproductive constraints. *Ibis* 126:177–87.

Axelrod, Robert. 1981. The emergence of cooperation among egoists. *American Political Science Review* 75:306–18.

————. 1984. *The evolution of cooperation*. New York: Basic Books.

Axelrod, Robert, and Hamilton, William D. 1981. The evolution of cooperation. *Science* 211:1390–96.

Bachman, C., and Kummer, Hans. 1980. Male assessment of female choice in hamadryas baboons. *Behavioral Ecology and Sociobiology* 6:315–21.

Baldwin, John D., and Baldwin, Janice I. 1979. The phylogenetic and ontogenetic variables that shape behavior and social organizations. In Irwin S. Bernstein and Euclid O. Smith, eds., *Primate ecology and human origins*, 89–116. New York: Garland Press.

Barash, David. 1982. *Sociobiology and behavior*, 2nd ed. New York: Elsevier.

Barnard, Alan. 1983. Contemporary hunter-gatherers: Current theoretical issues in ecology and social organization. *Annual Review of Anthropology* 12:193–214.

Barnard, Chester J., ed. 1984. *Producers and scroungers: Strategies of exploitation and parasitism*. London and Sydney: Croom Helm; N.Y.: Chapman and Hall.

Barnard, Chester J., and Sibly, R. M. 1981. Producers and scroungers: A general model and its application to captive flocks of house sparrows. *Animal Behaviour* 29:543–50.

Barner-Barry, Carol. 1977. An observational study of authority in a preschool peer group. *Political Methodology* 4:415–99.

————. 1978. The biological correlates of power and authority: Dominance and attention structure. Paper presented at the annual meeting of the American Political Science Association, New York.

————. 1979. The utility of attention structure theory and the problem of human diversity. Paper presented at the world congress of the International Political Science Association, Moscow.

————. 1981. Longitudinal observational research and the study of the basic forms of political socialization. In Meredith Watts, ed., *Biopolitics: Ethological and physiological approaches*, 51–60. San Francisco: Jossey-Bass.

————. 1982. An ethological study of leadership succession. *Ethology and Sociobiology* 3:199–207.

Barry, Brian. 1970. *Sociologists, economists, and democracy*. London: Macmillan.

Beck, Benjamin. 1982. Chimpocentrism: Bias in cognitive ethology. *Journal of Human Evolution* 11:3–17.

Becker, Gary S. 1976. Altruism, egoism, and genetic fitness: Economics and sociobiology. *Journal of Economic Literature* 14:817–26.

Beckstrom, John H. 1985. *Sociobiology and the law*. Urbana: University of Illinois Press.

Bernstein, Irwin S. 1981. Dominance: The baby and the bathwater. *The Behavioral and Brain Sciences* 4:419–57.

Bernstein, Irwin S., and Ehardt, C. 1985. Agonistic aiding: Kinship, rank, age, and sex influences. *American Journal of Primatology* 8:37–52.

Bernstein, Irwin S., and Sharpe, L. 1966. Social roles in a rhesus monkey group. *Behaviour* 26:91–103.

Bertram, C. R. 1975. Social factors influencing reproduction in wild lions. *Journal of Zoology, Proceedings of the Zoological Society of London* 177:463–82.

Bigelow, Robert S. 1969. *The dawn warriors: Man's evolution towards peace.* Boston: Little, Brown.

Birdwhistell, Raymond L. 1970. *Kinesics and context.* Philadelphia: University of Pennsylvania Press.

Birke, Lynda. 1986. *Women, feminism, and biology: The feminist challenge.* Brighton, Eng.: Harvester Press.

Blanc, A. C. 1961. Some evidence for the ideologies of early man. In Sherwood L. Washburn, ed., *Social life of early man*, 119–36. Viking Fund Publications in Anthropology no. 31. Chicago: Viking Fund.

Bleier, Ruth. 1984. *Science and gender: A critique of biology and its theories on women.* Elmsford, N.Y.: Pergamon.

Blurton Jones, Nicholas G. 1984. A selfish origin for human food sharing: Tolerated theft. *Ethology and Sociobiology* 5:1–3.

———. 1986. Fitness returns from resources and the outcome of contests: Some implications for primatology and anthropology. *Proceedings of the Tenth Congress of the International Primatological Society* 3:389–402.

———. 1987. Tolerated theft: Suggestions about the ecology and evolution of sharing, hoarding and scrounging. *Social Science Information* 26:31–54.

Blurton Jones, Nicholas G., and Konner, Melvin J. 1973. Sex differences in behaviour of London and Bushmen children. In R. P. Michael and John H. Crook, eds., *Comparative ecology and behaviour of primates*, 689–750. London: Academic Press.

Boese, G. 1975. Social behavior and ecological considerations of West African baboons. In R. Tuttle, ed., *Socioecology and psychology of primates.* The Hague: Mouton.

Boggess, Jane. 1979. Troop male membership changes and infant killing in langurs. *Presbytis entellus. Folia Primatologica* 32:65–107.

Bond, J., and Vinacke, W. 1961. Coalitions in mixed-sex triads. *Sociometry* 24:61–75.

Bonner, John Tyler. 1980. *The evolution of culture in animals.* Princeton, N.J.: Princeton University Press.

Boorman, Scott A., and Levitt, Paul R. 1973. A frequency-dependent natural selection model for the evolution of social cooperative networks. *Proceedings of the Natural Academy of Science* 70:187–89.

———. 1980. *The genetics of altruism.* New York: Academic Press.

Borgia, Gerald. 1980. Human aggression as a biological adaptation. In J. Lockard, ed., *The evolution of human social behavior*, 165–91. New York: Elsevier.

Brace, C. Loring. 1979. Biological parameters and Pleistocene hominid lifeways. In Irwin S. Bernstein and Euclid O. Smith, eds., *Primate ecology and human origins*, 263–89. New York: Garland Press.

Breines, Wini, et al. 1978. Social biology, family studies, and antifeminist backlash. *Feminist Studies* 4:43–67.

Brewer, S. 1978. *The forest dwellers.* London: Collins.

Busse, C. D. 1976. Chimpanzee predation on red colobus monkeys. Unpublished manuscript.

Busse, C. D., and Hamilton, William, III. 1981. Infant carrying by male Chacma baboons. *Science* 212:1281–83.

Bygott, J. D. 1974. Agonistic behaviour and dominance in wild chimpanzees. Ph.D. diss., University of Cambridge.

————. 1979. Agonistic behaviour, dominance, and social structure in wild chimpanzees of the Gombe National Park. In David A. Hamburg and Elizabeth R. McGown, eds., *The great apes*, 405–28. Menlo Park, Calif.: Benjamin/Cummings.

Byrne, R., and Whiten, A. 1987. The thinking primate's guide to deception. *New Scientist* 1589:54–57.

Cacioppo, John T., and Petty, Richard E. 1979. Attitudes and cognitive response: An electrophysiological approach. *Journal of Personality and Social Psychology* 37:2181–99.

Callon, M., and Latour, Bruno. 1981. Unscrewing the big leviathans: How do actors macrostructure reality and how sociologists help them. In K. Knorr and A. Cicourel, eds., *Advances in social theory and methodology*. London: Routledge & Kegan Paul.

Campbell, Bernard. 1979. Ecological factors and social organizations in human evolution. In Irwin S. Bernstein and Euclid O. Smith, eds., *Primate ecology and human origins*, 291–12. New York: Garland Press.

Campbell, Donald T. 1965. Variation and selective retention in socio-cultural evolution. In H. Barringer, G. Blanksten, and H. Mack, eds., *Social change in developing areas*, 19–49. Cambridge: Schenckman.

————. 1972. On the genetics of altruism and the counter-hedonic components in human culture. *Journal of Social Issues* 28:21–37.

Caplan, Arthur M. 1978. *The sociobiology debate*. New York: Harper & Row.

Caporael, Linnda R.; Dawes, Robyn M.; Orbell, John M. and van de Kragt, Alphons. 1989. Selfishness examined: Cooperation in the absence of egoistic incentives. *Behavioral and Brain Sciences* 12 (4):683–737.

Capouya, Emile; and Tompkins, Keitha. 1975. *The essential Kropotkin*. New York: Liveright.

Carneiro, Robert. 1970. A theory of state. *Science* 169:733–38.

Cattani, Richard J. 1981. Monitor poll of political scientists. *Christian Science Monitor* 11 September: 3; 15 September: 6; 16 September: 7.

Chagnon, Napoleon A. 1968. Yanomamo social organization and warfare. In M. Fried, M. Harris, and R. Murphey, eds., *War: The anthropology of armed conflict and aggression*, 109–59. Garden City, N.Y.: Natural History Press.

Chagnon, Napoleon, and Irons, William, eds. 1979. *Evolutionary biology and human social behavior*. N. Scituate, Mass: Duxbury Press.

Chance, Michael R. A. 1976a. Attention structures as the basis of primate rank orders. In Michael R. A. Chance and Ray R. Larson, eds., *The social structure of attention*. New York: John Wiley.

————. 1976b. Social attention: Society and mentality. In Michael R. A. Chance and Ray R. Larson, eds., *The social structure of attention*, 315–33. New York: John Wiley.

————. 1976c. The organization of attention in groups. In Mario von Cranach, ed., *Methods of inference from animal to human behavior*. The Hague: Mouton.

————, ed. 1989. *Social fabrics of the mind*. Hillsdale, N.J.: Lawrence Erlbaum.

Chance, Michael R. A., and Clifford, J. J. 1970. *Social groups of monkeys, apes, and men*. New York: E.P. Dutton.

Chance, Michael R. A., Emory, G., and Payne, R. 1977. Status referents in long-tailed macaques *Macaca fascicularis:* Precursors and effects of a female rebellion. *Primates* 18:611–32.

Chapais, B., and Schulman, S. 1980. An evolutionary model of female dominance relations in primates. *Journal of Theoretical Biology* 82:47–89.

Chase, Ivan. 1980. Social process and hierarchy formation in small groups: A comparative perspective. *American Sociological Review* 45:905–24.

Cheney, Dorothy L. 1977. The acquisition of rank and development of reciprocal alliances among free-ranging immature baboons. *Behavioral Ecology and Sociobiology* 2:303–18.

———. 1983. Extrafamilial alliances among vervet monkeys. In R. Hinde, ed., *Primate social relationships*. Sunderland, Mass.: Sinauer Associates.

Cheney, Dorothy L., and Seyfarth, Robert M. 1988. Another "Just So" story: How the leopard-guarders spot. *Behavioral and Brain Sciences* 11:506–7.

Cheney, Dorothy L.; Seyfarth, Robert M.; Smuts, Barbara B.; and Wrangham, Richard W. 1987. The study of primate societies. In Barbara B. Smuts et al., eds., *Primate societies*, 1–8. Chicago: University of Chicago Press.

Chepko-Sade, B. Diane. 1974. Division of group F at Cayo Santiago. *American Journal of Physical Anthropology* 41:472.

Chepko-Sade, B. Diane, and Olivier, T. 1979. Coefficient of genetic relationships and the probability of intragenealogical fission on *Macaca mulatta*. *Behavioral Ecology and Sociobiology* 5:263–78.

Chepko-Sade, B. Diane, and Sade, D. 1979. Patterns of group splitting within matrilineal kinship groups. *Behavioral Ecology and Sociobiology* 5:67–86.

Cherfes, J., and Gribbin, J. 1981a. The molecular making of mankind. *New Scientist* 91:518–25.

———. 1981b. Descent of man—or ascent of ape? *New Scientist* 91:582–95.

Chevalier-Skolnikoff, Suzanne; Galdikàs, Biruté; and Skolnikoff, Alan Z. 1982. The adaptive significance of higher intelligence in wild orang-utans: A preliminary report. *Journal of Human Evolution* 11:639–52.

Chevalier-Skolnikoff, Suzanne, and Poirier, Frank E., eds. 1977. *Primate bio-social development: Biological, social and ecological determinants*. New York: Garland Press.

Chism, J. B., and Rowell, Thelma E. 1986. Mating and residence patterns of adult male patas monkeys. *Ethology* 72:31–39.

Chism, J. B.; Rowell, Thelma E.; and Olson, D. K. 1984. Life history patterns of female patas monkeys. In M. Small, ed., *Female primates: Studies by women primatologists*, 175–92. New York: Alan R. Liss.

Ciochon, Russell L. 1983. Hominoid cladistics and the ancestry of modern apes and humans: A summary statement. In Russell L. Ciochon and Robert S. Corruccini, eds., *New interpretations of ape and human ancestry*, 781–843. New York: Plenum Press.

Ciochon, Russell L., and Corruccini, Robert S., eds. 1983. *New interpretations of ape and human ancestry*. New York: Plenum Press.

Ciochon, Russell L., and Fleagle, John G., eds. 1987. *Primate evolution and human origins*. Menlo Park, Calif.: Benjamin/Cummings.

Clutton-Brock, Thomas; Guinness, F. E.; and Alban, S. D. 1982. *Red deer: Behavior and ecology of two sexes*. Chicago: University of Chicago Press.

Cohen, Mark Nathan. 1977. *The food crisis in prehistory*. New Haven, Conn.: Yale University Press.

Cole, Sonia. 1975. *Leakey's luck: The life of Louis Seymour Bazett Leakey*. New York: Harcourt Brace Jovanovich.

Cords, Marina. 1984a. Mating patterns and social structure in redtail monkeys. *Zeitschrift für Tierpsychologie* 64:313–29.

————. 1984b. Mixed species groups of Cercopithecine monkeys in the Kakemega Forest, Kenya. Ph.D. diss., University of California–Berkeley.

————. 1987. Forest guenons and patas monkeys: Male-male competition in one-male groups. In Barbara B. Smuts et al., eds., *Primate societies*, 98–111. Chicago: University of Chicago Press.

Cords, Marina; Mitchell, B. J.; Tsingalia, H. M.; and Rowell, Thelma E. 1986. Promiscuous mating among blue monkeys in the Kakamega Forest, Kenya. *Ethology* 72:214–26.

Cords, Marina, and Rowell, Thelma E. 1987. Birth intervals of blue and redtail monkeys in the Kakamega Forest, Kenya. *Primates* 28:277–81.

Corning, Peter A. 1970. Theory of evolution as a paradigm for the study of political phenomena. Ph.D. diss., New York University.

————. 1977. Human nature *redivivus*. In J. Ronald Pennock and John W. Chapman, eds., *Human nature in politics*, 19–68. New York: New York University Press.

————. 1983. *The synergism hypothesis: A theory of progressive evolution*. New York: McGraw-Hill.

Corning, Peter A., and Hines, Samuel M. 1988. Political development and political evolution. *Politics and the Life Sciences* 6:141–55.

Corruccini, Robert S., and Ciochon, Russell L. 1983. Overview of ape and human ancestry: Phyletic relationships of Miocene and later Hominoidea. In Russell L. Ciochon and Robert S. Corruccini, eds., *New interpretations of ape and human ancestry*, 3–19. New York: Plenum Press.

Cox, C. R., and LeBoeuf, Bernard J. 1979. Female incitement of male competition: A mechanism. *American Naturalist* 111:317–35.

Cronin, John F. 1983. Apes, humans and molecular clocks: A reappraisal. In Russell L. Ciochon and Robert S. Corruccini, eds., *New interpretations of ape and human ancestry*, 115–35. New York: Plenum Press.

Crook, John H. 1970a. Social organization and the environment: Aspects of contemporary social ethology. *Animal Behavior* 18:197–209.

————. 1970b. *Social behaviour in birds and mammals: Essays on the social ethology of animals and man*. London: Academic Press.

Crook, John H., and Gartlan, John. 1966. On the evolution of primate societies. *Nature* 210:1200–1203.

Crook, John H., and Goss-Custard, J. 1972. Social ethology. *Annual Review of Psychology* 23:277–312.

Curie-Cohen, M.; Yoshihara, B.; Blystad, C.; Luttrell, L.; Benforado, K.; and Stone, W. H. 1981. Paternity and mating behavior in a captive group of rhesus monkeys. *American Journal of Primatology* 1:335.

Curtin, R., and Dolhinow, Phyllis. 1978. Primate social behavior: In a changing world. *American Scientist* 66:468–75.

Dahlberg, Frances, ed. 1981. *Woman the gatherer*. New Haven, Conn.: Yale University Press.

Darling, Frank F. 1937. *A herd of red deer*. London: Oxford University Press.

Darlington, Cyril D. 1969. *The evolution of man and society*. New York: Simon and Schuster.

Darwin, Charles. 1977. *The collected papers of Charles Darwin*. P. Barett, ed. Chicago: University of Chicago Press.

————. [1872] 1965. *The expression of the emotions in man and animals*. Chicago: University of Chicago Press.

Datta, S. 1983. Patterns of agonistic interference. In Robert Hinde, ed., *Primate social relationships*. Sunderland, Mass.: Sinauer Associates.

Davies, James C. 1980. Biological perspectives of human conflict. In Ted Robert Gurr, ed., *Handbook of political conflict: Theory and research*, 19–68. New York: Free Press.

Dawkins, Richard. 1976. *The selfish gene*. New York: Oxford University Press.

Day, Clarence [1920] 1936. *This Simian World*. New York: Knopf.

Dennett, Daniel C. 1988. Précis of *The intentional stance*. *Behavioral and Brain Sciences* 11:495–546.

d'Entrèves, Alexander Passerin. 1967. *The notion of the state*. Oxford: Clarendon Press.

DeVore, Irven. 1965a. Male dominance and mating behavior in baboons. In F. Beach, ed., *Sex and behavior*. New York: John Wiley.

———, ed. 1965b. *Primate behavior: Field studies of monkeys and apes*. New York: Holt, Rinehart & Winston.

DeVore, Irven, and Hall, K. R. L. 1965. Baboon ecology. In Irven DeVore, ed., *Primate behavior*. New York: Holt, Rinehart & Winston.

DeVree, J. K. 1982. Foundations of social and political processes. *The dynamics of human behavior, politics, and society*. Bilthoven, Netherlands: Prime Press.

DeWaal, Frans B. M. 1975. The wounded leader: A spontaneous temporary change in the structure of agonistic relations among captive Java-monkeys, *Macaca fascicularis*. *Netherlands Journal of Zoology* 25:529–49.

———. 1977. The organization of agonistic relationships within two captive groups of Java-monkeys *Macaca fascicularis*. *Zeitschrift für Tierpsychologie* 44:225–82.

———. 1978. Exploitative and familiarity-dependent support strategies in a colony of semi-free living chimpanzees. *Behavior* 66:268–312.

———. 1982. *Chimpanzee politics: power and sex among apes*. London: Jonathan Cape.

———. 1984. Sex differences in the formation of coalitions among chimpanzees. *Ethology and Sociobiology* 5:239–55.

———. 1985a. Coalitions in monkeys and apes. In H. Wilke, ed., *Coalition formation*, 1–27, 263–67. Amsterdam: North Holland.

———. 1985b. The exportation of biopolitics: a review of Heiner Flohr and Wolfgang Tonnesmann, eds., *Politik und Biologie*. In *Politics and the life sciences* 3:206–7.

———. 1986a. The brutal elimination of a rival among captive male chimpanzees. *Ethology and Sociobiology* 7:237–51.

———. 1986b. The integration of dominance and social bonding in primates. *Quarterly Review of Biology* 61:459–80.

———. 1987a. Dynamics of social relationships. In Barbara Smuts et al., eds., *Primate societies*, 421–29. Chicago: University of Chicago Press.

———. 1987b. Conflict resolution in monkeys and apes. In K. Benirschke, ed., *Primates: The road to self-sustaining populations*, 341–50. New York: Springer-Verlag.

———. 1989. *Peacemaking among primates*. Cambridge: Harvard University Press.

De Waal, Frans B. M., and van Hooff, Jan A. R. A. M. 1981. Side-directed communication and agonistic interactions in chimpanzees. *Behaviour* 77:164–98.

De Waal, Frans B. M.; van Hooff, Jan A. R. A. M.; and Netto, W. 1976. An ethological analysis of types of agonistic interaction in a captive group of Java-monkeys *Macaca fascicularis*. *Primates* 17:257–90.

De Waal, Frans B. M., and van Roosmalen, A. 1979. Reconciliation and consolation among chimpanzees. *Behavioral Ecology and Sociobiology* 5:55–66.

De Waal, Frans B. M., and Yoshihara, D. 1983. Reconciliation and redirected affection in rhesus monkeys. *Behavior* 85:224–41.

Dewsbury, Donald A. 1982. Dominance rank, copulatory behavior, and differential reproduction. *Quarterly Review of Biology* 57:135–59.

Dickemann, Mildred. 1979. Female infanticide, reproductive strategies, and social stratification: A preliminary model. In Napoleon A. Chagnon and William Irons, eds., *Evolutionary biology and human social behavior.* North Scituate, Mass.: Duxbury Press.

Dixson, A. F., and Herbert, J. 1977. Gonadal hormones and sexual behavior in groups of adult talapoin monkeys. *Hormones and Behavior* 8:141–54.

Drickamer, L. 1974. Social rank, observability and sexual behavior of rhesus monkeys. *Journal of Reproduction and Fertility* 37:117–20.

Dunbar, Robin, I. M. 1983. Life history tactics and alternative strategies of reproduction. In P. Bateson, ed., *Mate choice.* Cambridge: Cambridge University Press.

———. 1988. *Primate social systems.* Ithaca, N.Y.: Cornell University Press.

Dunbar, Robin I. M., and Dunbar, Patsy. 1975. *Social dynamics of Gelada baboons.* Basel: Karger.

Duncan, S. D.; Brunner, L. J.; and Fiske, D. W. 1979. Strategy signals in face-to-face interaction. *Journal of Personality and Social Psychology* 32:302–13.

Durham, William H. 1976. Resource competition and human aggression. Part I: A review of primitive war. *Quarterly Review of Biology* 51:385–415.

———. 1979. Toward a coevolutionary theory of human biology and culture. In Napoleon C. Chagnon and William Irons, eds., *Evolutionary biology and human social behavior,* 35–59. North Scituate, Mass.: Duxbury Press.

Durnin, J. V. G. A.; Edholm, O. G.; Miller, D. S.; and Waterlow, J. C. 1973. How much food does man require? *Nature* 242:418.

Duvall, S. W.; Bernstein, Irwin S.; and Gordon, T. P. 1976. Paternity and status in a rhesus monkey group. *Journal of Reproductive Fertility* 47:25–31.

Eckholm, Erik. 1984. New view of female primates assails stereotypes. *New York Times,* 18 September: C-1, C-3.

*Economist.* 1984. August: 34.

Edinger, J. A., and Patterson, M. L. 1983. Nonverbal involvement and social control. *Psychological Bulletin* 93:30–56.

Eibl-Eibesfeldt, Irenaus. 1975. *Ethology: The biology of behavior.* 2d ed. New York: Holt, Rinehart & Winston.

———. 1979a. Human ethology: Concepts and implications for the sciences of man. *Behavioral and Brain Sciences* 2:1–26.

———. 1979b. Ritual and ritualization from a biological perspective. In Mario von Cranach, K. Foppa, W. Lepenies, and D. Ploog, eds., *Human ethology,* 3–55. New York: Cambridge University Press.

———. 1979c. *The biology of peace and war.* New York: Viking.

———. 1980. Too many jumping on the bandwagon of sociobiology. *Human Ethology Newsletter* 29:7–10.

———. 1989. *Human Ethology.* New York: Aldine de Gruyter.

Eisenberg, J.; Muckenhirn, N.; and Rudan, R. 1972. The relation between ecology and social structure in primates. *Science* 176:863–74.

Ekman, Paul. 1972. Universal and cultural differences in facial expressions of emotions. In J. Cole, ed., *Nebraska symposium on motivation, 1971.* Vol. 19. Lincoln: University of Nebraska Press.

————. 1979. About brows: Emotional and conversational signals. In Mario von Cranach, Klaus Foppa, Wolf Lepenies, and Detlev Ploog, eds., *Human ethology*, 169–249. New York: Cambridge University Press.

Ekman, Paul, and Friesen, Wallace V. 1975. *Unmasking the face: A guide to recognizing emotions from facial cues*. Englewood Cliffs, N.J.: Prentice-Hall.

————. 1976. Measuring facial movement. *Journal of Environmental Psychology and Nonverbal Behavior* 1:56–75.

————. 1978. *The facial action coding system*. Palo Alto, Calif.: Consulting Psychologists Press.

————. 1982. Felt, false and miserable smiles. *Journal of Nonverbal Behavior* 6:238–52.

Ekman, Paul; Friesen, Wallace V.; and Ancoli, S. 1980. Facial signs of emotional expression. *Journal of Personality and Social Psychology* 39:1125–34.

Ekman, Paul, and Oster, Harriet. 1979. Facial expressions of emotion. *Annual Review of Psychology* 30:527–54.

Eldredge, Niles, and Tattersall, Ian. 1982. *The myths of human evolution*. New York: Columbia University Press.

Ellsworth, Phoebe. 1975. Direct gaze as a social stimulus: The example of aggression. In P. Pliner, T. Alloway, and L. Krames, eds., *Nonverbal communication of aggression*, 53–75. New York: Plenum Press.

Englis, Basil G.; Vaughan, K. B.; and Lanzetta, John T. 1982. Conditioning of counter-empathetic emotional responses. *Journal of Experimental Social Psychology* 18:375–91.

Erikson, E. H. 1966. Ontogeny of ritualization in man. *Philosophical transactions, Royal Society of London*, series B 251:337–49.

Everitt, B. 1977. *The analysis of contingency tables*. London: Chapman and Hall.

Falk, Dean. 1987. Brain lateralization in primates and its evolution in hominids. *Yearbook of Physical Anthropology* 30:107–25.

Fedigan, Linda M. 1982. *Primate paradigms: Sex roles and social bonds*. Buffalo, N.Y.: University of Toronto/Eden Press.

Feinman, S. 1979. An evolutionary theory of food sharing. *Social Science Information* 18:695–726.

Ferguson, N. 1977. Simultaneous speech, interruptions and dominance. *British Journal of Clinical Psychology* 16:295–302.

Feyerabend, Paul K. 1975. *Against method: Outline of an anarchistic theory of knowledge*. London: NLB; Atlantic Highlands, N.J.: Humanities.

Fichtner, Margaria. 1988. Jane Goodall weaves a life around chimps. *Sunday Star-Bulletin and Advertiser* [Honolulu], 15 May: D-4.

Fisher, Elizabeth. 1979. *Women's creation: Sexual evolution and the shaping of society*. New York: McGraw Hill.

Fisher, Helen. 1982. *The sex contract*. New York: William Morrow.

Fisher, Ronald A. 1930. *The genetic theory of natural selection*. Oxford: Clarendon Press.

Flannery, Kent. 1972. The cultural evolution of civilizations. *Annual Review of Ecology and Systematics* 3:339–426.

Fleagle, John G. 1988. *Primate adaptation and evolution*. New York: Academic Press.

Flohr, Heiner. 1986. Bureaucracy and its clients: Exploring a biosocial perspective. In Elliott White and Joseph Losco, eds., *Biology and bureaucracy*, 57–116. Lanham, Md.: University Press of America.

Foley, R. A., and Lee, P. C. 1989. Finite social space, evolutionary pathways, and recon-structing hominid behavior. *Science* 243:901–6.

Fossey, Dian. 1983. *Gorillas in the mist*. Boston: Houghton Mifflin.

Foucault, Michel. 1965. *Madness and civilization*. New York: Pantheon.

Fox, Michael. 1982. Are most animals mindless automatons? A reply to Gordon G. Gallup, Jr. *American Journal of Primatology* 3:341–43.

Fox, Robin. 1975. *Biosocial anthropology*. London: Malaby.

Frank, Robert. 1988. *Passions within reason*. New York: Norton.

Freeman, D. 1964. Human aggression in anthropological perspective. In J. D. Carthy and F. J. Ebling, eds., *The natural history of aggression*, 119–30. Institute of Biology Symposium no. 13. New York: Academic Press.

Fridja, N. H. 1973. The relation between emotion and expression. In Mario von Cranach and Ian Vine, eds., *Social communication and movement*, 325–40. New York: Academic Press.

Fridlund, A. J., and Izard, Carroll E. 1983. Electromyographic studies of facial expressions of emotion and patterns of emotion. In John T. Cacioppo and Richard E. Petty, eds., *Social psychophysiology: A sourcebook*, 243–86. New York: Guilford.

Fried, Morton H. 1967. *The evolution of political society*. New York: Random House.

Friedrich, Carl J. 1963. *Man and his government*. New York: McGraw-Hill.

Frost, S. W. 1959. *Insect life and insect natural history*. New York: Dover.

Galdikàs, Biruté. 1975. Orangutans, Indonesia's "People of the Forest." *National Geographic* 1484:444–73.

———. 1984. Adult female sociality among wild orangutans of Tanjung Puting Reserve. In Meredith F. Small, ed., *Female primates: Studies by women primatologists*, 217–35. New York: Alan Liss.

Gambaryan, P. P. 1974. *How mammals run*. New York: John Wiley.

Gardner, R. Allen; Gardner, Beatrix T.; and van Cantfort, Thomas E., eds. 1989. *Teaching sign language to chimpanzees*. Albany: SUNY Press.

Garfinkel, Alan. 1981. *Forms of explanation*. New Haven, Conn.: Yale University Press.

Garfinkel, Harold. 1967. *Studies in ethnomethodology*. Englewood Cliffs, N.J.: Prentice-Hall.

Gartland, J. 1968. Structure and function in primate society. *Folia Primatologica* 8:89–120.

Gazzaniga, Michael. 1985. *The social brain*. New York: Basic Books.

Geist, Valerius. 1978. *Life strategies, human evolution, environmental design: Toward a biological theory of health*. New York: Springer-Verlag.

Ghiglieri, Michael Patrick. 1984. *The chimpanzees of Kibale Forest: A field study of ecology and social structure*. New York: Columbia University Press.

———. 1988. *East of the Mountains of the Moon: Chimpanzee society in the African rain forest*. New York: Free Press.

Gianos, Phillip. 1982. *Political behavior: Metaphors and modes of American politics*. Pacific Palisades, Calif.: Palisades Publishers.

Gilmore, H. 1980. A syntactic, semantic and pragmatic analysis of baboon vocalization. PhD diss., University of Pennsylvania.

Goffman, Erving. 1961. *Asylums*. Garden City, N.Y.: Doubleday.

Golembiewski, Robert T., ed. 1978. *The small group in political science: The last two decades of development*. Athens: University of Georgia Press.

Goodall, Jane. 1971. *In the shadow of man*. Boston: Houghton Mifflin; London: Collins.

————. 1975. Chimpanzees of Gombe National Park: Thirteen years of research. In Irenaus Eibl-Eibesfeldt, ed., *Hominisation und Verhalten*, 74–136. Stuttgart: Gustav Fisher.

————. 1977. Infant killing and cannibalism in free-living chimpanzees. *Folia Primatologica* 28:259–82.

————. 1979. Life and death at Gombe. *National Geographic* 155:592–621.

————. 1986. *The chimpanzees of Gombe: Patterns of behavior.* Cambridge: Harvard University Press.

Goodall, Jane; Bandora Adriano; Bergmann, Emile; Busse, Curt; Matama, Hilali; Mpongo, Esilom; Pierce, Anne H.; and Riss, David. 1979. Inter-community interactions in the chimpanzee population of the Gombe National Park. In David A. Hamburg and Elizabeth R. McCown, eds., *The great apes*, 13–53. Menlo Park, Calif.: Benjamin/Cummings.

Gould, Stephen Jay. 1977. *Ontogeny and phylogeny.* Cambridge: Harvard University Press.

Gould, Stephen Jay, and Eldredge, Niles. 1977. Punctuated equilibria: The tempo and mode of evolution reconsidered. *Paleobiology* 3:115–51.

Gouzoules, Sarah. 1984. Primate mating systems, kin associations and cooperative behavior: Evidence for kin recognition. *Yearbook of Physical Anthropology* 27:99–134.

Graber, Doris. 1982. Have I heard this before and is it worth knowing? Variations in political information processing. Paper presented at the annual meeting of the American Political Science Association, Denver.

Green, Halcott P. 1986. *Power and evolution.* Columbia: Institute of International Studies, University of South Carolina.

Griffin, Donald R. 1981. *The question of animal awareness.* New York: Rockefeller University Press.

————. 1984. *Animal thinking.* Cambridge: Harvard University Press.

————, ed. 1982. *Animal mind—human mind.* New York: Springer-Verlag.

Grine, Frederick E., ed. 1988. *Evolutionary history of the "robust" australopithecines.* New York: Aldine de Gruyter.

Hall, Edward T. 1959. *The silent language.* Greenwich, Conn.: Fawcett.

Hall, J. A. 1980. Voice, tone and persuasion. *Journal of Personality and Social Psychology* 38:924–34.

Hall, K. R. L. 1963. Variations in the ecology of the Chacma baboon, *Papio ursinus. Symposia of the Zoological Society of London* 10:1–28.

Hall, K. R. L., and DeVore, Irven. 1965. Baboon social behavior. In Irven DeVore, ed., *Primate behavior*, 53–110. New York: Holt, Rinehart & Winston.

Hall, Roberta L., ed. 1982. *Sexual dimorphism in Homo sapiens: A question of size.* New York: Praeger.

————. 1985. *Male-female differences: A bio-cultural perspective.* New York: Praeger.

Hall, Roberta, and Sharp, Henry, eds. 1978. *Wolf and man: Evolution in parallel.* New York: Academic Press.

Hamilton, William D. 1964. The genetic evolution of social behaviour: Parts 1 and 2. *Journal of Theoretical Biology* 7:1–52.

————. 1971. Geometry for the selfish herd. *Journal of Theoretical Biology* 31:295–311.

Hamilton, William D.; Buskirk, R.; and Buskirk, W. 1975. Chacma baboon tactics during intertroop encounters. *Journal of Mammalogy* 56:857–70.

Hammer, Signe. 1988. Debunking the "Killer Ape" myth. *MS* 16 (7):78.

Hammerstein, P., and Parker, G. A. 1982. The asymmetric war of attrition. *Journal of Theoretical Biology* 96:647–82.

Haraway, Donna. 1978. Animal sociology and a natural economy of the body politic. Part 1: A political physiology of dominance. Part 2: The past is the contested zone: Human nature and theories of production and reproduction in primate behavior. *Signs* 4:21–60.

———. 1983a. Signs of dominance: From a physiology to a cybernetics of primate society. *Studies in History of Biology* 6:129–219.

———. 1983b. The contest for primate nature: Daughters of man the hunter in the field, 1960–1989. In M. Kann, ed., *The future of American democracy*, 175–207. Philadelphia: Temple University Press.

———. 1986. Primatology is politics by other means. In Ruth Bleier, ed., *Feminist approaches to science*, 77–118. New York: Pergamon.

———. 1989. *Primate visions: Gender, race, and nature in the world of modern science*, London: Routledge, Chapman & Hall.

Harding, Robert S. O., and Teleki, Geza, eds. 1981. *Omnivorous primates: Gathering and hunting in human evolution*. New York: Columbia University Press.

Harpending, Henry; Rogers, Alan; and Draper, Patricia. 1987. Human sociobiology. *Yearbook of Physical Anthropology* 30:127–50.

Harris, Marvin. 1968. *The rise of anthropological theory*. New York: Crowell.

———. 1977. *Cannibals and kings*. New York: Random House.

Harvard Crimson. 1985. Anthropology professor dies in Japan: Glynn L. Isaac known for study of human origins. 7 October.

Hausfater, Glenn. 1975. Dominance and reproduction in baboons: A quantitative analysis. *Contributions to Primatology*. Basel: Karger.

Hausfater, Glenn; Altmann, Jeanne; and Altmann, Stuart. 1982. Long-term consistency of dominance relations among female baboons. *Science* 217: 752–55.

Hawkes, K.; O'Connell, J. F.; Hill, K.; and Charnov, E. L. 1985. How much is enough?: Hunters and limited needs. *Ethology and Sociobiology* 6:3–16.

Hayden, B. 1981. Subsistence and ecological adaptations of modern hunter/gatherers. In Robert S. O. Harding and Geza Teleki, eds., *Omnivorous primates: Gathering and hunting in human evolution*. New York: Columbia University Press.

Hearne, Vicki. 1987. *Adam's task*. New York: Viking.

Henley, Nancy M. 1977. *Body politics: Power, sex and nonverbal communication*. Englewood Cliffs, N.J.: Prentice-Hall.

Henley, Nancy M., and Freeman, Jo. 1984. The sexual politics of interpersonal behavior. In Jo Freeman, ed., *Women: A feminist perspective*, 3d ed., 465–77. Palo Alto, Calif.: Mayfield.

Henley, Nancy M., and Harman, Sean. 1985. The nonverbal semantics of power and gender: A perceptual study. In Steve L. Ellyson and John F. Dovidio, eds., *Power, dominance, and nonverbal behavior*, 151–64. New York: Springer.

Hill, K., and Hawkes, K. 1983. Neotropical hunting among the Ache of eastern Paraguay. In R. Hames and W. Vickers, eds., *Adaptive responses of Native Americans*. New York: Academic Press.

Hinde, Robert A. 1972. *Non-verbal communication*. Cambridge: Cambridge University Press.

———. 1978. Dominance and role: Two concepts with dual meanings. *Journal of Social and Biological Structures* 1:27–38.

———. 1982. *Ethology*. Glasgow: William Collins.

———. 1987. Can nonhuman primates help us understand human behavior? In Barbara B. Smuts et al., eds., *Primate societies*, 413–20. Chicago: University of Chicago Press.

———, ed. 1983. *Primate social relationships*. Sunderland, Mass.: Sinauer Associates.

Hladik, C. M. 1977. Chimpanzees of Gombe and the chimpanzees of Gabon: Some comparative data on the diet. In T. H. Clutton-Brock, ed., *Primate ecology*, 481–501. New York: Academic Press.

Horr, David A. 1977. Orang-utan maturation: Growing up in a female world. In Suzanne Chevalier-Skolnikoff and Frank E. Poirier, eds., *Primate bio-social development*, 289–321. New York: Garland.

Hrdy, Sarah Blaffer. 1974. Male-male competition and infanticide among the langurs *Presbytis entellus* of Abu, Rajasthan. *Folia Primatologica* 22:19–58.

———. 1977a. Infanticide as a primate reproductive strategy. *American Scientist* 64:40–49.

———. 1977b. *The langurs of Abu*. Cambridge: Harvard University Press.

———. 1979. Infanticide among animals: A review, classification, and examination of the implications for the reproductive strategies of females. *Ethology and Sociobiology* 1:13–40.

———. 1981. *The woman that never evolved*. Cambridge: Harvard University Press.

———. 1986. Empathy, polyandry, and the myth of the coy female. In Ruth Bleier, ed., *Feminist approaches to science*, 119–46. New York: Pergamon.

Hrdy, Sarah Blaffer, and Whitten, Patricia L. 1987. Patterning of sexual activity. In Barbara B. Smuts et al., eds., *Primate societies*, 370–84. Chicago: University of Chicago Press.

Hubbard, Ruth; Henefin, Mary Sue; and Fried, Barbara, eds. 1979. *Women look at biology looking at women*. Cambridge, Mass: Schenkman.

Hummel, Ralph P. 1973. The psychology of charismatic leaders. Paper presented at the world congress of the International Political Science Association, Montreal.

———. 1974. Freud's totem theory as complement to Max Weber's theory of charisma. *Psychological Reports* 35:683–86.

Hummel, Ralph, and Isaak, Robert. 1980. *Politics for human beings*. 2d. ed. North Scituate, Mass.: Duxbury Press.

Isaac, Glynn. 1978a. The food-sharing behavior of protohuman hominids. *Scientific American* 244:90–108.

———. 1978b. Food sharing and human evolution: Archaeological evidence from the Pliopleistocene of East Africa. *Journal of Anthropological Research* 34:311–25.

Itani, Junichero. 1983. Intraspecific killing among nonhuman primates. In Margaret Gruter and Paul Bonannan, eds., *Law, biology, and culture*, 62–74. Santa-Barbara, Calif.: Ross-Erikson.

Izard, Carroll E. 1972. *Patterns of Emotions*. New York: Academic Press.

———. 1977. *Human emotions*. New York: Plenum Press.

Izard, Carroll E.; Hembree, Elizabeth A.; and Huebner, Robin R. 1987. Infants' emotion expressions to acute pain: Developmental change and stability of individual differences. *Development Psychology* 213:105–13.

Jaros, Dean, and Grant, Lawrence. 1974. *Political behavior: Choices and perspectives*. New York: St. Martin's Press.

Jay, Phillis. 1968. *Primates: Studies in adaptation and variability*. New York: Holt, Rinehart & Winston.

Jolly, Allison. 1985. *The evolution of primate behavior*. New York: Macmillan.

Jones, Diane C. 1983. Power structures and perceptions of power holders in same-sex groups of young children. *Women and Politics* 3:147–64.

Kagan, Jerome; Reznick, J. Steven; Snidman, Nancy. 1988. Biological bases of childhood shyness. *Science* 240:167–71.

Kaplan, Abraham. 1964. *The conduct of inquiry: Methodology for behavioral science.* San Francisco: Chandler.

Kaplan, H. 1983. The evolution of food sharing among adult conspecifics: Research with Ache hunter-gatherers of eastern Paraguay. Ph.D. diss., University of Utah.

Kaplan, H., and Hill, K. 1985. Food sharing among Ache foragers: Tests of explanatory hypotheses. *Current Anthropology* 26:223–45.

Kaplan, H.; Hill, K.; Hawkes, K.; and Hurtado, A. 1984. Food sharing among the Ache hunter-gatherers of eastern Paraguay. *Current Anthropology* 25:113–15.

Kaplan, J. 1978. Fight interference in Rhesus monkeys. *American Journal of Physical Anthropology* 49:241–50.

Kavanagh, Dennis. 1983. *Political science and political behavior.* London: George Allen and Unwin.

Kempf, E. 1917. The social and sexual behavior of infra-human primates, with some comparable facts in human behavior. *Psychoanalytic Review* 4:127–54.

Kinder, Donald R., and Abelson, Robert P. 1981. Appraising presidential candidates: Personality and affect in the 1980 campaign. Paper presented at the 1981 meeting of the American Political Science Association.

Kinzey, Warren G., ed. 1987. *The evolution of human behavior: Primate models.* Albany: SUNY Press.

Kitcher, Philip. 1985. *Vaulting ambition.* Cambridge: MIT Press.

Kleiman, D. 1979. Parent-offspring conflict and sibling competition in a monogamous primate. *American Naturalist* 114:753–60.

Knorr, K., and Cicourel, A. 1981. *Advances in social theory and methodology: Towards an integration of micro and macro sociologies.* London: Routledge & Kegan Paul.

Knorr, K., and Mulkay, M. 1983. *Science observed: Perspectives in the social study of science.* London and Los Angeles: Sage.

Köhler, Wolfgang. 1925. *The mentality of apes.* London: Routlege and Kegan Paul. Reprint New York: Liveright, 1976.

Konner, Melvin. 1982. *The tangled wing: Biological constraints on the human spirit.* New York: Holt, Rinehart & Winston.

Kortlandt, Adrian. 1972. *New perspectives on ape and human evolution.* Amsterdam: University of Amsterdam, Department of Animal Psychology and Ethology.

Kraut, R. E., and Johnston, R. E. 1979. Social and emotional messages: An ethological approach. *Journal of Personality and Social Psychology* 37:1539–53.

Krebs, J. R., and Davies, N. B. 1981. *An introduction to behavioral ecology.* Sunderland, Mass.: Sinauer Associates.

Kropotkin, Peter A. 1925. *Mutual aid.* London: Heinemann.

Kuhn, Thomas. 1970. *The structure of scientific revolutions.* 2d ed. Chicago: University of Chicago Press.

Kummer, Hans. 1967. Tripartite relations in hamadryas baboons. In S. Altmann, ed., *Social communication among primates.* Chicago: University of Chicago Press.

———. 1968. The social organization of hamadryas baboons. *Bibliotheca Primatologica* 6:1–189.

———. 1971. *Primate societies.* Chicago: Aldine-Atherton.

———. 1973. Dominance versus possession: An experiment on hamadryas baboons. In Emil Menzel, ed., *Precultural primate behavior.* Basel: Karger.

————. 1978. On the value of social relationships to nonhuman primates: A heuristic scheme. *Social Science Information* 17:687–705.

————. 1982. Social knowledge in free-ranging primates. In Donald R. Griffin, ed., *Animal mind—human mind*, 113–50. Berlin: Springer-Verlag.

Kummer, Hans; Goetz, W.; and Angst, W. 1974. Triadic differentiation: An inhibitory process protecting pair bonds on baboons. *Behavior* 49:62–87.

Kummer, Hans, and Goodall, Jane. 1985. Conditions of innovative behaviour in primates. *Philosophic Proceedings of the Royal Society of London*, series B 308:203–214.

Kummer, Hans, and Kurt, F. 1965. A comparison of social behavior in captive and wild hamadryas baboons. In H. Vagtborg, ed., *The baboon in medical research*, 1–16. Austin: University of Texas Press.

Kuo, Zing Yong. 1967. *The dynamics of behavior development*. New York: Random House.

Kurland, J. A., and Beckerman, S. J. 1985. Optimal foraging and hominid evolution: Labor and reciprocity. *American Anthropologist* 87:73–93.

Kurtén, Björn. 1986. Neanderthals and transubstantiation. In B. Kurtén, *How to deep-freeze a mammoth*, 84–98. New York: Columbia University Press.

Kurth, Gottfried. 1976. Neencephalization, hominization, and behaviour. *Journal of Human Evolution* 5:501–9.

Lack, David. 1966. *Population studies of birds*. Oxford: Clarendon Press.

La Lumiere, L. P. 1981. Evolution of human bipedalism: A hypothesis about where it happened. *Philosophical Proceedings of the Royal Society of London*, series B 292: 103–7.

Lancaster, Jane Beckman. 1978. Carrying and sharing in human evolution. *Human Nature* 12:82–89.

————. 1984. Introduction. In Meredith Small, ed., *Female primates: Studies by women primatologists*, 1–10. New York: Alan Liss.

————. 1985. Evolutionary perspectives on sex differences in the higher primates. In Alice S. Rossi, ed., *Gender and the life course*, 3–27. New York: Aldine.

Landau, Martin. 1961. On the uses of metaphor in political analysis. *Social Research* 28:331–53.

Lanzetta, John T., and Orr, Scott P. 1980. Influence of facial expressions on the classical conditioning of fear. *Journal of Personality and Social Psychology* 39:1081–87.

Laponce, Jean. 1987. Relating physiological, physical and political phenomena: Center and centrality. *International Political Science Review* 8:175–82.

Larsen, Ray. 1976. Charisma: A reinterpretation. In Michael R. A. Chance and Ray Larsen, eds., *The social structure of attention*, 253–72. New York: John Wiley.

Lasswell, Harold Dwight. 1930. *Psychopathology and politics*. Chicago: University of Chicago Press.

————. 1936. *Politics: Who gets what, when and how*. New York: McGraw-Hill.

————. 1948. *Power and personality*. New York: Norton.

Latour, Bruno. 1986a. The powers of association. In J. Law, ed., *Power, action and belief: A new sociology of knowledge*, 264–80. Keele, England: Sociological Review Monograph.

————. 1986b. Visualization and cognition: Thinking with eyes and hands. *Knowledge and Social Studies: Past and Present* 6:1–40.

————. 1987. *Science in action*. Cambridge: Harvard University Press. 2d ed., 1987. Milton Keynes, England: Open University Press.

Latour, Bruno, and Strum, Shirley. 1986. Human social origins: Please tell us another story. *Journal of Sociological and Biological Structures* 9:169–87.

Law, John, ed. 1986. *Power, action and belief: A new sociology of knowledge.* Keele, England: Sociological Review Monograph.

Leacock, Eleanor, and Lee, Richard, eds. 1982. *Politics and history in band societies.* New York: Cambridge University Press.

Leakey, Mary D. 1981. Tracks and tools. *Philosophical Transactions of the Royal Society of London,* series B 292:95–102.

———. 1984. *Disclosing the past.* Garden City, N.Y.: Doubleday.

Leakey, Mary D., and Harris, John M. 1987. *Laetoli: A Pliocene site in northern Tanzania.* Oxford: Clarendon Press.

Leakey, Richard E., and Alan Walker. 1985. Homo erectus unearthed. *National Geographic* 1685:624–29.

LeBoeuf, Bernard J. 1974. Male-male competition and reproductive success in elephant seals. *American Zoology* 14:163–76.

———. 1978. Social behaviour in some marine and terrestrial carnivores. In E. S. Reese and F. J. Lighter, eds., *Contrasts in behaviour.* New York: John Wiley.

LeBoeuf, Bernard J., and Peterson, R. S. 1969. Social status and mating activity in elephant seals. *Science* 163:91–93.

LeBoeuf, Bernard J.; Riedman, M.; and Keyes, R. S. 1982. White shark predation on pinnipeds in California costal waters. *Fishery Bulletin* 80:891–95.

Lee, Richard B. 1969. Eating Christmas in the Kalahari. *Natural History* 78, no. 10:14–22, 60–63.

———. 1972. !Kung spatial organization: An ecological and historical perspective. *Human Ecology* 1:125–47.

———. 1979. *The !Kung San: Men, women, and work in a foraging society.* London and New York: Cambridge University Press.

———, eds. 1968. *Man the hunter.* Chicago: Aldine Press.

Lee, Richard B., and DeVore, Irven. 1976. *Kalahari hunter-gatherers.* Cambridge: Cambridge University Press.

Leighton, Donna R. 1987. Gibbons: Territoriality and monogamy. In Barbara B. Smuts et al., eds., *Primate societies,* 135–45. Chicago: University of Chicago Press.

Leutenegger, Walter. 1982. Sexual dimorphism in nonhuman primates. In Roberta L. Hall, ed., *Sexual dimorphism in Homo sapiens: A question of size,* 11–36. New York: Praeger.

LeVine, K. A., and Campbell, Donald T. 1971. *Ethnocentrism: Theories of conflict, ethnic attitudes, and group behavior.* New York: John Wiley.

Lewin, Roger. 1987. *Bones of contention: Controversies in the search for human origins.* New York: Simon and Schuster.

Llewellyn-Davies, M. 1978. Two contexts of solidarity. In P. Caplan and J. M. Bujra, eds., *Women united, women divided.* London: Tavistock.

Lockard, Joan S., ed. 1980. *The evolution of human social behavior.* New York: Elsevier.

Lopreato, Joseph. 1984. *Human nature and biocultural evolution.* Boston: Allen and Unwin.

Lorenz, Konrad Z. 1966. *On aggression.* New York: Harcourt Brace Jovanovich.

———. 1970–71. *Studies in animal and human behaviour.* 2 vols. Cambridge: Harvard University Press.

Lorenz, Konrad Z., and Leyhausen, Paul. 1973. *Motivation of human and animal behavior.* New York: Van Nostrand Reinhold.

*Los Angeles Times* Service. 1989. Chimps are declared an endangered species. *Sunday Star-Bulletin and Advertiser,* [Honolulu] 26 March: D1.

Loy, J. 1975. The descent of dominance in *Macaca:* Insights into the structure of human societies. In R. H. Tuttle, ed., *Socioecology and psychology of primates,* 153–80. The Hague: Mouton.

Lumsden, Charles J., and Wilson, Edward O. 1981. *Genes, mind, and culture: The coevolutionary process.* Cambridge: Harvard University Press.

————. 1983. *Promethean fire: reflections on the origin of the mind.* Cambridge: Harvard University Press.

McGrew, William C. 1977. Socialization and object manipulation of wild chimpanzees. In Suzanne Chevalier-Skolnikoff and Frank E. Poirier, eds., *Primate bio-social development,* 261–88. New York: Garland.

————. 1981. The female chimpanzee as a human evolutionary prototype. In Frances Dahlberg, ed., *Woman the gatherer,* 1–39. New Haven, Conn.: Yale University Press.

McGrew, William C.; Baldwin, P. J.; and Tutin, C. E. G. 1981. Chimpanzees in a savanna habitat: Mt. Asserik, Senegal, West Africa. *Journal of Human Evolution* 10:227–44.

McGuinness, Diane, and Pribram, Karl. 1980. The neuropsychology of attention: Emotional and motivational controls. In M. C. Wittrock, ed., *The brain and psychology* 95–129. New York: Academic Press.

McGuire, Michael T. 1982. Social dominance relationships in male vervet monkeys: A possible model for the study of dominance relationships in human political systems. *International Political Science Review* 3:11–32.

McGuire, Michael T., and Raleigh, Michael J. 1986. Behavioral and physiological correlates of ostracism. In Margaret Gruter and Roger D. Masters, eds., *Ostracism: A social and biological phenomenon,* 39–52. New York: Elsevier.

McHugo, Gregory J.; Lanzetta, John T.; Sullivan, Denis G.; Masters, Roger D.; and Englis, Basil G. 1985. Emotional reactions to expressive displays of a political leader. *Journal of Personality and Social Psychology* 49:1513–29.

McHugo, Gregory J.; Smith, C. A.; and Lanzetta, John T. 1982. The structure of self-reports of emotional response to film segments. *Motivation and Emotion* 6:365–85.

MacIver, Robert. 1947. *The web of government.* New York: Macmillan.

Mackenzie, William. 1967. *Politics and social science.* Harmondsworth, Eng.: Penguin.

McRae, Michael. 1986. The poacher's revenge: The final battles of Dian Fossey. *Outside* 11, no. 5: 34–38, 86–90.

————. 1988. Dilemma at Gombe. *Outside* 13, no. 3: 44–49, 86–88.

Madsen, Douglas. 1985. A biochemical property relating to power-seeking in humans. *American Political Science Review* 79:448–57.

Mainardi, Danilo. 1980. Tradition and the social transmission of behavior in animals. In George W. Barlow and James Silverberg, eds., *Sociobiology: Beyond nature/nurture?* 227–55. Boulder, Colo.: Westview Press.

Manheim, Jarol. 1982. *The politics within: A primer in political attitudes and behavior.* Rev. ed. New York: Longman.

Manicas, Peter T. 1982. The human sciences: A radical separation of psychology and the social sciences. In P. F. Secord, ed., *Explaining human behavior: Consciousness, human action and social structure,* 155–73. Beverly Hills, Calif.: Sage.

————. 1983. Reduction, epigenesis and explanation. *Journal of the Theory of Social Behaviour* 13:331–54.

Marais, Eugene N. 1956. *My friends the baboons*. London: Methuen.

————. [1934] 1969. *The soul of the ape*. New York: Atheneum.

Markl, Hubert. 1985. Manipulation, modulation, information, cognition: Some of the riddles of communication. *Fortschritte der Zoologie* 31:163–94.

Marshall, Abraham. 1920. *Principles of economics*. 8th ed. London: Macmillan.

Maslow, Abraham. 1936. The role of dominance in the social and sexual behavior of infrahuman primates. Part 2: An experimental determination of the behavior syndrome of dominance. *Journal of Genetic Psychology* 48:310–38.

Massey, A. 1977. Agonistic aids and kinship in a group of pigtail macaques. *Behavioral Ecology and Sociobiology* 2:31–40.

Masters, Roger D. 1967. La redécouverte de la nature humaine. *Critique* 245:857–76.

————. 1968. *The political philosophy of Rousseau*. Princeton, N.J.: Princeton University Press.

————. 1970. Genes, language, and evolution. *Semiotica* 2:295–320.

————. 1973a. On comparing humans—and human politics—with animal behavior. Paper presented to the ninth world congress of the International Political Science Association, Montreal.

————. 1973b. Functional approaches to analogical comparisons between species. *Social Science Information* no. 12, 4:7–28.

————. 1974. Ethological comparisons between animal and social behavior. Paper presented at the Conference on the Relations Between Biological and Social Theory, American Academy of Arts and Sciences, Brookline, Mass.

————. 1975. Political behavior as a biological phenomenon. *Social Science Information* 14:7–63.

————. 1976a. The impact of ethology on political science. In Albert Somit, ed., *Biology and politics*, 197–233. Paris: Mouton.

————. 1976b. Exit, voice, and loyalty in animal and human behavior. *Social Science Information* 15:855–78.

————. 1977. Human nature, nature, and political thought. In J. Roland Pennock and John W. Chapman, eds., *Human nature in politics*, 69–110. New York: New York University Press.

————. 1978. Attention structures and political campaigns. Paper presented at the annual meeting of the American Political Science Association, New York.

————. 1979. Beyond reductionism: Five basic concepts in human ethology. In Mario Cranach et al., eds., *Human Ethology*, 265–84. Cambridge: Cambridge University Press.

————. 1981. Linking ethology and political science: Photographs, political attention, and presidential elections. In Meredith Watts, ed., *Biopolitics: Ethological and physiological approaches*. New Directions for Methodology of Social and Behavioral Sciences no. 7, 61–89. San Francisco: Jossey-Bass.

————. 1982a. Evolutionary biology, political theory, and the state. *Journal of Social and Biological Structures* 5:433–50.

————. 1982b. Is sociobiology reactionary? The political implications of inclusive fitness theory. *Quarterly Review of Biology* 57:275–92.

————. 1984. Explaining male chauvinism and feminism: Cultural differences in male and female reproductive strategies. In Meredith Watts, ed., *Biopolitics and gender*. New York: Haworth Press.

———. 1989a. *The nature of politics*. New Haven, Conn.: Yale University Press.

———. 1989b. Gender and political cognition. *Politics and the Life Sciences*. 8:3–39.

Masters, Roger D., and Sullivan, Denis G. 1989a. Nonverbal displays and political leadership in France and the United States. *Political Behavior* 11:121–54.

———. 1989b. Facial displays and political leadership in France. *Behavioural Processes* 19:1–30.

Masters, Roger D.; Sullivan, Denis G.; Lanzetta, John T.; McHugo, Gregory J.; and Englis, Basil G. 1986. The facial displays of leaders. *Journal of Social and Biological Structures* 9:319–43.

Mauss, Marcel. 1967. *The gift*. Trans. I. Cunnisson. [1925. *Essai sur le don, forme archaïque de l'échange*.] New York: Norton.

Maynard-Smith, John. 1978. Evolution and the theory of games. *American Scientist* 64:41–45.

Maynard-Smith, John, and Parker, G. A. 1976. The logic of asymmetric contests. *Animal Behaviour* 24:159–75.

Maynard-Smith, John, and Price, G. 1973. The logic of animal conflicts. *Nature* 246:15–18.

Merchant, Carolyn. 1980. *The death of nature: Women, ecology, and the scientific revolution*. New York: Harper & Row.

Mills, C. Wright. 1959. *The sociological imagination*. New York: Oxford University Press.

Montagner, Hubert. 1978. *L'enfant et la communication*. Paris: Stock.

Montagner, Hubert; Restoin, A.; Rodriguez, D.; and Kontar, F. 1988. Aspects fonctionels et ontogénétiques des interactions de l'enfant avec ses pairs au cours des trois premières années. *Psychiatrie de l'enfant* 31:173–278.

Montagu, Ashley M. F. 1968. *Man and aggression*. New York: Oxford University Press.

Moore, J. 1984a. Female transfers in primates. *International Journal of Primatology* 5:537–90.

———. 1984b. The evolution of reciprocal sharing. *Ethology and Sociobiology* 5:5–14.

Morris, Desmond. 1956. The function and causation of courtship ceremonies. In Autuori et al., eds., *L'instinct dans le comportement des animaux et de l'homme*. Paris: Masson.

———. 1967. *The naked ape*. New York: McGraw-Hill.

———. 1977. *Man watching*. New York: Harry N. Abrams.

Morris, R., and Morris, Desmond. 1966. *Men and apes*. New York: McGraw-Hill.

Mowat, Farley. 1987. *Woman in the mists: The story of Dian Fossey and the mountain gorillas of Africa*. New York: Warner Books.

Murnighan, J. 1978. Models of coalition behavior. Game theoretic, social psychological, and political perspectives. *Psychology Bulletin* 85:1130–53.

Nacci, P., and Tedeschi, J. 1976. Liking and power as factors affecting coalition choices in the triad. *Social Behavior and Personality* 4:27–32.

Nash, L. 1976. Troop fission in free-ranging baboons in the Gombe Stream National Park, Tanzania. *American Journal of Physical Anthropology* 44:63–77.

Newton, James; Masters, Roger D.; McHugo, Gregory J.; and Sullivan, Denis G. 1988. Making up our minds: Effects of network coverage on viewers' impressions of leaders. *Polity* 20:226–46.

Nieuwenhuijsen, K., and de Waal, Frans B. M. 1982. Effects of spatial crowding on the social behavior of chimpanzees. *Zoology and Biology* 1:5–28.

Nishida, Toshisada. 1979. The social structure of chimpanzees of the Mahale Mountains. In David Hamburg and Elizabeth McCown, eds., *The great apes*. Menlo Park, Calif.: Benjamin/Cummings.

———. 1983. Alpha status and agonistic alliance in wild chimpanzees. *Primates* 24:318–36.

Nishida, Toshisada, and Hiraiwa-Hasegawa, Mariko. 1987. Chimpanzees and bonobos: Cooperative relationships among males. In Barbara B. Smuts et al., eds., *Primate societies*, 165–77. Chicago: University of Chicago Press.

Nishida, Toshisada; Hiraiwa-Hasegawa, Mariko; and Takahata, Y. 1985. Group extinction and female transfer in wild chimpanzees in the Mahale National Park, Tanzania. *Zeitschrift für Tierpsychologie* 67:284–301.

Noë, Ronald; de Waal, Frans; and van Hooff, Jan. 1980. Types of dominance in a chimpanzee colony. *Folia Primatologica* 34:90–110.

Omark, Donald R. 1980. The group: A factor or an epiphenomenon in evolution. In Donald R. Omark, Fred F. Strayer, and Daniel G. Freedman, eds., *Dominance relations*. New York: Garland Press.

Omark, Donald R.; Strayer, Fred F.; and Freedman, Daniel G., eds. 1980. *Dominance relations: An ethological view of human conflict and social interaction*. New York: Garland Press.

Orr, Scott P., and Lanzetta, John T. 1980. Facial expressons of emotion as conditioned stimuli for human autonomic responses. *Journal of Personality and Social Psychology* 38:278–82.

Osgood, Charles E. 1966. Dimensionality of the semantic space for communication via facial expression. *Scandinavian Journal of Psychology* 7:1–30.

Packer, C. 1979. Male dominance and reproductive activity in Papio Anubis. *Animal Behavior* 27:37–45.

———. 1980. Male care and exploitation of infants. *Animal Behavior* 28:512–20.

Packer, C., and Pusey, A. 1982. Cooperation and competition within coalitions of male lions: Kin selection or game theory? *Nature* 296:740–42.

Parker, G. A. 1974. Assessment strategies and the evolution of fighting behavior. *Journal of Theoretical Biology* 47:223–43.

Parker, G. A., and MacNair, M. 1978. Models of parent-offspring conflict. Part 1: Monogamy. *Animal Behavior* 26:97–110.

Parker, G. A., and Rubenstein, D. I. 1981. Role assessment, reserve strategy, and acquisition of information in asymmetric animal conflicts. *Animal Behavior* 29:221–40.

Parker, Sue Taylor, and Gibson, Kathleen Rita. 1979. A developmental model of the evolution of language and intelligence in early hominids. *Behavioral and Brain Sciences* 2:367–407.

Perlez, Jane. 1988. Tourists are mixed blessing for gorillas in Rwanda wilds: Visitors preserve habitat, but introduce disease. *The Contra Costa [Calif.] Times*, 26 December: B4.

Peterson, Steven A. 1982. Neurophysiology and rationality in political thinking. Paper presented at the annual meeting of the American Political Science Association, Denver.

———. 1983a. The psychobiology of hypostatizing. *Micropolitics* 2:423–51.

———. 1983b. Biology and political socialization: A cognitive developmental link? *Political Psychology* 4:265–88.

———. 1983c. Why policies don't work: A biocognitive perspective. Paper presented at the annual meeting of the American Political Science Association, Denver.

Peterson, Steven A., and Lawson, R. 1982. Cognitive psychology and the study of politics. Paper presented at the annual meeting of the American Political Science Association, Denver.

Peterson, Steven A.; Somit, Albert; and Brown, Barbara. 1983. Biopolitics in 1982. *Politics and the Life Sciences* 2:76–80.

Peterson, Steven A.; Somit, Albert; and Slagter, Robert. 1982. Biopolitics: 1980–81 update. *Politics and the Life Sciences* 1:52–57.

Pettersson, Max. 1978. Acceleration in evolution before human times. *Journal of Social and Biological Structures* 1:201–6.

Pettman, Ralph. 1975. *Human behaviour and world politics*. New York: St. Martin's Press.

Pierce, Ann H. 1978. Ranging patterns and associations of a small community of chimpanzees in Gombe National Park, Tanzania. In David C. Chivers and John Herbert, eds., *Recent advances in primatology* 1:59–62. New York: Academic Press.

Pitt, Roger. 1978. Warfare and hominid brain evolution. *Journal of Theoretical Biology* 72:551–75.

Plate, Elise. 1984. The double-bind phenomenon in politics: The influence of nonverbal expressive behavior of male and female political candidates on impression formation. Senior honors thesis. Dartmouth College.

Plotnik, R. 1974. Brain stimulation and aggression: Monkeys, apes, and humans. In R. L. Holloway, ed., *Primate aggression, territoriality, and xenophobia*, 123–58. New York: Academic Press.

Plutchik, Robert. 1980. *Emotion: A psychoevolutionary synthesis*. New York: Harper & Row.

Popp, J. 1978. Male baboons and evolutionary principles. Ph.D. diss., Harvard University.

Popp, J., and DeVore, Irven. 1979. Aggressive competition and social dominance theory: Synopsis. In David Hamburg and Elizabeth McCown, eds., *The great apes*. Menlo Park, Calif.: Benjamin/Cummings.

Post, D.; Hausfater, Glenn; and McCuskey, S. 1980. Feeding behavior of yellow baboons: Relationship to age, gender and dominance rank. *Folia Primatologica* 34:170–95.

Potts, Richard. 1987. Reconstructions of early hominid socioecology: A critique of primate models. In Warren G. Kinzey, ed., *The evolution of human behavior: Primate models*, 28–47. Albany SUNY Press.

———. 1988. *Early hominid activities at Olduvai*. New York: Aldine de Gruyter.

Pribram, Karl, and McGuinness, Diane. 1975. Arousal, activation, and effort in the control of attention. *Psychological Review* 82:116–49.

Pusey, A. E. 1977. The physical and social development of wild adolescent chimpanzees. Ph.D. diss., Stanford University.

Ra, Chong Phil. 1989. Individual development, political socialization, and biopolitics: The ontogeny of political behavior. Ph.D. diss., University of Hawaii–Manoa.

Raleigh, Michael J., and McGuire, Michael T. 1986. Animal analogues of ostracism: Biological mechanisms and social consequences. In Margaret Gruter and Roger D. Masters, eds., *Ostracism: A social and biological phenomenon*, 53–66. New York: Elsevier.

Ralls, K. 1976. Mammals in which females are larger than males. *Quarterly Review of Biology* 51:245–76.

Ransom, T. 1984. *The baboons of Gombe*. Lewisburg, Penn.: Bucknell University Press.

Ransom, T., and Ransom, B. 1971. Adult male-infant relations among baboons *Papio anubis*. *Folia Primatologica* 16:179–95.

Rasmussen, D. 1979. Correlates of patterns of range use of a troop of yellow baboons: Sleeping sites, impregnable females, birth and male emigrations. *Animal Behavior* 27:98–112.

Reader, John. 1981. *Missing links: The hunt for earliest man*. Boston: Little, Brown.

Reichs, Kathleen J. 1983. *Hominid origins*. Washington, D.C.: University Press of America.

Reiter, J.; Simpson, N. L.; and LeBoeuf, Bernard J. 1978. Northern elephant seal development: The transition from weaning to nutritional independence. *Behavioral Ecology and Sociobiology* 3:337–67.

Reynolds, Vernon. 1984. Primate social thinking. Paper presented at the tenth congress of the International Primatological Society, Nairobi, Kenya.

Rhine, R. 1975. The order of movements of yellow baboons. *Folia Primatologica* 23:72–104.

Rhine, R., and Owens, N. 1972. The order of movement of adult male and black infant baboons *(Papio anubis)* entering and leaving a potentially dangerous clearing. *Folia Primatologica* 18:276–83.

Rhine, R., and Westlund, B. 1978. The nature of the primary feeding habit in different age-sex classes of yellow baboons. *Folia Primatologica* 30:64–79.

Richard, Alison F. 1985. *Primates in nature*. New York: W. H. Freeman.

Riker, William H. 1962. *The theory of political coalitions*. New Haven, Conn.: Yale University Press.

Riker, William H., and Ordeshook, Peter C. 1973. *An introduction to positive political theory*. Englewood Cliffs, N.J.: Prentice-Hall.

Riss, D., and Goodall, Jane. 1977. The recent rise to the alpha rank in a population of free-living chimpanzees. *Folia Primatologica* 27:134–151.

Rodman, Peter S., and Mitani, John C. 1987. Orangutans: Sexual dimorphism in a solitary species. In Barbara B. Smuts et al., eds., *Primate societies*, 146–54. Chicago: University of Chicago Press.

Rosenbaum, Walter. 1975. *Political culture*. New York: Praeger.

Rosenberg, Alexander. 1980. *Sociobiology and the preemption of social science*. Baltimore, Md.: Johns Hopkins Press.

Rossi, Alice S. 1977. A biosocial perspective on parenting. *Daedalus* 106:1–31.

Rousseau, Jean-Jacques. 1964. *Discourse on the origin of inequality*. Roger D. Masters, ed. New York: St. Martin's Press.

———. 1990. *Rousseau, judge of Jean-Jacques. Dialogues*. In Roger D. Masters and Christopher Keeley, eds., *The collected writings of Rousseau*, 1. Hanover, N.H.: University Press of New England.

Rowell, Thelma E. 1966. Forest living baboons in Uganda. *Journal of Zoology* 149:344–64.

———. 1969. Intra-sexual behavior and female reproductive cycle of baboons. *Animal Behavior* 17:159–67.

———. 1972. *Social behaviour of monkeys*. Baltimore, Md.: Penguin.

———. 1974. The concept of social dominance. *Behavioral Biology* 11:131–54.

Rowell, Thelma E., and Dixson, A. F. 1975. Changes in social organization during the breeding season of wild talapoin monkeys. *Journal of Reproductive Fertility* 43:419–36.

Rowell, Thelma E., and Olson, D. K. 1983. Alternative mechanisms of social organization. *Behaviour* 86:31–54.

Rubenstein, R., and Lasswell, Harold D. 1966. *The sharing of power in a psychiatric hosptial*. New Haven, Conn.: Yale University Press.

Sahlins, Marshall D. 1965. On the sociology of primitive exchange. In M. Banton, ed., *The relevance of models for social anthropology*. ASA Monograph 1. London: Tavistock.

———. 1972. *Stone age economics*. Chicago: Aldine.

Sapolsky, R. 1982. The endocrine stress-response and social status in the wild baboon. *Hormones and Behavior* 16:279–92.

———. 1983. Individual differences in cortisol secretory patterns in the wild baboon: The role of negative feedback sensitivity. *Endocrinology* 113:2263–68.

Sarich, Vincent M. 1983. Retrospective on hominoid macromolecular systematics. In Russell S. Ciochon and Robert L. Corruccini, eds., *New interpretations of ape and human ancestry*, 137–50. New York: Plenum Press.

Sarich, Vincent M., and Wilson, Allan C. 1967. Immunological time scale for hominid evolution. *Science* 158:1200–1203.

Schaller, George B. 1963. *The mountain gorilla: Ecology and behavior.* Chicago: University of Chicago Press.

Scherer, Klaus R. 1979. Personality markers in speech. In Klaus R. Scherer and H. Giles, eds., *Social markers in speech.* New York: Cambridge University Press.

———. 1982. Methods of research on vocal communication: Paradigms and parameters. In Klaus R. Scherer and Paul Ekman, eds., *Handbook of methods in nonverbal behavior research.* New York: Cambridge University Press.

Schubert, Glendon. 1967. Academic ideology and the study of adjudication. *American Political Science Review* 61:106–29.

———. 1973. Biopolitical behavior: The nature of the political animal. *Polity* 6:240–75.

———. 1978. Cooperation, cognition, and communication. *Behavioral and Brain Sciences* 1:597–600.

———. 1979. Ethology: A primer for political scientists: Part 2. *Center for Biopolitical Research Notes* 2, no. 2 (April).

———. 1980. Review of J. A. Kurland, *Kin selection in the Japanese monkey* (New York: S. Karger, 1977). *Journal of Social and Biological Structures* 3:391–95.

———. 1981a. Glaciers, neoteny, and epigenesis: A review essay. *Journal of Social and Biological Structures* 4:287–96.

———. 1981b. The sociobiology of political behavior. In Elliott White, ed., *Sociobiology and human politics*, 193–238. New York: Heath-Lexington.

———. 1981c. The use of ethological methods in political analysis. In Meredith Watts, ed., *Biopolitics: Ethiological and physiological approaches.* 15–32 San Francisco: Jossey-Bass.

———. 1982a. Epigenesis: The newer synthesis? *Behavioral and Brain Sciences* 5:24–25.

———. 1982b. Infanticide by usurper hanuman langur males: A sociobiological myth. *Social Science Information* 21:199–244.

———. 1982c. Political ethology. *Micropolitcs* 2:51–86.

———. 1982d. Nonverbal communication as political behavior. In Mary Ritchie Key and Donald Preziosi, eds., *Nonverbal communication today: Current research*, 69–85. The Hague: Mouton.

———. 1983a. The structure of attention: A critical review. *Journal of Social and Biological Structures* 6:65–80.

———. 1983b. Theory, empiricism, and disciplinary chauvinism. *Journal of Social and Biological Structures* 6:83–84.

———. 1983c. The evolution of political science: Paradigms of physics, biology, and politics. *Politics and the Life Sciences* 1:97–110.

———. 1983d. Evolutionary politics. *Western Political Quarterly* 36:175–93.

———. 1983e. Psychobiological politics. *Canadian Journal of Political Science* 16:535–76.

———. 1984a. Variations on a theme by Chance: Social behavior and the psychology of attention. *Journal of Social and Biological Structures* 7:377–86.

————. 1984b. Promethean fireflies and foxfire: Reflections on the permutation of coevolutionary theory. *Politics and the Life Sciences* 2:219–23.

————. 1985. Epigenetic evolutionary theory: Waddington in retrospect. *Journal of Social and Biological Structures* 8:233–53.

————. 1986a. Scientific creation and the evolution of religious behavior. *Journal of Social and Biological Structures* 9:241–60.

————. 1986b. Primate politics. *Social Science Information* 25:647–80.

————. 1987. Banishment as biosocial behavior. *Human Ethology Newsletter* 5, no. 4: 5–8.

————. 1989a. *Evolutionary Politics*. Carbondale: Southern Illinois University Press.

————. 1989b. Catastrophe theory, evolutionary extinction, and revolutionary politics. *Journal of Social and Biological Structures* 12:259–79.

————. In press. *Sexual politics and political feminism*. Greenwich, Conn.: JAI Press.

Schubert, Glendon, and Somit, Albert, eds. 1982. *The biology of primate sociopolitical behavior*. DeKalb: Northern Illinois University, Center for Biopolitical Research.

Schubert, James N. 1983. Ethological methods for observing small group political decision making. *Politics and the Life Sciences* 2:3–41.

————. 1984a. Dominance and influence in small group decision-making. Paper presented to a conference on ethological contributions in political science, Tutzing, Federal Republic of Germany, 25–28 June.

————. 1984b. Dominance and influence in small group decision-making: An ethological approach to verbal and paralinguistic aspects of behavior. Paper presented at the annual meeting of the American Political Science Association, Washington, D.C.

Schubert, James N.; Wiegele, Thomas C.; and Hines, Samuel M. 1986. Age and political behaviour in collective decision making. *International Political Science Review* 8:131–46.

————. 1987. Age, age structure, and political decision making. Final report to the U.S. National Institute on Aging.

Schwartz, G. E.; Fair, P. L.; Salt, P.; Mandel, M. R.; and Klerman, G. L. 1976. Facial muscle patterning to affective imagery in depressed and nondepressed subjects. *Science* 192:489–91.

Schwartz, Jeffrey H. 1984a. The evolutionary relationships of man and orang-utans. *Nature* 308:501–5.

————. 1984b. Hominoid evolution: A review and a reassessment. *Current Anthropology* 25:655–72.

Scott, John P. 1958. *Aggression*. Chicago: University of Chicago Press.

Scott, William. 1820. *Lessons in elocution*. Leicester. Hori Brown.

Sebeok, Thomas A. 1985. A scientific quibble. *Semiotica* 57:117–24.

————. 1987. On a high horse. *Semiotica* 67:141–45.

Sebeok, Thomas A., and Jean Umiker-Sebeok, eds. 1980. *Speaking of apes*. New York: Plenum Press.

Secord, Paul F. 1982. *Explaining human behavior: Consciousness, human action and social structure*. Beverly Hills, Calif.: Sage.

Service, E. R. 1962. *Primitive social organizations: An evolutionary perspective*. New York: Random House.

Seyfarth, R. 1976. Social relationships among adult female baboons. *Animal Behavior* 24:917–38.

————. 1977. A model of social grooming among adult female monkeys. *Journal of Theoretical Biology* 64:671–98.

———. 1980. The distribution of grooming and related behaviors among adult female velvet monkeys. *Animal Behavior* 28:798–813.

Shaw, R. Paul; Wong, Yuwa; Goldstein, Joshua S.; and Kitcher, Philip. 1987. Symposium: Human evolution and war. *International Studies Quarterly* 31:5–31.

Sibly, R. M. 1983. Optimal group size is unstable. *Animal Behavior* 31:947–48.

Sigg, H. 1980. Differentiation of female positions in Hamadryas one-male groups. *Zeitschrift für Tierpsychologie* 53:265–302.

Silk, J. 1980. Kidnapping and female competition in captive Bonnet macaques. *Primates* 21:100–110.

Simon, Herbert Alexander. 1983. *Reason in human affairs*. Palo Alto, Calif.: Stanford University Press.

———. 1985. Human nature in politics. *American Political Science Review* 79:293–304.

Simonton, Dean K. 1984. *Genius, creativity and leadership: Historiometric inquiries*. Cambridge: Harvard University Press.

Simpson, George Gaylord. 1969. *Biology and man*. New York: Harcourt, Brace and World.

Slobodkin, Lawrence B. 1964. The strategy of evolution. *American Scientist* 52:342–57.

Slocum, Sally. 1975. Women the gatherer: Male bias in anthropology. In Rayna R. Reiter, ed., *Toward an anthropology of women*, 36–50. New York: Monthly Review Press.

Small, Meredith F., ed. 1982. *Female primates: Studies by women primatologists*. New York: Alan Liss.

Smith, Eric A. 1981. The application of optimal foraging theory to the analysis of hunter-gatherer group size. In B. Winterhalder and E. A. Smith, eds., *Hunter-gatherer foraging strategies*. Chicago: Chicago University Press.

———. 1985. Innuit foraging groups: Some simple models incorporating conflicts of interest, relatedness, and central-sharing. *Ethology and Sociobiology* 6:27–48.

———. 1987. On fitness maximisation, limited needs, and hunter-gatherer time allocation. *Ethology and Sociobiology* 8:73–85.

Smuts, Barbara B. 1982. Special relationship between adult male and female olive baboons. Ph.D. diss., Stanford University.

Smuts, Barbara B., et al., eds. 1987. *Primate societies*. Chicago: University of Chicago Press.

Somit, Albert. 1984. Review of *Chimpanzee politics*. *Politics and the Life Sciences* 2:211–13.

———, ed. 1976. *Biology and politics*. Paris: Mouton.

Somit, Albert, and Peterson, Steven A. 1980. Cost benefit analysis, shifting coalitions, and human evolution. *Human Ethology Newsletter*. 31:16–18.

Somit, Albert; Peterson, Steven A.; Richardson, W. D.; and Goldfischer, D. S. 1980. *The literature of biopolitics*. DeKalb: Northern Illinois University, Center for Biopolitical Research.

Sommer, V., and Mohnot, S. M. 1985. New observations on infanticides among hanuman langurs *Presbytis entellus* near Jodhpur (Rajasthan/India). *Behavioral Ecology and Sociobiology* 16:245–48.

Spiro, Melford E. 1975. *Kibbutz: Venture in Utopia*. Cambridge: Harvard University Press.

Stack, Peter. 1989. Rwanda's gorillas—without the mist. *San Francisco Chronicle*, 16 January: E1, E5.

Stammbach, Eduard. 1987. Desert, forest and montane baboons: Multilevel societies. In Barbara B. Smuts et al., eds., *Primate societies*, 112–20. Chicago: University of Chicago Press.

Stanley, Steven M. 1986. Is human evolution punctuational? In B. J. Williams, ed., *On evolutionary anthropology*, 77–89. Malibu, Calif.: Undena Publications.

Stein, D. 1984. *The sociobiology of infant and adult male baboons*. Norwood, N.J.: Ablex Publishing.

Stern, B. R., and Smith, D. G. 1984. Sexual behaviour and paternity in three captive groups of rhesus monkeys *Macaca mulatta*. *Animal Behavior* 32:23–32.

Stewart, Kelley J., and Harcourt, Alexander H. 1987. Gorillas: Variation in female relationships. In Barbara B. Smuts et al., eds., *Primate Societies*, 155–64. Chicago: University of Chicago Press.

Stoltz, L., and Saayman, G. 1970. Ecology and behaviour of baboons in the northern Transvaal. *Annales of the Transvaal Museum* 26:99–143.

Strayer, Fred F. 1981. The organization and coordination of asymmetrical relations among young children: A biological view of social power. In Meredith Watts, ed., *Biopolitics: Ethological and physiological approaches*, 33–99. San Francisco: Jossey-Bass.

Struever, Steven, ed. 1971. *Prehistoric agriculture*. Garden City, N.Y.: Natural History Press.

Struhsaker, Thomas. 1969. Correlates of ecology and social organization among African Cercopithecines. *Folia Primatologica* 11:80–118.

Strum, Shirley C. 1975a. Life with the "Pumphouse Gang." *National Geographic* 147:672–91.

———. 1975b. Primate predation: Interim report on the development of a tradition in a troop of olive baboons. *Science* 187:755–57.

———. 1981. Processes and products of change: Baboon predatory behavior at Gilgil, Kenya. In Robert Harding and Geza Teleki, eds., *Omnivorous primates: Gathering and hunting in human evolution*, 255–302. New York: Columbia University Press.

———. 1982a. The evolution of political behavior and sexual differences among primates. Paper presented at the annual meeting of the Western Political Science Association, San Diego.

———. 1982b. Agonistic dominance in male baboons: An alternative view. *International Journal of Primatology* 3:175–202.

———. 1983a. Why males use infants. In David Taub, ed., *Primate paternalism*. New York: Van Nostrand Reinhold.

———. 1983b. Use of females by male olive baboons *Papio anubis*. *American Journal of Primatology* 5:93–109.

———. 1983c. Baboon cues for eating meat. *Journal of Human Evolution* 12:327–36.

———. 1987. *Almost human: A journey into the world of baboons*. New York: Random House.

———. In press. Are there alternatives to aggression in baboon society?

Strum, Shirley C., and Mitchell, William. 1987. Baboon models and muddles. In Warren G. Kinzey, ed., *The evolution of human behavior: Primate models*, 87–104. Albany: SUNY Press.

Sugiyama, Yokimaru. 1976. Life history of male Japanese monkeys. *Advances in the Study of Behaviour* 7:255–84.

Sullivan, Denis, and Masters, Roger D. 1988. "Happy Warriors": Leaders' facial displays, viewers' emotions and political support. *American Journal of Political Science* 32:345–68.

———. In press a. Nonverbal cues, emotions, and trait attributions in the evaluation of political leaders: the contribution of biopolitics to the study of media and politics. In Albert O. Somit and Steven A. Peterson, eds., *Research in Biopolitics*. Greenwich, Conn.: JAI Press.

———. In press b. Nonverbal behavior, emotions, and democratic leadership. In George E. Marcus and John L. Sullivan, eds., *Reconsidering American democracy.* Chicago: University of Chicago Press.

Sullivan, Denis; Masters, Roger D.; Lanzetta, John T.; Englis, Basil G.; and McHugo, Gregory J. 1984. The effect of President Reagan's facial displays on observers' attitudes, impressions, and feelings about him. Paper presented at the annual meeting of the American Political Science Association, Washington, D.C.

Susman, Randall L. 1987. Pygmy chimpanzees and common chimpanzees: Models for the behavioral ecology of the earliest hominids. In Warren G. Kinzey, ed., *The evolution of human behavior: Primate models*, 72–86. Albany: SUNY Press.

Szasz, Thomas. 1965. *Madness and civilization.* New York: Pantheon.

———. 1970. *The manufacture of madness.* New York: Harper & Row.

———. 1973. *The age of madness.* Garden City, N.Y.: Anchor Press.

Talmon, Jacob L. 1961. *The origins of totalitarian democracy.* New York: Praeger.

Tanner, Nancy Makepeace. 1981. *On becoming human.* New York: Cambridge University Press.

———. 1987. Gathering by females: The chimpanzee model revisited and the gathering hypothesis. In Warren G. Kinzey, ed., *The evolution of human behavior: Primate models*, 3–27. Albany: SUNY Press.

Tanner, Nancy Makepeace, and Zihlman, Adrienne L. 1976. Women in evolution: Innovation and selection in human origins. *Signs* 1:585–608.

Teleki, Geza. 1973. *The predatory behavior of wild chimpanzees.* East Brunswick, N.J.: Bucknell University Press.

Templeton, Alan R. 1984. The evolution of man. Seminar sponsored by the University of Hawaii at Manoa, Department of Genetics and Hawaian Evolutionary Biology Program.

Terrace, Herbert S. 1979. *Nim: A chimpanzee who learned sign language.* New York: Knopf.

Testart, A. 1982. The significance of food storage among hunter-gatherers: Residence patterns, population densities, and social inequalities. *Current Anthropology* 23:523–37.

Thomas, D. K., 1961. The Gombe Stream Game Reserve, *Tanganyika Notes Rec.*, 56:34–39.

Thompson, Philip R. 1975. A cross-species analysis of carnivore, primate, and hominid behavior. *Journal of Human Evolution* 4:113–24.

Tiger, Lionel. 1969. *Men in groups.* New York: Random House.

———. 1979. *Optimism: The biology of hope.* New York: Simon and Schuster.

———. 1987. *The manufacture of evil: Ethics, evolution, and the industrial system.* New York: Harper & Row.

Tiger, Lionel, and Fox, Robin. 1971. *The imperial animal.* New York: Holt, Rinehart & Winston.

Tiger, Lionel, and Shepher, Joseph. 1975. *Women in the kibbutz.* New York: Harcourt Brace Jovanovich.

Tinbergen, Niko. 1968. On war and peace in animals and man. *Science* 160:1411–18.

Trivers, Robert L. 1971. The evolution of reciprocal altruism. *Quarterly Review of Biology* 46:35–57.

———. 1972. Parent-offspring conflict. *American Zoologist* 14:249–64.

Trivers, Robert, and Willard, D. 1973. Natural selection of parental ability to vary the sex ratio of offspring. *Science* 179:90–91.

Tsingalia, H. M., and Rowell, Thelma E. 1984. The behavior of adult male blue monkeys. *Zeitschrift für Tierpsychologie* 64:253–68.

Van de Sande, J. 1973. Speltheoretische onderzoekingen naar gedragdverschillen tussen mannen en vrouwen. *Nederlands Tijdschrift voor Psychologie* 28:327–41.

Van Hooff, Jan A. R. A. M. 1969. The facial displays of the Catyrrhine monkeys and apes. In Desmond Morris, ed., *Primate ethology*, 9–81. New York: Anchor Books.

———. 1972. A comparative approach to the phylogeny of laughter and smiling. In Robert A. Hinde, ed., *Non-verbal communication*, 209–41. New York: Cambridge University Press.

———. 1973. A structural analysis of the social behavior of a semi-captive group of chimpanzees. In Mario von Cranach and Ian Vine, eds., *Social communication and movement*. New York: Academic Press.

———. 1982. Coalitions and positions of influence in a chimpanzee community. In Glendon Schubert and Albert Somit, eds., *The biology of primate sociopolitical behavior*, 2–15. DeKalb: Northern Illinois University, Center for Biopolitical Research.

Vehrencamp, S. L. 1983. A model for the evolution of despotic versus egalitarian societies. *Animal Behavior* 31:667–82.

Vogel, Christian R. 1979. Der Hanuman-Langur *Presbytis entellus*, ein Parade-Exempel für die theoretischen Konzepte der 'Soziobiologie'? In *Verhandlungen Deutsche Zoologische Gesellschaft*, 73–89. Stuttgart, West Germany: Gustav Fischer Verlag.

Vogel, Christian R., and Loch, H. 1984. Reproductive parameters, adult-male replacements, and infanticide among free-ranging langurs *Presbytis entellus* at Jodhpur Rajasthan, India. In Glenn Hausfater and Sarah Blaffer Hrdy, eds., *Infanticide: Comparative and evolutionary perspectives*, 237–55. New York: Aldine.

Von Cranach, Mario, ed. 1976. *Methods of inference from animal to human behavior.* The Hague: Mouton.

Von Cranach, Mario; Foppa, Klaus; Lepenies, Wolfgang; and Ploog, Detlev, eds. 1979. *Human ethology: Claims and limits of a new discipline.* Cambridge: Cambridge University Press.

Vrba, Elisabeth S. 1988. Late Pliocene climatic events and hominid evolution. In Frederick E. Grine, ed., *Evolutionary history of the "robust" australopithecines*, 405–26. New York: Aldine de Gruyter.

Waddington, Conrad Hal. 1957. *The strategy of the genes.* London: George Allen and Unwin.

Walker, Alan. 1984. Extinction in hominid evolution. In Matthew H. Nitecki, ed., *Extinctions*, 119–52. Chicago: University of Chicago Press.

Walker, S. 1983. *Animal thought.* London: Routledge & Kegan Paul.

Walters, J. 1980. Interventions and the development of dominance relationships in female baboons. *Folia Primatologica* 34:61–89.

———. 1981. Inferring kinship from behavior: Maternity determinations in yellow baboons. *Animal Behavior* 29:126–36.

Washburn, Sherwood, and DeVore, Irven. 1961. The social behavior of baboons and early man. In Sherwood Washburn, ed., *Social life of early man*, 91–105. Chicago: Aldine.

Washburn, Sherwood, and Hamburg, David Allan. 1965. The study of primate behavior. In Irven DeVore, ed., *Primate behavior.* New York: Holt, Rinehart & Winston.

———. 1968. Aggressive behavior in old world monkeys and apes. In Phyllis Jay, ed., *Primates: Studies in adaptation and variability*, 458–78. New York: Holt, Rinehart & Winston.

Washburn, Sherwood; Jay, Phillis; and Lancaster, Jane. 1965. Field studies of old world monkeys and apes. *Science* 150:1541–47.

Washburn, Sherwood, and Lancaster, C. 1968. The evolution of hunting. In Richard B. Lee and Irven DeVore, eds., *Man the hunter.* Chicago: Aldine.

Wasser, S. 1981. Reproductive competition and cooperation: General theory and a field study of female yellow baboons. Ph.D. diss., University of Washington, Seattle.

―――. 1982. Reciprocity and the trade-off between quality and relatedness. *American Naturalist* 119:720–31.

Wasser, S., and Barash, David. 1981. The "selfish" allomother. *Ethology and Sociobiology* 2:91–93.

Watanabe, K. 1979. Alliance formation in a free-ranging troop of Japanese macaques. *Primates* 20:459–74.

Watts, Meredith, ed. 1981. *Biopolitics: Ethological and physiological approaches*. San Francisco: Jossey-Bass.

―――. 1983. Symposium on biopolitics and gender. *Women and politics* 3, 2–3:1–210.

Weber, Max. 1964. *The theory of social and economic organization*. Trans. and ed. by T. Parsons, New York: Free Press.

Wellman, Paul I. 1947. *Death on horseback*. Garden City, N.Y.: Doubleday.

Western, Jonah David, and Strum, Shirley C. 1983. Sex, kinship, and the evolution of social manipulation. *Ethology and Sociobiology* 4:19–8.

Wheatley, B. P. 1982. Adult male replacement in *Macaca fascicularis* of East Kalimantan, Indonesia. *International Journal of Primatology* 3:203–19.

Wheeler, Harvey, and Danielli, James. 1982. Constructional biology. *Journal of Social and Biological Structures* 5:11–14.

White, Elliott. 1980. The end of the empty organism: Human neurobiology, classical social science, and political learning. Paper delivered at the annual meeting of the Midwest Political Science Association, Chicago.

―――, ed. 1981. *Sociobiology and human politics*. New York: Heath-Lexington.

White, Tim D. 1988. The comparative biology of "robust" *australopithecus:* Clues from context. In Frederick E. Grine, ed., *Evolutionary history of the "robust" australopithecines*, 449–83. New York: Aldine de Gruyter.

Whiten, A., and Byrne, R. W. 1988. Tactical deception in primates. *Behavioral and Brain Sciences* 11:233–73.

Wiegele, Thomas C. 1979. *Biopolitics: Search for a more human political science*. Boulder, Colo.: Westview Press.

Wight, Martin. 1946. *Power politics*. London: Royal Institute of International Affairs.

Willhoite, Fred. 1976. Primates and political authority: A biobehavioral perspective. *American Political Science Review* 70:1110–26.

Williams, George C. 1966. *Adaptation and natural selection: A critique of some current evolutionary thought*. Princeton, N.J.: Princeton University Press.

Wilson, Edward O. 1975. *Sociobiology: The new synthesis*. Cambridge: Harvard University Press, the Belknap Press.

―――. 1980. *Sociobiology: The abridged edition*. Cambridge: Harvard University Press, the Belknap Press.

―――. 1988. Symposium on the creative mind. *Journal of Social and Biological Structures* 11:1–189.

Wingerson, Lois. 1982. Nice guys finish first. *Discover* 3–4 (March): 66–67.

Winterhalder, B. 1985. Diet choice, risks, and food sharing in a stochastic environment. Paper delivered at the conference on Risk and Uncertainty: Ecological and Economic Perspectives, University of Washington, Seattle.

Wittenberger, J. F. 1981. *Animal social behavior*. North Scituate, Mass.: Duxbury Press.

Wolpoff, Milfrod H. 1983. Ramapithecus and human origins: An anthropologists's perspective of changing interpretations. In Russell S. Ciochon and Robert L. Corruccini, eds. *New interpretations of ape and human ancestry*, 651–76. New York: Plenum Press.

Woodburn, J. 1968. Stability and flexibility in Hadza residential groupings. In R. B. Lee and Irven DeVore, eds, *Man the hunter.* Chicago: Aldine.

———. 1972. Ecology, nomadic movement, and the composition of the local group among hunters and gatherers: An East Africa example and its implications. In P. J. Ucko et al. eds., *Man, settlement, and urbanism.* London: Duckworth; New York: Schenman.

———. 1982. Egalitarian societies. *Man* n.s. 17:431–51.

Woodruff, G., and Premack, David. 1979. Intentional communication in the chimpanzee: The development of deception. *Cognition* 7:333–62.

Wrangham, Richard W. 1974. Artificial feeding of chimpanzees and baboons in their natural habitat. *Animal behavior* 22:83–93.

———. 1975. The behavioral ecology of chimpanzees at Gombe Stream National Park, Tanzania. Ph.D. diss., Cambridge University.

———. 1979. Sex differences in chimpanzee dispersion. In David Hamburg and Elizabeth McCown eds., *The great apes.* Menlo Park, Calif.: Benjamin/Cummings.

———. 1981. An ecological model of female-bonded primate groups. *Behaviour* 75:262–300.

———. 1983. Ultimate factors determining social structure. In Robert A. Hinde, ed., *Primate social relationships*, 255–62. Sunderland, Mass.: Sinauer Associates.

———. 1987. The significance of African apes for reconstructing human social evolution. *The evolution of human behavior: Primate models*, 51–71. Albany: SUNY Press.

Wrangham, Richard W., and Smuts, Barbara. 1980. Sex differences in behavioural ecology of chimpanzees in Gombe National Park, Tanzania. *Journal of Reproduction and Fertility* (supplement) 28:13–31.

Wright, Quincy. 1955. *The study of international relations.* New York: Appleton-Century-Crofts.

Yerkes, Robert M. 1943. *Chimpanzees: A laboratory colony.* New Haven, Conn.: Yale University Press.

Yunis, Jorge, and Prakash, O. 1982. The origins of man: A chromosomal pictorial legacy. *Science* 215:1525–29.

Yunis, Jorge; Sawyer, J. R.; and Dunham, K. 1980. The striking resemblance of high-resolution G-banded chromosomes of man and chimpanzees. *Science* 208:1145–48.

Zihlman, Adrienne L. 1981. Women as shapers of the human adaptation. In Frances Dahlberg, ed., *Woman the gatherer*, 75–120. New Haven, Conn.: Yale University Press.

———. 1982. *The human evolution coloring book.* New York: Barnes and Noble.

———. 1983. A behavioral reconstruction of australopithecines. In Kathleen J. Reichs, ed., *Hominid origins*, 207–38. Washington, D.C.: University Press of America.

———. 1987. Sex, sexes, and sexism in human origins. *Yearbook of Physical Anthropology* 30:11–19.

Zihlman, Adrienne L., and Lowenstein, Jerold M. 1983. *Ramapithecus* and *Pan paniscus*: Significance for human origins. In Russel S. Ciochon and Robert L. Corruccini, eds., *New interpretations of ape and human ancestry*, 677–94. New York: Plenum Press.

Zihlman, Adrienne L., and Tanner, Nancy. 1978. Gathering and the hominid adaptation. In Lionel Tiger and Heather Fowler, eds., *Female hierarchies*, 163–94. Chicago: Beresford Book Service.

Zinnes, Dina. 1970. Coalition theories and the balance of power. In S. Groennings, E. Kelley, and M. Leiserson, eds., *The study of coalitions*, 357–68. New York: Holt, Rinehart & Winston.

Zivin, Gail. 1977. Facial gestures predict preschoolers' encounter outcomes. *Social Science Information* 16:715–29.

Zuckerman, Solomon. 1932. *The social life of monkeys and apes*. London: Routledge & Kegan Paul.

# Notes on Contributors

Nicholas G. Blurton Jones, who received a doctorate at Oxford University and studied ethology with Niko Tinbergen, taught at the University of London while conducting research on child development in England and also among the San in Namibia. Since 1981 he has been at the Graduate School of Education at the University of California in Los Angeles, as co-editor of the journal *Ethology and Sociobiology*, and teaches jointly in the departments of anthropology and psychiatry. He currently conducts fieldwork in Tanzania on children in regard to their subsistence.

Frans B. M. de Waal conducted his dissertation research on aggressive behavior and coalition formation among captive macaques at the Laboratory for Comparative Physiology of the University of Utrecht. This work served as a methodological preparation for a more extensive study of similar issues in the unique chimpanzee colony of the Arnhem Zoo. The observations were reported in a series of technical articles as well as in a popular book, *Chimpanzee Politics* (1982). Since 1981, de Waal has been a research scientist at the Wisconsin Regional Primate Research Center in Madison, working on reconciliation behavior and conflict resolution in a number of primate species. This resulted in his recent book, *Peacemaking among Primates* (1989).

Jane Goodall is the leading authority on chimpanzee behavior; a pioneering female field primatologist; and a renowned teacher as well as a researcher through her hosting of scores of students and fellow professionals at her work station at Gombe on Lake Tanganyika, plus the dozens of television programs, books, and articles by her and by others based on her research. Her Ph.D. in zoology (1965) is from Cambridge University. She has long maintained close associations with the preeminent researchers in primate evolution and behavior, including the late Dr. Louis Leakey of Kenya, Dr. Robert Hinde of Cambridge, and Dr. Sherwood Washburn of Stanford; as well as with the National Geographic Society in Washington, D.C., and the Jane Goodall Foundation in Los Angeles. Her best known work includes *In the Shadow of Man* (1971) and *The Chimpanzees of Gombe* (1986).

Bruno Latour is a professor at the Ecole Nationale Supérieure des Mines de Paris and at the Science Studies Program of the University of California, San Diego. He is a member of the Centre de Sociologie de l'Innovation of the Ecole des Mines. He is the author of *Laboratory Life* (1979), *Science in Action* (1987), and *The Pasteurization of France* (1988). He coedited with Michel Callon many books on sociology and the history of science. He is the author of numerous articles in philosophy, history, and sociology of science or technology. He is currently working on a social history of French science.

Roger D. Masters is professor of government at Dartmouth College, and editor of the "Biology and Social Life" section of *Social Science Information*. His latest publications are *The Nature of Politics* (1989) and (co-edited with Christopher Kelly) *Rousseau: Judge of Jean-Jacques*, the first volume of *The Collected Writings of Rousseau* (1990). In addition to his work in biopolitics, earlier publications have included editions of Rousseau's *Discourses* (1964) and *Social Contract* (1978), *The Nation Is Burdened* (1967), and The *Political Philosophy of Rousseau* (1968).

Thelma E. Rowell, after obtaining B.A. and Ph.D. degrees from Cambridge University in England, worked in Uganda on baboons both in the wild (in the Queen Elizabeth National Park) and in captivity (at Makerere University, where she also studied reproductive cycles and behavior in captive groups of several other species). In 1969, she moved to the University of California at Berkeley, where she is now professor of zoology. Subsequently she has done primatological research on talapoins, cotton-top tamarins, and patas monkeys, concentrating since 1982 on a field study of blue monkeys in Western Kenya.

Glendon Schubert grew up in upstate New York and received his degrees from Syracuse University. His forty-year postdoctoral teaching career began at UCLA, and includes appointments at Howard University, Syracuse University, Rutgers University, Franklin and Marshall College, the University of Minnesota, the University of Oslo, and Michigan State University; and also academic chairs as the William Rand Kenan, Jr., Professor at the University of North Carolina at Chapel Hill, and University Professor at York University in Toronto. During the past twenty years he has been a biobehavioral political scientist with a principal interest in a life-science approach to politics, emphasizing primatology, feminism, and psychology. This approach is exemplified by his work as associate or advisory editor to such interdisciplinary and international journals as *The Behavior and Brain Sciences*, the *Journal of Social and Biological Structures*, and *Politics and the Life Sciences*. The author of more than one hundred articles published in professional journals, and the author or editor of twenty-five books, his recent books include *Evolutionary Politics* (Southern Illinois University Press, 1989) and *Sexual Politics and Political Feminism* (JAI Press, in press). Presently he is University Professor at the University of Hawaii, Manoa, and Research Professor at Southern Illinois University at Carbondale.

James N. Schubert teaches at Alfred University in the western New York State southern tier. His doctorate (1975) is in political science from the University of Hawaii at Manoa. He worked for a postdoctoral year at the Survey Research Center of the University of Michigan, and taught at Southern Illinois University at Carbondale; and was a research associate at the Center for Biopolitical Research of Northern Illinois University in 1981–82. Throughout the 1980s he was an active researcher and the author of critical studies of the politics of food aid, famine politics, and the politics of human longevity. He was the principal investigator and director of multi-university research under contracts from the National Science Foundation and the National Institute of Aging, on field survey human ethological studies of dominance behavior and also of age-related behavioral differences in village councils of several states. He was president of the Association for Politics and the Life Sciences (1987–89). Currently he is directing further multi-university and ethological research, under a grant from the National Science Foundation, on nonverbal in relation to verbal behavior as oral argument in decision-making by justices of the United States Supreme Court.

Shirley S. Strum took her doctorate in physical anthropology at Stanford University with Sherwood Washburn, and has worked continuously as a pioneer female field primatologist in Kenya with "The Pumphouse Gang" of baboons for almost two decades. She has collaborated in other research with Bruno Latour and with her husband, field ecologist Jonah David Western. She teaches anthropology at the University of California-La Jolla; and her book *Almost Human* (1987) is a leading contribution to feminist (as well as to field) primatology.

Denis G. Sullivan is Remson Professor of Government at Dartmouth College, and coauthor of *The Politics of Representation* (1974), *Explorations in Convention Decision Making* (1976), and articles on party nominating conventions. More recently, he has written on the role of political leaders' facial displays in eliciting emotions and cognitions.

# Name Index

# Subject Index

ping of, 97, 98, 105; extinction among, 13, 230; home bases of, 14, 89, 98, 99; survival among, 99; vertical posture of, 105. *See also* Hominid behavior

Hominoids *(Hominoidae)*, 8, 12–13; intelligence of, 14; *Sivapithecus*, 12, 96. *See also* Hominid behavior; Hominids; *Homo* genus; Hylobatids; Modern primates; Pongids

*Homo* genus, 13–14; *Archaic Homo sapiens*, 8, 13; *H. erectus*, 8, 13–14; *H. habilis*, 13–14; *H. sapiens*, 9, 35, 55, 164; *H. sapiens neanderthalensis* (Neanderthals), 8, 13, 23; *H. sapiens sapiens* (modern humans), 8, 15, 230, 243, 244. *See also* Human behavior; Human evolution; Human nature; Human thinking

Human behavior, xvi, 8–9, 22, 23–24, 31, 99, 169, 221; aggressive, xv, 19, 170; cannibalism, 163; cultural, 230; deception, 167, 182, 227; direct observation, 32, 34, 166; domestication, 55; emotionality, 166; food cultivation, 58; food sharing, 35–36, 164–65, 170–87, 244; food storage, 170–71, 178–80, 187; food transportation, 35; foraging, 171, 180–83; gathering, 20; gender, 30, 168, 205, 206, 240; hunting, 20, 172, 177, 180–84, 186; individual, 21, 43, 74, 164, 170, 207, 246; injury avoidance, 173, 174, 176, 177, 186, 226; international peace making, 95; intrafamilial, 52; intragroup social relations, 207; killing, 19; kin grouping, 31; marriage, 62, 65; militarism, 21; neurotic/psychotic, 39, 49, 91; predation, 23, 68; rapprochement, 95; religious, 224; scavenging, 186; scrounging, 170, 178, 180–83, 187; sex differences in, 56, 159–60; and sex dimorphism, 20; sex roles in, 20, 56; sexual, 32, 56, 99, 166 (*see also* Sexual behavior); in small groups, 25, 166, 168, 185, 207, 210, 218–19, 230; social, 165, 169 (*see also* Primate behavior, social; Social behavior); speaking, 25, 51, 56, 81, 221, 229, 245; "tolerated theft," 170–87, 244; tool use, 34; warfare, 19, 95, 136–37; written language, 53, 230

*Human Behavior and World Politics* (Pettman), 44

Human evolution, 33, 36, 99, 168, 170–87, 224; of the brain, 56, 106; of gathering-hunting bands, 48–49, 98–99, 171, 176, 186 (*see also* Gathering-hunting bands); homology in, 8, 30, 36, 38, 49, 51, 53, 55, 56, 73, 94–95, 106, 226, 240; neoteny, 56

Humanities, 22, 29

Human nature, xiii, xv, 11, 25, 36, 164, 165, 221–23, 226, 228, 232, 234, 240, 247; empathy, 106; female, 21, 159–60; male, 21, 159–60; political, xv, 223–25; and the political animal, 228; selfishness, 21, 159, 164, 171, 176, 226–27, 244; social Darwinism and, 21, 164

Human thinking, 31, 50; anticipation of the future, 98; conceptualization, 9, 33, 50, 222; emotional effects in, 40, 50, 52, 99, 166–67,

222; female, 21, 159; ideological, 32, 41, 73, 183, 187, 226, 242; intelligence, 33; learning, 172 (*see also* Socialization, human); male, 57; memory, 50, 97–98; perception, 9, 25, 56, 166; projection, 10, 31–32, 33, 34, 41, 57, 59, 225, 246; self-conciousness, 96, 98, 118, 172, 236; use of language, 118, 137, 166

*Human Zoo, The* (Morris), 42

Hylobatids *(Hylobatidae:* Gibbons, Simiangs), 12. *See also* Ape(s)

International Primatological Society, xii, 37n, 48, 73n, 207n

Kakombe Valley, Tanzania, 90, 99
Kekopey Ranch, Kenya, 39
Kenya, xv, 39, 47
Koobi Fora, Kenya, 14

Lake Nyassa, Malawi, 89
Lake Tanganyika, 89, 90, 99, 101
Lake Victoria, 39
*Leviathan* (Hobbes), 92, 225
Linguistics, xiii, 9; evolutionary theory of, 14; grammar, 50; paralinguistics, 25, 246

Macaque(s), x, xii, 18, 21, 64, 65; Japanese (*Macaca fuscata*), 68; long-tailed, 38, 55; rhesus, 56, 240

Mammalian behavior, 231; competitive, 5, 11, 18, 19, 20–21, 23, 31–32, 33, 43, 52, 59, 60, 62, 65, 70–72, 93, 94, 138, 164, 207, 208, 223, 224, 226, 231, 234, 240; conception, 32, 60; conspecific perception of, 61–63; cooperative, 5, 11, 17, 20, 21, 31, 43, 44, 48, 52, 62, 65, 68, 72, 77, 93, 138, 164, 172, 208, 222, 223, 226, 227, 231, 240, 244; female grouping, 61, 63–64, 69; gregarious breeding, 60; harems analogized, 16, 18, 23, 31–32, 57–72, 159, 243; infanticide, 44 (*see also* Primate behavior, infanticide); predator avoidance, 69, 71; social, 189, 233; visibility of, 62–64, 70

Mammals, 7–8, 17, 23, 34, 90, 94, 222, 229; dimorphism of, 61; domesticated, 59; female, 57–72; longevity, 62; male, 57–72; mortality of, 62; predation by, 62, 78; predation on, 63; survival of, 62, 69, 71, 164, 184. *See also* Animal attributes; Mammalian behavior; Modern primates

Methodology, 9, 13, 22, 23, 24, 25, 50, 51, 73, 74, 76, 94, 163, 167, 168, 189, 206, 209–11; ethnomethodology, 33, 74, 79, 233; observation, 16, 31, 33, 57, 62–63, 64–65, 77, 80, 91, 106, 140–41, 163, 176, 208, 229, 233

Modern primates (*see also* Primate behavior; Primate groups; Primate[s]; Psychobiology): humans, 21, 33–34, 94, 221–22, 229–33 (*see also* Human behavior; Human evolution; Human nature; Human thinking); prosimians, 12, 14; simians, 53, 54, 55, 229–30, 244 (*see also* Ape[s]; Monkey[s]; Primate [nonhuman] habitats)